A DIFFERENT STORY:
AESTHETICS AND THE HISTORY OF WESTERN MUSIC

by Olle Edström

AESTHETICS IN MUSIC No. 8

PENDRAGON PRESS
HILLSDALE, NY

Other Titles in the Aesthetics in Music Series

No. 1 *Analysis and Value Judgment* by Carl Dahlhaus, translated by Siegmund Levarie (1983)

No. 2 *Arts, Science/Alloys: The thesis defense for his doctorate d'Etat* by Iannis Xenakis (1985)

No. 4 *Musical Aesthetics: A Historical Reader* (3 volumes) by Edward A. Lippman
Vol. I: From Antiquity to the Eighteenth Century (1986); Vol. II. The Nineteenth Century(1988); Vol. III: The Twentieth Century (1991)

No. 5 *Contemplating Music: Source Readings in the Aesthetics of Music* (4 Volumes) by Ruth Katz and Carl Dahlhaus; Vol. I: Substance (1987); Vol. II: Import (1989); Vol. III: Essence (1992);
Vol. IV: Community of Discourse (1994)

No. 6 *Images and Ideas in Modern French Piano Music: The Extra-Musical Subtext in Piano Works by Ravel, Debussy, and Messiaen* by Siglind Bruhn (1997)

No. 7 *A Humanistic Philosophy of Music*, Revised Edition, by Edward Lippman (2006)

Olle Edström has also published the following books:
Den Samiska Musikkulturen en översikt, Diss., Göteborg, 1978
På Begäran Svenska Musikerförbundet 1907-1982, Kristianstad,1982
Schlager i Sverige 1910-1940, Göteborg, 1989
Michael Jackson Dangerous och dess mottagande, Göteborg, 1992
Göteborgs Rika Musikliv en översikt mellan världskrigen, Göteborg, 1996
Harmoniskt Samspel Sjuttiofem år med STIM, Göteborg, 1998

Library of Congress Cataloging-in-Publication Data

Edström, Karl-Olof, 1945-
 [Annan berättelse om den västerländska musikhistorien, och det estetiska projektet. English]
 A different story : aesthetics and the history of Western music / by Olle Edström ; edited by Joel Speerstra.
   p. cm. -- (Aesthetics in music ; no. 8)
 Includes index.
 ISBN-13: 978-1-57647-123-4
 1. Music--Philosophy and aesthetics. 2. Music--History and criticism. I. Speerstra, Joel. II. Title.
 ML3845.E2913 2007
 781.1'7--dc22
                              2007048625

copyright 2008 Pendragon Press

FOREWORD

This project grew out of a conference in Umeå, a small university town in the north of Sweden, where I met several distinguished aestheticians. I realized that, to a greater extent than most of the participants, I felt I understood aesthetics as primarily a social process rather than as a transcultural and a historical phenomenon. I felt a need to follow the trajectory of the concept of the aesthetic at the same time as I wrote a personal meta-narrative of the history of Western music. The book was originally published in Swedish under the title, "En ANNAN berättelse om den västerländska musikhistorien – och det estetiska projektet" (2002). The present book has been translated by Joel Speerstra in collaboration with the author. The translation was made possible through support from the Swedish Research Council.

Göteborg, March 2007

Olle Edström

TABLE OF CONTENTS

Introduction
    A Declaration of Intent   11
    A Controversial Term   11
    How Common is the Term in Music Today?   15
    A Presentation of the Problem   18
    Material, Method and Purpose   19
    The Organization of This Text   21

Chapter 1 Homo Aestheticus
    Other Voices   23
    Ellen Dissanayke's Anthropology   24
    Speech as a Precondition For, and Analogy to Music   27
    Steven Pinker's Perspective   29
    "Music is an Enigma"   32

Chapter 2 The Greeks
    In Black and White   35
    Three Thousand Years Ago   38
    An Unusually Revolutionary Time   41
    A Summary Discussion   43
    The Loadbearing Capacity of a Thought   47

Chapter 3 The Age of Enlightenment
    The Birth of Aesthetics   51
    On Music's Breadth and Function   52
    Socio-cultural Conditions   54
    What Counts as Art?   58
    Aesthetics as Ideology   60
    Visits in Time   64
    A Contemporary Journey   65
    A Few Other Journeys   67
    In Germany   69
    Swedish Observations   73
    Music's Structures—Music's Functions   74
    Listening to Music in Concert   82
    The Formation of a Code of Values   84
    Sing Burghers, Farmers and Workers   89
    Instrumental Music Between the Inner and Outer World   94
    In the Work "Itself"   101

Other Social Models: Habermas and Luhmann	106
From Theory to Social Empire	110
Beethoven's Public	117
New Structures	120
Aesthetic II: A Summary Discussion	122

Chapter 4 A Time of Consolidation

Introduction	129
The Difference Becomes Set in Stone	132
Four Thousand Wandering Virtuosi	134
A Swedish Example from Göteborg	137
Swedish Music Journalists	140
Music in the Salons—Intimate Scenes of Home	142
Use and Status	144
The Schumanns and Salon Music	146
From 1850 Towards the Twentieth Century	152
Different Ways of Listening	155
A Common Bourgeois Form	163
More on Song's Underrated Importance	167
Autonomous Discussion	170

Chapter 5 A Period of Expansion

Introduction	177
Changes in Art Music	180
Some Knew	184
Many Disembark	187
Music Spreads Out	189
Mass Media—New Ways to Use Music	191
Listening to Music on the Radio	195
Ethereal Music and Aesthetics	198
Education—and—or—Enjoyment	201
Is it possible to define art or the aesthetic experience?	209
Consumption and Aesthetics	218
Personal Use	221

Chapter 6 The Present: The Use of Music—the Transformation of Aesthetics

Introduction	227
Youth Music and Aesthetics	232
"The Aesthetics of Rock"	235
Wicke—East Germany	237
Postmodern Times	240
Simon Frith's "approach to music and society"	245

TABLE OF CONTENTS

Everyday Aesthetics in Youth Culture	250
A Sociological View of Aesthetics	253
Social Change Leads to New Aesthetic Ground Rules	254
Late Modern Changes	258
The Thoroughly Aesthetified Society	260
From æI to æ?	262
Society of Experience	263
One—or the Other	267
Both—And	270
Conclusion: Tying Up Loose Ends	275
Bibliography	287
Index	303

Aesthetics is for the artist what ornithology is for the birds.
Barnett Newman

INTRODUCTION

A Declaration of Intent

This book is not just another story about western music history. It is an attempt to use a word, aesthetics, as a key to unlock historical rooms filled with music and song, where an ethnological approach toward song's and music's social and aesthetic meaning can be sought. We will undertake a musicological journey from the deep past to our own time, observing the term aesthetics, and determining what it collectively meant for those who used and transformed it. The journey starts early in human history and takes us through a developing landscape symbolically marked by aesthetic I (æI), aesthetic II (æII), aesthetic III (æIII) and so forth. These shorthand symbols, to be explained later, create a methodical path to help us understand our music history and the "aesthetic project," a social process that begins in earnest during the Age of Enlightenment and continues into our own time.

The word "aesthetics" is rarely used in normal conversation, partially because it is hard to get a grip on it. But, it is one of the most important terms within all of western cultural history. Like other words such as art, objective, and subjective, it is a controversial term.[1]

A Controversial Term

On the same day that I began to sketch this work, I read an internet discussion on a music theory site. The author, Larry Solomon, was pondering

---

[1] The idea of controversial terminology arises from the philosopher Walter G. Gallie (1956). "Essentially contested concepts" are, writes Gallie, "concepts the proper use of which inevitably involves endless disputes about their proper uses on the part of the users" (1956:169). Among the factors that, taken together, can be categorized as controversial can be mentioned that it must have value, stand for something/mean something that has a complex character, and that those who use the term should be aware that other groups use the term in a different way. Gallie uses examples such as art, democracy, and justice.

the differences between objective and subjective music analysis.[2] For him, music analysis was interesting only if it was objective and resulted in observations that all persons, using the same methods could agree about. All other observations were subjective and therefore of little value to him. Instead of reading subjective analyses, he would rather listen to subjective performances of the analyzed music.

The long musical debate that followed on the site brought about no mediation between the two contrary positions. Furthermore, we had no general agreement about what sort of analysis tools could be used. The idea that an objective analysis method would be controversial comes as no surprise for anyone who works within the humanities and social sciences. Actually I was only surprised that someone could believe that it was possible to find objective analysis tools at all. The concept of "objectivity" becomes even more challenging whenever one attempts to analyze art music scores. The larger and more complex the structure of the music becomes, the greater the risk of seeing structures on the page that one cannot hear in performance. If we turn to a sister discipline, art history, we see that the relationship is somewhat different. For an art historian, it is probably self evident that a layperson's oral description of what one can see in a painting, for example Jackson Pollock and an extensive written description and analysis of the same will be different. However, unlike music, analyzing a painting does not depend upon one's hearing. Musicology has developed analysis methods that are not only dependent upon hearing but also upon the role visual analysis of the text plays.[3]

Value judgments mask even the most innocent objective terms. No word can stand isolated from others, which is why within language, we build up a net of meanings, a net so thickly woven that we seldom, if ever, are capable of seeing through it. For example, within the functional analysis system that slowly became the dominating method in Sweden in the 1950s, a C major chord in C Major is called the tonic (from the Greek word *tonos* = tension), while a G Major chord gets labeled dominant (from the Latin *dominari* = to control or rule). Both of these descriptive terms' etymologies give us clear associations. The problem with these descriptive terms' meanings is that, of course, they really should be reversed,

---

[2] SMT-list@boethius. music.ucsb.edu, Sat. 30 Oct 1999.
[3] To give three examples: a) in Heinrich Schenker's music theory, the term prolongation assumes that the listener can experience structures over a long time period, a period that one can more easily see in a score than hear; b) analysis methods within twelve-tone techniques, for example show that it is possible to visually identify, but hardly possible to aurally identify a retrograde inversion of a series spread over different instruments; as well as c) analysis methods that involve toneclass theories in which there is little or no possibility of hearing the delimitations within groups on which the methods are based. See also footnote 9, below.

because that is how we hear the functions of these two chords: the dominant chord creates tension, while the tonic chord has an underlying, minating function.[4]

If instead, we turn to the Roman Numeral analysis system that is used today in the U.S., and was used earlier in Sweden, in C Major, a C Major chord is symbolized with a Roman numeral I and a G Major Chord with a V. It doesn't take long, however, for the musicology student to discover that music theoreticians, since at least the eighteenth century, have been improving the descriptive value of these terms with pedagogically designed metaphors. Riepel (1755) describes the C Major chord as "der Meyer" (God's owner), G as "der Oberknecht" (the Highest servant) and C minor as "Schwarze Gredel" (Black Margareta).[5] As late as during the 1960s a translation of Ernst Tittel's *Harmonilehre* (1965) was published, where this Roman Numeral system had developed a pedagogical superstructure: G Major was the father, D major, the grandfather, E Major the Father-in-law and so on.

While the word pair *objective-subjective* is fairly well-known, *autonom* is unusual in everyday speech. Those who study art history often meet that word, as well as *aesthetic*, a word that has long fascinated me. This work began because of Ingmar Bengtsson's important book *Musikvetenskap* [Musicology] (1973). It became a starting-point for my further explorations of aesthetics, and its opposite--resigning and leaping into the void. With Bengtsson one could read about aesthetics and about the following compounds: aesthetic evaluations, functions, messages, experiences, qualities, communications, and so forth. The heading for one large section of the text, "Meaning-Expression-Value-Aesthetics," gave an overview of the term "aesthetic" and its history. Bengtsson's broad definition of music aesthetics, placed it near music philosophy, and incorporated music psychology, and sociology. Here also belonged:

> [a]ll the eternal and continually new questions about music's meaning, being, and expression, as well as its attitudes, and the science surrounding it all. In this way, borders are unavoidably crossed between aesthetic and hermeneutic, however one wants to draw this distinction; furthermore a vagueness is also found between an aesthetic and a general music-semiotic way of contemplation. (1973:290)

Bengtsson told how a beautiful piece of sculpted wood that one might find on the beach could be both an aesthetic object as well as carry an inner intended aesthetic message. The human observer could understand that message only in the context of a value judgment, where a "transition from hermeneutic

---

[4]With thanks to Bengt Edlund for the reminder!
[5]Compare with Ratner (1980:50). Schwarze Margaretha was a local German nickname for a Swedish [sic] Queen whose swarthy face led to her being taken for a man.

to aesthetic" took place. This could happen only if the thing one judged was something one also understood.

But, I wondered, how could there be an "indwelling intention" in a piece of wood? My question marks pepper the margins, most particularly on the pages where Bengtsson tried to bring order to it all by introducing qualitative judgments, chiefly in the spirit of the natural sciences.[6]

A footnote in the text pointed to an inquiry into aesthetics by the ethnomusicologist Alan Merriam (1964). His work, *The Anthropology of Music*, was also very important during the 1960s and 70s. The purpose of the chapter on aesthetics was to research whether thoughts surrounding aesthetics had any relevance for music other than art music, for instance traditional music (folk music). Merriam found that to a great extent this was not the case.[7] The six Western aesthetic factors were:

1) That there exists a physical as well as psychological distance between object and subject

2) that [music's] form could be manipulated for its own sake

3) that music, like sound could be ascribed to and could act as an intermediary to emotional qualities

4) that beauty is ascribed to, and is mediated by, art

5) that there was a conscious intent to formulated as aesthetic, and

6) that there was an aesthetic intellectual structure. (after Merriam 1964:261-269)

For nearly thirty years I have continued to ask musicians, students, doctoral candidates, and others, what they understand by the term "aesthetic" and constructions like "aesthetic music," "aesthetic experience" and so forth.[8] The answers vary from silence, through various doubtful suggestions, to a few firm opinions. I have learned *aesthetic* falls within a confusingly large semantic field.

---

[6]Bengtsson made a distinction between "real feeling experiences and mood experiences." If they were intended and real, they were marked (EmR+) and if they were temporary and private (EmR–). These terms could be given the prefix (L) for listener or (K) if it applied to the composer. Because music (M) itself could not cause its own expression, M(EmR+), the term emotive qualities was introduced, EmQ, for the "character" or "expression" that music had, independent of the composer's intention. There were also value qualities (VQ) and aesthetic qualities (EQ). This system generated many possible combinations. Bengtsson's attempt to use the clarity of the natural sciences had its pedagogical benefits, but was off-putting in the work itself (1973:305ff).

[7]I found later concerning my own source studies regarding Sami jojks also very little that indicated that aesthetics was a relevant category within the traditional Sami culture (1978). Since then, new research about similar aesthetic awareness among the first peoples have changed our Western view. Pioneering work in this respect was carried out by the ethnomusicologist Steven Feld's work (1982) on the Kaluli peoples' sound- and music performances (see also Dissanayake,1992:118-119, among others).

[8]See also my article on experiencing music in *Svensk Tidskrift för Musikforskning*, /STM/ 1986.

People find it easier to give an example of aesthetic music than a definition of the word. A typical example is Beethoven's fifth symphony. But if I ask what music would you *not* describe as *aesthetic*? The answer the common responses are folk music, popular music, Burl Ives, psalms, Elvis Presley. But there are music researchers, especially those born after 1950 who will give aesthetic examples from rock music genres.[9]

How Common is the Term in Music Today?

We need not doubt that the discussion about *aesthetics* (what is included within the term, the term's history, and so forth), is to a high degree, a living discipline within musicology. For several decades now, the term *aesthetic* appears within studies of almost every musical form. This change has come at the same time folk and popular music have claimed their places within writings on music, especially in the last decades of the twentieth century.[10]

Today if you look up the word "aesthetic" in the musicological database RILM, you find 13,063 suggestions (sic) of articles. In philosophical journals such as the British Journal of Aesthetics and The Journal of Aesthetics and Art Criticism, many articles discuss aesthetics and music. Among others, the following recent books discuss aesthetics: Finn Benestad (1978), Huray & Day (1981) and Bojan Bujić (1988). Other larger studies worth mentioning here are Edward Lippman (1986), Carl Dahlhaus (1988), Enrico Fubrini (1987/1997), Roger Scruton (1998) and Lippman (1999 /collection of articles/). There is more to read on this topic than one could wish.[11]

Turning to musicological literature, the use of the word "aesthetics" seems to be more common in American musicology than in Swedish. In a culture like the American one, it is less problematic than within European music, to use the word *aesthetic* for both art music and popular music. Within American culture there is likely to be more of an egalitarian approach to class and art than in Europe.

[9]Within current rock research we find the word aesthetic already in a book titled *The Aesthetics of Rock* by Richard Meltzer (1970). At the same time as these changes, we also find that tone class theory's inventor, Allen Forte (1995), uses a modified version of Schenker's theory apparatus in his studies on melodies by Jerome Kern, George Gershwin, Richard Rodgers among others, as well as rock music researcher Allan Moore (1998) who does something similar in his analysis of Beatles' songs.

[10]If I confine myself to Swedish music historical writings, very little information about folk music and popular music can be found in Tobias Norlind (1922), Jeanson & Rabe (1927-31/1945/1966), while Jan Ling has given both folk music and popular music a substantial space, partly in a music history up to 1730 (1983), and partly in a separate book on Europe's folk music (1989). in the handbook series *Musiken i Sverige* (del I-IV) both folk and popular music forms are given their entitled space.

[11]The number of introductions within the larger field of aesthetics is naturally very large. I am confining myself to naming one example only from the Danish idea historian Søren Kjørup "Kunstens Filosofi" (2000).

Classical aesthetics	Romantic aesthetics
"A sense of restraint, order, tradition and economy of forms.	"A sense of unrestrained and often innovative artistic activity.
Form tends to be clear and traditional.	Extended use of all available resources and often a search for something new.
The composer functions within chosen boundaries of restraint.	Form tends to be less clear and more innovative.
Traditional form and musical language more important than personal expression."	The composer throws off all restraint and seeks any means of self-expression.
	Personal expression more important than form and musical language." (1982:228)

Here, aesthetics clearly closely resembles something like "style and spirit." Manoff shows how the term is both bound to its own time, but also has a timeless dimension. "Altherdoc Blues" with The Heath Brothers (1978) and Hindemith's Trauermusik are all listed under classical aesthetic. This common use of aesthetics both levels and legitimatizes different music styles. If we research everyday music-making and look for ways the word is used in daily speech, in magazines and newspapers, and in the mass media, we rarely find aesthetics. A closer search of "estet*" in Swedish daily newspapers in 1997 (Spraakbanken, GU, Press 97), a search of 12 million words, produced only 355 hits, of which only 25 deal with music (http://spraakdata.gu.se). A clear majority of the examples refer to architecture, art, artistic handcraft, and literature.

- A campy nostalgia preceding the late English nineteenth-century aestheticism and William Morris's tradition-bound handcraft ideology.
- Gospel music is also a fermenting of group aesthetics, like blues, classic rock…
- But with the Romantic comes a revolutionary change. Most clearly we see it perhaps within aesthetics.
- But with the Romantic comes a revolutionary change. Most clearly we see it perhaps within aesthetics.
- But that he applies a laughing-out-loud aesthetic when he depicts this community makes the picture hardly less worthy.
- Even if Patrick Carnbäck scored correctly it was no aesthetic highpoint [ice hockey, sic!].
- Popular music lies at the bottom. I can imagine that the new modernists take that for granted. Aesthetic elitism is not the worst of it.

INTRODUCTION

In Tom Manoff's (1982) broadly competent music history one finds, for example, after the section "Mozart's Natural Genius," another passage called "The Classical Aesthetic" and later another called "The Romantic Aesthetic." A pedagogical chart shows aesthetics, aesthetical, etc. used in common musicological ways: What is clear from these citations is that *aesthetic* is used today in areas that lie outside the traditional artistic disciplines: writings on sport, road building, etc. As far as I have been able to find, with very few exceptions, the word can be directly replaced by "art" or related concepts like "artistry," "an artistic view," "artistic doctrines," or with "artistic," or "stylistic." The meaning might have been clearer if the authors had chosen words like these instead. The readers of the sports page, for instance, would probably have been more content with a formulation like "no artistic highpoint" than "no aesthetic highpoint."

This work is not designed to study the use of *aesthetics* in daily discourse, but we can assume it is seldom used in common conversation. A study of how high school students speak with each other supports this assumption.[12]

What comes from this overview inventory is that *aesthetic* is both a controversial term and a seldom-used word within a wide area. We can also assume that the word in daily use has something to do with "science about beauty" and that "aesthetic" can be translated into the phrase "concerning beauty, or something that is "tasteful," according to the Swedish Academy's wordlist. The current general article (Estetik) by the philosopher Göran Hermerén in the *Nationalencyklopedien* (NE, 1992), divides the study of aesthetics into five related topics:

1) the study of perception
2) the doctrine of beauty and its modifications, for instance the sublime, the comic, the tragic, and so forth
3) philosophical study of the problem, the term, and the conditions under which it affects the discussion of art and artistic experience
4) empirical studies of factors that affect aesthetic preferences and experiences of beauty
5) the understanding and circumstances surrounding appearance and expression in art, nature, daily life, etc.

---

[12]Within the project GSM (Gymnasieungdomars språk- och musikvärldar, or "Highschool Students' Spoken and Music Worlds" Göteborgs universitet) we studied how high school students talked about music examples. Apart from the primary observation that many of the young people shared a large resistance to talking about music at all, we found that the word "estet*" did not appear and that discussion that points semantically toward this term's general area only was touched upon in two music examples, Mozart's 40th symphony and the Beatles' '*She loves you*.' both music examples were experienced as "classical music" (see also Lilliestam, 2002). Probably most of the high school students in larger communities have at least seen the word aesthetics, if nowhere else when they chose classes for school ("estetiskt program").

Because the English language is a dominant world language within today's humanities, it may be helpful to take note of how Merriam-Webster defines the word:

1) a branch of philosophy dealing with the nature of beauty, art, and taste and with the creation and appreciation of beauty;
2) a particular theory or conception of beauty or art: a particular taste for or approach to what is pleasing to the senses and especially sight;
3) a pleasing appearance or effect.

These definitions come closest to Hermerén's second and third sections.

For the adjective, aesthetic, the following definitions are given:

1) a) relating to, or dealing with aesthetics or the beautiful
   b) artistic
   c) pleasing in appearance
2) appreciative of, responsive to, or zealous about the beautiful; also responsive to or appreciative of what is pleasurable to the senses.

Another philosopher, T. F. Diffey (1995), points out that when one studies aesthetics, one can do it with a point of departure in a mother discipline like philosophy, psychology, or sociology, in which case one studies:

The nature and defining characteristics of art, the meaning of works of art are said to have, how they may be judged, valued or interpreted, the nature of imagination and of creativity, the kinds of experience offered by art etc. (1995:60)

"Aesthetic" on the other hand, he writes, has throughout history had three general meanings: "the perceptual, the beautiful and the artistic." He calls attention to the fact that the first meaning (Hermerén's first section) has been all but forgotten. The adjective "aesthetic" normally refers now to something that is considered beautiful, and or artistic. Diffey calls attention to the importance of separating the noun "aesthetics" (a study of the substances of aesthetics) with the adjective "aesthetic" and adds: "Confusion is born of the failure to pay proper regard to the differences" (1995:60).[13] But Diffey also establishes that the term *aesthetic* today is no longer always found within its traditional semantic area (compare with the examples from the *spraakbanken* above):

The term 'aesthetic' is now taking on in general usage meanings and resonances which cannot by captured by restriction to that which pertains only to art and/or beauty... We should regard the term 'aesthetic' as a term that extends

---

[13]Compare with the art historian Jacques Maquet (1986), who writes that art and aesthetics are separated in this way: "*Art objects* are man-made... and selected for display. *Aesthetic objects*, man-made or natural, stimulate a total disinterested vision" (1986:33).

thought by pointing *to new and not as yet entirely understood territory.* (1995:65 /my italics/)

All of Hermerén's subdivisions will be touched upon again to some extent, but in the next section I will deal with them from my own perspective as an ethnomusicologist.

A Presentation of the Problem

For a musicologist, there is an apparent divide between how our discipline uses the term *aesthetic* and its common use. There is almost nothing that would lead us to believe that the situation would have been so much different fifty or a hundred years ago. The difference in education levels in Sweden in 1900 between on the one hand, a small educated group within the bourgeoisie and the upper class, and on the other hand, everyone else's level of education (industrial workers, those in the handcrafts, farmers, office workers, etc.) makes it hard to imagine that the word was used or even known among 90 per cent of the population. Although there are many terms in humanities and sciences that never make their way into everyday speech, the term aesthetic did have its own life within upper-class society in the eighteenth and nineteenth centuries. It was used inversely to devalue other musical forms as opposed to art music, that was seen as more valuable. Music that a large majority of the people used over time, took on a "lower aesthetic value," "lacking depth," and considered "only entertainment." The general study of aesthetics shows oppositions around that word have existed in Western culture for at least three centuries. Aesthetics can be seen as a key term in the study of the relationship between the subjective taste of the individual and the correct taste dictated by a society. An overarching question is when, how, and why did the term *aesthetics* develop, and what driving forces lay behind it? What needs and interests are hiding there? Why, over time, have different kinds of music been assigned different aesthetic values? Does it have to do with the different structures of different kinds of music? Does the aesthetic confusion lie within social relationships, within the music itself, or directly with the people? Can theories about music's possible adaptive advantages, seen from an evolutionary perspective, cast any light on the meaning of the term *aesthetics*? This long list of problems should be studied both diachronically and synchronically. How, then, should one set about understanding aesthetics, its use and its meaning? And how far back in history can one go to research a word understood and used until the 1970s only by a small elite to describe art music?

Material, Method, and Purpose

True to my perspective as an ethno-musicologist I take a bottom-up perspective based on how music is actually used. Ideas, thoughts, and actions in human history, as well as objects created by people, as they appear to us, cannot be fully understood, if an analysis does not include the object's social use, function, and meaning.[14]

The task, then, is to find information about where/when/how/and with whom, song and music[15] was played and listened to. To do this, one must examine the following factors: a) the social context, b) the references of individuals in groups, c) the music and d) the presentation of music in an intimate ensemble. These four create the framework for the use and reception of music, as well as its roll, function, and meaning.[16] Any narrative about aesthetics should be placed within this thought matrix. To further our understanding of aesthetic listening, experience and attitudes, we depend on empirical knowledge and a hermeneutically experienced perspective.

This book does not pretend to be a description and analysis of music-aesthetic's history. Rather, it is an outline of the process of a changing aesthetic matched against a reading of the descriptions of musical daily life in European society. In the following chapters, historical writings describing music's use will meet thoughts about aesthetics and it is my hope that these meetings can generate new understandings. To do this, it will be necessary to go outside the world of the music researcher and draw from many sources including philosophers, speech researchers, sociologists, and idea historians.[17] The academic disciplines found

---

[14] Our capacity to perform and to empathize is always being tested with every interpretation of information. This is true especially of information from earlier developments within our cultural sphere and information about current modern tribal people. Compare for example the writings of ethnomusicologist Hans Oeschs describing the Orang Asli and the Senoi, a modern tribal (cont.) people in Malaysia. Orang Asli have no abstract words. Senoi know only four counting words: "1 (näi), 2 (narr), 3 (näq) und viel (lembek)" (1987:273f).

[15] I use the pair of words "song and music" in this book to remind the reader that the balance between our awareness of sung music and instrumental music has been very different in different eras. Song is always a separate branch of music. Music is an umbrella term for both sung and instrumental music but it is not used that way in our language. Other languages do have a term that really functions as an umbrella including all song and instrumental music. In the nineteenth century and backwards in time song was more in the foreground and afterwards instrumental music has become more foregrounded.

[16] My thought here is that a single discrete individual is a solipsistic point of departure, that leads nowhere within sociological and ethnological studies. We are individuals within a group, i.e. group-individuals. The sociologist Norbert Elias (1968/1989:51-73), who in different circumstances developed the concept, and described the idea of the individual isolated person, *homo clausus,* and her opposite, *homo aperti.*

[17] Compare with Allen's commentary (1962/1939) in his long description and comparison of cultural and music history since the seventeenth century: "The plea in these pages is for abandonment of monistic philosophies of music history; for a return to the tolerant spirit of...

within the world of the University are more or less arbitrary divisions of reality. The authors referenced here advance our discussion of aesthetics but their inclusion does not mean that I always agree with them.

In addition to the main text, readers will find rich footnotes intended to make it easier for those who wish to read the side commentaries, the clarifying criticisms, or to compare the text with other authors' work.

In summary, then, the purpose of this text is to thoroughly explore the many facets of aesthetics. Through a tour of western music history, we begin a dialog between the description and the analysis of the term and its *musical* life-path on one hand; and on the other, we compare it with music's use on normal days and holidays, exploring its function and meaning. It is my hope that the reader will find this to be a *different* picture of western music history and culture. It is not intended to cover composers and their lives and it presupposes a general knowledge of western music. Behind this purpose sits a hope of weaving together the many threads of aesthetics, even the confusing ones, into a better carpet of thought on which to stand. Simply put, I would like to act as an intermediary for a deeper understanding of how it all hangs together.

The Organization of This Text

This work begins with a discussion of previous as well as current work that lies within closely related research fields. We will meet different hypotheses about art and music's biological roots. We will explore closely related research fields such as anthropology, sociology, psychology, and linguistics. This survey is based, in part, on the idea that the demands of Neo-Darwinism have generated new explanatory models that can also be applied to art. We will meet an essential aesthetic behavior for humans, that we have carried with us since the beginning of time, and that I have chosen to call æI. What this and the following aesthetic definitions stand for, I will more clearly define in their respective contexts.

We begin with music's use and its meaning in Greek high culture. We will examine the roles philosophers such as Plato and Aristotle played, and how they reacted to the development of Greek society. In this section we meet a number of Greek words including aisthesis, whose use in Greek culture will be studied. Our next stop will be the eighteenth century. This period is so decisive in western culture and, therefore, aesthetics history, that it receives extensive discussion and analysis. In contrast to the Greek cultural history, the eighteenth century offers rich material that enables us to discuss the life of the members of the court, as well as music's use, the Age of Enlightenment's changing society, the philosophical discussion of good

---

Michael Praetorius, who could enjoy all kinds of music, ancient and modern, and music for all kinds of social use and communication" (1962:182).

taste, and not least, by extension, an understanding of the modern meaning of aesthetics. It is here that we meet a new dimension of aesthetic experience that will be referred to as æII. In the nineteenth century, the web of relationships described by aesthetics broadened, but at the same time divisions within bourgeoisie music became more evident. Through these distinct cultural eras, we will explore whether or not the function of music changed in some conclusive way. We will see how a broader aesthetic way of experiencing music became more common among the bourgeoisie. This form of aesthetic experience will be referred to as æIII.

Sweeping twentieth century changes in the role and function of music altered the content and the meaning of the aesthetic experience. The general level of education rose, changing expectations about how culture was understood and used. At the same time, broadcast media began to have a strong influence on the way music was used and discussed, and not always in the way that cultural and political authorities wished for. An account is given of different philosophical attempts to define what art is, and how, for example, aesthetic experiences can be understood. In this final section, I will introduce theories on how the current culture of affluence and excess has affected the way in which we experience music, and how that, in turn, affects the aesthetic experience. We will encounter other kinds of aesthetic experience, æIV and æV^n, but that does not mean that the earlier aesthetic experiences have disappeared.

To say that artists and the arts can be dangerous at least accords with the seriousness of their origins and customary uses. To say they are superfluous and only for an elite requires a lack of acquaintance with the arts and other societies as well as an unwillingness to accept their manifold forms in our own.

Ellen Dissanayake

CHAPTER 1: HOMO AESTHETICUS

Other Voices

We have a plethora of research today—more than we can possibly read. During the 1990s more literature was published than all other periods combined. In addition, some young research fields, such as bio-musicology are not even cohesive fields yet, but are developing concurrently in multiple disciplines. In 1977 the East German musicologist Georg Knepler published a very large work on the history of our human understanding of music, a work that to some extent is linked to many later works (see below). Knepler tried to go back to human beings' pre-history in order to ground music history and the aesthetics of music. Human speech, he said, developed as a continuation of the need to communicate ideas about unknown objects, situations and events. Knepler wanted to understand the internal and emotional structure that resulted in the communication we call music (Knepler 1977, 36). Knepler began with experimental psychological research, neurophysiology, and psychology, semiotics, archeological research etc., and discussed the similarities between human and animal behavior. He also tied his study to a hope of his own time: semiotic theory. Because of the East German antagonism to the west, his book also had a materialist-political side mirroring his time and place. Parts of Knepler's publication are still very interesting, but its strength lies more in his analysis of the development of the field of music history and musicology from the eighteenth century and forward, than in music's pre-history.

The Austrian musicologist Wolfgang Suppan and his book *Der musizierende Mensch* (Suppan 1984) has earned at least a mention in this context. He presents in his book's introduction, three postulations that could also serve as guiding lights for the present text:
    a) ethnomusicology does not proceed from a western understanding of
        music, but rather from the music-making and the music-listening person;
    b) music is a part of the human world of symbols; and

c) music is a human everyday utilitarian artifact (*Gebrauchsgegenstand des Menschen*).

For this present work, however, some newer research is of even larger importance.

Ellen Dissanayake's anthropology

In the beginning of the 1990s two books were published with the title: *Homo Aestheticus*. The subtitle of one was *The Invention of Taste in the Democratic Age* (Ferry 1990)[1] and the other, *Where Art Comes From and Why* (Dissanayake 1992). Both are important, but the American anthropologist Ellen Dissanayakes's broad anthropological and biological sense must first be discussed. I judge her writings to be both convincing and informative.

As an anthropologist and ethologist, Dissanayake begins from the position that behavior we call "artistic" and/or "symbolic" has many parallels with animal behavior that generally is referred to as ritual.[2] If some temporary behavior and expression led to the experience of satisfaction, then during humans' evolution, some behaviors/expressions came to be permanent and were experienced as symbolic:

> [S]atisfying human bodily feelings of security and mastery that arose naturally from acts of patterning and elaborating at some point became 'symbolic': they looked like or brought to mind something else (Dissanayake 1992, 89).

Over the course of our development, symbols (whether the signs have a visual similarity to that which is symbolized or not), sound, movement, the shape of an object (rock paintings, figures, signs etc.) were culturally transmitted from generation to generation and were in a close relationship to that which was being symbolized. There was no separation between thought and feeling. When one separates out some dimension, something is always lost.[3]

One of philosophy's most cited and influential sentences comes from the French philosopher René Descartes. In 1644 he said: "Je pense donc je suis," or in Latin, "cogito ergo sum." This implied separation between body and soul/spirit.

---

[1] For a discussion of similar writings that lie between "philosophical aesthetics and aesthetic theories" see Åhlberg 2000.

[2] For a detailed description of the place of ritual and its function in relationship to art, see also Dissanayake 1988. For a newly published work with many different articles that take up human and human cultural development from a primarily neo-Darwinist perspective, see Dunbar, Knight, and Power 1999.

[3] Compare with her formulation: "Every mental state has cognitive, perceptual, motivational, and emotional dimensions and cannot be properly understood if only one aspect is considered at the expense of the others" (Dissanayake 1992, 30).

HOMO AESTHETICUS

It seemed so rational, but for current neurologists this idea is completely passé. The body and the spirit are one. That means that among other things our feelings have been rehabilitated. Neurologist Antonio Damasio shows that our feelings are controlled by earlier areas of the brain (sub-cortexes) and at the same time are just as cognitive as other processes (Damasio 1994).

Descartes was basically completely wrong in divorcing soul and body.[4] Dissanayake suggests that which feels good for us as humans *is*, as a rule, good for us. What we experience as positive, gives us a sign about what we need. Humans invest time and energy in these universal symbolic behaviors because they have also shown themselves to be beneficial for our development.

Dissanayake describes as "making special" the activities we experience as something over and above the normal. These behaviors are then added to earlier natural behaviors. Through cultural transmission they are refined, controlled and learned. This *making special* has a great deal in common with human play and rituals, and lies partly outside of the everyday. In a summary statement, she says:

> Along with gaining better control of the means of subsistence... humans took an additional remarkable and unprecedented evolutionary step... Thus, in the history of the human species... [it] is not only the development of language or the invention of technological means of production that has made us anomalous or unique. Our invention and application of what might be called the 'means of enhancement' or 'means of refinement'—or an infinity of possible objects and occasions—is deeply engrained in human nature (Dissanayake 1992, 95).

Dissanayake uses the term "making special" as an alternative to our modern term "art." At their roots, both terms stand for very similar behaviors and objects. These behaviors and happenings that are culturally impressed upon our primary biological foundation can be called aesthetic, but they are something much more than an added skill such as learning about English poetry or learning

---

[4] The clarification is cited in Damasio's book: "The soul by which I am what I am, is entirely distinct from my body." How wrong Damasio considers this to be, can be understood by the tone of his noisy summary: "This is Descartes' error: the abyssal separation between body and mind, between sizable, dimensioned, mechanically operated infinitely divisible body stuff on the one hand, and the unsizable, undimensioned, un-pushpullable, nondivisible mind stuff; the suggestion that reasoning, and moral judgment, and the suffering that comes from... emotional upheaval might exist separately from the body" (Damasio 1994, 249). Analytical philosophers have made many frontal assaults on Descartes' dualism (Ryle 1949, Dennet 1991). Sociologist and historian Norbert Elias in his extensive production, seldom missed an opportunity to engage with Descartes from a sociological perspective. In the introduction to Elias 1987, he writes for instance: "'*Cogito ergo sum.*' What can be more absurd! Merely in order to say it, one had to learn a communal language; and why say it if no one was there to listen, to accept or to reject it? The man of straw presented by Descartes has lately acquired some fig leaves, such as 'intersubjectivity' or 'validity for all human beings', providing the lonely subject of knowledge *a posteriori* with some shadowy company. They do little to save it from its basic solitude, or transcendental theories of knowledge from their built-in solipsistic tendency" (Elias 1987, xviii).

to play the viola. *They are what we are*, writes Dissanayake, and refers to the title of her book: *Homo Aestheticus*.

But what can this concept of the aesthetic mean? Which psycho-biological prerequisites can explain this "extra action" in our existence? They are, according to Dissanayake, about our capacity to be empathic in order to experience a sounding course of events.[5] Another partial explanation lies in what she calls the aesthetic conditions that we categorize using binary (male-female, good-bad, etc.) and spatial (left-right, up-down etc.) terms.[6] These in-programmed abilities allow us to experience a heightened level of expression when used in "out-of-the-ordinary" moments. What is called "cognitive universals" are, therefore, a kind of basic organizational framework, one if manipulated in different ways generates "emotionally toned associations":

> Even though closure, division, similarity, repetition, and so forth have their fundamental *raison d'être* in natural endowments that contribute to survival, the vital ability to recognise these cognitive universals is extended in humans to their deliberate manufacture, refinement, and elaboration. [...] In humans, what is special, i.e. distinctive, contrastive, may acquire metaphysical significance... as well as perceptual and cognitive relevance (Dissanayake 1992, 164f).

Dissanayake believes our brains code different sense impressions at the same time, but our conscious processes filter out much of the actual conscious experience. With the help of language, we learn to express these impressions as analogies by metaphoric speech. This capacity is something we are apparently born with. Dissanayake references the child psychologist Daniel Stern who has written about mother-child integration in a cross-modal exchange, in which the child answers and strengthens a mutual reaction pattern. Taken together, the visual, the tactile, kinesthetic, aural, and olfactory concepts in every language can be used metaphorically to describe psychological qualities (Dissanayake 1992, 174).

---

[5] Dissanayake cites a latter-day philosopher, Susanne Langer, because she intuitively formulated what contemporary psychologists within empathy research have also pronounced: "Music sounds the way emotions feel." A similar formulation comes from the pen of the music aesthetician Kivy: "[Music is] expressive in virtue of its resemblance to expressive human utterance and behavior" (Dissanayake 1992, 147). See also Suppan 1984, 180ff.

[6] The ethnomusicologist Hans Oesch instructively discusses the native Orang Asli people's binary thoughts. He also suggests that our current thoughts about the relationship between character and symbol must be reassessed in this context: "The logic of preliterate peoples...depends much more on contrary perceptions of the attributes of the objects, i.e., the difference between raw and cooked, male and female, dry and wet [...] In order to understand and discern sacred and secular experiences, you have to understand this duality, and to address the function of music has in religious and everyday activities [...] If every natural object and every social action has two dimensions, the profane and the cosmic, you have to ask yourselves *if our concept of the symbol has any use whatsoever.*" (Oesch 1987, 273-275 [my italics]).

Among other proto-aesthetic prerequisites that are discussed are analogies between temporality and spatiality within song.[7] As with previous behaviors, Dissanayake asserts that song causes an affective addition. It is apparently difficult to prove to what degree these reactions played a distinct survival-role in human evolution, she writes, but also adds that it isn't absurd to point out:

> [t]hat the building blocks of aesthetic experience (sensitivity to changes in tempo, dynamics, size, quality, and so forth) evolved in selectively useful contexts and possess intrinsic optimal stimulation levels (e.g. fast/slow, loud/soft, large/small, strong/weak) that are relevant to our biological nature (Dissanayake 1992, 180).

The different qualities and factors that suggest that humans have a psycho-biological predisposition toward aesthetic empathy have, in the course of human development, manifested themselves in different behaviors with specific characters. When we describe these activities in western culture, we call them dance, painting, music, and today we hold them under the umbrella term of art.

Dissanayake also asserts that if our feelings towards the objects were seen earlier to project from subject to object, our current neurological research suggests that the process is exactly the reverse:

> [t]he work of art writes itself on the perceiver's body: electrochemically in the signalling patterns of activity that comprise the brain's cortical maps, which may in turn have concomitant physiological and kinesthetic effects (Dissanayake 1992, 185).

But as long as aesthetics are not analyzed as neuro-psychological processes, they will not be seen as something with a biological basis (Dissanayake 1992, 185).

It is part of the rules of the game that the kind of text Dissanayake has written takes theories from a very wide range of fields, and that some arguments apparently are not from a completely developed empirical starting point. At the same time, her conclusions and arguments are quite reasonable and add to a more complete discussion. It is also possible that the "making special" that Dissanayake talks about may have a corollary "experiencing special" that happens when one sings/plays/listens to song and music. This basic human aesthetic experience will be referred to in the following pages as *aestheticI*, shortened to æI.

---

[7]From a study of the songs of the Australian aborigines, we learn there was a close melodic-geographic relationship between the melodic contours of a song and the landscape, as well as between melodic rhythm and human walking (Dissanayake 1992, 179). Similar reflections have been made by observers of Sami jojks since the eighteenth century (see Edström 1978).

Speech as a precondition for, and analogy to music

The musicologist Ulrich Volgsten assumes that if music listeners say and write about what they can hear, this is what, in fact, we do hear. And even though language can hardly capture only a part of the listener experience, the meaning of the experience, in its widest sense, must be understood as ideological. We must skip over much of what Volgsten says about problematizing, and focus, instead, on how he developed a theory of how music "can sound the way we say we think it does." His errand is to show that music has an affective influence on us even before we consciously develop cognitive thoughts about it. How should we, in other words, explain a fundamental sound-categorizing mechanism?

Like Dissanayake, Volgsten turns to babies in his attempt to see how the pre-cultural categorization can be better understood. Part of the answer lies in the fact the we are pre-programmed to code along figural lines; mother's voice is recognized outside the deviations that can be called "good forms" (Volgsten 1999, 107). Another partial explanation could be that the happiness associated with, for example, positively categorizable sound is a reaction that does not subside, but rather rises linearly. Volgsten relies upon research that points out that the perception of something is dependent upon which cognitive brain areas are activated, "whereas *aesthetic* pleasure has to do with the net amount of activation of these units" (my italics).[8]

A third partial explanation—and perhaps the most important—comes from Daniel Stern, who showed that babies have the ability, very early on, to answer and react to rhythm, intensity, timeframes, forms, and dynamics. The reaction patterns between mother and child have an "attunement" and an "activity and intensity contour."[9] Volgsten focuses on Stern's discussion of the concept of attunement, and couples it together with Stern's study to show how the baby's self-awareness is formed in this mother-child process:

> Though the main reason for invoking Stern's idea is to show the fundamentally social character of music, a quality of music which inevitably makes it ideological, the stages of self-development may also be suggestive as an outline for a future functionalist theory of music experiences... In other words, we can take the notion of affect contour for granted here, as that which constitutes the input to the functional system we are considering—the musical mind (Volgsten 1999, 123).

Volgsten describes how this early interaction creates prerequisites for intentionality in peoples' reactions and an intuitive understanding of the others'

---

[8] Volgsten adds that this rise of contentment does not diminish according to the often-observed inverse U-curve (Volgsten 1999).

[9] Compare with Dissanayake: "The infant might accelerate the *intensity contour* of its psychical movement to match the mother's vocal effort or gesture with its arm in the same temporal beat as the mother's head-nodding" (Dissanayake 1992, 167).

affective condition. These prerequisites are, in the end, channeled and expressed through the baby's developing language ability. And it is here that Volgsten finds a parallel in understanding music's own channels of development (Volgsten 1999, 127ff).

Both Dissanayake and Volgsten comment on music's universal place in all known societies. But the thought that one could somehow prove the existence of a universal aesthetic is long gone. In order to trace an in-programmed aesthetic critical ability, psychologists research babies' reactions.

The psychologist Nathan Kogan asserts in an article that babies at the age of six months can discern between different kinds of musical stimuli in a way that cannot be explained by reference to any cultural stimulus (Kogan 1994). The question arises: what adaptive function could this represent from a developmental perspective? One possible answer can be taken from Dissanayake who points out that this ability has a positive influence on individuals and therefore also for the group. In ritual situations dance and music creates this satisfaction and have an adaptive value for both parties:

> At the individual level, participation would be expected to enhance positive states of emotional arousal: at the collective level, participation would be expected to strengthen interpersonal bonds and identification with one's group (Dissanayake 1992, 147).

Another explanation may be that a baby's musical sensitivity is a consequence of other fundamental adaptive behaviors. Kogan—here we can also return to Stern—attributes this sensitivity to a special baby language that exists between mother and child.[10] Kogan, therefore, explores the possibilities that can be found in the psycho-biological field, a question that researchers are especially interested in from the perspective of human evolution. No one has yet gone on a hunt after a special gene for music or for an aesthetic gene. But there are, in fact, a number of researchers interested in evolution. We turn now to the socio-linguist Steven Pinker, who has a good deal to say about music as a "special event" and a *special experience*.

Steven Pinker's perspective

Like a number of humanists and community researchers, socio-linguist Steven Pinker has adopted ideas emanating from Charles Darwin, ideas that

---

[10]Dissanayake has recently argued that "because of increasing infant altriciality during hominization, the primate propensity for relationship or emotional communication… became so crucial, that special affiliative mechanisms evolved… these in turn could be further developed (as temporal art, including music) to serve affiliative bonding among adults" (Dissanayake 2000, 388).

experienced a new Renaissance at the end of the twentieth century. This research direction falls under different headings depending on which fundamental outlook one has about it: "neo-darwinism," "evolutionism," "biologism," etc. It interests many important researchers including the philosopher Daniel Dennet (1995), the sociologist Walter G. Runciman (1998) and the philosopher Peter Singer (2000).[11]

Pinker tries, of course, to bring the discussion about aesthetics to an even more fundamental level, i.e. a biological level, than Dissanayake. What Pinker does is to test the procedure of "reverse engineering" on the mental organs (sight, sound, etc.) we are born with, and whose function and design are dependent on genetically-steered programs. He tests first which goals these mental organs should reach and if one could trace backwards, one might understand how, over millions of years, a biological process has developed, and what that means for us today. But, writes Pinker, even if the ultimate goal that our intellect was constructed for was to maximize:

> [t]he number of copies that created it... the gene-centred theory of evolution does *not* imply that the point of all human striving is to spread our genes (Pinker 1997, 43).

Our daily human goals—whether they are unconscious or conscious—are not about our genes, but about our quality of life, our health, family, friends, children, etc. Within this scientific field, we discover a strong urge to test new theoretical models.[12]

---

[11] For a critical illumination see, for example, Rose and Rose 2000. For a well-balanced survey of how this research field has come to be received, see Knight et al 1999. One writes: "Initially, social anthropologists and indeed most social scientists saw the new Darwinism not as a science but as a right-wing ideology... With the rise of post-modern influence within social anthropology during the 1970s and 1980s, not only Darwinism but Western science itself became viewed as little more than an ideological construct designed to serve the dominant political powers. This view licensed... the anthropologist to treat social constructs as the only phenomena accessible to study [...] But what precisely is 'a social construct'? Under what selection pressures did...[taboos, supernatural sanctions etc.] become invented, believed in? [...] As the paradigm-change of which this book is a small part unfolds, social anthropology will inevitably undergo profound restructuring" (Knight et al 1999, 6ff).

[12] So that the reader can understand what it can include, I offer one example: the biologist Margie Profet wondered why many women during their first term of pregnancy often feel an aversion to some foods. According to the traditional Freudian analysis, this has to do with the woman's loathing for the man and her unconscious will to abort the fetus. Profet hypothesised that what women didn't eat and couldn't tolerate during pregnancy was, in fact, harmful for the development of the fetus. This theory was supported when Profet went through hundreds of separate studies over the whole world. Because women in these studies avoided things that were unhealthy for their fetuses, without having any knowledge themselves about substances that were unhealthy for fetal development, Pinker draws the natural conclusion that the biological-adaptive explanation is more plausible (Pinker 1997, 39). From a biological perspective it is not always the point that we should know why we naturally behave the way we do.

Together with Pinker, we ask ourselves if it is possible to give an evolutionary answer as to why humans engage in "making special" within the frame that we today label art. Pinker offers some answers to this question under the associative rubric of "The Meaning of Life." A first problem, he says, is that the concept of art not only concerns aesthetics but also is about status:

> The very uselessness of art that makes it so incomprehensible to evolutionary biology, makes it all too comprehensible to economics and social psychology… The value of art is largely unrelated to aesthetics: a priceless masterpiece becomes worthless if it is found to be a forgery… The banality that the psychology of the arts is partly the psychology of status has been repeatedly pointed out (Pinker 1997, 522).

The point of these formulations—which are a bit unexpected for a humanist—is surely to get the reader to see art through "objective" biological eyes. It is a given, writes Pinker, that we experience pleasure and even elation when we engage with the arts, but in order to give a biological answer to the original question, we must distance all [sic] social/psychological explanations.[13] It is the brain that registers different input and that gives us experiences of well-being. Other parts of the brain assure that we use our knowledge and skills to reach goals. Even though it was not necessary from an evolutionary perspective that an organism should invest a great deal of energy to combine these two behaviors, it is precisely what humans have come to do. We use, therefore, our intellect to have as good a biological health as possible, but also for artistic activities. We have an intellect that:

> [r]ises to a biologically pointless challenge: figuring out how to get at the pleasure circuits of the brain and deliver the jolts of enjoyment without the inconvenience of wringing bona fide fitness increments from the harsh world… Now, if the intellectual faculties could identify the pleasure-giving patterns, purify them, and concentrate them, the brain could stimulate itself (Pinker 1997, 524).

Pinker concludes that the intellect engages itself in this "self stimulation" with the help of three different strategies. Art is one of them, and thereby one of many "pleasure technologies." Other activities include what the intellect thinks about, such as "Where does the universe come from?" Or, to pose a modern question, "What is good and bad art?" But, Pinker writes, we are possibly not created to solve problems of this kind at all. For him, religion and philosophy engage "in part [in] the application of mental tools to problems they were not

---

[13] One can well feel that it must be difficult to fulfill these goals. The fact that we think and write in a social context is after all difficult to get past [sic]. We are not only a biological thought experiment because we think in a social context.

designed to solve." Therefore religion and philosophy can be seen as technology for the future.[14]

"Music is an Enigma"

Against the background of these preparatory expositions, it is perhaps not so strange that Pinker described music as an enigma. Compared with our language, our senses, etc., music could disappear from our history without changing our lives at all. Therefore, Pinker asserts that song/music is not an adaptive behavior, but rather a technology, a cocktail of recreational drugs that we take in through our ears in order to stimulate a number of pleasure centers in the brain.

Pinker then makes an attempt to delineate deviancies and similar qualities between speech and music. He writes first that music "communicates nothing but formless emotion" and cannot tell a story in and of itself, not even "a plot as simple as 'boy meets girl, boy loses girl.'" Likewise, Pinker finds that music has a number of parallels to speech and discusses it with the help of music theoreticians, Schenker, Jackendorff and Lerdahl among others (Pinker 1997, 529-34). This review contains no new news for a musicologist. In fact the opposite is true, Pinker's relative lack of knowledge within this field rings rather harshly in the ears.

Pinker concludes that a normal piece of music is a sounding cake of ingredients that are attractive for at least six of our mental processes:

1) Speech—that music borrows its "mental machinery" from language—"in particular, from prosody." He reminds us that music is sometimes called "heightened speech" and gives some examples of this.
2) "auditory scene analysis"—that our mental ability to discriminate between different types of sound and to be able to hear from where a sound comes is used and coded through these adaptive capacities.
3) emotional cry—a verbal expression that goes back to an earlier stage of development like "crying, whining... growls, moans... cracks, hesitations."[15]
4) "habitat selection"—precisely as we noted, to make an environment safer; with the help of our senses we can also recognize stylized natural sounds

---

[14]Influenced by the criticism of the philosopher Colin McGinn (1993), Pinker says that when it comes to our understanding the terms consciousness, free will, knowledge, morals, basically nothing has been attained. He writes: "Maybe philosophical problems are hard not because they are divine or irreducible or meaningless or workaday science, but because the mind of Homo sapiens lacks the cognitive equipment to solve them... our minds are not the pipelines to truth" (Pinker 1997, 561). Compare also with McGinn 1993:149ff.

[15]Such emotional outbursts are something that Charles Darwin and moreover, many musicologists (myself among them: see Edstrom 1978) speculate over. Compare Wallin et al 2000 and Allen 1962, 183f.

in program music—"simplified templates of evocative environmental sounds."

5) motor control—that music lies near and uses our abilities for motor control and movement. Pinker refers to the fact that music psychologists think that "music recreates the motivational and emotional components of movement."

6) something else [sic!] –here Pinker uses the holistic trick: saying that the whole is more than the sum of its parts. But he repeats that music is not thought to be, from an evolutionary standpoint, an adaptive behavior (Pinker 1997, 527-38).

Pinker's musicological tour adds fairly little. Similarities and differences between the syntax of music and speech, and the *phoneme/morpheme* pair in relationship to *musem*,[16] and so forth is well known.[17] What seems new, albeit speculative, are points two and four, but again, what these add to the discussion is difficult to verify. Because it is equally easy or very difficult to discuss point number seven, Pinker's view on music reinforces the view that it is a non-adaptive behavior.

Dissanayake begins with the view that humans, during their phylogenesis, have developed into "aesthetic" animals, and that music, like other "special events" were included among the art-related behaviors. Volgsten prefers the ontogenetic connection and similarity between speech and musical development. Pinker, on the other hand, views music as the clearest example of an accrued technology. He does not, as Dissanayake does, make any attempt to show that other primates and other animals (beasts and birds) have aesthetic behaviors or artifacts such as colorful bird songs or gibbons' sound signals, which raise and strengthen a behavior's *communicative* function. We also know that Neanderthal people, among other behaviors, decorated graves and made patterns on tools.[18] Many ethnomusicologists have also written about the differences between folk and functional aesthetics that does not lie too far from the theories that are put forth in zoological semiotics.[19]

If it were possible for Pinker to answer the question of why humans enjoy certain forms, colors, jokes, myths, and sounds, he would still remain skeptical about general theories about art. This is above all, due to his assertion that we have

---

[16]Compare with Tagg 1979.

[17]For general discussions see de la Motte-Haber 1989, and Sloboda 1985.

[18]For a rich experimental map of the current knowledge and hypotheses surrounding sound communication between primates and the development of song/music etc, see Wallin et al 2000. Among other authors who see music's development differently than Pinker, turn to Brown, Falk, Freeman, Merker, Miller and Richman in Wallin et al 2000.

[19]Compare with Merriam 1964, 271f and the semiotician Thomas Seboek in Seboek 1979. Compare also what Suppan writes on music's biological roots, that it is less about researching "die Biologie der Musik" than "die Biologie in der Musik" Suppan 1984, 192.

a difficult time staying on purely biological grounds; instead, we wind up in a labyrinth of social impulses about power and status. His final sentence concludes: "theories of art carry the seeds of their own destruction" (Pinker 1997, 523). The crucial difference between Dissanayake's and Pinker's views lies in the fact the Dissanayake describes human musical "special events" as a necessity, while Pinker sees them as accidents. Research continues.

We will now turn our attention to a time for which the sources are more substantial, and focus on the relationship between the use of music in western culture and the aesthetic discourse that begins several hundred years before our own time. As Dissanayake points out "To the primitive and to the traditional religious devotee everywhere, the statue *is* the god…as the word *oak* is an oak" (Disssanayake 1992, 207). Whether the same is true in later times is no longer self-evident, which Dissanayake claims is due to the entrance of a very important and new medium:

The embeddedness of preliterate society in its environment, the coherence and interpenetratedness of word and referent, image and reality, began to be lost to mainstream Western philosophy from the time of Plato… the first great philosopher to speak from a full *literate* perspective when he demonstrated how images *contrast with* reality (Disssanayake 1992, 207). So therefore with æI in our baggage we *head* for the old Greeks, for here we will meet much that changes history.

*Philosophy arose in ancient Athenian culture
by aggressively defining itself in contrast
to art as the source of superior wisdom.*
Richard Shusterman

CHAPTER 2: THE GREEKS

In Black and White

This heading conceals a socially constructed truth: we believe most in the written word.[1] Of course, it hasn't always been so. We must go back to the earliest high cultures to find the spoken word written down, i.e., a written language. New survival strategies like agriculture, with their increased division of labor leading to specialization and skills are important causes for the development of written communication technologies. As described by the linguist Walter J. Ong, writing, in time had a sweeping impact on peoples' understanding of reality and the ways by which the cultures changed (Ong 1982).[2]

In Ancient Greece, several hundred years before our timekeeping, only a small minority was able to both read and write. A fundamental separation developed between those that could speak and those that could write the words down, between those that could read and write and those that couldn't. Thanks to writing, one could see and hear what someone had thought or done recently or in the distant past, and share in the thoughts or events that even the one affected had a limited memory of, or even no memory at all.

People could now, with their sight, change the flow of time, i.e., read about certain events, jump here and there in the text, iron over, change the text in a way that an oral culture could not. One saw text with external objective eyes, instead of remembering the spoken with the inner subjective ear.

---

[1] Many current musicologists and philosophers, for example Nelson Goodman, have analogously believed more in the written note picture than in sounding music. The oral transmission of music (folk music, schlager, dance music, jazz, etc.) was up until the end of the previous century also from this perspective seen as "lower" than the traditions tied to the written page. Cf. musicologist Lars Lilliestam's work (1995).

[2] I am making a conscious demarcation here and am not going to go into the vast amount of research that exists about the indigenous peoples' music culture (gatherers, hunters, nomads, and farmers). Cf. Suppan's excellent study of music's function and meaning, music specialists, dance, music instruments, and so forth (Suppan 1984, 32-152).

In 400-300 B.C.E., when Plato and later Aristotle wrote their texts, people had sung, played, danced, drawn, engaged in ritual, and so forth, for hundreds of generations. What was new now, was that for a couple of generations, a small elite group also discussed and analyzed these phenomena in written form, like other basic questions, such as *what a thing is* and *in what sense do we exist*. Some generations before Plato, Pythagoras also came to a detailed exposition of music's acoustic qualities, which gave music a theoretical position that earlier had no philosophical context.[3]

As Dissanayake formulated it, it only became possible *at this time* for a philosopher like Plato to ponder how a picture of something could contrast with reality:

> In his view, a painter or sculptor made works that were *images* or *representations* of an ideal reality that was forever separate and removed from any individual instance of it. In other words... they made 'art' (Dissanayake 1992, 207).

The Greek word that Plato used to describe the shoemaker's task, *techné*, is however, not identical with our current word *art*. For the Greeks, *techné*, was an overarching concept that could be used both for that which a singer, and a shoemaker or sculptor did: their skills.[4] While for the shoemaker, "art" was built on earlier experience, that a shoe should look like a shoe, a singer could be inspired by the gods and sometimes also add something extra above and beyond her skill. It was as if the gods themselves were singing.[5]

---

[3] Pythagoras discovered that the relationship between certain intervals came to represent an analogous correspondence to the planets' relationships to one another. But even though, according to musicologist Finne Benestad, Pythagoras rejected the thought of a music that sounds in the universe, many other philosophers, among them Plato, were not foreign to the idea: "The doctrine of the harmony of the spheres developed a very large importance and not just for the Greek philosophers, but also for the musical teaching system all the way to the Renaissance. These points of departure were probably of oriental origin, but were natural for every [sic!] Greek" (Benestad 1978, 21).

Pythagoras' discoveries are in the background of the late antique division of the arts between *artes liberales* where music, or rather music theory came to be included in the *quadrivium* together with astronomy, arithmetic, and geometry. In this group there were also fragments of music theory and it took until the seventeenth century before a new music theory slowly changed this picture. Music theory came slowly to be associated more with grammar, rhetoric and dialectics and be included in the other group, the *trivium*. During the eighteenth century more and more terms and methods of analysis entered from speech analysis. During the twentieth century, also a mathematical system, Fortes *pitch-class theory*, has won some successes. For a thorough discussion of this historical development see the work of the musicologist Hroar Klempe (1998).

[4] *Techné* translates to English often as art, craft, or skill, but is, of course, also the root word in *technique*. Cf. Hanfling 1992, 5.

[5] See Tatarkiewicz 1980, 99f. The literary scholar Gerhard Plumpe points out that the individual's contribution was not thought of as subjective: "For Plato, however, this phenomenon of inspiration had nothing to do with subjectivity and individuality. What we understand by these concepts, the Greek thinkers probably would not have recognized." ["Aber für Platon hatte das Phänomen der Inspiration nichts mit Subjektivität und Individualität zu tun. Was wir mit diesen Begriffen

THE GREEKS

Aisthesis is generally chracterized as an ability to experience something with the senses, but was not something that was only attributed to art:

It referred to both sensation and perception... and had no special application to the perception of works of arts and beauty... and it marked out one side of a division that was important in Greek thought, namely, the division between the sensory perception of things and the intellectual apprehension of them (Collinson 1992, 112).

Aisthesis thus stood in contrast to *noesis*, that is, sense and knowledge.

Plato and Aristotle wrote metaphorically about the aisthetic process as qualities in what we see, hear, feel, etc., that transmit their individual forms and qualities to people through the sense organs" (Sörbom 1994, 37).

The culture of writing made it possible for those who discussed these aspects of reality not only to distance themselves from it through the power of the written word, but there was also a similar distance or status distinction between those who thought and those who wrote (Plumpe 1993, 27f). This meant that the philosophers, as the high priests of thought, could demarcate themselves from the other professional groups, at the same time as the roots of our present-day concept of art and view of art sprang through the crust of the earth and developed green shoots. According to the philosopher Richard Shusterman, Socrates and Plato tried at once both to define themselves apart from the sophists and poets by placing philosophy at the pinnacle of thought and society. For those who understood philosophy's exposition and also could participate in their wisdom through the written word, this was not only the best direction they could receive, writes Shusterman, "but the noblest and most intense joys of contemplation" (Shusterman 1992, 35).[6]

Another delimitation that was also obvious in Athenian society was that many slaves worked within the handcraft professions. In the city state of Athens that Plato experienced, there were about 45,000 free men and about 100,000

---

meinen, hätten griechische Denker wohl kaum verstanden"] (Plumpe 1993, 33). There seems to be a connection from idea to idea that in the end leads us back to an *Ursprungsposition*: from a) Dissanayake's thesis that sculptures of gods *are* Gods, to b) Plato's idea that an unusually inspired poet was directly affected by the Gods, to c) the late, romantic variant that this inspiration only could be found in the human gods, i.e. the geniuses, to d) a current fundamentalist-deductive and Darwinist idea where artistic gift is seen as a mainly genetically determined thing, i.e., as something that is found in the gods = the people themselves. A full circle?!

[6]Cultural sociologist Martin Jay discusses an alternative way that was suggested by Martin Heidegger "when he defended the Nazi revolution as a realization of Promethean action and exhorted his students to join their 'knowledge-service' to the labor and military service" (Jay 1998). What Heidegger claimed was that for the Greeks, theory was not something that one philosophized over for its own sake "but the other way round to understand theory as the supreme realization of genuine practice" (Jay 1998, 23). Even if this view contained some truth, it led in practice to a separation between practice and theory already in the Greek society.

slaves. Women had no political rights and lived largely within the four walls of the home.

For the classical philosophers, the concept of *mimesis* was a point of departure in their discussions on Art. Mimesis can be translated in different ways, for example as the "presentation/description of something," and the meaning varies between "imitation" or "copy," in the second case "representation," "exact mimicking" and sometimes "performance" (Hurtshouse 1992, 241).

Plato's famous comparison with the prisoners in the cave gives a picture of how he thought. People, Plato explained, can only see the shadows on the wall in front of themselves, which means that the true world lay apart—behind the backs of—people's power of imagination. In the world the people experienced, concrete and abstract objects/thoughts were only an illusion. The *philosophical* thought came closer to the ideal world, where ideas and forms always existed unchanged.

The fact that artists therefore imitated an illusion did not increase their social status. Plato established:

> The artist's representation is… a long way removed from truth… [The artist is] merely manufacturing shadows at third remove from reality… We may assume, then, that all poets from Homer downwards have no grasp of reality, but merely give us a superficial representation of any subject they treat including human goodness (Hurtshouse 1992, 247).

The most concrete discussion on the mimetic properties of art can be found not in Plato, but in his student Aristotle. Even though there undoubtedly are differences between Plato's and Aristotle's views, both uphold the thought of art's mimetic information.[7]

Three thousand years ago

For our present needs, let me draw out the contours of the Greek song/music tradition that we will meet up until Aristotle's time. The Greek language that was spoken made certain demands on the bard who sang or recited long epic texts like the *Iliad*:

---

[7] Aristotle represents, in opposition to Plato, the view that ideas and forms existed as essences of the objects we perceive. Aristotle claimed also that a painting of something was not only a slavish reproduction, but that an artist also could improve the motive. Cf. Hurtshouse 1992, 256. The most concrete description that Aristotle gave about art and its fuctions concerns a rather concrete art form, tragedy. Here we also meet the concept of *catharsis*, that should be understood as a contemplative, cleansing experience. If we fully experience the development of the tragedy and, for example, experience the feeling of fear, but do not react as if it were a real situation, but rather experience it in a cognitive way, we can release or cleanse ourselves of this feeling (Collinson 1992, 119f).

Ancient Greek was a pitched language, so melody had to be an outgrowth of the natural inflections of the spoken language. Greek vowels had long and short values that corresponded to long and short notes in the musical settings. Thus musical rhythms were derived from metric forms, and melodic movement was governed by the natural rise and fall of the text (*Encyclopædia Britannica Online*).

We understand from this, and the Greek word *mousiké* that stood for both song text, song/music and dance, that there was a close conceptual connection between these activities and other ways of thinking in the Greek music culture.[8] Plato, for example, connected the Greek scales, the modes, with different Greek populations. Different melodic formulas and scale uses early in Greek history came to be associated with different moods and textual content. It was therefore obvious for Plato that hypolydian mode was useful for songs of mourning, ionic mode for drinking songs, and so forth.[9] There were also good conditions for a mimetic thought process within music culture. The philosopher Göran Sörbom clarifies:

> For Plato and Aristotle and many others, but not all ancient thinkers it was natural to use the conceptual framework of *aesthesis* and *mimesis*... A piece of music is not, for instance, anger in itself in abstraction, nor is it an example of anger... but it is an image of anger. [...] This knowledge and praxis tied up to it is to a large extent culturally established and acquired by the members of the culture in a process... in which we learn which things are images and imitations and how to react in front of them and how to use them (1994:42).

One sang about gods, heroes, historical events, and praised the families in whose service one was bound.[10] These bards, who had exulted status and great importance, sang to their own accompaniment on the lyre. They probably did so in a special song speech, that fewer and fewer could exculpate, and by the middle of the millennium, had also become distorted.[11]

Normal people sang and danced in a number of different social contexts: parties, processions, rites, offerings, and so forth. There was also a close connection between songs and their areas of use. Women had for example special songs when they weaved. As another example, boys and men engaged in exercise to certain songs with instrument accompaniment. There is a rich daily repertoire for different

---

[8] For us today music = music, song = song, and dance = dance, but with the addition that song can be a part of the concept of music. It is however doubtful that music can be understood as a subdivision of the concept of song, cf. the question "is music a kind of song?" See also page 169.

[9] Cf. Benestad 1978, 23f for a longer citation of Plato's *The States* where it describes what qualities the different modes were supposed to have exhibited.

[10] For a comprehensive introduction to Greek music culture during Antiquity, see Mathiesen 1999.

[11] Observe that the inspired bard's recitation was seen to a greater degree as a result of the influence of the gods than his own skill. During these "inspired" moments, the prestige of the bard, the poet, the singer/musician, was higher. Cf Hanfling 1992, 6f.

uses (Zaminer 1989, 123).[12] Plato called attention to the importance within *mousiké* that one learned songs in a correct way and that boys received a physical and spiritual education in school that met the demands society would place upon them. Song/music had an importance for society's wellbeing and continued existence. Moral "mousikal" and military practices went hand in hand.

In Plato's dialog *The Laws* it is postulated that there exists *nothing beautiful in and of itself*. This means that the musical thought in Ancient Greece did not concern aesthetic value as such.[13] It would even have been blasphemous to state that music's purpose was to give the soul pleasure, rather the decisive quality was that it was made according to the mimetic rules and laws that governed *mousiké*. The correct ways to perform songs had a refining quality on human character.[14] Plato's discussion can be compared to a circular path: those who had interpretive precedence decided what gave pleasure, was entertaining and, what was good and right.[15]

When the song melody was interleaved with instrumental music, however, confusion was created:

> For when there are no words, it is very difficult to recognize the meaning of the harmony and rhythm, or to see that any worthy object is imitated by them... all this sort of thing... is exceedingly coarse and tasteless (Lippman 1986, 21).

The Greeks' love of sport also had parallels, in music competitions too. In one especially famous competition lyrical and dramatic songs as well as instrumental pieces were presented. The titles of the latter could be as fantasy-filled as "The Song of the Army Tank." Pieces could contain many musical illustrations that the *aulos* player Sakades gained victory with a description of Apollo's victory

---

[12] In a later Greek source from the 200s we find a division into fifty different dance styles and a register with innumerable shepherd's songs with different content, as well as worker songs for different tasks (Henderson 1957, 391). One also sang in choirs for rites, offerings, and official festivals. Unison singing was the most important and the most common form of musical expression. The free boys who went to school learned songs from a teacher who taught music specifically: "Boys of the upper classes went to a music-master, and in company there were expected to intone their piece of epic or to sing the classics at meals. 'Musical hoggishness' was a social and political insult" (Henderson 1957, 391).

[13] Cf. Lippman 1986, 3.

[14] Cf. Plato: "When anyone says that music is to be judged of by pleasure, his doctrine cannot be admitted... but only that other kind of music which is an imitation of the good, and bears resemblance to its original (Plato as cited in Lippman 1986, 19). The opposite was also true: the wrong music had a negative influence on people. Suppan states that in general, when one examines the fundamental functions that song/music has in indigenous cultures, one finds that "everywhere there is, within the framework of cultural value systems, a clearly pre-assigned and socially controllable order" ["überall besteht eine im jeweiligen Rahmen der kulturellen Wertvorstellungen festgelegte und sozial kontrollierte Ordnung"] (Suppan 1984, 68).

[15] Plato defined the competence that such a person should have: "In the first place, of what the imitation is; secondly, he must know what is true; and thirdly, that it has been well executed in words and melodies and rhythms" (as cited from Lippman 1986, 19).

over the Python. Here the audience could hear both the "roaring of the monster" and "the god's victory." According to the musicologist Carl-Allan Moberg, "it was a program-music and mimetic instrumental art" of the highest order (Moberg 1973, 34).[16]

An unusually revolutionary time

When Plato and Aristotle wrote their texts, a slow change within music culture reflected that the broader culture found itself within a time of crisis. It was probably to a high degree, against these persistent winds that obstinately kept blowing in the same direction, that Plato and Aristotle, among others, reacted to. The Athenian society went through a dramatic and politically turbulent period, which affected everyone's vision.

From the 490s to the 480s Athenians were at war with Persia. The advantage in the war went back and forth. At one point at the end of the 480s Athens, completely destroyed by the Persians, but the Greeks shortly thereafter, won a key sea battle and the Persians retreated. Then came the rebuilding of the city. Athens was in coalition with other city-states, began an aggressive and war-like foreign policy against Persia and Sparta. This period of expansion ended first in 446 B.C.E. with a peace treaty. The war against the hereditary enemy of Sparta was taken up by 431, however, and continued with a few pauses until 404:

> In 405 the Athenian navel power was completely annihilated...Afterwards Athens was starved out through a naval blockade.... and the Athenian government at the end of 404 was forced to make a humiliating peace (Thomsen 1983, 167).

The century was thus characterized by sometime victories and setbacks and with a relatively long and relatively quiet period for the population around the middle decades of the century. It was during this time that Pericles came to power in Athens and introduced a form of democracy for the free men. Culture thrived. One paid for example, for tickets for the poor free men who wanted to go to the theater. During the three-day-long festival of Dionysus, dramas were produced, a tradition that had great importance and popularity for the times. Because no reprises were allowed, productions were large. But at the same time there was a thorough and deep change in the spirit of the society. While traditionally one had to rely on the benevolence of the controlling gods, around the middle of the century an enlightenment movement sprang up that was a constant irritation with its rational thoughts, questioning traditional religious and collective norms

---

[16]Moberg also mentions that program music on the *aulos* had been strongly influenced by a similar tradition on the Lyre. Even poets were inspired to similar mimetic effects. Moberg names a "word painting" with "imitation of, among other things, tremolo effects on the *aulos* [which] was seen to describe the battle at Salamis (480)" (Moberg 1973, 35).

of value. Therefore, the Danish historian Rudi Thomsen, writes that in the last decades of the century there was a *serious cultural crisis*:

> It was increased further through the accidents of war, and among thinking people disturbed the belief in a divine guidance of the world and also undermined respect for all the societal norms—both moral and legal... Therefore the individual lost his old anchoring in society... and a thus far unknown individualism gained approval. Cultural life lost its earlier hallmark of harmonic balance, and instead more feeling based but also realistic attitudes became foregrounded (Thomsen 1983, 185).

It is these events and societal changes that create the background for Plato and Aristotle's writings. While musical life had earlier mainly relied upon an individual practice, gradually the idea was introduced that it was socially acceptable to be merely a listener. The practicing musicians multiplied in number and developed a more independent function in a cultural climate where one began to experiment outside the traditional frames.[17]

The dissolution of traditional values, vocal music's reduced role as well as instrumental music's increased one, combined with a more individualistic view of song and music's expressive possibilities all lead within the realm of the school to the long period of education that boys began to doubt. At the same time as instrumental music became more common and practitioners more professional, they lacked the support of the highest levels of society. Both Plato and Aristotle complained about the changes underway:

> Our music was once divided in its proper forms... 'hymns'... 'dirges'... 'paeans'... It was not permitted to exchange the melodic styles of these established forms... But later, an unmusical anarchy was led by poets who... were ignorant of the laws of music... their works and their theories infected the masses. So our theatre, once silent, grew vocal, and aristocracy of music gave way to a pernicious theatrocracy (Plato, from the *Laws* as cited after Henderson 1957, 395).

Virtuosity, the actors' outgoing style, and the emphasis on superficial effects were other developments that Plato and Aristotle viewed negatively.[18] The development that Plato lamented over, is mirrored also in the comedies that entertained the Athenian viewers.[19]

---

[17] Music historian Max Wegner writes that "in the course of [music] becoming more full and refined, it was also more selfevident, presumptuous, excessive and hybrid" ["Indem sie [die Musik] sich vervollkomnete und verfeinerte, wurde sie alsbald allzu selbstbewusst, überheblich, masslos und hybrid"] (Wegner 1963, 19). Even if meaning implies that music is an independent being, it states that music changed as a result of the socio-cultural development.

[18] As the music historian Isobel Henderson cites, melodies that were new for Aristotle for his student Aristoxenos they had already become conventional: "Contemporary music to him, is not shocking but sugary" (Henderson 1957, 397). Cf. Mathiesen who gives music theory a generous place (Mathiesen 1999, 287-607 [sic!]).

[19] Henderson and the musicologist Crossley-Holland both refer to Aristofanes' *The Frogs* that

Aristotle's writing that music is probably not completely necessary for children's upbringing can also be seen as a sign of change. Aristotle questions the qualities possessed by different kinds of music and how the senses are affected by that music. He also questions the social uses and functions of music and the appropriate employment of instruments. *Mousiké* had a high reputation, instrumental playing, a low one. We are reminded again of the general division between theory and practice that existed everywhere in Greek culture.[20]

The musicologist Albrecht Riethmüller (1989) suggests that in Aristotle's writings on music culture, we find a classical Greek musicology. Like Plato, Aristotle looked back, but accepted also some features of the new time. Riethmüller maintains that Aristotle's use of *mousiké* shows that he did not think about *mousiké* in terms of its earlier combined meanings, but thought about it in ways that come closer to our modern concept of music (1989:126). Moberg adds that the resolution of the concept of *mousiké* not only led to an aesthetically emancipated tonal art but also the poetry and music developed itself according to its own laws (1973: 30). Moberg does not go further into how this self-development could be possible. He also gives no further idea of what the aesthetic could be in this process.

A Summary Discussion

As this overview has shown, song dominated in the Greek culture. Thanks to the close syntactic and semantic relationships that existed between speech and melody in the Greek songs, these songs have been compared to another language.[21] Song could also be accompanied by different instruments. There was a broad understanding about which instruments could be used and by whom and in what contexts. In much higher numbers than within the vocal culture, there were professional practitioners, that sometimes had the opportunity to compose pieces of program music.

---

describes this development in the form of comedy (see Henderson 1957, 392-5). Cf. the comedy *The Clouds,* where an important theme is also that it was "better before" (for a short citation see Ling 1983, 33). Musical incompetence, that was once seen as a sign of the lower classes now became generally "a plume of the new snobbery" (Henderson 1957, 339).

[20] A thorough discussion of Aristotle's texts can be found in Riethmüller 1989, 216-37. Aristotle writes generally that music concerns a) "amusement and relaxation" b) "tends in some degree to virtue" or c) "contributes something to intellectual entertainment and culture"(cited from Rackham 1932). Aristotle made the comparison that because one didn't need to know how to prepare good food (like a professional chef), but that one was happy to eat good food, one didn't need to be a professional musician either in order to enjoy instrumental music (Rackham 1932, 651f).

[21] Henderson suggests that this relationship "is perhaps unparalleled in Europe" (Henderson 1957, 385).

One can find that there is a certain amount of contradiction in the discussions of Plato and Aristotle that we have revisited here when it comes to the social importance of music. I experience this as a consequence of the clear socio-cultural changes that occurred during this period. Because Plato/Aristotle saw the old song/music as an expression of the right and the true—including how music was used and what it meant—their writings appear logical. But one finds in Aristotle the argument that song and music's power in its differing functions clearly was experienced as the "making special" that Dissanayake spoke of. The *fundamental aesthetic experience æl, existed here in a socially developed form.* It was important that children should learn to participate in song/music—though not generally to learn to play instruments. The receiver's sense changed in relationship to music's character and ethos (cf. Sörbom 1994, 43):

> Since we accept the classification of melodies made by some philosophers, as ethical melodies, melodies of action, and passionate melodies [i.e. representative of character, of action and of emotion]... we say that music ought to be employed not for the purpose of one benefit... but on account of several (for it serves the purpose of both education and of purgation, and thirdly... for amusement... yet not employ them all in the same way, but use the most ethical ones for education, and the active and passionate kind for listening to when others are performing (Aristotle from Rackham 1932, 671).

Plato and Aristotle were dismissive of the taste of the common man, regarded instrumental music as being on a lower plane, and experienced the new music styles as degenerating. They also were critical of those who were practically engaged in music. At the same time, it was perfectly normal for free men to engage in "mousikal" activities in the earlier Greek society. There was, in other words, an unresolved conflict between a skepticism of praxis and an expectation of participation in song. In a time when instrumental music emancipated itself and the demands of virtuosity rose, this unresolved conflict solved itself from a philosophical standpoint (neither Plato nor Aristotle propagandized for youth to become virtuosi).

The earlier association between mode and textual content changed and must therefore have defended the traditional requirements of a mimetic art, but at the same time instrumental music's mimetic possibilities *were* smaller. Moberg suggests that the prejudice against instrumental music was motivated by the listeners' experience of "helplessness and vexation" because the music itself gave no "directions about its 'content,' but rather had to be understood with the help of a series of conventions" (Moberg 1973, 30).

Against this background we can now present the conclusions that Shusterman and Dissanayake have drawn. Dissanayake maintains that Plato was the first great philosopher, who, thanks to the mental mechanisms that the written language made possible, among other things, wrote about the difference between pictures/representations and reality. Because the Greeks with few exceptions did not notate their single-voiced melodies, there was hardly a similar process within song/music's field as found in the literary one. On the other hand, one used one's written language and rational thought to describe in detail acoustic relationships and melodies/tonal relationships.[22] We find therefore that while the literary tradition is preserved in writing, the singing/instrumental tradition continued according to the conditions of oral culture.

One development, that must be described as important for music culture was that individualism, which had become more common, even had an impact on music. From the fourth century the employers of musicians would rather have heard a virtuosic performance than a new song. While text and music were composed earlier by the same person, now there was a division of labor:

> Sophisticated poets were growing incapable of making music, and musicians of writing sophisticated verse. When the classical unity of music was broken, the "music" (in our narrow sense of the term) was supplied by a professional engaged in the performance (Henderson 1957, 400 [cf. the above opinion of Riethmüller on the development from *mousiké* to music]).

One result of this division was that the musician's/composer's status changed for the worse. At the same time a gradual fragmentation of Athenian society began. Thomsen talks about how society began to be permeated with class divisions between a rich upper class and a large and poor proletariat (Ling 1983, 183). Instead of a cohesive culture and within the free classes a co-operative spirit, we find an increasing division of labor and individualism. Plato and Aristotle's search to place themselves highest had naturally enough both a socially and intellectually delimiting function. That they distanced themselves in this from the cultural development that occurred around them, can also be seen as an expression of—to borrow ways of thinking from the contemporary French sociologist Pierre Bourdieu—their internal struggle to defend their positions within the Greek philosophical field.[23]

With the exception of the close connections among poetry/song/dance that the concept of *mousiké* describes, there is otherwise little in the existing description up to this point that seems strange for our idea of music's use and

---

[22] Ling returns to the music historian Donald J. Grout's frustrated sigh in the introduction to his Greek section in *A History of Western Music* (Grout 1960), i.e., that "no area within musicology has produced a richer harvest of dissertations from a more meager field of facts" (as cited in Ling 1983, 36; cf. also Benestad 1978, 17f). One can also establish that the section that takes up Greek music theory as it is described by Aristoxenos not infrequently is repeated as the main bulk of what is said about Greek music (cf. Henderson 1957 and Riethmüller 1989).

[23] Thoughts from Bourdieu will appear now and then in this writing. Fundamental to his thorough sociological theory are, among other things: the idea that a person's socialized way of thinking and acting guides daily actions and that we judge and process different positions within the different fields of activity in which we are involved.

function. We find admittedly no detailed descriptions of how song/music is used in the culture and only general discussion on music's function. But it is not difficult to imagine that music in the power of its use could have the functions that Merriam found generally important. Those functions are all, with the exception of the second, relevant in this case, as "the function of":

1) Emotional expression, 2) Aesthetic enjoyment,[24] 3) Entertainment, 4) Communication, 5) Symbolic representation, 6) Psychical response, 7) Enforcing conformity to social norms, 8) Validation of social institutions and religious rituals, 9) Contribution to the continuity and stability of culture, [and] 10) Contribution to the integration of society (Merriam 1964, 219-26).

As the reader noted "aesthetic enjoyment" is the second function. Nowhere in the thorough writings of Merriam can there be found, however, that something that can be interpreted as an understanding of the concept of aesthetics in its modern meaning from the eighteenth century (see Chapter 3).

Some writers (Riethmüller and Henderson) suspect that during this time a change from *mousiké* to music began. As mentioned it was above all a social development that brought a division between song and instrumental music when it came to their inner development, position, and status. Generally, instrumental music gradually developed a stronger position, but at the same time the professional musicians' esteem sank among trendsetting writers and philosophers. We can presume that this evaluation pattern gradually was also taken over by the general population. But it must have taken time before the mimetic ideal within *mousiké techné* lost its meaning.

To return to Dissanayake's expression, we have met different forms of "making special" and "special experience" that I refer to as æI. Aesthetics, i.e. *aesthesis*, in Greek culture concerned whether one, for example, could perceive with the senses the different qualities of the modes, the mimetic dimensions of programmatic instrumental music, etc., as opposed to intellectual thought about the music's acoustic properties: the composition of intervals in different modes, an so forth. Aristotle defined art's most important forms as "order, symmetry and definiteness."[25] One didn't expect something beautiful in and of itself. *Aisthesis* was

---

[24] On this function, "aesthetic enjoyment," Merriam writes that whether or not it is found in non-literary cultures "is a moot point." He means that this function exists without question in many high cultures, and that it probably is found in others (Merriam 1964, 223). It is obvious that all discrete divisions of music's function are rough constructions. For different individuals the same music piece can have different functions of varying weight and importance. The difficulty lies in the ability to distinguish and identify them. Also take note that there must be a large communal basis of functions within a culture in order for this to be experienced as a separate fellowship. We are not 'singular individuals" but rather group individuals. Cf. Ch. 1, footnote 16.

[25] Cf. Sörbom who writes in summary, "music can give hedonistic pleasure, structural pleasure (beauty), and pleasure from learning." Concerning the hedonistic variation he also says that, "there is a great disagreement about the value of such pleasure and the role it should play in human life"

no overarching concept. For the Greeks, art meant something other than what the concept came to mean later in history.

The Loadbearing Capacity of a Thought

In Riethmüller there is an astonishing train of thought. He suggests that Plato's ideas surrounding art in relationship to Aristotle, who came after him, corresponds to Hegel's views in relationship to Kant (Riethmüller 1989, 216). Despite the fact that mutual chronologies between the respective pairs are not the same (Hegel's writings come after Kant's Plato's before Aristotle), one always must be careful with comparisons between how different people think, especially when those comparisons concern space in time of over 2000 years. It is easy within the philosophical tradition to think that the eternal questions are just that. This is difficult for me to accept I can understand that two questions formulated in writing from different time periods can look quite similar on paper, but I see this similarity as a fairly deceitful one.

One fundamental position for me is therefore that what we understand/experience (concretely or abstractly) is grounded in our biological abilities, interacting with our socially learned and culturally inherited approaches and behaviors. Further, I see our speech as a communication form with which we share these experiences, feelings, and understandings. Because speech changes syntactically and semantically, it makes it possible to formulate other experiences, states, judgments, and opinions spread over time. At the same time this process makes it more difficult to access earlier experiences, judgments, and opinions.

Language stands therefore in a procedural relationship to the culture in which it is spoken. The semantic fields within which a word's meaning is located, can shrink or expand with time, they can even expand outside of their original areas and mutate into something completely different. The same word—art, for example—partly relates to a constellation of other words, but also can relate to the entire network of judgments and experiences present in a given time and culture. The same word can therefore have different impact and meaning, phenomena have different functions, abstract ideas have different meanings in different times and in different cultures.

The answer to what a word like art or aesthetic means must therefore always be related to time and place. In principle there are just as many answers as there are times/places/cultures within which the question is asked. Whatever we choose to take as an example, we understand that which is said/thought/done within its time/context. Concretely put: Aristotle lived in his conceptual world with his idea about how the sun rose (a geocentric worldview), about the rights of

---

(Sörbom 1994, 37).

slaves, the origin of species, women's role, music's development, the emergence of disease, and so forth. Hegel also lived in his own conceptual world. All peoples' thoughts, judgments, conclusions, and so forth come from these premises. The analog in Plato–Aristotle and Kant–Hegel is therefore a seductive one, but a theoretical minefield because the distance in time creates widely different cultural points of comparison.

This, of course, is more or less what Karl Mannheim said:

Each idea acquires a new meaning when it is applied to a new life situation. When new strata take over systems of ideas from other strata, it can always be shown that the same words mean something different to the new sponsors, because these latter think in terms of different aspirations and existential configurations. This social change of function, then, is...also a change of meaning (Mannheim 1968, 188).

Another way to illuminate this process is to make a free connection to the German historian and sociologist Norbert Elias's concepts, psychogenesis and sociogenesis. People are a cumulative project. Our culturally inherited knowledge and our behavior form us in different ways. Simply put: there is a close connection between structural changes within a culture and how peoples' ways of thinking and acting can change (see further below concerning the nobility).[26] The following was formulated by the sociologists Stephen Mennel and Johan Goudsblom, both important interpreters of Elias's thought:

Philosophers no longer speak of a pre-given 'reason', but they use 'logic' or 'language' in an equivalent way to denote a pre-given unchanging and eternal form behind the changing contents of knowledge... This conception of one, unchanging logic of rationality, Elias remarks, gives the impression that, by means of it, the theory of relativity could as well be discovered by Albertus Magnus as by Albert Einstein... and [uses this] analogy for how scientific knowledge actually grows—by successive small advances over currently knowledge, stimulated by pressures of social competition (Elias 1998, 34).

That I found it necessary to take this argument into my narrative is not just in order to compare it with Plato/Aristotle, Kant, and Hegel. Rietmüller compares Aristoxenos's writings on music theory with Johann Mattheson's introduction to his *Der vollkommene Capellmeister* from 1737 and finds them to be very similar. Mattheson sometimes used the pseudonym "Aristoxenos der jüngere" (Reitmüller 1989, 238, 244)! But as we have seen, there are also a number of other changes during Greece's classical period: instrumental music became more disseminated, song/music was seen as more emotional, the earlier

---

[26]This is basically what Elias's monumental works, *The Court Society* (Elias 1983) and *The Civilization Process* (Elias 1978) are concerned with. These thoughts are also central to Elias's work on Mozart (Elias 1991). I have discussed Elias's pioneering research earlier in a larger article (Edström 1995). For introductions to Elias, see Mennel 1989 and van Krieken 1998.

THE GREEKS

rule system was loosened. Some of these changes we will meet in the next chapter. This has presumably meant that many researchers have repeatedly the analogous sirens when they have compared the Classical Greek period with the European seventeenth and eighteenth centuries.

Even though it is difficult to avoid these false "parallel" fifth sirens, we must be on our guard against their seducing contents. With these words of warning in mind we will take a huge step in time to Europe in the Age of Enlightenment. By doing this we will be skipping over a not inconsequential amount of music, that in other contexts would earn our attention. But for the overall goal of our narrative all of this music within an enormous span of time has no definitive meaning for the "aesthetic project." Without giving away too much, it can already be said that the word aesthetic *became* highly relevant during Mattheson's time, instrumental music developed a create importance and human emotion bloomed. The word aesthetic became a concept whose meaning we will continue to hunt after.

If man is ever to solve that problem of the politics in practice he will have to approach it through the problem of the aesthetic, because it is only through beauty that man makes his way to freedom.

Friedrich Schiller[1]

CHAPTER 3: THE AGE OF ENLIGHTENMENT

The Birth of Aesthetics

The German literary critic Gerhard Plumpe notes that there are at least two kinds of authors in the history of writing about aesthetics. One group maintains that such phenomena have always existed, and that the concept of aesthetics itself is unproblematic. Moberg for instance writes on the Greek "aesthically free tonal art," and "the aesthetics of Antiquity," as well as "the Aesthetics of the Middle Ages," i.e. about aesthetics within specific fields and time-periods before the eighteenth century. The other group of authors point out that the use of the concept of aesthetics is not simple, and that it should be researched further. Most, including Plumpe, set the birth of the concept at 1750, when Alexander Baumgarten's work *Aesthetica* was published. But the first definition actually can be found in his earlier work *Meditationes philosophicae de nonnullis ad poema pertinentibus*, where he says:

> Therefore, things known are to be known by the superior faculty as the object of logic; things perceived are to be known by the inferior faculty, as the object of the science of perception, or aesthetic (Aschenbrenner 1954, 78).[2]

During the Middle Ages, the concept of sensory perceptions (*aesthesis*), art, and beauty were not bound up together. When the concept of aesthetics

---

[1] The section in Schiller's own formulation that is similar to this English paraphrase (taken from Woodmansee 1994, 58) is: "Ich hoffe, Sie zu überzeugen, dass die Materie, weit weniger der Bedürfnis als dem Schmack des Zeitalters fremd ist; ja, dass man, um jenes politische Problem in der Erfahrung zu lösen, durch das ästhetische den Weg nehmen muss, weil es die Schönheit ist, durch welche man zu der Freiheit wandert."

[2] Thanks to Göran Sörbom, Uppsala, who reminded me that Baumgarten in this paragraph begins by saying that, already with the Greeks and the Fathers of the Church, there was a distinction between "things perceived" and "things known," and between perception and clear thought (compare with the above, page 33).

resurfaced during the eighteenth century, it was associated with *art* (Plumpe 1993, 26).[3]

Several questions arise: "How long did this concept gestate before the pregnancy was carried to term?" And, "Who impregnated what?" For it is clear that when Baumgarten "newly-defined" the word aesthetic in the 1730s, a prior socio-cultural process had been going on for some time. Baumgarten recovered a word that stood for something that he experienced and felt compelled to give it linguistic form. An experienced practice gave birth to a theoretical awareness.[4] Aesthetics became more than a word; it became a concept. Let us therefore look more closely at the causes that lie behind the process that led to the twin births of art and aesthetics during the Enlightenment.

On Music's Breadth and Function

The picture painted by general music historians about music history in the seventeenth and eighteenth centuries shows, above all, a musical life centered around the court, and within the church and the cities. Folk music during this time, dependent as it is on the researcher's attitude and existing source material, is seen very little. One notable exception is the Swedish musicologist Jan Ling's history of music in which folk music is given a considerable coverage. One of his chapters is called "Music in the European Autocratic States" (Ling 1983, 459-606). It is clear from this large chapter that music communities were extremely diversified. Ling breaks it down this way:

Music and power: music's role in the autocratic ideology

Baroque and thorough bass

Italy as a musical center of production

Musical spaces and musical styles

A musical form develops

---

[3]We shall soon take up this point again, where it will be seen that it includes a number of problems of delimitation. If there was art, then there was also non-art. If there was something beautiful, then there must also have been something that was ugly.

[4]The idea historian Sven-Eric Liedman gives a background to the concept's development. Concerning Baumgarten, an account is given for his connection backwards in time with philosophers like Christian von Wolff and forwards like Gottfried Wilhelm Leibniz (Liedman 1997, 356-9). Also Luc Ferry (1993, 33-76) gives a great deal of place for these connections and different pre-stages of the history of aesthetics. Concerning the dating of the Enlightenment, Liedman shows that there are many different opinions about what that movement contained, where it began and how it developed. One thinks today not only of the French tradition but also reckons with Scottish, English, German, and North American Enlightenment (Liedman 1997, 43). An overarching definition like the one that Liedman formulated after Seyla Benhabib is that the Enlightenment Project consists of a "striving to connect scientific-technological progress with human freedom and happiness" (Liedman 1997, 42).

THE AGE OF ENLIGHTENMENT

- Opera—a symbol of absolutism and the beginning of a public musical
- Life in the service of the middle classes
- The new musical styles and the church
- Instrumental concerts
- Music instruments and their function
- Musical understanding—the learned musical world view and the absolutist states
- Music among farmers, gentlemen, and handcraft workers

With Ling's help, we can refresh our memories about the function and variation of music. In the chapter's introduction, Ling contrasts two examples of how music forms were separated from one another: a courtly opera is set in an antique mythical world that glorified autocracy. It was written by a composer (Cesti) who clawed his way up to "the famous court composer's dizzying heights"; the other, a simple song about the misery of war, could have been performed by vagrant "wandering singers and hurdy-gurdy players." The difference in social status and economic conditions can hardly ever have been greater.

We find, therefore, on one hand that the vast majority of people–farmers, rural workers, sailors, and hand craft workers (including manufacturers)–sang simple songs about life's joys and sorrows, psalms and hymns. They danced circle games to songs and music performed by individuals and sometimes by parish musicians, or city musicians and their apprentices. Most people lived in the countryside, or in small villages and only a small minority in large cities. Rural people grew up with their music and it held a functional place in their lives. Song and music had its functional place as "making special," as æI, during holidays and festivities. One gradually became familiar with the music that one heard as one passed through life.

On the other hand, in contrast to the folk music, we find a rich flowering of music styles and genres developed by music specialists within the church and at court (singers, cantors, organists, instrumentalists), and in the cities, as well (with guilds of multifaceted city musicians). Even this song and music had a structure and, where appropriate, a written content that corresponded to its function. Both folk song and "music for nobility" functioned as a transmitter and idealization of the message of their respective worldly and religious ideologies. It had a structure and in many cases a written content corresponding to its function, or as a decorative entertainment, or supporting sound source during processions, audiences, banquets, dinners, etc. It functioned also as dance music, and as concerted music at social gatherings, where it drew greater attention to itself within different kinds of closed societies within the court, in city academies, and "concert societies."

On a "third hand" we also find that traditional folk music could be performed among the nobility and bourgeoisie. It was made by amateur musicians and could be heard within the universities as well as at certain courts. Because folk music could be performed by the nobility, it was used in a different context than its original one, one of the reasons why song and music's meaning and function partly changed.

A person's worldview determined how one connected to the music of the time as well as to what music was chosen and what it meant. At least as sure as it is that music's structure and form had a functional connection to situations for which it was written or played, it is equally sure that the music that was played, what was chosen and what meaning it had, stood in a close relation to a person's total worldview, how that person thought and reacted as a social being. In order to better understand peoples' conditions as cultural beings during this period, and in order to better understand the relationship between music's use and function for the people living in the seventeenth and eighteenth centuries, it is necessary to fix our gaze on the processes and powers that created the basic conditions for this relationship, their aesthetic sense. Otherwise it is not possible to understand why Baumgarten raised the aesthetic flower in his garden.

Socio-cultural Conditions

Norbert Elias's description of the rise and fall of court societies gives ample room to the changing behaviors and needs of the nobility during the seventeenth and eighteenth centuries (Elias 1983). The point of departure for Elias is his theory that an increasing division of labor, and a generally rising level of knowledge within society together with a slowly increasing standard of living, gradually affected the *figurations*, or the social networks, that people moved within. More and more people came into contact with one another. For historical reasons, within this process a special form of government developed. Governments were formed in which all decisions were taken by one person: the king or queen, the prince, duke, or some other person of high nobility, and sometimes also higher dignitaries within the church. These changes meant that a geographical area developed a central government, which in turn led to a court and an administration. As the king ruled over his family, he also ruled over his court and his lands. Within the larger powerful noble society that surrounded power, work time and leisure time melded into one and public figures were constantly surrounded by various servants, among them musicians and singers. One didn't divide the day into work time and leisure time. One did not have a profession in any modern sense. One was always a public person.

THE AGE OF ENLIGHTENMENT

For Elias it is important to show that the courtly societies created a personality type that had to maneuver completely in public, but whose behavior was at the same time very carefully regulated. They were always exposed to the gaze of others. Above all, they felt they must maintain their prestige and standing and this prevailing etiquette informed their various art forms. It was important to control one's emotional life, not primarily for economic reasons, but rather to maintain the prestige and standing that one had achieved.

In this world one was surrounded by various art forms that one related to according to prevailing etiquette. The refined taste that one bore had a demarcating function downwards. Everyone's prestige was the most important socio-economic resource. Elias describes how prestige became fetishized:

> The fetish character of every act in the etiquette was clearly developed at the time of Louis XIV [...] Etiquette and ceremony increasingly became… a ghostly perpetuum mobile that continued to operate regardless of any direct use-value (Elias 1983, 86).

Fettered within this highly regulated world—and clearly in many cases, fettered within the system—people viewed external objects differently than we do today. Everything, including art and music, played their roles in a never-ending power drama. Things in and of themselves, art and music, for example, meant less objectively, than what they connoted in relationship to the never-ending power drama:

> Again we see the meaning that etiquette and ceremonial had for the court nobility. This apparatus is apt to appear meaningless to us because we miss in it a practical use or purpose outside itself to which it relates…While we like to objectify or reify everything personal, court people personify the objective; for it was always with people and their positions relative to each other that they were primarily concerned…To enact their existence, to demonstrate their prestige, to distance themselves from lower ranking people and have this distance recognized by the higher-ranking—all this was purpose enough in itself (Elias 1983, 100).[5]

Many factors, both within and outside the closed court societies, would change the balance of power. Louis XIV's finance minister, Jean-Baptiste Colbert initiated a set of reforms that promoted a better regulation of the state's finances. Trade and commerce, handcraft and small-scale industry were afforded better conditions, but with the King's death in 1715, war caused financial problems. finances were very troubling, due to many war concerns. As has been noted by the Swedish historian Kurt Ågren (1985), however, it is striking that France soon recovered and became competitive with other trading powers like England and

---

[5]Compare with Burke 1994, 271f. One was not always successful in behaving as etiquette demanded. Here is a Swedish example. Peter Englund tells about the Swedish king Karl X Gustav: "The 1600s were a time possessed with etiquette… On one occasion, he found himself placed to the right of the Queen, and that was enough for him to leap away passionately, which resulted in surprise among the observers and irritation among the advisors" (Englund 2000, 53).

Holland.[6] This was important, particularly for the growing bourgeoisie and handcraft classes. The court culture changed, both internally as well as through external innovative ideas and intellectual efforts, leading to a number of new openings and questionings within the etiquette structure.[7]

Elias sees a parallel between the features of the French court and artistic sensibilities that became standardized under the *ancien régime*. He takes as an example the classical French dramas, which like the court itself, were carefully controlled and calculated. Plays were not to be understood primarily as entertainment, but rather as an exclusive part of the all encompassing social game.[8]

Although Elias in this context does not mention music specifically, his outlook and discussion clearly show the value of applying an ethnological (sociological) perspective to art. The encoding of art and the practice of art was not an add-on, but rather encoded into all of life. It was as much a part of one's life as seeing one's reflection in a mirror. Art was always part of a larger ceremony. Opera, for example, was not an activity of leisure because leisure time in the modern sense did not exist. Like other art forms, it was a way to maintain social relationships and was not seen as having importance in itself, but as an object of etiquette (all objects within their life-experience were treated in a similar way), with whose help one set oneself apart from others.[9]

* * *

---

[6] Elias also touches upon similarities and differences among the court societies in England, the German speaking areas, and France. The English societies were centered around London, but not to such a high degree as the French around Paris. In the German societies there were a number of courts of different sizes and with different backgrounds. Elias points to the number of differences that developed due to the different cultural relationships. As, for example, conversation was important in France, the book had a more important place in Germany. The noblemen in Prussia chose in large numbers to be active as officers while the French nobility mainly warred in words (compare with diplomacy!). For the German societies a certain amount of study of the law was not uncommon, while in France a more natural alternative was to turn to higher Church positions (Elias 1983, 146ff).

[7] As an example, Elias cites the changes that were brought about by Marie-Antoinette and the meaning of Voltaire's writings and deeds (Elias 1983, 86, 106). For a detailed description of an ethnological-mental perspective of the socio-political and intellectual process during the time of Louis XIV see Burke 1992.

[8] Elias sees large similarities between the classicist court culture that was found in Weimar in Germany during Goethe's time there: "Here too we find, admittedly in the context of a quite different relationship of rising bourgeois strata to the court than in seventeenth century France, a good many of the court characteristics we have referred to, at least as ideals: the serenity, the moderation of effects, the calm and circumspection and not least the specific solemnity by which court people stood out from the mass" (Elias 1983, 112).

[9] Elias writes: "What matters at court is not the thing itself but what it means in relation to certain people," and refers in turn to Saint-Simon (cf Elias 1983, 100 footnote 29).

How this process concerning *taste* developed into a weapon, among other things, can be read about further in *Homo Aestheticus*. Like Elias, the book's author, the philosopher Luc Ferry begins his story more than a century before Baumgarten published his book in 1735.

Ferry finds *taste*, as a general concept, appeared earliest in Italy in the middle of the seventeenth century, and then he follows it to France, England, and Germany. In the succession of French philosophers and writers after Descartes, Ferry sees two lines of development concerning the discussion around *taste*, and *beauty*. One line ties back to the concept of *mimesis*, or that which mimics nature, and therefore is true, and the other line follows the *feelings* of the subject:

> Behind these two conceptions of beauty—whose conflict goes on through the eighteenth century—two visions of subjectivity are confronting each other: one, issued from Cartensianism, locates the essence of the cogito in reason while the other, Pascalian or even sensualist, places the essential elsewhere, in the heart or the feelings (Ferry 1993, 26).[10]

For both of these conceptions there is a point of departure where each individual is thought of as an isolated unit.[11] Agreement between different persons' experience of what is beautiful, stemmed from the highest source, from God who guaranteed the social congruence between individuals.

Tensions between French and Italian music, perhaps most obvious in opera, continued to surface throughout Louis XIV's reign. Poetry and word took precedence in the more rational tradition of French music; melody and form surfaced in the more emotional tradition of Italian music.[12] The long fight within the French culture between French and Italian opera can be seen as an application of the tension between the French rational tradition and the Italian emotional tradition of opera. It was no accident that it was opera, a vocal music form, that was debated. Discussions of music always started with vocal music. Johann Mattheson (1739), as one of many, saw instrumental music as a child

---

[10] One can compare with Elias, who states that people who defied etiquette by showing feelings in the wrong context lost face and therefore lost power. It was not until Rousseau that thoughts about naturalness and feelings were more widely accepted. Elias talks about "a degree of emancipation of spontaneous emotional impulses, accompanied by a theoretical assertion of the autonomy of 'feeling'" (Elias 1983, 113).

[11] Ferry noted that Leibniz's concept that every person was an isolated being, a monad, is the background to this thought, and added that this individualist perspective culminated with Leibniz's rationalism and Berkeley's and Hume's empiricism (Ferry 1993, 27). We will return to the last-named empiricist soon.

[12] This well-known fight between the Italian and the French for superiority within Opera in France is taken up in all the major histories of music. For a description of a historical-aesthetical perspective, see Fubini 1997, 133-178, and from an historical perspective, see Allen 1962, 40f.

of vocal music.[13] These struggles continued through different parts of the music field during all of Louis XIV's reign, during the ancien régime, and on to the middle of the eighteenth century culminating in the War of the Buffons.[14] While poetry and word took precedence in French culture, melody and form stood in the foreground in Italian music. The question of whether music or poetry was the driving element in opera was often coupled with a discussion of music's mimetic capabilities, which were apparently viewed as of a lesser caliber than the mimetic capability that served an artist who painted a canvas of a well-known landscape

What Was Counted as Art?

During the *ancien régime's* last decades, many French philosophers wrote about the different art-forms' relationships to one another. They also touched upon the antagonisms found between the visions of how different tastes could be legitimized. The writer Jean-Baptiste Du Bos is considered the first banner bearer of the aesthetics of feeling in France.[15] Of all the art forms, Du Bos argued that music was the one that spoke most directly to the heart. This, however, did not mean that he had given up on the idea of the mimetic, or that instrumental music was superior to vocal music. Tones, he believed, were inferior to words:

> Music then effects its imitations by means of melody, harmony and rhythms... The natural signs of the passions that music evokes and which it artfully uses to increase the impact of the words to which it is set, must then make these words more able to touch us. For these natural signs have a marvelous power to move us... Thus, the pleasure of the ear becomes the pleasure of the heart (Huray and Day 1981, 17).

One condition for all valuable music was that it should move the listener, that it should speak directly to the feelings of the listener.[16] Du Bos, however, did not see *the beautiful* as something that was only decided by *the public*, but rather as something that was relative. This meant that taste was something that was *subjective and individual*. Du Bos' opinion thus stood in stark opposition to

---

[13] As will be seen, vocal music held hegemony during the eighteenth century. The old thesis about vocal music's superiority is repeated up until the beginning of the nineteenth century by several music theoreticians (see Ratner 1980, 4f).

[14] The word comes from bouffons, which, according to *Sohlmans musiklexikon* (1975), was a collection of French opera enthusiasts who took a position for the "the Italian reality-based opera-buffa and against the last expressions of the domestic, elevated and characterized Baroque opera."

[15] Ferry (1993, 42) writes that Rousseau saw Du Bos' production from 1719 as the most valuable within its field. Compare with Huray and Day 1981, 17.

[16] Music's meaning as the language of emotions is commented on by the music theoreticians of the time, perhaps above all on Sulzer whose theory about the beautiful art came out first in 1771: "Expression is the soul of music. Without it, music is but an entertaining diversion. But with it, music becomes the most expressive speech overpowering the heart" (Baker and Christensen 1995, 51).

THE AGE OF ENLIGHTENMENT

the earlier tradition and pointed the way forward, as we shall see. Du Bos along with many other French philosophers, was read both in Germany and in England. There was, on the whole, a richer exchange of texts between the central European countries than we think today.

The philologist Charles Batteux's later work (Batteux 1747) summarizes much of what has just been said, but we also find in his writings what has been called the modern *system* within which the art forms are placed (Hanfling 1992, 7f). Batteux formulated what many before him had felt was underway. The Medieval introduction to *artes liberals* had, in itself, functioned for a long time as material for critical analysis, which above all can be understood against the background of the bourgeois class's success.

As Plumpe formulated it, the communal process, whereby the position of art, and the process by which taste is established, must be contemplated first and foremost in relationship to the bourgeois class's social and economic advances. One no longer accepted the social value of handcraft and manufacturing in relation to the "free" arts.

The great significance of the pre-industrial techniques collided more and more with the old divisions of this social hierarchy (Plumpe 1993, 31).[17]

A description of this process can be found in Denis Diderot's famous article on art in the *French Encyclopedia*. If one no longer could use an unambiguous measure to define what was art, then another method was needed. It soon became the fashion to divide the arts into "the Beautiful" and "the Mechanical or Practical." Batteux argued that they could be reduced to one and the same principle (Les beaux-arts réduits à un même principe), the "Principle of Beauty". He now divided the arts into those whose purpose lay within themselves (music, painting, poetry, sculpture, and dance) as opposed to the practical, for example the art of gardening, which during this time came to lose its status as a fine art.[18] As the idea-historian Sven-Erik Liedman writes, it then became the fashion to discuss the relationship between the beautiful arts (Liedman 1997, 359). Similar modern systems regularly were constructed by many following generations of philosophers.

---

[17]Die immense Bedeutung der proto-industriellen Technik kollidierte mehr und mehr mit der alten Einteilung und ihrer sozialen Hierarchisierung.

[18]We shall not follow as industriously how Art with a capital A becomes something other than handcraft. This change is a twin process to the development of the concept of aesthetics. One writer who notices this change at the end of the eighteenth century is Karl Philipp Moritz, a person who we also meet later. He was a hat maker, later an actor, thereafter a reform-minded teacher and finally a professor (Huray and Day 1981, 185). In a letter to the philosopher Moses Mendelssohn he writes about handcraft production ("the mechanical arts") and art ("the fine arts"): "The purpose of a watch… is an extrinsic one, centered on the person whose convenience the object serves… Divorced from [its] function… a matter of total indifference… The opposite is the case with the beautiful. This has no extrinsic purpose. It is not there to fulfill anything else" (Huray and Day 1981, 187).

Underscoring the words of Batteux, Liedman emphasizes the beautiful arts should "not reproduce all nature, but rather the beautiful part of it. The Beautiful should mirror beauty" (Liedman 1997, 355).[19]

Aesthetics as Ideology

As a complement to Elias and Ferry, we now turn to a literary critic's assessment and will complement Elias's and Ferry's approach in part with literary critic Terry Eagleton's historical-materialist interpretation of the birth of aesthetics, and with philosopher Martha Woodmansee's analysis. Both will show us some of the reasons for "high" literature's claims to aesthetics. Eagleton says that the history of aesthetics, in large part, is the history of the middle class, where the function of art is determined only by the conditions of the marketplace. Aesthetic discussions have a central role in the creation of the new dominating ideology. Eagleton, among other things, returns to the strange idea that an artwork is a kind of *subject*.[20] And in his introduction he establishes:

> The aesthetic is at once the very secret prototype of human subjectivity in early capitalist society, and a vision of human energies as radical ends in themselves which is the implacable enemy of all dominative or instrumental thought. (Eagleton 1990, 9).

Through his description of the thinkers for which aesthetics were a key concept, Eagleton gives us in a concentrated form, his understanding of western society's development up to the turbulent European situation of the 1980s:

> The emergence of the aesthetic as a theoretical category is closely bound up with the material process by which cultural production, at an early stage of bourgeois society, becomes 'autonomous'—autonomous, that is, of the various social functions which it has traditionally served. Once artifacts become commodities in the market place, they exist for nothing and nobody in particular, and can consequently be rationalized, ideologically speaking, as existing entirely and gloriously for themselves (Eagleton 1990, 8f).

---

[19] Notice Liedman's comment that for Leibniz "fundamentals of German philosophy contributed to a different understanding of the concept of mimesis: it was not that the French art philosophers [like Batteux] upheld that a beautiful work of art must always mirror nature. The beautiful could be a construction of art itself, and thereby of the human imagination. This thought process culminated at the turn of the nineteenth century in the romantic idolization of the genius" (Liedman 1997, 357).

[20] From an ethnomusicologist's perspective one could think that it must have been most difficult to combine the thought of art as a subject with instrumental music. As a subject, instrumental music should lie far from the realm of the possible, where music's meaning is difficult to describe, and music in general as sounding material disappears over time, while a painting and a sculpture, on the other hand, survives through time. The social construction of music as a subject should therefore be a more difficult-to-formulate process than the comparable one within literature, painting, sculpture, etc. That it needed a new concept in order to make this construction possible is clear (see the discussion below on the Work).

Eagleton sees in the aesthetic project a political driving force that comes from a burger class intellectual elite, which in Germany had limited possibilities to change the absolutist power balance of the nobility. Baumgarten understood the aesthetic object's status and meaning as a sensual object rather than a rational or scientific one. Eagleton—250 years later—defined it more as a cultural process in which the burger classes had the distinct purpose and goal of gradually assuming the power held by the upper class. The "political/aesthetic project" developed a binding, internal function for the middle classes, as they stood together in contrast to the power apparatus of the nobility. Within the middle classes, conditions were created for shared habits, approaches, devotions, and feelings that developed within the middle classes: "This is equivalent to saying that power in such a [bourgeois] order has become *aestheticized*" (Eagleton 1990, 20).

Here it may be helpful to remember Elias's criticism: that the bourgeoisie at many of the individual German courts had little direct contact with the ruling class, implying that one did not take over all of the court's manners and ways of thinking to such a high degree:

> This exclusivity prevented the broad permeation of bourgeois circles from aristocratic form of behavior that can be observed for a time in both France and England (Elias 1983, 97).

According to Elias, the bourgeoisie was exposed to as many constraints as the members of court. The former (bourgeois men, for Elias speaks all too rarely about women) were formed above all by their professions. The demands and strains that were part of professional life for the bourgeoisie were completely different from those present during their leisure time (Elias 1983, 115).[21] Leisure can therefore be seen as a free zone in which a meaningful part of the musical aesthetic project could be developed, because the nobility had very little influence in this zone to press their values upon the bourgeois person's body and mind.

It is in this latter bourgeois-free zone that Woodmansee begins her new reading of how writers and poets of the eighteenth century developed aesthetics within the literary world. Because there was no functioning copyright law, authors were unprotected from pirate-copies, which meant that they could not count on any secure income even if their products became popular. While many authors had taken a pragmatic and populist attitude toward their audience, others seriously adopted the Enlightenment spirit and believed the thesis that the public should be educated and their taste raised. This difference of opinion, not least among poets,

---

[21]Compare with what Elias says gradually occurred when elite groups began to develop within the bourgeoisie: "As soon as exclusive, elitist tendencies appear in bourgeois strata, they also express themselves in prestige symbols directed at maintaining the group's distance from others, while transfiguring its existence. In these symbols the group's existence is presented as an end in itself surrounded by its aura of prestige, even though in the case of bourgeois strata utilitarian values and economic interests mingle with the prestige-values" (1983:103).

writes Woodmansee, often made great demands on the wider public. This is one of the reasons the concepts of "high and low culture" took shape in the second half of the eighteenth century, and are taken for granted today. She adds that many disappointed writers turned toward the public:

> Unable to reach the new broad-gauge audience on whose approval they depended, the *Aufklärer* decry the public for wanting only to be 'diverted', 'moved', 'stimulated'. Displaying a lack of fellow-feeling… they condemn the unwitting public for its addiction to the 'pleasant sensations' manufactured by the growing literature industry, and… turn their backs on it. "Since one cannot hope to build and to plant," Schiller remarks… "it is at least something to inundate and destroy. The only possible relationship to the public is war" (Woodmansee 1994, 29).

The "true" writer's escape out of this situation was partly to be demarcated from those who flirted with the wide bourgeois public power, partly to turn the focus of the work inward, towards literature itself. As a result of this thinking, the idea of the artist's mimetic mission also slowly receded. If there was not a clear external relation, it was natural to turn one's interest in the other direction, toward theinner structural qualities. As a result, it was possible for these educated and Latin-speaking authors to connect themselves to Baumgarten and his philosophical colleagues as they began to describe their books, writings, poetry, dramas, and so forth, as works located within a distinct literary sphere, one that was *artistic and aesthetic*: "The task of the poet is to 'arouse aesthetic feelings'—not to teach or to preach" (Woodmansee 1994, 95). In our further discussion of musical narrative we will draw correlations to Woodmansee's observations regarding literature.

In summary, we find ourselves in a time where 99% of the people, depending on the values and beliefs sto which they adhere, can hardly set aside, let alone abandon, the thought of an almighty God. The nobility lived principally in a world where all of life's events, including one's natural and social needs, were to a great extent regulated by the special power structure within powerful court society. One lived in a milieu and context where artfully designed gardens, representational art, music, and splendid palaces, etc., formed a clear and present part of daily life. Music was experienced within this milieu primarily as a sounding object, through which one could position oneself within the noble field. It was a game to be played. Through one's performance, one's actions, and one's carefully weighed comments, one gambled in this game, following presupposed rules of etiquette, or consciously obstructing them, in the hopes of elevating one's personal prestige. During the latter half of the seventeenth century, a prevailing classical and rational view of art characterized the leading representative arts: drama and opera. One also found factors and developments both within and without the court societies that led to changes.

THE AGE OF ENLIGHTENMENT

The bourgeoisie, who lived principally in both the professional and the private worlds, found themselves in the shadow of a noble hegemony, which at the same time blocked their ambitions to change their future prospects. The people within this process, that persisted for many generations, managed to navigate within the temporary fields that opened and were changed through personal points of view. This process depended upon how they engaged and accepted the noble values of the time, as well as the different rationality and thought processes that their mercantile professional lives brought about.[22]

As Luc Ferry showed, this process led people to change their views and attitudes towards art gradually. As they slowly escaped the iron grip of the rules of etiquette, they began to see and hear music from a more personal and emotional point of view. And at the same time, the millennia old thoughts and concepts about art's important mimetic mission and ideas about that word as centrally important, began to break up. People fumbled to find a new path.

For Ferry, this is further confirmation that the history of aesthetics is a key to the understanding of the history of modernism. But he also poses the question: how can we—except through God—we understand and contemplate the sensual? Philosophers have pondered this question since the birth of the concept of the aesthetic. Ferry also stacks up the many questions that are related to this one:

> How is one to come up with an 'objective' answer to this matter once the foundations of the beautiful have been situated within the most intimate subjectivity, that of taste?… how to ground objectivity using representations of the subject as starting point? … how to ground the collective on individual volition? (Ferry 1993, 19).

But it must be said that very few people during this period contemplated the issues of taste, aesthetics, art systems, subjectivism or objectivism. Answers to these questions must, until later on, be open-ended, but it must be emphasized again, that during this period the percent of the population who experienced *and* thought about concepts and phenomena like taste, aesthetics, the system of the arts, subject/subjectivism, object/objectivism, and so forth, was very small (2%, 8% or X%?).[23] At any rate: Baumgarten's tender plant grew slowly and "enlightendly."

---

[22] Elias discusses in this context a citation from Hippolyte Taine (1828-1898), where it becomes clear that gradually as the generations followed one another, the successful burghers became "cultivated in heart and mind, tactful versed in literature, philosophy, good manners." Of the sons of the bourgeoisie, it is said that "[they] throw money out of the window just as elegantly as young dukes with whom they take supper" (as cited in Elias 1983, 65, footnote 43).

[23] As will later be touched upon, the problem is that it is complicated to find the things that humans might have had ideas about, but had not yet conceptualized (see below p. 92).

Visits in Time

To better understand the developing concept of the aesthetic and how music functioned during the eighteenth century, we turn to the ethnomusicologist Jens Henrik Koudal's magnificent work on the life of city musicians in Denmark between 1600 and 1800, and thereafter we will have a look at several travelers' stories from the period. The point, as stated earlier, is to better understand what is included under the developing concept of the aesthetic.

Although Koudal draws from a Danish example, his analysis holds for most of the German speaking areas of the time, as well as in Sweden (Koudal 1999, 30-33). He reports that in Denmark the nobility in 1600 made up only 0.25% [sic!] of the population, priests circa 2%, the bourgeoisie (merchants, officials, members of handcraft guilds) circa 20%, farmers/country folk circa 75-80%. Apart from playing in the city where they had their official position, city musicians during the eighteenth century also were responsible for a good part of the festival music that was performed in the countryside.[24] In some cities, tower music was played at official ceremonies, and bourgeois festivals, also for farmers but to a lesser extent at the year's harvest festivals. City musicians also instructed the children of the bourgeoisie as well as their own apprentices in playing instruments. During the second half of the eighteenth century, musicians began to play in different societies in more concert-like settings, which led in Odense for example,, to the establishment of an official concert society.

City musicians were an intermediary upward link to the court and military spheres as well as downwards "to the farmers." In order to practice their profession, they were forced to be competent on several instruments, which is why there were seldom virtuosi or genuine composers. But many both wrote arrangements and adapted compositions in accordance to the taste of the time. Music, as Koudal describes it, functioned in processions and ceremonies, as well as for dancing, background music for inns and at parties, and so forth.

At the same time Koudal shows that these musicians had a very broad, regularly renewed repertoire. In their music, the gallant style and the *empfindsamer Stil* (see below) were becoming as common as in Germany. Some music was carried out into the countryside contrasted with older folk styles:

> What the musicians that came from outside presented, the farmers experienced as new norms, new instruments and new music. Among these new norms, they had to pay for the music that became, as it were, a commodity (Koudal 1999, 543).

---

[24] In 1800, the professions of organist and city musician were combined into one position in Denmark, making it impossible to maintain the profession in the countryside.

This, then, formed the context in which value judgments about music were made: how well it lived up to the norms, and thereby how suitable it was. It was expected that city musicians at the university in Copenhagen could play fanfares, solemn brass music and perhaps also cantatas, sonatas and sinfonias, as well as the so-called perfected music for well-born folk (Koudal 1999, 396).

People then, as they do today, longed for novelty and musicians provided it. Influenced by what was happening on the continent, people began dancing the minuet rather than the polska. And the violin became country folks' most popular instrument. Musicians own value judgments changed. Within this milieu there was always a tight relationship between consumers and producers of music.

Organists and other city musicians were invited to play with musically interested members of the bourgeoisie. Ensemble playing, by both amateurs and professionals, peaked during the eighteenth century. In the larger picture, perhaps amateur and professional musicians played together in ensembles more during the eighteenth century than at any time earlier or later in western history.

A Contemporary Journey

Let us journey through Germany, France and Italy with a lawyer and amateur lutenist who wrote about his experiences. In the early 1700s, Johann Friedrich Uffenbach made music wherever he traveled. Once on a visit to Tübingen, he met another lutenist, an apothecary who ran a coffee house. Together they sang and played German opera arias for evening café guests (Preussner 1949, 18). Whether in opera performances, concert halls, or with other musicians in people's homes, Uffenbach loved to entertain. Apart from his visits to opera performances and concerts, we also find him alone and with other music makers at home. Here, he sang opera arias and accompanied himself on the lute, played duets, played songs and other simple party music. Uffenbach also took part in weddings at the homes of burgers and farmers, where he danced and entertained with music (Preussner 1949, 18).

Influenced by the city musicians from his student days in Strassbourg, he traveled around Europe, composing music and providing fellow musicians with new compositions.[25] Later on in 1715, during Carnival time in Venice, he regaled his readers with wonderful descriptions of the unbelievable pranks and spectacles that took place in the confusion of carnivals and masked balls.

---

[25] The reaction to Uffenbach's appearance is an example of peoples' sensitivity for correct etiquette, deeply anchored even among the bourgeois citizens: he was laughed at because of his German clothing. In Strassburg, one dressed after the Paris fashion. Because he did not want to attract such attention, he went directly to the tailor and ordered new clothing. Preussner writes "until they were ready, he stayed at home" (Preussner 1949, 21).

He once visited the church of St. Salvatore where he attended a great funeral. Unobserved by the confusion of the carnival, more than forty musicians gathered there, including the best castrati in Venice:

> The music was wonderful. The castrato Sinesino moved the prayerful congregation with his fulsome song in a much more sympathetic way than he had done for the opera mob[26] (Preussner 1949, 66).

In Italy, as elsewhere, Uffenbach sought out chamber music concerts in private noble or bourgeois houses as often as he could.[27] In Rome, for example, he visited the concerts that were given every week in the Rospolis palace. People sat in chairs along the long gallery walls, listening to the musicians and singers gathered in the center to perform large works including Oratorios. The musicians and the singers (castrati) sat in the middle of the room. The new music, composed and directed by Antonio Caldara, chapel master to the Pope, was in one instance so beautiful that it moved Uffenbach to say he was convinced that he had never experienced anything like it (Preussner 1949, 77).

He added that all were so quiet one could have heard a fly buzzing –in the rests, one presumes.

Apart from numerous descriptions of smaller musical happenings that Uffenbach participated in, he also visited the Paris Opera. There he found that the audiences knew some of the arias so well, that they sang along. Some of the best loved opera arias were available in printed or handwritten versions (Preussner 1949, 144ff).[28]

---

[26]"Die Musik war herrlich, besonders der kastrat Sinesino, den die andächtige Gemeinde hier sympatischer berührt haben mag als der Opernmob, sang mit trefflicher Stimme und Gelehrsamkeit" (Preussner 1949, 66). Uffenbach had heard Sinesino at the Opera some time earlier. There were two main types of positions for castrati. The castrati that were employed by the church where often stationary, while the other group had shorter terms of employment, and traveled from court opera to court opera. The latter were also often well-known as virtuosi and had better terms of employment giving them higher status in relation to the permanently employed musicians' lower status (compare with Neitzert 1990, 33f).

[27]When Uffenbach visited Lyon, he found that the bourgeoisie had established a special music room in the city where music loving amateurs played together every week (Preussner 1949, 11). It should be noted that on one of these occasions he managed to get a ticket to be allowed to enter.

[28]The audience was allowed to sing along during certain well-known songs at operas and other similar musical dramatic works, apparently common behavior in many places from this time. Such was the case, for instance, when Johann Abraham Peter Schulz's opera was performed in Copenhagen at the end of the eighteenth century (compare with Karevold 1996, 27ff). This form of sing-along is also found, of course, at English Music Halls from the beginning of the nineteenth century.

A Few Other Journeys

Like Uffenbach, another traveler, the Englishman Charles Burney, didn't think very much of French Opera. Burney made two long journeys on the continent during the 1770s, the first to France and Italy, and the second mainly to Germany and Austria. Like Uffenbach, Burney also played himself, and composed. If one looks at the critiques he gives, one gets the impression that he had a normal conservative musical taste for his time. The musicologist Warren Dwight Allen writes that as a critic, Burney loved "grace and elegance, symmetry, order, and naturalness" and he was "thoroughly representative of eighteenth century taste" (Allen 1962, 81).[29]

Burney once had a discussion with the opera composer Grétry and they agreed that an opera aria should have only *one* subject or *affekt* (Burney 1959a, 32). He generally remarked on how careful singers and musicians were with intonation. His commentaries about badly tuned organs are numerous. He held the musically educated in great admiration, and often sought them out during his travels, as he enjoyed hunting for older music, manuscripts and treatises. Likewise, the portraits and descriptions from his journeys are very valuable because he wrote with diligence and care about musical life as he met it. The music milieus that Burney describes most often were in churches, opera houses, private salons, as well as somewhat less frequently, the rarer public concert locations.

If we begin with the most grandiose, the opera house, it is clear that it was very popular to visit the opera, that the simple bourgeoisie could be found below on the parquet level, while the upper classes had their own box seats. On visiting the Théâtre Italien in Paris, Burney remarks on how the public makes just as much noise there as it does in London. On another occasion in Turin, he has this to say about a comic opera:

> The Italians hold these performances in no very high estimation; they talk the whole time, and seldom attend to any thing but one or two favourite airs… the only two that were applauded were encored, and I observed that the performer does not take it as such a great favour to be applauded here as in England (Burney 1959a, 57).

He made similar comments about opera audiences in other places in Italy.[30]

---

[29]Burney also wrote a history of music, as did his contemporary John Hawkins. Allen makes an important point that since the eighteenth century historians have often had the idea that they should also play the role of critic: "A general historian of music, according to this theory, (cont.) must select from the great mass of available material only that which is 'important'. Unfortunately, however, the importance of the material can be determined only by esthetic [aesthetic] judgement of the critic-historian… the significance of music in relation to the society in which it emerges is of vastly greater importance than the esthetic judgement of the historian concerning that music" (Allen 1962, 65).

[30]In connection with his visit to Naples, Burney notes: "Indeed, music at the theatres, and other

Burney often heard choir and ensemble music performed "to the glory of God" in churches and monasteries, but it is clear from his writings that he believed music was to the greatest extent for the contemplation and betterment of people. In Milan, he visited, among other places, a convent in order to hear music at a service for their yearly festival. The music was introduced with an *adagio* in the motet style of the time:

> [w]hich was truly divine, and divinely sung by one of the sisters, accompanied by the organ only, by another. It was by far the best singing, in every respect, that I have heard since my arrival in Italy; where there is so much, that one soon grows fastidious (Burney 1959a, 77).

Later during the service he heard a piece that satisfied him beyond all measure and was performed with a voice that created the impression that "went deeper into his soul than tones from an instrument could ever do."

Burney also wrote of street musicians on every corner, about concerts performed by orphan girls in the large educational institutes in northern Italy, and about the songs of gondoliers whom he found superior than other people within their class, something that he attributed to the fact that they are were allowed to attend the theater in Venice free.

There were also many occasions where Burney visited "Academies" in upper class private homes to hear music performed by both amateur and professional musicians. At these meetings performers usually presented solo songs and duets, and the instrumentalists played mainly chamber music–duets and trios, and solo pieces.

On occasion he also visited regular public concerts. From a Sunday Concert in Paris (Concerts spirituelles) he reported that once the audience applauded and expressed their appreciation loudly. One Saturday morning in Turin, he heard Pugnani play a solo concert in the Royal Chapel, and in Bologna, the Philharmonic Society had a yearly performance on a grand scale. He wrote:

> There is a... public performance, morning, evening, on the 13th of August in the church... This year... the band was very numerous, consisting of near a hundred voices and instruments. There are two large organs... and beside these, a small

---

public areas in Italy seems but an excuse for people to assemble together, their attention being chiefly placed on play and conversation even during the performance of a serious opera" (Burney 1959a, 257). It becomes clear later (from another contemporary, De Brosses) that renting opera boxes created a feeling of being at home. One listened absent-mindedly, although it was seen as well-mannered to at least listen carefully to the passages that were thought of as very interesting. During long-winded recitatives, however, people were often playing chess! Sensational information can also be found in Sharp: "Notwithstanding the amazing noisiness of the audience... the moment the dances begin, there is universal silence... Witty people therefore, never fail to tell me, the Neapolitans go to see, not to hear, an Opera" (as cited in Weiss and Taruskin 1984, 233).

one was erected for the occasion... The performers were placed in a gallery, which formed a semi-circle round the choir. (Burney 1959a, 163).

Burney recounted who made music for the different parts of the mass and added that "the morning service was finished by a symphony, with solo parts." Burney stated that the church was full to overflowing for the evening event:

> Upon the whole I was well entertained; and the variety of styles and masterly composition were such as reflected honour, not only on the Philharmonic society, but upon the Society of Bologna itself (Burney 1959a, 165).

In Germany

Later that same summer, when Burney traveled along the banks of the Rhine, he noted that contrary to what he had become accustomed to in Catholic countries, he heard hardly any song or music. In general, though, Burney met a similar music culture: operas, songs, music in churches, solo concerts, symphonies, chamber music, ensemble song, music at inns, songs on the street, and so forth. There were some differences, however, between the German and Latin countries. When he visited Mannheim he was very satisfied with the orchestra (apart from the intonation of the brass instruments). The Prince was a good flutist and also played the cello. Every evening–except when there was an opera–the Prince organized a concert in his palace, where not only his own subjects but also foreign guests, had free entrance. In Würtemberg, Burney found that the reigning duke had such a passion for music that the duchy's finances had been affected. The Duke was described as a good harpsichordist.[31]

In Munich, Burney was impressed by the Prince's royal family. The Prince played the harpsichord. His sister was a well-known cultural personality. Among other accomplishments, she had written two Italian operas (both text and music!). Here Burney was also invited to a supper after one of the opera performances where the Italian singers performed a trio: "Sung in such a way, as one never can hope to hear in public, and the chances are many against it in private" (Burney 1959b, 47).

---

[31] Even though the sovereign had reduced his musical forces, there were still a large number of musicians and singers (including "at present fifteen Castrati"). Burney even writes that it can be harmful for a community if interest in art goes too far: "music becomes a vice... For that nation, of which half the subjects are stage-players, fiddlers, and soldiers, and the others beggars, seem to be ill governed. Here nothing is talked of but the adventures of actors, dancers and musicians" (Burney 1959b, 38). The English publisher (in the 1959 edition) comments that Burney's critique of the Duke of Würtemberg was not included in the German translation of the book that was already released in 1772!

When Burney visited Berlin, he was allowed to speak with some of Fredrick II's famous musicians and composers. He also heard the king himself play the flute, although not any of his own compositions.[32]

Burney attached great importance to the congregational singing when he visited various churches, judging its overall musical culture (apparently he heard folk music less often):

> And it seems as if *the national music of a country was good or bad, in proportion to that of its church service;* which may account for the taste of the common people of Italy, where indeed the language is more musical than any other country in Europe, which certainly has an effect upon their vocal music; by the excellent performances that are every day heard for nothing in the churches, by the common people, more contribute to refine and fix the national taste for good music, than any other thing that I can at present suggest (Burney 1959b, 78 [my italics]).

Several weeks after Burney wrote this in Vienna he praised a three-thousand person strong congregation in a church in Dresden calling it perhaps the best unison psalm singing he has heard (compare with Sulzer's opinion below).

Even if Burney was most fascinated by the Italian music culture, he shows in his writings that he found both depth and breadth in the song and music he encountered in Germany. The music of Protestant churches played a prominent cultural role, hosting both congregational singing, and liturgical and concerted music. Burney, as usual, offered no detailed descriptions of how music was understood by anyone other than himself. But his writings do show that among many regents there was an active interest in music. It is not difficult to imagine that this interest, to a great extent, was disseminated among their bourgeois subjects. Those who stood *over* someone in the social hierarchy were seen regularly also to be bearers of a *higher* culture. The Enlightenment as an educational project within which every person, on a rational basis, would develop an opinion about their culture's customs and conventions, had barely begun during this time.

Burney included no details about how spectators and participants related to music, so it is difficult to know if the fact that Burney does not comment that

---

[32]Burney is impressed by the position of music in Berlin, and writes quite thoroughly about it (he was in Berlin for nine days). On the other hand he was also disappointed. He found an intolerance to music that the King did not personally like, and wrote in general: "The music of this country, is more truly German than that of any other part of the empire" (Burney 1959b, 207). Burney's opinions of musical life in Germany were not always generously accepted in German reading circles. Johan Friedrich Reichardt is especially critical of the way Burney writes about Berlin's musical life, and suggests that Burney talked with a great number of people and saw a great deal, but heard less (Reichardt 1976, 35). As Reichardt's publisher points out, there was a clearly rivalry between Reichardt and Burney, where the former also published musical travel journalism (Reichardt 1976, 11). For more about Reichardt see below.

THE AGE OF ENLIGHTENMENT

German and Austrian audiences were not noisy at opera performances meant that they listened more carefully.[33]

We shall also follow a third writer, composer, Johann Friedrich Reichardt, who described the music culture of Vienna and Paris from the last decades of the eighteenth century. Reichardt fought partly for the old ideal. He wanted, for example, the same *affekt* to be maintained through an entire movement. But as a true apostle of the Enlightenment, Reichardt also preached in his writing that peoples' knowledge should be deepened, their senses and customs refined. The musical taste would thereby be improved and the true art of music be spread to one and all (Reichardt 1976, 27).

When Reichardt wrote about the changes in musical life, he often used the phrase, "true music." By that, he meant music that was not unnecessarily virtuosic.[34] Reichardt composed songs for young children. In his essay "To Youth" he pointed out that it was important to learn how to sing beautifully and correctly. By that, he meant that the youth should learn to observe and appreciate the beauty of nature so they would be protected from bad taste and bad habits. They did not

---

[33] Funnily enough, there is a similar commentary in his daughter Fanny Burney's novel *Evelina*: "Indeed I am quite astonished to find how little music is attended to in silence; for though everyone seems to admire, hardly anybody listens" (as cited in Weber 1975, 3). It is clear from the Schumann couples' journals that audiences in the 1840s could be completely silent at a Gewandhaus concert. The Swedish composer Jacob Axel Josephson also speaks about the prayerful audiences in Leipzig (Ander 2000, 39). During the Schumanns' tours in Russia in 1844, it is clear, however, that the audience listened very distractedly. In the former case, the audience was most likely mainly bourgeois, and in the latter case, nobility. A well-known story about inattentive noble listeners was also told by Louis Spohr (Cf. Schumann 1987, 188, 332, 380). The musicologist William Weber warns that one should not attach too much importance to the descriptions that one did not listen carefully to opera music during the eighteenth century. He suggests that it was good manners to say that one didn't listen carefully (Weber 1997, 683). As we just witnessed, Uffenbach said that the audiences in Paris could sing along with well-known arias. For a comparison with the situation in Göteborg in the 1860s, see Anders Carlsson 1996, 141ff. As I will also touch upon in the next chapter, when it comes to listening to music, changes came at different speeds in different countries. We must also always be careful to delineate between different music forms in different contexts.

[34] The musicologist Hanns-Werner Heister writes in his work on the development of the concert that virtuosity is a non-bourgeois element that slowly crept in to the bourgeois concert: "as it relates to the moment of musical-technical maximum efficiency, whose model comes originally above all from the sphere of the court and theater" (Heister 1983, 213). As was mentioned, the virtuoso castrati traveled most often from one court opera to the next during the eighteenth century. The number of virtuoso instrumentalists that traveled around and gave concerts goes up during this century until it becomes an "industry" after the beginning of the nineteenth century (see below). Plato already complains, as we have seen, about the masses' fascination with virtuoso musicians. It would be difficult to argue that human fascination with a fast and complex performance has fundamentally changed. My thoughts turn to the pianist Art Tatum, the violinist Itzak Perlman and the guitarist Yngwie Malmsteen.

have to understand the text completely, for the melody itself would be enough to move the heart.[35]

Reichardt's many letters from Vienna at the beginning of the nineteenth century bear witness to the fact that the number of public concerts, and at the same time, private musical evenings, rose in frequency and scope. He commented on how the structure of music had gradually changed. It was no longer true that music at court or among the nobility was necessarily of a different kind or had other qualities other than the music that one enjoyed among the bourgeoisie. In Vienna's musical salons Reichardt heard, in addition to works by Haydn, Romberg, Mozart, Moscheles, and Beethoven, chamber music works by Prince Louis Ferdinand as well as Prince Lobkowitz who sang songs including arias from the latest Italian operas (Reichardt 1976, 281, 289).

These music-loving bourgeoisie and people within the nobility did not take music for granted; rather, it was something that was meaningful *in itself*. One paid an entrance price to public concerts, one subscribed to chamber music concerts, one was invited to salons where one knew that chamber music of both amateur and professional caliber would be performed. Among the forms that were also present, Reichardt describes, for example, a quartet, led by Herr Schuppanzigh, a wonderful violinist, who during the winter of 1808 on Thursdays from twelve o'clock until two o'clock, gave subscription concerts in a private home. Attendees were most likely part of the bourgeoisie or the nobility. People from the lower classes could not pay or set aside work time for this, or and, often for social reasons, find themselves at home within this milieu.[36]

---

[35]Reichardt writes in the often lengthy style of his time: "Why does one bring to you contemplations over the thousand-fold beauties of Nature in Verse and Rhyme? To make you more aware, more important, more distinguished, more pleasant, through true Love to preserve you, to protect beautiful Nature from the false taste in Art and Manners…here therefore are well ordered tones, comprehensible and pleasant to the ear, and moving to the heart, a very powerful medium… you perhaps do not at first understand the words, you at least do not grasp them, only the Melody presses itself upon you, and is each time thereby displaced in the emotions, where the poetry and the melody of the song should be confraternally affected." ["Warum bringt man euch Betrachtungen über die tausendfache Schönheit der Natur in Verse und Reime? Eben um sie euch merkbarer, wichtiger, bedeutender und angenehmer zu machen, euch durch wahre Liebe zur wahren, Schönen Natur von dem falschen Geschmacke in Kunsten und Sitten zu schützen….hiezu sind wohlgeordnete Töne, die dem Ohre fasslich und angenehm sind und die das Herz rühren, ein sehr kräftiges Mittel… dass ihr die Worte vielleicht nicht einmal verstandet, sie wenigstens nicht behieltet, allein die Melodie prägte sich bei euch ein, und ihr lallt und trüllert sie euch itzt oft vor und wendet jedesmal dadurch in die Empfindung versetzt, die die Poesie und Melodie des Liedes gemeinschaftlich haben erregen sollen."] That we recognize Plato's ideas is not an accident; the Platonic legacy was very much alive among the educated bourgeoisie. "The Greeks," writes Reichardt, "understood this better" (Reichardt 1976, 165).

[36]It would take a long time before people from the worker classes would visit orchestra and chamber music for similar socio-economic reasons. I treat this issue thoroughly in my book on Göteborg (Edström 1996).

Swedish Observations

Sweden, including Göteborg, enjoyed a rich musical life during the eighteenth century. The function of music and its changes that have been described on journeys through the central cultural lands of Europe, can to a large extent also be observed in Sweden. Even here, and not least in Göteborg, a rich musical life developed during the eighteenth century.[37] The writer Wilhelm Berg describes a visit in the 1770s by the German violinist Benedictus Schindler:

> A richer musical life developed, and it is from this time that one can date its origin in Göteborg where individual music lovers gave more public performances, as well as the contributing forces who gave their own concerts (Berg 1914, 10).

One of these "contributing forces" was a wealthy businessman and a musical amateur, Patrik Alströmer, who after he had played an important role in the consolidation of Stockholm's musical life, later had a similar role in the musical life of Göteborg. Berg paints a picture of a multifaceted man with an "aesthetic interest, a lover of music and, also a composer" (Berg 1914, 14). From Berg's description, one comes away with the impression that many within the upper classes of the community invested much interest and energy in music making. There were public concerts with larger ensembles and vocal performances. They played chamber music, and concerts were arranged with varied programs featuring visiting musicians or singers (Berg 1914, 14-25).

We can complement this picture with information from Jan Ling's study that covers the same time period and place, where we find many other examples of the importance of music making, which was measured as both a social and artistic pursuit. Among other things–and mainly thanks to Alströmer–a list of musicians including Ferdinand Zellbell the younger, Johann Gottlieb Naumann, Georg Joseph Vogler, Bartolomeo Campagnoli, visited the city. Through his reading of Alströmer's journal, Ling offers a detailed and rich description of the place musicians held among the bourgeoisie in Göteborg. He estimates that the group of people referred to in the journal could have been up to "several hundreds of people" or at the most a thousand people. Göteborg's population at that time was around 10,000. He described one month of 1778:

> This month of March is rich with musical events where musicians were invited to dinners and music making with Patrick [Alströmer]: for example on Sunday the 8th, where he made music with Misters Mancioli, Mengelin and Martini. Music happened also on Monday the 9th, where Mrs. Hall stayed and ate dinner. On Tuesday it was time for an evening at Vauxhall, where one danced, ate and played whist. There was dancing again on Monday the 12th. A dinner with the organist

---

[37] For a way in, see, *Musiken i Sverige* II (Jonsson and Jonsson 1993) and the cited literature there. For a later description of the rich Opera culture in Sweden during the end of the eighteenth century, see the musicologist Anna Ivarsdotter's section in Skuncke and Ivarsdotter 1998.

Bäck took place on the 13th, and on the 17th it's the first East India Company Directorate, followed by dinner and "an evening Concert at my home where Mr. Lolli played a Solo concert" (Ling 1999, 77).

Ling points out that our ability to understand the inhabitants and their musical life "is limited to those possibilities that can be found to compare their different aesthetic [sic] and social relationships to one another" (Ling 1999, 91). It was clear that music lovers had a different relationship to art music than the one that exists today. Then, people seemed preoccupied with the new, and uninterested in the old. At the same time, he also states that the level of the music life was high, perhaps higher than we would expect today.

Clearly, the European bourgeois played and sang in ever-larger numbers, and often attended events where music played a role, or was the main attraction. Individual youths from the bourgeoisie, especially girls, spent many hours singing or practicing their instruments, . As we have noticed elsewhere, within the nobility, the concept of art and music changed. Music held a central place, as Uffenbach described, in the home. In Reichardt's formulation, Haydn's music, however difficult it sometimes seemed, was a complete expression of purity and blending in situations where music friends met to take part in shared enjoyment (Reichardt 1976, 267).

For all of the contemporary traveling writers, it was a natural thing to pass judgment constantly. It seems to have been particularly important for the writers to place compositions in their context, by function and style. One valued, in other words, the music that one heard. But, as has been clearly shown, one did not expect that the music being performed would be carefully listened to at the Opera. And even if one made a concerted effort to focus on the Music, often the noise and intrigues of the opera audience laid obstacles in the way. Concentrating on music may have been easier in the churches. Whatever the case, both song and music were to the highest degree, a part of a culture's social and religious context, respectively.

We know—in contrast to what we have heard about relationships in classical Greek society—much about what music was performed during this time. On the other hand, other than these travel documents, there is very little written about the relationship between music's *structure* and the social functions it played for different groups of people. Could the analysis of musical structure, help us to draw a frame around the aesthetic?

Music's Structures—Music's Functions

The eighteenth century marked a time when the nobility and the church became less dominant in people's lives, and people even began to wonder if they could trust in an all-powerful and determining God. Obviously some of those people wondered, how they could define and explain what "beautiful" meant.

When Reichardt outlined what a *Liebhaber* (a lover of music), had to learn, he remarked that they often took liberties when it came to fifths and octaves. Above all, they overstepped the rules of art, which in fact "are grounded in the nature of our ears and of our feelings" (Reichardt 1976, 69).[38] Many philosophers and empiricists from Anthony Shaftesbury to David Hume struggled with this Platonic notion that rules can be found in the world of ideas or in nature.[39] As Ferry formulated it, Hume determined that "rules of art exist, and that those rules translate an agreement concerning what has been universally found to please in all countries and in all ages" (Ferry 1993, 56). Ferry is, of course, cognizant of Hume's philosophical solution that taste was to be grounded in our experience, and that *the beautiful* (see below) was dependent upon the qualities of the object itself that conveyed pleasant feelings.[40] Like other empiricists, Hume formed a list of qualities that made the experience of beauty more accessible. He conceded that some variation of opinions depended upon the person's age and temperament, and the fact that certain people had better judgment than others. Put simply, one can say that Hume thought beauty was found, in the eyes of the beholder, or the ears of the listener.

Ferry, however, shows that neither a rational-deductive argument ("a thought process combined with a derivation from top-down"), nor an empirical-inductive argument ("observations of reality combined with a derivation from bottom-up") can serve as a useful means of measuring the legitimacy of taste.[41] If Hume, using the empirical-inductive argument, came to a different opinion than another colleague using the same method, how could a universal norm of value ever be formulated? Ferry writes:

---

[38] Reichardt apparently referred to the ban of parallel fifths and octaves in multi-voiced works.

[39] With Shaftesbury we find two tenacious ideas, the thought that when we contemplate a painting we do not do it out of selfish motives but rather disinterestedness, and the idea of a special faculty for taste (see the discussion below concerning Kant and cf. Dickie 1997, 11f).

[40] I have taken this from Dickie who is citing Hume: "Though it be certain, that beauty and deformity, more than sweet and bitter, are not qualities in objects, but belong entirely to the sentiment, internal or external; it must be allowed, that there are certain qualities in objects, which are fitted by nature to produce those particular feelings" (Dickie 1997, 18).

[41] Ferry uses and often comments upon the philosopher Ernst Cassirer's work on Enlightenment, especially the difference between Descartes' deduction and Newton's observation (compare with Ferry 1993, 33, 41 among other places).

Since within a Humean perspective there is no term external to the expert's judgement, we can't even make out by what right someone could decide that this or that judgement is or not tainted by prejudice… the discussability of the beautiful reveals itself to be impossible… *every one being in the end reinstituted in the untransgressable particularism of his monadic individuality* (Ferry 1993, 61).

Shortly after Hume, another philosopher, Immanuel Kant, offered his solution to the dilemma. His simplified solution was that it was normal for everyone to be able to judge what was truly beautiful, since what was beautiful was normative also for others.

However, in a larger sense, the societal construction of values was completely uninfluenced by both the English empirically interested philosophers and the German philosophers. Still, the structure of music was changed to a great degree, which we can assume is closely related to:

(a) The function and meaning of music were changed by society's transformation primarily because of the development of knowledge, the transfer of power, the division of labor, and the development of technology, and so forth.
(b) Music and its functions and meanings changed for people.
(c) People's personalities and ways of thinking changed depending upon (a).

If we have previously devoted our attention to (a) and to (c), we will now take up (b), the structure of music.

The beautiful was an impoertant concept of evaluation in the period. But beautiful is, of course, far too imprecise a concept to use in our study of how music changed, as we shall now see. Our assignment will be, therefore, to give an overview of stylistic changes in music and set these in relation to the situations where music was performed and the functions that music fulfilled. In Denmark, as we have discussed, during the first half of the eighteenth century, they played music in the gallant style as well as the *empfindsamer Stil*.

The word *galant* can be traced in French literature back to the Middle Ages, and came to stand for the refined taste in certain noble salons during the seventeenth century, where the concept became synonymous with intelligence, amorous conversation, elegant clothes, *bon goût*, and a courteous and entertaining manner (Farstad 2000, 47). Even though the gallant man emanated from the French noble culture, it is from within the German culture that a new *music style*, the "galant style," developed:[42]

---

[42] The term was introduced by the musicologist Ernst Bücken (1927, 13-88). Mattheson speaks during the 1720s about the *galant homme* as a music loving amateur, and in Mattheson's "Der vollkommendene Kapellmeister" (1739) we also find the concept of the galant style (Bücken 1927, 61).

It was not until mid-century, long after the *galant* literary and social movement in Germany was spent, that *galant* was raised to the status of a theoretically recognised and defined musical style, the *galant* or free style as opposed to the *gearbeitet* (elaborated, contrapunctal, church) or *gebunden* (strict, bound) style (Sheldon as cited in Farstad 2000, 48).

The German musicologist Lutz Neitzert wrote a brilliant dissertation in 1989 that supports this understanding and will support further discussion about how this stylistic transformation can have been understood.[43] Neitzert begins with an analysis of Baroque music, the musical style that we earlier described as an important part of the etiquette of the courtiers. Referring to Elias, Neitzert finds that there are postulate parallels between the structure of conversation and the structure of instrumental music (Neitzert 1990, 32). The preservation of distance between the people of the court stabilized society. Everything was predefined, even musical compositions. That way, contexts could be controlled and conflicts avoided. A composer's work had to fit within its predetermined place and not be emphasized as a composition in and of itself. Neitzert shows that a composer's handiwork resulted in his or her disappearance as an individual. Concerning the music, Neitzert notes that:

(a) musical movements have *one* basic expression;
(b) individual voices enter in turn;
(c) soloists appear in solo sections that are interspersed with tutti sections;
(d) there is a single prevailing controlled *affekt*.

These musical parameters Neitzert points out appear in a typical Baroque work such as Händel's Concerto Grosso op 6:5 (Neitzert 1990, 33-50). As will be clear from the music example below, the concerto is introduced with a unison melody phrase for solo violin 1 and violin 1 ripieno (the other first violins). This musical idea is extended further for two measures and prepares for the next entrance that follows in measure 4. Here unannounced enters the solo violin 2 in unison with violin 2 ripieno playing the same melody a fourth lower while the first violins spin on along similar paths. Thereafter, in measure nine, a third voice enters in the same way, in unison with the oboes, the alto viol, and the contrabasses, after which the movement continues in the same spirit, concluding in measure 62.

---

[43]Neitzert's dissertation is just as important as it is dense and difficult to digest. His theoretical framework is built on ideas from Elias as well as the sociologists Jürgen Habermas and Niklas Luhmann. If the first two names are well-known, Luhmann has as yet had little influence at least within Swedish musicology. Within the humanities, in the fall of 1999 when I began this work, I had only come across his name in the work of the literary critic Erland Lagerroth (1994, 100). A broad presentation of Luhmann's work in English can be found in New German Critique, no 61, 1994. Danes, who regularly are the first in the North to present the "latest," published an anthology in 1992 with texts about Luhmann (see *Autopoiesis*…). I will return later in this text to Habermas and Luhmann.

Example 1: Händel's Concerto grosso op 6:5

Since art was a part of etiquette, compositions, too, became part of the social game. Because of this courtly art idea, no one was necessarily surprised by completely unexpected musical structures. Rather, compositions were calmly balanced and as moderate, as their delivery at the court. The social game demanded that one not be disturbed by completely unexpected musical structures, but rather that compositions have a calming and moderate affect. Music mirrored this. Neitzert points out there was, ideally only *one* mode of reception (Neitzert 1990, 30). The last-mentioned discussion Neitzert combines with a review of the importance of the arguments of *Affekten* and the *Figurenlehre*. The arguments are based on the idea that the affects were objective to such an extent that they were thought to be obvious for the people who could encode them. They were, like formulas, a part of etiquetteand therefore minimally subjective. The different musical parameters in a piece of instrumental music were all there to underscore the same affective idea.

Although Neitzert focuses on secular instrumental music, he asserts that sacred music functioned in the same way: composers wrote for the glory of the most high and were in His service.[44] The congregation was not going to a concert, either, but to a service with more or less the same interest in the music as in the sermon. Neitzert refers to Johann Georg Sulzer, who wrote at the end of the eighteenth century that the liturgical musical forms were unchanged within the Catholic Church, while the Protestant Church had developed new forms that were tasteless and not always successful.[45] As has been pointed out, despite these criticisms, the music life of Protestant churches was of great import for the development of a rich worldly music culture.

If we generally compare the structure of baroque music with galant music, we find that much has changed. The musicologist Per Kjetil Farstad writes:

> The *galant* style... expressed elegance, contained singable melodic phrases, short motifs, light textures, simple harmony, ornaments (short embellished figures, slurred notes, trills and appogiaturas). It also accommodated a more flexible treatment of dissonance, had formula-based cadences, and used frequent tempo and dynamic changes. The *galant* artist had to have 'taste', and be familiar with the latest Italian methods of playing and singing (Farstad 2000, 48).

Neitzert asserts it was because of the reduced importance of the nobility and the church, that new musical structures could emerge and be accepted. While public music and art once functioned as a representative confirmation of absolute power, gradually other music emerged that also became socially accepted. The new forms of music developed, both in response to the new *galant* nobleman's personality type, and also in response to the needs that the bourgeoisie experienced in their daily lives. These new musical structures did not function like a superior noble sound structure, where composers' handcraft skills were channeled toward the music's official function. Instead, the melody became a more and more important parameter in the musical structure, while other parameters developed

---

[44] Compare with what Christoph Wolff writes generally about Bach's music production: "An orientation toward the taste and needs of a wider public seems to have been entirely foreign to Bach" (Wolff 1991, 374).

[45] Sulzer formulates it this way: "Among the Protestants, however, poets and composers have permitted themselves new forms, and were not always successful...In some...Churches...they actually introduced the tasteless incursion of dramatizing Church Music" ["Bey den Protestanten aber haben Dichter und Tonsetzer sich neue Formen erlaubt, und sind nicht allemal glücklich dabey gewesen... In einingen... Kirchen.. ist man sogar auf den abgeschmackten Einfall gekommen, die Kirchenmusik bisweilen dramatisch zu machen"] (as cited in Neitzert 1990, 48). Sulzer's commentary shows again that Burney's opinion about the correlation between good church music and the condition of music in the country or city also must be related to which Christian philosophy prevailed in each area (see p. 70). In which case, now and then throughout music history, indications emerge that in Catholic countries, but more often in Protestant ones, people were used to sitting still and listening to God's word presented in instrumental form or with text. It can not be excluded that many peoples' way of listening to this music during this time shared parallels with the form of listening that we see later where people meet music during concerts.

a more supportive role. The individuality of the melody was therefore noted to a greater extent than earlier.[46]

In all the essentials, however, Neitzert does not see these changes as a countervailing style to the earlier representative noble polyphonic music style, but rather as a process of collapse (Neitzert 1990, 107).[47] The musicologist Charles Rosen, on the other hand, describes the quarter century from 1750 as a transition period that was "penetrated by eccentricity, [a] hit–or–miss experimentation" (Rosen 1980, 57). But he adds more clearly that what changed decisively was the function of the music:

> Toward the middle of the century, however, the symphonies and overtures written for *public performances*, and the sonatas, duos, and trios written for *amateurs* are notably different in style. The chamber music is more relaxed, diffuse, and simple... Public works began to be more formal. The string quartet, *for connoisseurs*, bridged the gap between the two styles (Rosen 1980, 45 [my italics]).

When new styles, such as *Empfindsamer Stil* and *Sturm und Drang* make inroads, there are naturally both functional causes and relevance on an individual level. *Empfindsamer Stil* and *Sturm und Drang* as styles, could function in different contexts and for music designed for different purposes.[48] Perhaps it was generally as d'Alembert wrote in 1751 in an introductory text to his great Encyclopedia, that of all the arts, music had made the greatest advances in recent years.[49]

Neitzert also sees these two styles as the two first *bourgeois* music styles. To a greater extent than in the *galant* style, we can observe an individualizing of expression and a splintering of the musical stream. This all leads to another way of listening. One listens partly to a clear melody, and partly to the music's different divisions in a more process-oriented way. There were a large number of tools that the composer could use in the last part of the eighteenth century. Individualizing meant at the same time emotionalizing. Carl Philipp Emanuel Bach's expressed it

---

[46] As the reader understands, I am speaking of Bach sons, like Carl Philipp Emanuel and Johann Christoph Friedrich, or for example in the sonatas of Haydn or Mozart (for a detailed description of all of the *topoi* and forms of this period see Ratner 1980).

[47] A commentary concerning Neitzert's choice of the phrase "process of collapse": that something is contemplated as either a change or as a collapse is naturally not insignificant. The choice of words clarifies a particular socio-historical position.

[48] For an account of different opinions on these styles see Farstad 2000, 46-78. The concept of *Sturm und Drang* was taken from Klinger's 1776 drama "Sturm und Drang," A musical demarcation of this term is given in Ratner 1980, 21f.

[49] In the same *Encyclopedia*, Rousseau defines music during the Baroque with the words "harmonie confuse, le chant dur et peu naturel" [confusing harmony, difficult songs with little naturalness] (cited in Stoljar 1985, 39).

this way: "wherein the musician cannot move others unless he himself is moved" {"*indem der Musickus nicht anders rühren kan, er sey denn selbst gerühret.*"}[50]

This individualizing, that followed in line with the entire enlightenment project, was predicated on the possibility that individual people could develop through education. And it also meant that the composer was no longer seen as practicing a handcraft that *discovered* something already existing, but as an artist who *invented* something new. Ferry talks about this change as a key to understanding the new modern world-view. When a person took things into his own hands:

> [h]e ceases to be he who modestly limits himself to discovering and expressing in a agreeable fashion the truths created by God and becomes he who invents. The genius appears and the imagination tends to become 'the queen of faculties,' the one that rivals the divine in the production of radically unprecedented works (Ferry 1993, 29).[51]

If we connect this to what Elias said, we can see how the European *bourgeois* person's altered living conditions, the division of time into work and leisure, the availability of education, economic power, and so forth, added to the changing processes in communal life. It eventually provided so much fuel during the eighteenth century's second half that it ignited a revolution. Enclosed in the same process we find that the new music styles were developed and categorized.

By now it is clear that through a review of Neitzert's work, we get a rich and informative picture of how the structure of music was formed within its socio-cultural context. Each change took place in a kaleidoscopic relationship with one another, and all factors were part of the socio-musical process of change. Among these factors were: a) the public concert; b) the *bourgeois* audience's origins, structures, and languages; c) music making at home and chamber music; as well as d) institutions that acted as intermediaries and dispensers of value judgments: music critics and music journalists, publishing entities and pedagogues.

From a music technology perspective, all these factors have an important bearing on our discussion of taste, beauty, and the aesthetic. We will enlarge our discussion of these respective factors and also tie in the concerts and the music making at home that Uffenbach, Burney and Reichardt described and gave opinions about.

---

[50] This belief that one cannot "move" others if one is not personally "moved" is not a new discovery. Aristotle already specifically expressed this (compare with Nässén 2000, 20).

[51] This development has a parallel in what Allen calls "the great-man theory" that slips in during the eighteenth century, and becomes fully visible during the nineteenth century: "Historians began to return to supernatural explanations… the history of music began to be written more and more in the terms of great names" (Allen 1962, 86. See also 198).

Listening to Music in Concert

The social pressure that made it more and more important to reflect on taste and opinion in a society where traditional value patterns began to slowly give way, led to more and more people expressing themselves in writing and speech: one wrote down one's reflections ("philosophy") and one's judgments ("criticism") concerning different art forms. Writing pedagogical studies and composing music for amateurs increased significantly during this time. Reichardt combined all these four activities in his professional life, with less emphasis on philosophizing than composing and making music. He was also a critic, as we have seen in his travel letters. He was, however, not terribly engaged as a philosopher, but rather mostly as a musician and a composer. After visiting a bourgeois music evening, or having visited a public concert he often made his opinions public, as we have seen, through his published travel letters.

If we look at the development of the concert form, we initially find concerts for private society and academies. In some larger cities, some of these concerts were open to the public. There were a large number of different variations on how these concert enterprises were organized. The division between amateurs and professional musicians also varied. Our three traveling music journalists reported being invited to private concerts, and attended public concert-like events performed in noble palaces or churches. They received tickets for "partly private" concerts, or bought tickets for public concerts and performances. The speed with which this process led to the founding of orchestral institutions with permanent professional musicians during the nineteenth century, varied throughout Europe. Seen from a distance, there was therefore, a change from:

(a) concerts with a completely demarcated and chosen audience, to

(b) subscription concerts with a mix of nobility and bourgeoisie in the audience; to

(c) concerts for which everyone could buy tickets set at market prices to

(d) concerts for which everyone could buy tickets at prices reduced through community support (summarized from Heister 1983, 35ff).[52]

In this process we can see a number of relationships that mutually influenced and were dependent upon one another. As audience sizes grew, there were more potential consumers of information about the music presented at concerts. Concert goers wanted to know what they could expect in any given program and afterwards, they wanted to see their critical opinions mirrored in a

---

[52]Alternative forms with these principal differences are legion. How concerts are supported today differ from country to country: through state, or community tax revenues, and/or business (state or private) and/or private giving. This affects different concert organizations' programming politics (see also Ch. 4, footnote 71).

reporter's or even in a music critic's published opinion of the concert. Periodical and newspaper reviewers became a new agent in the service of serving the social construct. Later, this role grew into an institution; a single critic's judgment, with god-like dispensation, contributed to the construction of the "right taste." The musicologist Hanns-Werner Heister calculates that about 80% of Germany's people could not be counted upon as potential audience members at the beginning of the nineteenth century, while about 5% of a city's population could visit concert halls simultaneously (Heister 1983, 168).

Although the servants most often offered refreshments and sweets during the private concerts that Uffenbach attended in Italy, that was not the case at public concerts. Going out to a social event where one sat or stood to hear what the musicians and singers had to offer resulted in the audience's attention becoming focused on the performance and on its new and unfolding the musical structures, which in turn, had developed somewhat different characteristics. Heister explains that in these situations people now listened in a more concentrated and a process-oriented way to a sequence of events, and experienced music with the help of their emotions. From an earlier phase, where it wasn't unheard of that those who subscribed to a music series also participated in music making now and then, it became more and more the norm later in the nineteenth century to leave the music making to the professionals, and assume a passive listening role (Heister 1983, 188).

The different factors in this social process mutually affected one another in an intricate interplay: the changes in the structure of music resulted in new options of listening differently. At the same time, a greater focus on making music/song more accessible in concert situations led, in turn, to more people being able to listen in a different way than at the beginning of this process. This further changed the language with which music was performed, and led some composers to try new musical solutions. All of this spiraled to serve the socio-political needs of various status groups, which created new options for listening differently, and the spiral continued—and this was perhaps most unanticipated—serving the socio-political needs of a socially demarcated group to maintain their status, this, in turn meant that....which led to...(and so forth).

One of Norbert Elias's important ideas is that social development, like nature's development, is blind. This network of factors that mutually affect one another bring about changes one cannot foresee, nor fully describe afterwards.

How music is thus used, affects how it is listened to, and what it means, which in turn affects the structure of music, which in turn stands in relationship to people's methods of dealing with and thinking about the changing development of society. It is within this spiraling network that our old word *aisthesis* took on a new shape, and afterwards became known, within the newly constructed semantic field, as the *concept* of aesthetics. What the word meant exactly and for whom it had meaning during the latter half of the eighteenth century certainly varied a great deal. 99% of people had never encountered the word: perhaps only those few who were so interested in philosophy that they had read Baumgarten's books in Latin. But it was not a foregone conclusion that one immediately used or accepted the new word. Immanuel Kant writes, for instance, in a note in his *Critique of Pure Reason*:

> The Germans are the only ones who now employ the word 'aesthetics' to designate that which others call the critique of taste. The ground for this is a failed hope, held by the excellent analyst Baumgarten, of bringing the critical estimation of the beautiful under principles of reason, and elevating its rules to science. But this effort is futile. For the putative rules or criteria are merely empirical as far as their sources are concerned, and can therefore never serve as *a priori* rules according to which our judgment of taste must be directed, rather the latter constitutes the genuine touchstone of the correctness of the former. For this reason it is advisable again to resist from the use of this term and save it for that doctrine which is true science (Kant 1998, 156).[53]

Kant disapproved of Hume's method and was not eager to link aesthetic academic status to a discussion of taste. However, other countries besides Germany also began using the word, usually connecting it to earlier discussions of taste. The discussion of the aesthetic is connected therefore to an earlier discussion on taste, the critical judgment of the music forms of the time and how music's meaning and function changed based in part on the new ways in which it was used.

It took some time before the concept was accessible through written discourse. Let me make this more clear through a a survey of the reviews of music in German periodicals during the last part of the eighteenth century show. Does the word appear at all?

The Formation of a Code of Values

In the educational climate that prevailed during the latter part of the eighteenth century, it became important for *bourgeois* culture and those in culturally interested circles to take part in discussions about literary products

---

[53]Kant's philosophy turned many of the previously accepted perspectives upside down. Ferry writes: "The Kantian movement is... a veritable revolution... Kant invites us to reverse the relation that existed between finiteness and the Absolute since the dawn of modern metaphysics. Instead of first positing the absolute in order then to situate the human condition within the order of lesser Being, of limitation, Kant begins with finitude to then go up, but only as a second step, toward the Absolute. [...] the divine figure of the Absolute is in turn relativized and brought down to the simple rank of a simple 'Idea' of reason whose objective reality is forever in demonstrable by theory" (Kant 1998, 78). Kant's stake within philosophy can be compared, therefore, with a Copernican conversion: if Copernicus showed that the earth went around the sun (and not the other way around), Kant begins with the assumption that it is our conceptual apparatus that structures the world and not the reverse.

and new music and song. The sociologist Jürgen Habermas places this interest squarely within a rambling *bourgeois* general public, with its concerts, literary salons, eighteenth-century writings, lending libraries, book clubs, and so on, all having given places.

The development of a shared system of values and a language for the same, was, when it came to new forms of music, neither a fast nor an easy process in a low-tech and pre-mass-media society. Old opinions lingered long and, as the musicologist Susan Morrow shows in her review of a large number of German periodicals from the 1760s, new ways of thinking are shared with old ones over a long span of time. The following long quotation from a local newspaper from 1792 is a surprisingly good summary of many of the factors, and relationships that we have just touched upon:

> Music is nothing more than a succession of tones intended to express certain sentiments, or to arouse them in others, or to entertain... Just as music is born through sentiment, in the same manner it affects only sentiment, the heart is the actual target of music. Words affect reason, producing in it special ideas which can, of course, then produce feeling again. But music affects the feelings directly...No matter how brilliant, no matter how artfully woven together, if it is not a true artistic product it does not arouse sentiments. Purely instrumental music can certainly make, in and of itself, a very lively impression: a beautifully performed Haydn sonata can do a lot. But in this type of music always lies a great deal that is vague, ambiguous, uncertain, and you have to have a certain amount of training to get true pleasure from it (cited from Morrow 1997, 12).

Morrow suggests these basic thought forms came out of a coincidence of cultural circumstances, social factors and prevailing ideas, rather than from a few influential writers articulating new thought. Articles in periodicals of the time commented on one another and publicly compared different opinions creating a "group think." Articles were written by both amateurs and professional musicians (for example Reichardt):

> The practical nature of this enterprise writing forced the reviewers… to come up with realistic standards that would allow them to do their job. Precisely because they were not trying to write about aesthetic theory, the reviewers could think about instrumental music in new and different ways. Collectively their discourse took a form and shape (Reichardt 1997, 18).

It is clear then that music was something that one judged critically on the basis of new points of departure like music's "own" rules and gradually many older patterns of thought became erased. Morrow writes: "If mimesis could not help, other avenues would have to be explored" (Reichardt 1997, 44).

In the community that developed, the need for recommendations and opinions grew large. The choice of words and the way of formulating oneself, and opinions and evaluations spread to the wider readership through these periodicals.

It is estimated that about 15% of Germany's population around 1770 and about 25% around 1800 could read. Because many of the periodicals were bought by subscription from reading societies, or could be found at periodical libraries, several people, including whole families, could read the same periodical. Besides (something Morrow forgets to report), one read aloud more often in private contexts, whereby not just men, but also women and other family members could share in the written word. The number of editions varied greatly. Print runs of most periodicals varied from 1000 to 5000 to 10,000 copies, while the largest, the ones with the and broadest content, like the *Hamburgischer Correspondent* was printed in 25,000 copies. The profile of individual periodicals varied. Some periodicals focused on general culture, while others focused on literature or on the general community. Regardless of the subject matter, it was not uncommon to find notices, announcements, reviews, and other articles about musical life. Opinions and recommendations were, thus, widespread.

Morrow shows how certain key words, metaphors and opinions hold sway for a time, only to be replaced by others. One wave of value judgments rolls in, flattens out and is followed by another. From the middle of the century it becomes clear that value judgments were being made to delineate, for example, German music from Italian, especially in relation to the shortcomings of Italian music when it came to compositional work. While German music was heavy and serious, Italian music was light and fleeting. This value judgment became gradually less important, or more succinctly, self-evident. German music was thought to mirror particularly masculine qualities. Words like "wahr" and "echt" appeared more and more.[54] Instrumental music was perceived to bear *inner* value.

Morrow shows that reviews from the 1760s to 90s, revolved around four main themes: compositional correctness, order and completeness, the creative genius, and expressivity (Morrow 1997, 72ff).[55] The two first rational factors were written about most during the 1760s; the two latter factors—the irrational ones—

---

[54]These words, exactly like "objective" and "aesthetic," developed a delimiting function, and functioned clearly within music history as exclusionary words (compare with Kjørup 1999, 100). A typical way these words are used is to apply them to music that one is personally fond of. Music journalists in Göteborg often used words like "real" and "true" in the inter-war period as concepts for music that particularly captured them, and for music that had serious ambitions. So it is even sometimes today. When the Icelandic artist Björk's latest album ("Vespertine") was recently reviewed in the daily newspaper *Göteborgs-Posten* (010923) the reviewer wrote that "she doesn't want to be difficult and smart. Precisely the opposite. But in order to create real and true music demands…" (my italics).

[55]Observe that the concept of genius had a broad meaning: "They used the word Genie as defined in Sulzer's *Allgemeine Theorie der schönen Künste*, to designate a composers' talent or gift for composition, reserving the superlative *Original = Genie*, a specific term traceable to Shaftesbury, for special cases—for C. P. E. Bach, Haydn, Mozart" (Morrow 1997, 74). Morrow also shows (from Sulzer) that one associated genius with intelligence, humor, and innovative music (Morrow 1997, 76).

dominated during the two following decades. At the end of the century, a balance between all four factors was sought. These four main themes were valued most when the unexpected was skillfully presented within the frame of the known.

Musicians worked to balance the *beautiful* and well-known with the *sublime*, the magnificent, and unknown. In this, Mozart succeeds Haydn as the most important model of the 1790s (Morrow 1997, 135f).

This idea of balance carried with it the implication that one listened to the piece's totality—*das Ganze*—which also can be experienced as a reaction to the fact that pieces became longer and longer, resulting in the rewarding of process-oriented listening. This stood in contrast to a textual way of listening. According to the musicologist Carl Dahlhaus, listening to song permits a fragmentary way of listening, whereas, in instrumental music one needs to keep track of what happens in the flow of the music in order for it to be meaningful:

> While listening to an aria or Lied, one lends ones ears mostly to the musical details—and allows these to affect oneself, irrespective of the context in which they fulfill a function: This system of relationships—in which the expressive glance of the eyes plays a role—is determined by the text, and not by the overarching musical form, that admittedly exists, but that passes unnoticed (Dahlhaus 1988, 74).[56]

A total vision also emerged in compositional treatises, as well as the philosophical writings. Younger writers could most clearly articulate these changes.[57] Morrow shows that Karl Philip Moritz was one of the first to liberate art from its social function:

> Moritz strictly separated the art work itself from its effect and purpose, dismissing the latter as irrelevant, thus freeing art from any social function (*something reviewers had been doing implicitly for decades*). Like Goethe, he insisted that it should then be judged as a formal unity within its own self-referential system. Thus, aesthetic pleasure would reside partly in the perception of musical form (Morrow 1997, 148 [my italics]).[58]

---

[56]"Beim Hören einer Arie oder Liedes neigt man vielmehr dazu, musikalisches Details unabhängig von dem Kontext, in dem sie eine Funktion erfüllen, auf sich wirken zu lassen; das Bezugssystem, dem die expressiven Augenblicke angehören, stiftet der Text, nicht eine übergreifende musikalische Form, die zwar vorhanden ist, aber in der Regel kaum wahrgenommen wird."

[57]Morrow refers to the third part of Heinrich Christoph Koch's treatise on composition from 1793 (Morrow 1997, 135). Compare also with Baker 1995, 111-133, where there is a more detailed discussion of Koch's reading and choice of music examples.

[58]Compare with Woodmansee 1994, 18-22. Woodmansee points especially to the contemplative attitude toward art that, as Moritz describes it, had a parallel within a pietistic Christian view of God: "The mode of reception described here follows just as necessarily for Moritz from the nature of the work of art as does the religious piety from the nature of the Deity. God is an end in Himself… we are thus enjoined to love God disinterestedly, for His own sake. An analogous relationship is established between the work of art and the 'aesthetic' attitude" (1994, 20 [my italics]).

One finds, on the whole, in Moritz's writings, most of the ideas that concerned music culture at the end of the eighteenth century. Dahlhaus has summarized these as:

    (a) thoughts about music's abilities to express feelings become meaningful,

    (b) opinions that music can express that which words are not capable of,

    (c) the idea that a piece exists for the sake of music, and not for the listeners, and

    (d) that art's meaning develops a spiritual dimension and is understood as a religion (Dahlhaus 1988).

Not least, Moritz expressed a distancing from the old idea of mimesis, and touched in the following quotation, what Eagleton earlier named the curious thought of the object as subject: "When I contemplate a beautiful object, I deflect the aim from myself back on the object itself. I consider it as something that fulfills not me, but *itself*" (Huray and Day 1981, 186).

* * *

Morrow's instructive analysis of the empirical material, shows clearly how the collective of writers, while at the same time traveling across unknown territory, created a map of the terrain and come nearer to a shared basic set of values. Reviews were read by a large number of people, including the standard-bearers of the society at the time.[59] While older thoughts about music as a mimetic art lived on, music gradually was seen as an independent phenomenon that was an expression of an inner emotional world. And one still associated different forms of music with given social functions. But during this process, certain words and concepts completely and naturally became associated with one another in a new way: concepts that stood for the new and the contemporary, that the genius was a bourgeois man that found new solutions, and that music was seen as an independent phenomenon that was an expression of an inner emotional world.

A very important point to remember is that all this was done by and large without using the word *aesthetic*. "Before the 1790s, the word 'aesthetic' had

---

[59]The musicologist Lutz Lesle (1984, 23) emphasizes that critics, thanks to Kant's idea of the Universal in all purely aesthetic judgments, could appear as spokespersons for the general public (see below). The concept of taste received, if one can put it this way, its democratic interpreters. The best educated and most clever critics' opinions came to be seen as objective, and the critics themselves saw their socio-cultural power increased. Those who read the papers gradually learned the arguments for the value of music: "To be capable of making aesthetic judgment is to be capable of entering the relevant sorts of support for ones' judgment, of recognizing entered objections to it, and of making appropriate responses to those objections" (Mulhall 1994, 25). Aesthetic debate constituted therefore "a way of constructing or discovering community through the articulation and development of individuality" (Mulhall 1994, 29).

occurred only twice in collective discourse" (Morrow 1997, 149). A somewhat more frequent "experimental" use appeared first in the 1790s.[60]

Morrow's analysis pertains, primarily, to German language speaking areas. However, we can be sure similar patterns were repeating themselves in other areas as well. If we take Josef Haydn's two London visits as an example, of this process, we find that his symphonies were met with enthusiasm by the *bourgeois* audiences. What was appreciated in this music was its "tendency towards "trick, artifice, surprise and difficulty" that while at the same time obeying conventions (Lessem 1988, 141). The English also found the music from Germany and Austria as to be very exciting in contrast to the Italian music. As people began listening to longer pieces, they began discussing its form and content. Some people in London even heard the same symphony more than one time, perhaps listening in different ways and finding pleasure in again and again. The musicologist Alan Lessem points out that one result of listeners hearing longer pieces was that questions about music's form and content began to be discussed. One could possibly listen in a different way and find pleasure in rediscovering its joy. Lessem summarizes:

> While the 1790s was a time of fresh responses to new impressions, its dominant social groups were also embracing an ideology of power, which, as a product of a quickly spreading industrial capitalism, began to call for the marshalling of such impressions, and their direction towards long-term goals. If Haydn's audiences, immersed in their senses and feelings, were only somewhat aware of the order in what they were hearing, we today have made that order into an absolute. (Lessem 1988, 143)[61]

It follows from Morrow's reviews that one to a great extent devoted one's interest to instrumental music. Instrumental music, as we have seen, grew in importance and scope during the eighteenth century. But songs like Reichardt's also grew in popularity.

Sing Burghers, Farmers and Workers

Reichardt is normally placed as only one of many composers within the Berlin *Lieder* school, along with Johann Abraham Peter Schultz and Carl Friedrich Zelter. As a musical form, Lieder, and above all songs accompanied by the clavichord, the harpsichord or the lute, were a musical form that grew in

---

[60] The word "aesthetic" occurs, however, in descriptions of a more encyclopedic character. Sulzer writes in 1771 concerning aesthetics: "This is a new term that has been coined to identify a science that came into being only a few years ago" (Huray and Day 1981, 121).

[61] As my colleague Bengt Edlund pointed out in a personal communication, Lessem's opinion is that only a limited group of listeners today can follow the course of events in a symphony. Compare with Cook 1990 who argues that there is a normal and a musicological way of listening. Music aesthetician Jerrold Levinson 1997 takes us to task for our inability to hear larger forms when we listen to music. We listen, as the title of his book has already suggested "in the moment."

popularity. What did these swarms of song books, editions of well-known operas and musical plays signify? Songs and pedagogical books intended for a culturally interested bourgeois society were published for the same nascent musical market, sonatas for both professionals and music lovers, arrangements and excerpts of well-known operas and musical plays, and so on. Not least, there appeared a stream of songs for an undefined bourgeois/noble audience, as well as collections of songs for children and women. It becomes necessary therefore to study what this signified. In what context was this music performed, and how was it experienced?

In her study of burgher traditions in Germany during the last half of the eighteenth century, the musicologist Margaret Stoljar explains this in a fashion that is underscored in our discussion:

> If we wish to study the nature of song at any historic moment, to uncover the ways in which its musical and verbal communication actually worked, we need to understand how listener and performer perceived its function and realized it. Only then will a sound foundation be established upon which analysis of form and style can be based (Stoljar 1986, 3).

Stoljar suggests how one understood music's function determined how one listened and what the song and music meant to the listener depended upon how one understood music's function. By the middle of the eighteenth century, it became increasingly common in a *bourgeois* home to read aloud from novels, read poems, and as we know, make music together.[62] In the realm of poetry the writer Friedrich Gottlieb Klopstock[63] succeeded in connecting to the new emotional thoughts of the times in a way that, according to Johann Gottfried Herder, was completely new for the German language. Herder in his turn "discovered" among the German people a tradition of songs and ballads (*Von deutscher Art und Kultur*, 1773) and published two collections of folk songs at the end of the 1770s.

Herder's "discovery" was itself a result of a long process. His discovery signaled that an interested middle class began documenting Europe's folk culture around 1800. Whereas in the sixteenth century, writes Peter Burke (1994), "popular culture was everyone's culture; a second culture for the educated," by the end of the eighteenth century, society's upper classes had, in effect, retreated from "the culture of the people" so much so that it could now be "discovered," a development that was also the case in Sweden:

---

[62] It should be observed that these novels often pertained to the life of the bourgeoisie (note for instance one of the earliest novels of all time, Samuel Richardson's *Pamela* from 1740 is not about the nobility).

[63] Klopstock published *Geistliche Lieder* in 1758, a work, according to the Swedish national encyclopedia (1993), that is "enthusiastic and strongly colored by pietism." Liedman points out, by the way, that pietism in Germany "with its passion for human Innerlichkeit, was a condition for the later rise of the romantic world view" (Liedman 1997, 357).

THE AGE OF ENLIGHTENMENT 91

Civilisation had its price… if we look back over the three hundred years [1500s-1700s]… the change in the attitudes of educated men seems truly remarkable. By 1800… they were in the process of rediscovering popular culture as something exotic and therefore interesting. They were even beginning to admire "the people" (Burke 1994, 285f).

During the eighteenth century, many more poets emerged from the newly created middle classes, together with advocates, priests, teachers, for whom the ideals like of freedom and brotherhood were important virtues. Without "past obligations" to the nobility, the middle classes could now reinvest some of their newly earned wealth in time and money, ploughing back their "winnings," as it were, into their cultural soil. They often founded literary societies where they read their own poems to like-minded people, and encouraged others to publish.

They also met in private homes as well as in unions, various societies and clubs to sing and make music. Their simple songs of friendship were sung *a cappella* or to simple accompaniment. The musical movements no longer were comprised of a melody that was followed by a thorough bass voice, but rather by Alberti basses and simple chordal patterns. One such preferred pattern made much of a singable melody and gave weight to music that was experienced as natural and immediate. Composers created songs and sonatas with this whole new population of female musicians in mind. As Reichardt points out in his later writings, many *bourgeois* and noble women were experienced pianists, an evolution that continued for a long time. Even though from the nineteenth century as a rule, most of the leading professional pianists were men, a complete assessment of quantity and quality would give women a great lead. Therefore, there have been a *much greater number of women than men* who have played the piano at a high technical level.

With time, demands were raised for song's style, breadth, and content. Solos and songs for music lovers, *Liebhaber*, were written, as well as for music experts, or *Kenner*. The demand for more complex music, both in the solo voice and the piano accompaniment grew. This context eventually included both folk songs, and *Lieder* in a folk style, as well as *Lieder* in other styles (*Sturm und Drang*, Vienna Classicism, Romantic, and so forth), and opera arias became very popular.[64] With time, the texts developed a similar breadth: from the most solemn to the most everyday things, like a child getting its first tooth. The personal experience of feelings take on new and important dimensions(as in the *empfindsamer Stil*).

---

[64]Stoljar discusses also the differences that were found within *Sturm und Drang*: from the uttermost simplicity in accompaniment and vocal lines to complex movements with vocal lines that demanded the highest technical ability. While composers like Neefe and André often find themselves at both of these extremes, others like Schulze and Reichardt land somewhere in between. One understood at the time this difference as the opposition between Nature and Art.

People listened therefore to a great extent bounded by the content of the text and their own personal emotions.[65]

Stoljar emphasizes that this song tradition explored the claims that Baumgarten had earlier made for the precedence of the senses when identifying the aesthetic:

> The particularity of each person's aesthetic experience...the focusing on the psychological content of art...the change in thinking about art from notions of form to those of expression was profound and revolutionary in character; the lyric poetry of Romanticism emerging... between 1770 and 1830, sprang ultimately from it...In this sense German poetry of *Sturm und Drang* was the first to articulate the demands of those who wrote the theory of art a generation before them (Stoljar 1985, 40).

Baumgarten's publication was written in 1735, and it would, however, be wrong to assume that his theoretical formulations would inevitably be given practical shape by future generations. Of course, before Baumgarten's publications, there were a number of other cultural expressions that also seemed to act as pre-cognitions of future events.[66] Stoljar's comments about *Sturm und Drang* underscore this. Hence, I see Stoljar's complaint more as a qualitative judgment. Generations had to pass before they had developed the social breadth to even talk about the cultivation of these art reflections. If we were to use the metaphor of culture as a broad landscape, we might see a new type of flower spring up. Then, miles away, a similar lonely flower begins to grow in comparable soil. And another. And another. Some, of course, wither before they are discovered. The flower species slowly spreads, creating their own flower-niche in the landscape. Finally, due to changes in climate, these flowers become well-rooted and spread quickly to cover huge areas.[67]

The picture that Stoljar paints of the song's repertory, of song's use and function, contributes to our understanding of the development of western music history. As we will see, song, as a part of music culture, is rarely accredited with the important role that it has played historically. The role of song has been severely undervalued within musicological research. What a paradox, because song, along with dance, is perhaps the most natural art practice that humans can engage in. As children, it comes naturally to us. As a culture, it is our backbone. We carry this

---

[65]Stoljar comments that song composers could directly transmit emotional moods, while instrumental music "[was] obliged to appeal to the imagination in less direct ways" (Stoljar 1985, 148).

[66]We touched lightly earlier on the French debate during the seventeenth century between Descartes and Pascal, a debate on the questions that would later by universally known (see further in Ferry 1990, 26, 33-77).

[67]For a less metaphorical description of this development, compare the conditions Lydia Goehr lays out within her philosophical discussion about the development of the Work concept (Goehr 1992, 89-119).

instrument with us and practice it naturally from early childhood. To exaggerate the point: the relation between the number of people within European culture—and this goes for folk, popular, and art-music—who sing as opposed to play an instrument has probably always been, let's guess, ten to one.

The fascination with social song and its sociability prevailed, not just in Germany, but also in many other countries across Europe. As printers could print music faster and cheaper, we entered the age of the modern music publisher which, in fact, affected the development of music culture.[68] It is virtually impossible to count the number of songs and romances that have been written since the beginning of the eighteenth century. Song became an equally important social activity as *bourgeois* men began singing in groups and choirs as students and in private gatherings.[69]

Lieder and popular melodies from school songs, musical theater and opera were linked to the pronunciation of folksongs, hymns, psalms, and other texts of ideological importance. As a result they further informed people's knowledge, attitudes and convictions. The meanings and functions of these songs for these bourgeois groups are not possible to separate from their private and public contexts:

> The real function of song in performance can be defined as its *use*, a term which is chosen in order to underline the fact that the process of song does not end with composition but performance and listening (Stojlar 1985, 15).

The private contexts and experiences people had when they sang and listened to music were the antithesis of the situation that occurred at public concerts. Both of these contexts were important areas within which peoples' understandings and experiences of song and music were cultivated.

But an important piece is still missing from western art music's aesthetic puzzle and it has to do with instrumental music's intimated advantage over vocal music. Up until now, we have seen that the understanding of the aesthetic has to do with:

(a) how a generally applicable taste was understood and discussed;

(b) a rich sensory experience and sense-oriented knowledge, recently added factors in this aesthetic process;

(c) the structures of music that changed in keeping with how the community

---

[68] In Sweden, for example, the hard-working Olof Åhlström, thanks to his Royal Privilege, could publish products like *Musikaliskt Tidsfördrif* [Musical Passtimes] (1789-1835) and *Skaldestycken satta i musik* [Poems Set to Music] (1793-1823).

[69] The meaning of human song from a bourgeois perspective is taken up clearly in Norlind's *Allmänna Musiklexikon* [*General Music Lexicon*] from the beginning of the twentieth century. He enthusiastically fills ten pages (19 paragraphs) about this word. The importance of student song has been thoroughly discussed in a series of dissertations in musicology from the twentieth century (Jonsson 1990, Kydland Lysdahl 1995, as well as Kvist Dahlstedt, 2001).

and the people in it evolved;

(d) a new language and new social mechanisms for the construction of value arose through the ways music was used (played and listened to) in new public concert situations, and

(e) above all, a singing "revolution" within the bourgeoisie created a different and individual point of departure for the function and meaning of music and song.

From an empirical-ethnological point of view, the practice of how instrumental music influenced the uses of this music in public as well as intimate contexts remains to be studied from an aesthetic perspective. As has been noted, instrumental music became a generally important form of music. We will therefore give the reception of instrumental music a short look.

Instrumental Music Between Inner and Outer Worlds

There were many from the early eighteenth century who agreed with the famous question posed by the secretary of the French Academy of Science: "Sonata, what do you want of me?" A hundred years later, programs were gradually compiled to facilitate the understanding of sonatas. As Stoljar makes clear, some philosophers were investigating the expressions and moods that distinguish the *Sturm und Drang* tradition already a generation before that tradition took hold. The classic and romantic music philosophy appears in Dahlhaus's last work (1988) and in some of his earlier accounts, as a long series of parallel main highways, crossed by smaller streets and a great number of cul-de-sacs. Dahlhaus treats the place of instrumental music in great detail. He shows that streams of thought do not always follow the well-marked roads. One often manages to get from one place to another through making false turns, misunderstanding the directions, or picking up a passenger who finds her own way.

At the same time as Haydn wrote his Russian quartets, Romantic music philosophy was being born. And, writes Dahlhaus "à la Stoljar," it can therefore be seen as strange that neither Haydn's nor Mozart's Classical music was accompanied by a Classical music philosophy. Furthermore, Wackenroder's and Tieck's Romantic music philosophy was not answered by Romantic music. Instead, in fact (Dahlhaus 1988, 86).[70]

Dahlhaus makes a clarification suggesting that paradoxes do sometimes get solved:

---

[70] "Reflection and compositional practice cancelled each other out" ["Reflexion und kompositorische Praxis klafften auseinander."] Cf. Niklas Luhmann's theory and description that philosophy and music, like many other social phenomena, be seen as separate systems (see below).

The fact that music and music aesthetics around 1800 do not completely agree, loses in any case its paradoxical sheen if one bears in mind that music aesthetics in general—which starts from music—as well as to a lesser degree is also supported by it, rather than starting from a philosophical and literary tradition, whose categories characterize it (Dahlhaus 1988, 90).[71]

A problem of this kind often solves itself by seeing it doubled: writers in different time periods may use the same word, but the word's *meaning* may not always be the same. Furthermore, the same music might be experienced differently in 1780 than in 1820, even though it sounded "the same"(Dahlhaus 1988, 107; cf. Ch. 3, footnote 118).

One also must, however, start with the assumption that if someone out of their own context and (musical) knowledge honestly describes something with certain concepts, this must be the researcher's point of departure, even if it is tempting, with today's results in mind, to state that "the wrong" concept was used, or the "wrong music" was cited.[72] People during this time did not live in a mass-media society. We sometimes forget that information about music and the music itself spread much more slowly than we are used to today. Just because we have access to various publications from that time, does not mean that musicians or composers back then, for example, had read Moritz. Some people had heard neither Haydn's or Mozart's music, but were well versed in Baumgarten's and Kant's writings. This means that, for example, a musician or composer's access to any particular author's thoughts and ideas, was random and limited. The possibility of variations within a limited stratum that "followed with its time" was therefore great. When we try to draw general conclusions on the basis of an overview of the publications of the time that we still have today, it is important to remember that their vision of the world was limited. In other words, people did not live in a mass-media society. Neither music, or opinions about the same, or new ideas spread terribly quickly. For example, Bedrich Smetana wrote at the end of the 1850s that Göteborg's inhabitants deified Mozart but did not understand his music, feared Beethoven, saw Mendelssohn's music as unenjoyable and that no one had ever heard Schumann before (Carlsson 1996, 73).

* * *

[71] ["Die Tatsache, dass Musik und Musikästhetik um 1800 auseinanderklaffen, verliert allerdings den Schein des Paradoxen, wenn man berücksichtigt, dass eine Musikästhetik im allgemeinen weniger durch die Entwicklung der Musik, die ihren Gegenstand bildet, als vielmehr durch die philosophische und literarische Tradition, aus der ihre Kategorien stammen, geprägt ist."]

[72] Science theoretician Jan Bärmark mentioned a superlative example at a 2000 seminar: in a biography of Goethe's life and works the contents of his journals are discussed. Goethe writes there that his first love was Elsa. The biographical researcher comments: "But there, Goethe was wrong."

The philosopher Lydia Goehr clearly summarizes how instrumental music advanced toward Parnassus' peak. She states that instrumental music (both playing and listening) could also open a transcendental or metaphysical dimension. The meaning of music lay in its ability to prove and elucidate the higher world's eternal truth. This meant, at the same time, that music's meaning could not be external, but rather—as we have already seen Moritz argue in the eighteenth century—must be found internally in the music itself:

> Theorists then argued that instrumental music, without particularized content, is the most plausible candidate for being 'the universal language of art'. Such music provides a direct path to the experience of a kind of truth that transcends particular natural contingencies and transitory human feelings. Schilling made the point: 'No aesthetic material is better suited to the expression of the ineffable than is sound' (Goehr 1992, 153f).

The coupling of music's *transcendent* and *inner meaning*, where the observation of music's structural, let alone its and formal qualities were written about more and more, led in turn, following Goehr, to the experience that instrumental music was something separated from the everyday. "The essence of fine art comprised the idea of severance from anything associated with the transient, contingent world of mere mortals" (Goehr 1992, 157). These similar "Romantic illusions" conveyed a concentration on the object that was missing earlier.[73] Goehr shows among other things how that composers reacted. Because listeners were not sufficiently quiet during a concert and that the demands for rehearsals were rising, composers' status grew, and they demanded more payment and successfully raised legal copyright issues.[74] Along with the idea that this music was something separated from reality, people also expected to express more of a detached, contemplative attitude while listening to music. This connects to what Dissanayake called the "detached aesthetic experience." She even writes:

> One can say that the highly detached kind of aesthetic response, as an ideal if not a perfectly achieved reality, is highly specialized and *un*natural and not available to untrained persons (Dissanayake 1989, 131).

---

[73] Cf. Christensen who, from his reading of Sulzer's extensive work from 1771, writes: "The task of finding an aesthetic justification for instrumental music was thus an urgent one in the eighteenth century... a solution was found precisely in the psychological processes studied so intently by the empiricist philosophers. It was only by enfranchising the sentient responses of a listener that the strictures of traditional mimetic theory could be countered. If instrumental music was ever to attain a worth commensurate to vocal music, a strong aesthetic of sentiment needed to be formulated and defended" (Baker and Christensen 1995, 5).

[74] Typically enough, it was operas—always nearest to the prevailing power—that theoretically as well as practically became protected by law first. France was, in this case, a precedent setting country, but it took until the middle of the nineteenth century before composers organized themselves into the SACEM in 1851. In Sweden, a similar organization was founded in 1923, STIM (see Edström, 1998).

What Goehr finds to be conclusive in this process that she describes, is what she calls "the aesthetic remainder." Based on the idea that an object can undergo an artistic conversion and then be experienced as an *art object*, Goehr conceives that through this process the object is imbued with completely new qualities, that the normative community—what Goehr calls "the institution of art"—saw as aesthetic:

> These properties constitute the aesthetic remainder; strip away (conceptually) the non-aesthetic properties (often an object's use or function) and the aesthetic remains. The romantic theorists had a formula at hand. The greater the aesthetic content, the less the worldly content, and, therefore, the more worthy the art (Goehr 1992, 167).

Here it is inevitable for us, as it was for Goehr, that we reconnect with Kant, as we now understand that thoughts from his philosophical accounts clearly appear, and initiate continuing change in the aesthetic project.[75]

In 1781 Kant wrote the fundamental distinction: "I call a science of all principles of *a priori* sensibility the transcendental aesthetic." Kant, like his earlier colleagues, brooded intently on how a judgment of taste, the critical assessment of the beautiful, could be reflected upon. Echoing Plato in some respects, Kant thought that we understand the object, for example music, not as music really is, but rather as it appears to us. Similar to the English empiricists, he tried to explain how the judgment of taste could be connected to aesthetic judgment's subjective and arbitrary character.[76] As we have seen, Ferry formulated this same problem as a question: "How is one to come up with an 'objective' answer to this matter once the foundations of the beautiful have been situated within the most intimate subjectivity, that of taste?" (Ferry 1993, 19).

Kant therefore, along with many of his other contemporaries, focused much of his energy on choosing and giving examples of what was beautiful and sublime, as well as scrutinizing how these choices could be reached. In his lectures during the 1780s, and in *Kritik der Urteilskraft (1790)*, he discussed in detail how taste is related to other concepts such as knowledge, freedom, and morals. I prefer, however, to quote an unusually illuminating passage from his 1782 lectures on metaphysics:

---

[75] Kant touches also on instrumental music's position in his discussion on free beauty and dependent beauty: "The first presupposes no concept of what the object ought to be" (Kant 1951, §16). In this division, Kant includes flowers, beautiful birds and other objects that do not represent anything in and of themselves. He adds: "We can refer to the same class what are called in music fantasies (i.e. pieces without any theme), and in fact all music without words. In the judging of a free beauty (according to the mere form), the judgment of taste is pure" (Kant 1951, §16). For a discussion about this passage see Dutton 1994.

[76] Cf. Norman Kreitman 1999, 189: "Perhaps the most important contrast between Kant's position and that of Hume is that though both are thoroughgoing subjectivists, Hume speaks of a consensus of mind, Kant of properties of Mind."

If something pleases in sensation, then it *gratifies*, and the object is agreeable... In order to distinguish the agreeable and disagreeable we need feeling; in order to distinguish the beautiful and ugly, we need taste; in order to distinguish the evil and good, we need reason. In the investigation of the agreeable and disagreeable we have no communal standard... Therefore one cannot engage in any dispute... But with the beautiful it is otherwise. There the beautiful is not that which pleases one, *but rather what has the approval of all* [my italics]... This communal sense arises thus: each private sensation of the one must accord with the private sensation of the other, and through this agreement we receive a universal rule. This is the communal sense or *taste*. Whatever then agrees, is beautiful... The universal agreement of sensibility is what constitutes the ground of satisfaction through taste... It is also like this with music. Sight and hearing are accordingly senses of taste and communal.... Agreeable is that which agrees with the private sense; but beautiful is that which agrees with the communal sense (Kant 1997, 66f).

Kant thought we organized our environmental stimuli with the help of our own imaginations, and then our intelligence took over and categorized what we sensed. People could *experience* the aesthetic. But it was illogical for Kant to say one thinks something was beautiful only for oneself. He assumed therefore that we all—*a priori*—bear the same inbuilt predispositions, or in today's terminology "preprogrammed software."[77]

Insights about *the beautiful* reached everyone through a free interplay or reciprocal action between our fantasy and our intelligence. As Kant wrote in his third *Kritik* in 1790, the judgment of the aesthetic comes about exactly because that which defines it is not a concept "but the feeling (or internal sense) of that harmony in the play of the mental powers, so far as it can be felt in sensation" (Kant 1951, §15). If we only analyze a musical work, we cannot reach a purely aesthetic judgment, because we have then rewarded *intelligence* at the cost of *fantasy* (the power of the imagination). Finally, the beautiful had no *purpose*. Kant, therefore, considered form to be the most important aesthetic criterion. *The beautiful* as we understand it through our form of reflection on the individual object—and which is shared by everyone else, thanks to the above-mentioned in-built "program"— constituted what for Kant was an aesthetic satisfaction. Or as Ferry formulates it:

---

[77]This formulation is also found in § 7: "It would... be laughable if someone who prided himself on his taste to justify himself by saying: 'This object....the concert we hear... is beautiful for me'. For he must not call it beautiful if it merely pleases him" (Kant 1951). In paragraph 5, Kant had earlier stated that "Taste is the faculty of judging of an object or a method of representing it by an entirely disinterested satisfaction or dissatisfaction. The object of such satisfaction is called beautiful." Kant replaces God as the highest judge of taste, but at the same time introduces a kind of Godly principle of the "pre-programmed" in us. As so many have pointed out, it seems strange that everyone must be in agreement that something is beautiful for it to count as a subjective aesthetic judgment . One could consider that someone found it "somewhat" ugly, but that this judgment was also aesthetic (cf. Plumpe 1993, 59f).

The feeling of beauty… and the aesthetic pleasure that accompanies it are born of a 'free' association of the imagination… this interplay is quite free in that it obeys no rule, everything nevertheless takes place *as if* it followed a certain 'logic'… In music, the art seeming the most distant from the theoretical sphere… the sound and images they bring forth in us seem to be organized… as if they wanted to say something (which is why music can so easily, without our understanding how, 'express feelings') (Ferry 1993, 91; cf. Kant 1951, §53).

If we cannot objectively consider ourselves from the outside, how can we guarantee the truth of our judgments, that of course—*from the beginning*—must be related to and "mediated" through the same environment? The basic problem that everyone, in a Kantian sense, can speak about music's beauty, without necessarily basing this value judgment in something other than a metaphysical belief, remained unsolved in Kant's work.[78]

If Kant had earlier seemed to have doubts about the word *aesthetic*, he used it now as one of his final points of departure in his third *Kritik*:

"The judgment of taste carries with it an aesthetic quality" (§8) "There can be no objective rule of taste which shall determine by means of concepts what is beautiful. For every judgment from this source is aesthetical" (§17) "The claim of an aesthetical judgment to universal validity for every subject requires, as a judgment resting on some *a priori* principle" (§30) "If art has for its immediate design the feeling of pleasure, it is called *aesthetical* art" (§44) (Kant 1951).

In his critique on the power of judgment, "*Kritik der Urteilskraft*" he created an epitome of aesthetics.[79] But music as an art form held a dubious position for Kant.[80] For something to be art at all, he thought it should *not* be a pure product of Nature, and have nothing to do with earning money in any way, and neither should it be only a form of sensory pleasure. It is thus in this light that we shall see his statement that music was perhaps more a "*Genuss*" than a "*Kultur*" (cf. Kant 1951, §51 ["enjoyment" than a "culture"]).

---

[78] I benefit here from Subotnik's excellent study from 1991.

[79] Cf. the philosopher Heinz Paetzold's summary: "He positions Aesthetics as Critique of Judgment. It is about the transcendental-critical problem of the prerequisites and validity of judgments and aesthetic judgments. In that way the critique of taste shows itself to be Aesthetics." ["Er (Kant) führt die Ästhetik als 'Kritik der Urteilskraft'. Es geht ihm darum, die transzendalkritische Fragestellung nach den Bedingungen der Möglichkeit und Gültigkeit von Urteilen auch auf ästhetische Urteilen anzuwenden. So erscheint die Ästhetik als Kritik der Geschmackurteile"] (Paetzold 1983, 426).

[80] The philosopher Kathleen Higgins points to an example in her reading of Kant that he had a very limited understanding of form aspects in music: "Again, in this discussion, we see Kant searching in vain for a musical form that he understands. Given Kant's premises, it is no wonder that he found music to be of dubious aesthetic worth. The only admissible ground for aesthetically valuing it—its formal characteristics—reveals little of interest to Kant. It took someone with more understanding of music's formal possibilities—namely—Hanslick to see Kantian formalism as a doctrine that could vindicate the status of music" (Higgins 1991, 65). For an instructive and newly published discussion on Kant and his vision of music see Herman Parret 1998.

In order to both have our cake and eat it too, that is, in order to understand and define how our collective adjustment between senses and reason functions when we pronounce judgment on what we consider to be beautiful, Kant assumes that we do this without cognitive ability, but with pure sensory expression containing no personal interest—as opposed to things that we find pleasant or good. Our judgment has further a contemplative character. That is, we see and hear without desire and experience that the object has an absence of function. That which is beautiful also contains innate formal qualities, qualities only the genius-artist who created it could bring forth, and a general value, something that above all the artist who created the object in his original genius could bring forth.[81]

According to Kant, a person who acted morally and ethically correct was a person who had an aesthetic ability to appreciate *the beautiful* and the higher value of life.[82] Kant insisted that the human intellect and our detailed conceptual apparatus played a very small role in experiencing the aesthetic. The beautiful was rather something in and of itself.

Dahlhaus (1988) points out that the theories of Kant—and others— would come to be built upon, criticized and misunderstood, likewise would nevertheless, have sweeping influence. My ethnological question is, then: For whom? I find it difficult to accept the thought of an idea-world off to the side of the observable-world, and the equally un-provable idea of an *a priori*-mechanism. It is tempting to compare this last thought with Dissanayake's idea of a pre-programmed ability "cognitive universal" and our biologically-based "making special" and "special behaviors." The conclusive difference for Dissanayake is, however, that these primary human primary qualities are formed into cultural behaviors through a cumulative process. Agreements of interpretation within a particular culture, in other words, are dependent upon a social process. Kant's solution was therefore, from this standpoint, a non-solution. At its roots, it denied what Elias, for example, contends: that every generation builds upon the previous one and knowledge is a social project. The eighteenth-century mind had a difficult time grasping this concept.[83] It was left, therefore, for the nineteenth-century

---

[81] See Kant 1951. A "musical" extract from Critique of Judgment is found in Huray and Day 1981, 216-29. Cf. also the summary in Goehr 1992, 168ff, or Subotnik 1991, 59ff. It can be added, somewhat dejectedly, that there seem to be hundreds of shelf-meters of explanations of Kant's gigantic system building, as well as works that discuss what Kant "actually" meant.

[82] Concerning the coincidence between a person's aesthetic interest and (good) morals see §42 (Kant 1951, 157ff).

[83] Elias writes that Kant's thought on an *a priori*-mechanism as a guarantee always leaves room for doubt, which means that the starting point becomes individualistic. Elias writes concerning Kant's and others' solipsism (that everything comes from one's own ego) and about Kant's idea world: "A long procession of books written on these lines, a tragicomic masquerade of wasted lives litters mankind's trail. If the world 'an sich' is unknowable, one wonders why their authors bother, or rather emphatically state their case. Resigned silence might be more appropriate" (cited from Mennell 1989, 190 – cf. also 1989, 15). Elias' view of Kant's *a priori*-concept is discussed

person to further develop a philosophical solution to the aesthetic problem. And two key questions remain: Does an individual's will ever become reconciled with life's transience, or does the solution lie in rising above this problem and defining for oneself what was Art?

In the Work 'Itself'

Now with Goehr's help we will further illuminate an innovative thought. she makes a comparison between music and art, and points out that paintings in the nineteenth century were taken out of their original context and hung next to one another in a museum. Because they were lifted out of their previous context, paintings were seen, therefore, with new eyes, as aesthetic objects that should be contemplated for their own sake. From a sociological point of view, we see how art's function has also changed. When the use of the object shifts, the function is also changed, as well as how it is regarded. When composers began to assign opus numbers to their musical works—and think differently about them—it meant they were, in fact, creating musical paintings—symphonies, for example, that should be experienced as unique works and performed in particular concert locations built specifically for that purpose.[84]

Everything collaborates to create a situation where one no longer talked only about compositions, but rather about the new music as *works* (Goehr 1992, 175, 202). Some *compositions* that were seen to have especially great value, were seen as *Works*, as we have seen, from the nineteenth century and have come to be regarded as independent "subjects."[85] Through "uninterrupted" repetition, these "famous masterpieces" came to be experienced in a *Work* history as living agents

---

thoroughly in Theory, Culture and Society, Vol 12, 1995, 42-145. Niklas Luhmann's (see below) special systems-thinking sees the same problem from another angle: "The Kantian solution is based on a petitio principii. We recognize the similarity of our own minds to other minds and then proceed from there. But how can a mind arrive at the idea that an 'interior' exists within the others that is similar to ones own 'interior', and that this 'interior' is different from other systems?... Finally, how is it that this has been going on for thousands of years with a stupendous regularity in all 'normal' people?" Luhmann concludes his article logically with a grimace toward both Kant and Descartes: "I don't know if I mean what I say. And if I knew, I would have to keep it to myself" (Luhmann 1994, 387).

[84]Goehr (1992) discusses a number of different factors that we have touched upon to different degrees. For instance, composers became important as personalities, one began to rehearse music pieces before they were performed, and one repeated them on different occasions, which meant that a focus on compositions in themselves, not experienced before, increased among contemporary musically-interested people.

[85]Goehr starts from the point that all of the factors that she discusses lead us to judge the use of the term Works for compositions before about 1800 as irrelevant (Goehr 1992, 8). Let us assume that there are twenty factors that together make the concept of a Work clear to a community. Obviously there exists a long transition stage before this concept of the Work is encoded, during which a composer like J. S. Bach, for example, writes some music that already fulfills many of these factors: the Brandenburg concertos for example.

in of a higher artistic world. The works became both the substance and the goal of Lady Music's advance during the Romantic Era.

If, however, we add to this description the results found by German musicologist Ulrich Tadday in his survey of how the new forms of music are described in the popular German cultural journals (Tadday 1993), a somewhat different understanding emerges. Not all instrumental pieces, of course, became *Works*.

Tadday shows that music's factual social function came into conflict with the experience within the idealistic autonomous aesthetic that art and life were different spheres (See Tadday 1993, 5; concerning autonomy see below p. 113 and 170). By deciphering the contents of some of the most influential of these periodicals, Tadday comes to the conclusion that there was a great need for cultural information that gave readers a broad overview even of music. The musical reviews and general information, however, were of course of a different type in the leading music trade papers such as *Allgemeine Musikalische Zeitung* (1798-1848) and the Neue Zeitschrift für Musik (not founded until 1834), in contrast to general weekly magazines and periodicals whose goal was to highlight music's pleasurable social function, while at the same time mediating a measure of bourgeois education.[86]

Tadday does not find any logic in Dahlhaus's assertion that people around the turn of the nineteenth century saw the absolute instrumental music as a part of the Enlightenment project's folk education.[87] Why would one have thought that music—which meant nothing in and of itself, or at the most, a kind of Romantic indefiniteness—would be appropriate as a knowledge-building object?[88] Tadday thinks, therefore, that this discourse, which one learned about through reading these periodicals, can be seen as the basis for a self-generating and cohesively broad bourgeois music culture. It was concerned less about music as Works, but rather more about who played where, what were the latest operas, and how well had the singers sung (Tadday 1993, 10f, 65ff and 98ff).

As Tadday formulates it, it was important within family circles and salons "*sich unterhalten zu können,*" basically, to be able to take part in conversations in this case about contemporary music. This also gradually increased the expected level of general knowledge about music. During this period a marked difference between the length and complexity of different instrumental pieces emerged. You

---

[86]Tadday divides his education concept in three parts: "1. Identifying, 2. Distinctive and 3. Compensatory" (Tadday 1993, 12). Tadday adduces that about 5% of the city populations can be identified as an educated bourgeoisie.

[87]Concerning absolute music see below p. 158.

[88]Cf. Tadday's critical view of Dahlhaus's assertion that instrumental music's function is the highest absolute music. Tadday writes in conclusion: "The educational function, that Dahlhaus ascribes to absolute music, emerges in its deepest meaning as dysfunctional" (Tadday 1993, 23).

needed to know more to even talk about the most complicated works. It was clear for the contemporary culture that within the symphonic tradition, there was a marked difference between even a late Haydn symphony and Beethoven's Third Symphony. (cf. Ch. 3, footnote 118). The differences between a short piece for piano–an entertaining German waltz of Schubert for example–and Beethoven's Ninth Symphony was even greater. Even before the turn of the nineteenth century, we have already seen that there was a proportional change between different kinds of books. There was a greater demand for entertainment literature. Literarily educated writers could establish that the range of entertainment literature quickly become much greater than the access to the literature that they considered the people should be reading (Tadday 1993, 60f). A similar change occurred within musical life. I have, therefore, replaced the word *literature* with *music* in the following quotation without changing the content of truth therein:

> Here also the Enlightenment's optimistic belief in the future quickly changed over to its opposite: the false hope that a massive, society-wide enlightenment through the exposure to [music] would become disillusioned by the market's own dynamics, a market that was steered by layers of profit and loss, by quantity not quality (Tadday 1993, 27).[89]

Tadday 1993, 210 offers the following comparative study of the contents of the general culture weekly periodicals and the *Allgemeine Musikalische Zeitung* in the year 1810:

	Weekly periodicals	AMZ
Opera	26%	24%
Concerts	17	25
Virtuosi, artists, composers	18	14
music publications	23	23
Music supplements	4	2

[89] ["Doch schlägt auch hier der Fortschrittsoptmismus der Aufklärung sehr bald in sein Gegenteil um, die trügerische Hoffnung auf eine massenhafte, volksweite Aufklärung über Bücherwissen [Music] wirt enttäuscht durch die Eigendynamik eines Marktes, der den Gesetzen von Gewinn und Verlust, von Quantität und nicht Qualität gehorcht."]

Instruments	7	3
Musical life	1	4
Music Institutions and organizations	3	2
Music aesthetics	0	1
Music theory, acoustics	0	2
Lied	1%	0%

Tadday also created a thematic index showing that 80% of the weekly periodicals contained "news/announcements/performances" and only 6% "reviews/articles," while the corresponding numbers for the *AMZ* are 60% and 17% respectively (Tadday 1993, 214). The contents of the two different types of periodicals, already mirror, therefore, the intimated division of music culture. As we see, the topic "music aesthetics," the contents that explicitly took up the question of the aesthetic, garnered 0% and 1%, respectively. The fact that some works developed the status of *Works* meant, as we have said, that other pieces were relegated to a lesser status. Or as Terry Eagleton put it, a need arose to differentiate the sheep from the goats. This legitimizing process had—at the beginning of the nineteenth century—somewhat different conditions than earlier. The ruling class—kings/queens, nobility, and the church—clearly continued to exercise an important control over the formation of taste far and wide, but other important driving mechanisms and power factors within the developing bourgeois society gradually came to represent a strong competition with the earlier groups' influence, and became all the more important. Because artists, at the same time, became less dependent on the nobility and the church, the modest market mechanisms that we noted during the eighteenth century grew in strength and formed a large framework within which the production of art came to occur. In Eagleton's words, it was an historical irony that the birth of the aesthetic as an intellectual discourse, coincided with degradation and sorrow caused by the beginning of the production of manufactured goods introduced within the cultural sphere. He continues (from a reading of how it *could have been* in the best of both worlds):

> The peculiarity of the aesthetic is in part a spiritual compensation for this degradation: it is just when the artist is becoming debased to a petty commodity producer that he or she will lay claim to transcendent genius. But there is another

reason for the foregrounding of the artifact which aesthetics achieves. What art is now able to offer, in that ideological reading of it known as the aesthetic, is a paradigm of more general social significance—an image of self-referentiality which in an audacious move seizes upon the very functionlessness of artistic practice and transforms it to a vision of the highest good (Eagleton 1990, 65).

If this definition focuses on the ideological function of aesthetics, Eagleton suggests that its individual basis lies, as Kant claimed, in the form of inter-subjectivity. The fact, however, that our experiences are shared by others is not enough in and of itself. We must add something in order to maintain this solidarity: "something which, while not strictly knowledge is nonetheless very like it… the aesthetic" (Eagleton 1990, 75). This shared link within the *bourgeoisie*, rested more likely in the unpronounceable, emotional, and intuitive level rather than in the cognitive:

And this is certainly one major reason why the aesthetic has figured so centrally in bourgeois thought. For the alarming truth is that in a social order marked by class division and market competition, it may finally be here, and only here, that human beings belong together (Eagleton 1990, 75).

Eagleton seems to understand the aesthetic as a compensation for something that was *expected to happen*. Couched in this definition of the aesthetic, however, lies the old opposition between an individual's freedom and a society's need to deprive individuals of that very freedom.[90] From the perspective applied here, the value of Eagleton's materialist explanatory model seems both enriching and limiting. The model assumes that something will occur based on the existing defined conditions and goals in a particular social situation. Formulated another way: peoples' thoughts and actions should produce expected results. Did they really have *control* over every interacting social factor present?

I would rather suggest that the process is blind, and that the causes and relationships between material things and abstract thoughts that exist at a certain moment, result in changes that no contemporary theoretical framework could completely explain. What is tested here, then, is an Elias variation of Ludwig Wittgenstein's advice: "All explanations must be removed, and only descriptions take their place" (Wittgenstein 1992, §109). This can be interpreted as follows:

---

[90] Eagleton returns many times in his discussion to formulations that contain the same point, for example: "The ultimate binding force of the bourgeois social order, in contrast to the coercive apparatus of absolutism, will be habits, pieties, sentiments and affection. And this is equivalent to saying that power in such an order has become aestheticized" (Eagleton 1990, 20), as well as: "The aesthetic is thus the wane hope, in an increasingly rationalized, demythologized environment, that ultimate purpose and meaning may not be entirely lost" (Eagleton 1990, 88). These thoughts can be found in the works of many writers with a fundamentally materialist view. The sociologist David Lloyd suggests in a survey article that it was in Germany "that aesthetics first came to represent a forestalled politics… the emergence of the aesthetic…can be succinctly formulated in a German rendering of the aphorism 'Aesthetics represents politics'" (Lloyd 1990, 120f).

different explanations and approaches must continuously be sought and compared with one another so that the fragmentary vision that we create of the past can be described. A healthy skepticism of the "Great Stories" does not keep us from using them and testing their descriptive value.

Other Social Models: Habermas and Luhmann

In the previous section, we focused mainly on how instrumental music's development led to new understandings about what the aesthetic could have meant for the limited number of people who actively participated in the social and cultural changes that occurred from the middle of the eighteenth century. Instrumental music compositions appeared as works that contained an inner and inaccessible meaning that could be interpreted. Moreover, works that had a metaphysical potential were seen as particular aesthetic objects. We have also touched on the rising interest in the song. And, we might add, the popularity of operettas and operas lasted far into the future.

Elias, as well as Ferry and Eagleton, depart from explanatory models that insist that social development can best be understood over time. We will next look at the different explanatory systems of two German sociologists, Jürgen Habermas and Niklas Luhmann, examining their thoughts in relation to our own time. Because this present work is neither a history of aesthetics nor of sociology, this discussion will be brief. In contrast to a third German, the sociologist and musicologist Theodor Wiesengrund Adorno who will soon cross our path, neither Habermas or Luhmann analyzed any music structure that can be compared to social conditions.

Habermas's name is well known within musicological circles. His descriptions of the way different arts during the seventeenth and eighteenth centuries were represented at public functions within the court and church (Habermas 1984) fits the picture painted by Elias of the French court society very well. Habermas adds to the musical functions Stoljar touched upon, claiming that music conforms to a market (concerts, music publishers, etc.). In this transitional process from a representative to a public (*bourgeois*) discourse, the discussion concerning judgments of taste became, as we have seen, an important point.

Habermas also looks forward in time to show how the *bourgeois* activities began by producing culture within the (*bourgeois*) public sphere, and gradually becoming more culturally consuming within its own private spheres.[91] This

---

[91] Looking ahead, we know that more and more private phenomena became public. The bourgeois groups that started orchestras and organized concerts during the nineteenth century—which can be seen as a transition from music-making in the home to larger salons, and then to concert houses—in many countries in Europe gradually received government support to operate concert activities. In Göteborg this development can be observed from the middle of the nineteenth

THE AGE OF ENLIGHTENMENT 107

process meant even a larger difference between work time and leisure time for the *bourgeois* person. Later, as structural changes continue, societies' administrative and judicial systems become more and more complex. As the division of labor continues, and market-driven mechanisms spread in a capitalist society, Habermas points out, as do many others, that the Enlightenment project did not meet expectations in changing everyone's quality of life, as the project's theoreticians originally envisioned. The structural changes that could have happened thanks to man's capacity for rational thought and his need to communicate, were not fulfilled.

Starting from the development that Habermas considers relevant for literature in the latter part of the nineteenth century, we can draw similarities to the development within music, which first began to take shape seriously at the beginning of the twentieth century. The following quotations are apt for both cultural areas:

> From the middle of the nineteenth century the institutions that had until then safeguarded the public's coherence as a reasoning community were shaken. The family lost its function as a "literary [musical] propaganda circle" (Habermas 1984, 209). The sounding board for an educated class developed for public use by reason had broken into pieces, and the public had splintered into a minority of non-public reasoning specialists and the broad mass of public receptive consumers (Habermas 1984, 225).

While Habermas finds that from the eighteenth century a conflict developed within the bourgeois culture, Luhmann suggests that there was a basic failure of society to develop a conception apparatus with which one could analyze arising situations.[92] But both writers are in agreement that an increasingly obvious divide has developed between professional art practitioners and their public. Luhmann terms it a catastrophic inequality.[93]

As Neitzert pointed out (following Luhmann) we can see that a number of asymmetrical relationships arose, that became more easy to see:

> Author–Public, Author–Interpreter, Critic–Public, Art Producer–Art Consumer, Art Producer–Art Handler, Virtuoso–Dilettante, Director–Orchestral Musician, Concert Music–House Music, Serious Music–Entertaining Music (Neitzert 1990, 166).

Luhmann further shows that an idealized communication between equally valued citizens is shredded by an increasingly self-contained *system*.[94] The

---

century when orchestra companies began, worked several years and were abandoned, until the permanent orchestra that was started in 1905 received support from the local government in 1908, a support that later would increase in scope (see Carlsson 1996, and Edström 1996).

[92] Cf. Neitzert 1990, 17.

[93] On the debate between Habermas and Luhmann concerning the different causes of the continued development during modernism see Outhwaite 1994.

[94] One might imagine that Luhmann would name his contemporary colleague Pierre Bourdieus's

first systems he names are the market economy and the judicial system, systems that both become instruments of power that made it possible to set aside the Enlightenment project's original goals: enlightenment, equality, and freedom. At the same time, Luhmann emphasizes that while people connected the good with *the beautiful*, they also underestimated the strange dynamics of the developing functional systems. Neitzert, who is the first musicologist I have found to have taken up Luhmann's thoughts, gives the following summary:

> One thought that a beautiful soul that was educated through contact with art, would in a natural way, also develop a good world. Logically one placed a greater value on an emotional communication coming from a shared life style much higher than an interactive mediation of functionally related information coordinated through a shared process. The marriage between the Good and the Beautiful did not survive the industrial revolution's social dynamizing (Neitzert 1990, 132).

Luhmann thinks that the modern world is characterized by many self-contained systems, of which art (and we can extend that to art music) is one. Here it is no longer about *the Beautiful* or dichotomies like true/false, or right/wrong, because these are members of completely different systems: science and the law, respectively. As explained by Harro Müller:

> In modernity, works of art are no longer regulated by rhetorics, or various conceptions of mimesis. Instead, works of art are designed to produce individuality effects and participate in a semantic evolution that is correlated to the transformation from a stratified to a functionally differentiated society. The system of arts plays a constant game of self-reference and external reference. External reference refers to various partial systems whose offerings serve as media which art may then work through for its own gain. The art system may also refer to itself (Müller 1994, 48ff).

Everything that functions within the system remains within the system. The wider world happens in a parallel place. But, Luhmann writes: "the wider world cannot contribute to the reproduction of the system with some form of operation" (Luhmann 1992, 14).[95] What began at the end of the eighteenth century, thanks to society's increasing differentiation, was that art's earlier social functions converted themselves into a self-contained systemic world: "The meaning of 'input' and 'output' in relation to parts of the social system gradually decreases" (Luhmann 1986, 621). It becomes irrelevant, therefore, to see art as a

---

field definition in this context. As far as I could see, none of these researchers cite one another, a good illustration of Bourdieus's idea of *meconnaissance*. One way to reduce the struggle over limited resources within the field can be to pretend that one is not in the same field.

[95]Luhmann tries to solve the problem of how different systems relate to their surroundings with the help of "self reference" and "foreign reference" as tools of thought (Luhmann 1992, 17). The Danish philosopher Ole Thyssen tries to define this deeply-rooted problem in chapter II of *Autopoiesis*, 1992, 21-56.

consequence of some external influence, which is why art comes to relate itself to itself. Contemporaneously with the art-system, a number of other social systems developed. The problem of how these systems—existing at the same time but parallel to one another—can in reality both exist in relationship to one another and at the same time seem to be closed, can be solved according to Luhmann through the concept of "interpenetration." The philosopher Ole Thyssen gives the following clarification:

> Two systems interpenetrate, when the one system makes it possible for the other, by making its complexity available without the other system needing to empty out the first system's complexity (Luhmann 1992, 26).

In contrast to Adorno (see below) Luhmann does not see art's independence as something *against* society, but rather *within* society. Art, including art music, therefore, shares the fate of modern society. The independent autonomous position that art has attained is now shared with the social system.[96] That matters stand this way can be clearly seen, according to Luhmann, in the vain traditional attempts to find criteria for art's beauty, art's educational possibilities, as well as symbolic qualities.

For Luhmann, unlike Adorno, art's function departs from its ability to *confront reality with another version of the same reality*. Art seems to find more inspiration in itself the farther forward in time one comes. "Artwork" as "l'art pour l'art"[97] is a strange concept for Luhmann, so far as it is *just that* that artwork *is* from the beginning within the art system. Art concerns affects experiences *within* a communication system (art as system).[98] In connection with Luhmann's statement that during the eighteenth century one could not solve the problem of what was good taste, he adds that aesthetics had not yet been developed into a theory of reflection upon the art system (Luhmann 1986, 638). One can therefore

---

[96]Luhmann sees this as a liberating process that is carried out thanks to the changes in society, and adds: "In a similar way, the recent attainment of the autonomy of art is not something that negates the dependence of society, not something that hopelessly positions Art to the side. Quite the opposite: Art shares the fate of modern society precisely because of its search to find its way in an autonomous system." ["Entsprechend ist die in der Neuzeit erreichte Autonomie der Kunst nicht etwas, was der Abhängigkeit von Gesellschaft widerstreitet; nicht, was die Kunst in ein hoffnungsloses Abseits treibt. Im Gegenteil: die Kunst teilt das Schicksal der modernen Gesellschaft gerade dadurch, dass sie als autonom gewordenes System zurechtzukommen sucht"] (Luhmann 1986, 623).

[97]This description from the middle of the nineteenth century can thus be compared with Moritz's comment that "the musical work exists for itself" (see above).

[98]With the help of his systems theory, Luhmann then goes through the history of art. It would be going too far to try to make a summary here of his equally fascinating and slightly astonishing conclusions. Those interested are invited to read his great work from 1995, *Die Kunst der Gesellschaft*. Nicholas Cook (1990) presents a parallel thought: that musicological methods exist in their own academic tradition, or, if one will, in their own system, and should not be blended together with science. Cf. also note 97.

assume that this gradually became the case. I find no other answer in Luhmann's texts. Aesthetics, a word Luhmann sets off with quotation marks, is a theory of reflection that developed within the auto-poetic system of art (meaning that the artwork produces the elements of which it is made within a self-referential system). To make doubly sure, in his summary Luhmann still places the concept within quotation marks: "Aesthetics."

The meta-level where Luhmann's texts often find themselves makes it difficult to bring them nearer our lives. He does not consider assigning any meaning to the contents of art music, nor does he worry over what music meant for people As Ulrich Tadday expressed it, Luhmann's rhetorical aesthetic system reduces art and music to its technical social dimension, within which there exists no depth of meaning, and within which the meaning of art is not applicable.[99] A terrifying conclusion.

From Theory to Social Empiricism

At the same time as Habermas describes how a structural transformation reshapes presuppositions for art's relationship and position in different social classes, he also points out how the human world is colonized by more and more refined economic, judicial, administrative, and mass media systems—something that threatens to undermine the everyday human world. In the wake of this process, "eternal" valuations that constituted a social bond, are fragmenting. Luhmann on the other hand, describes reality as consisting of a number of non-overlapping systems of which the art system is but one. Like all systems, it is only one of a number of ways to experience the present reality.

Since the 1930s, Adorno's theories have fascinated and bewildered generations of musicologists. In contrast to the researchers addressed above, Adorno is altogether too well-known within musicology to require further

---

[99]Tadday writes: "Luhmann's theoretical aesthetic system reduces Art and Music to a social-technological dimension, that in itself has no depth of meaning and doesn't confer deeper meaning to art." ["Luhmanns systemtheoretische Ästhetik reduziert Kunst und Musik auf eine sozialtechnische Dimension, der es selber an Bedeutungstiefe fehlt und die tiefere Bedeutungen von Kunst nicht zuläst"] (Tadday 1997, 30). Furthermore he says that substantial questions about music's semantic meaning and music's ideal value do not have any relevance for the judgment of an art work. Tadday further cites Luhmann's conclusion: "The system of art is a special system for societal communication with its own references (Self- and Other-references) whose forms denote that they only exist in the medium of art." ["Das Kunstsystem ist ein Sondersystem gesellschaftlicher Kommunikation mit je eigenen Selbst- und Fremdreferenten, welche Formen bezeichnen, die es nur in einem kunsteigenen Medium gibt"] (Tadday 1997, 33) — and questions, in summing up, what joy one has in hearing a pianist play if what happens only concerns form communication and answers: "Not a thing. Those who experience music in that way can only feel that it is an example of the modern, functionally diversified society, but that's all." ["Nichts. Wer Musik so erlebt, kann in ihr ein Paradigma der modernen, funktional ausdifferenzierten Gesellschaft wahrnehmen— mehr aber nicht"] (Tadday 1997, 33).

introduction.[100] He saw the modern world's development systems, including the Soviet and Western market economies, in a negative and gloomy light. People, he claimed, had lost their promised freedom through the fragmentation of our rational sense by the administrative (Soviet) and market economic (Western) systems and a distortion of the promise of the Enlightenment. While there was an idealistic vision of art-making in an early phase of the Enlightenment, the negative influence of the market imperceptibly entered the creative process and poisoned it.[101]

It seems as if Reason was already experiencing regret at the beginning of the humanist experiment and, in a spirit of dialecticism, gave up on itself in disappointment over humanity's handling of the experiment.[102] The unanswered question remains: How could music be spread if it weren't packaged in written form or presented within the market-dominated system?

Like Neitzert, Adorno has made thorough studies of the relationship between society and music culture. From a music technology perspective, however, a sense of uncertainty always arises when reading Adorno's analyses, particularly when he expresses himself on aesthetic questions, music's inner meaning, and the like. Adorno departs from the idea that art's relationship to society is one to one. Music as an artifact is a part of the same working process in society that produces other objects:

---

[100] See also Edström 1997, where I discuss Adorno's importance for the academic tradition of my own institution.

[101] Andreas Huyssen discusses Adorno's analysis of Wagner's work where this creeping poisonous field of problems is dealt with: "As the commodity form begins to invade all aspects of modern life, all aesthetic appearance is in danger of being transformed into phantasmagoria, into 'the illusion of the absolute reality of the unreal'"(Huyssen 1986, 39). Wagner succeeded, according to this opinion, in giving the opposition to developing industrialism a form that the bewitched public saw as an appealing German general artwork. Adorno then expands this thought to include the function that twentieth-century mass media culture is thought to have had, i.e., his perception that the culture industry maintained the social order. Cf. the sociologist Alan Swingewood (1998, 45f). The culture industry manipulated people from above, according to Dodd in his Adorno analysis: "The most basic function of the culture industry is stupification. It disables us psychologically and emotionally. It acts as psychoanalysis in reverse" (Dodd 1999, 71).

[102] Adorno's theoretical construction is both extensive and presented in an unusually complicated manner. The interpretation industry it has engendered is consequently large and difficult to summarize. Adorno departs from the opposing pair of subject—object, but interprets this negatively, i.e., that some final synthesis between them cannot be reached. Dodd explains: "Negative dialectics... rests on a distinction between a concept, that is, an idea, and an object, that is, the thing to which it refers... In modern society the relationship between concepts and objects is not identical... the point of negative dialectics, or what Adorno calls non-identity thinking, is partly to exploit this gap and thereby to understand something more of what objects in the world might potentially become"(Dodd 1999, 74). Adorno develops a long list of dialectical relationships that add up to a theory that is difficult to use. For an unusually readable presentation of Adorno's aesthetics, see Dennis 1998.

The productive power of the aesthetic is the same as that of useful work and contains within it the same Theology: that which is referred to as the aesthetic production-relationship, all that was contained in the power of production is found encapsulated there, and how it manifests itself, is the sediment and impressions of social interaction (Adorno 1970, 16f).

But how this process of interaction or mediation between music and society actually worked, Adorno, never satisfactorily succeeded in explaining (cf. Paddison 1993, Chapter 3).

As the Enlightenment Era came to an end, Adorno argues, art music relied on tones, as in Schönberg's twelve-tone world, to portray this course of events. Unlike the popular music from the nineteenth century, art music distanced itself from the marketplace. As a considerable number of researchers have criticized, however, Adorno never actually convincingly showed this course of events in an analysis of the relationships between society/person ⇔ music/structure. The reader is expected to depart from the idea that music analyses exist and are without reproach as well as that Adorno implicitly supports them. This seems strange, given his practical and theoretical knowledge of western music history. The leading interpreter of Adorno's music aesthetic, the philosopher Max Paddison, writes:

> It has to be admitted that there is a very real problem with Adorno's approach, because he often gives the impression that there is a smooth continuum between technical analysis, sociological critique and philosophical-historical interpretation, in spite of the calculatedly fragmented form in which he presents his ideas (Paddison 1993, 273).[103]

Adorno was a child of his time, as are we all, and in his case this meant that his conceptual apparatus seems to have been based more on a *bourgeois* life experience than a working class one.[104] Neitzert, departing from his reading of

---

[103] Dahlhaus found that Adorno's music analysis regularly rests on an all too highly abstract plane: "In his *Philosophie der neuen Musik* he illustrated his thesis of the historical movement of musical material by using *abstract* categories such as 'chords,' 'dissonance' and 'counterpoint' rather than analyses of works" (Dahlhaus 1983, 29 [my italics]).

[104] I commented on this in an earlier article: "Nowadays it is easier to understand his world of ideas...We now have a better understanding of how, as a gifted intellectual child of his time, he came to be the bearer of a German cultural tradition. Basically, these values had become second nature to him through the socialization process, but in his scientific work in the Frankfurt School he was, of course, constantly forced to reassess them. Put simply, the aims of the Frankfurt School were to understand and to establish a dialogue with the German working class. With such a background it is easy today to understand why he so obstinately chose such a thorny path. Like a stubborn dialectician, he launched an assault on everyone and everything in a bitter—not to say negative—aesthetic duel. Richard Wolin expresses this well: 'A dialectician's dialectician, he plays the apparent antagonism between culture and barbarism for all its worth. He tries to stake out a position between the aesthete or *Kulturmensch*, who invokes cultural privilege as a sign of superiority, and the modern-day philistine, who, upon hearing the word "culture," immediately

THE AGE OF ENLIGHTENMENT

Habermas, has pointed out that Adorno was spellbound by Hegelian thought. Even though Adorno will critically analyze the development of culture and later the cultural industry, he does this, according to Neitzert, from the perspective of the late *bourgeois* idea of an autonomous art, without reflecting enough over the origins of the concept (Neitzert 1990, 15).[105]

The musicologist Rose Rosengard Subotnik, one of the leading interpreters of Adorno's work in North American musicology, using Adorno's diagnosis of stylistic features in Beethoven, has tried to see what would be produced by a dialogue with musical structure in the spirit of Adorno. Subotnik's starting point is that a balance existed between the inner musical structure and society's judgments in the earlier Viennese Classic music. Haydn and Mozart had written in a "style that had produced the first great paradigms of a wholly autonomous music" (Subotnik 1991, 174). This balance was undermined by and through Beethoven because his compositions from his later period were more and more critical of society.

It was Beethoven's followers, writes Subotnik, that first experienced the complete loss of musical autonomy. That which happened in Beethoven's so-called second period, and above all through his late works, meant for Adorno:

[t]he irreversible bypassing of individual freedom as a possibility in concrete historical reality... the severing of subjective freedom... Implicit... is the eventual dissolution of all the values that made bourgeois humanism the hope of a human civilization (Subotnik 1991, 17).

Subotnik writes that the relationship between structure in Beethoven's music and culture surfaces through a complex form of mediation processes "which Adorno does not pretend to understand or elucidate adequately" (Subotnik 1991, 19). An implicit point of departure in whose thoughts is likewise, as has just been mentioned, that there can have been a balance between the creative individual's music and the receptive public: "A coincidence between purely musical meanings intended by the individual composer and those understood by society at large" (Subotnik 1991, 180). The relationship between art and society during Beethoven's middle period was, according to Adorno, especially favorable for a dialectical synthesis. As Subotnik formulates it:

---

reaches either for his revolver (reputedly, Göring) or checkbook (Hollywood). Both extremes must be foresworn'" (Edström 1997, 20).

[105] Cf. also with Neitzert's formulation: "Even if Adorno tries to rid aesthetic theory of the ideological individuality of the bourgeoisie art interpreters, to him the Work still remains (cont.) autonomous, that is a concept that is significantly removed from social life." ["Zwar unternimmt er [Adorno] es, die ästhetische Theorie vom ideologischen Individualismus der bürgerlichen Kunstexegeten zu befreien, doch bleibt auch ihm das Werk als solches ein autonomes, d.h. vom gesellschaftlichen Leben signifikant geschiedenes Gebilde"] (1989, 15).

Historical conditions provided Beethoven with a basis for thinking of musical structure as a totality that could accommodate a concept (e.g., subject, individual, or freedom) and its opposite (object, society, or form) in a resolution that preserved the essence of each (Subotnik 1991, 20).

That which is presented especially as new in the structure of the sonata movements during the middle period is the material that appears in the development and recapitulation sections. Adorno thought that there could have been a reconciliation between the opposing cultural forces (individual/freedom–society/coercion) that can be heard in this music. Beethoven's artistic interests and the artistic interests of the society coincided.[106] At the same time it is said that Beethoven began to understand that individual freedom would soon no longer be possible:

> In the second-period style... authentic music could maintain an affirmative character and still criticize society. Now [in the third period] to be authentic, music must become explicitly negative... to replace synthesis... with the impossibility of synthesis (Subotnik 1991, 25).

This means also that the more music became a part of reality, the more autonomous the music became.[107] The tragedy, according to Adorno, was that music would sooner or later become sounding ideology because of its social impotence (Subotnik 1991, 31).[108] Eagleton formulates this in a similar way in his own exposition on Adorno:

> Modernism is art forced into mute self-contradiction; and the source of this internal impasse lies in art's contradictory material status within bourgeois society. Culture is deeply locked into the structure of commodity production; but one effect of this is to release it into a certain ideological autonomy, hence allowing it to speak against the very social order with which it is guiltily complicit. It is this complicity which spurs art into protest, but which also strikes that protest agonized and ineffectual, formal gesture rather than irate polemic (Eagleton 1990, 348f).

---

[106] With Subotnik it should also be said that Adorno never explicitly states that a dialectical synthesis was reached in society during Beethoven's life, but rather "the possibility of a synthesis was a reality at this time, at least enough of a reality to suggest its own conceptual categories of form to the artist's imagination" (Subotnik 1991, 21). The problem for a reader with an author "type" like Adorno is that his labyrinthine use of language with its constantly creeping reversals, produces, in the end, intellectual exhaustion. The objections continuously hinted at, disappear before your eyes when you try to synthesize the threads of his argument in order to understand what Adorno actually wanted to say (Luhmann's and Habermas' writing style is, in the end somewhat easier to absorb).

[107] Note that for Moritz and the romantic interpreters that came afterwards, instrumental music's true worth lay beyond society's reality.

[108] Adorno and Subotnik's outlook is supported by Robert Witkin's reading of Adorno (1998, 30ff). As they discussed earlier, he sees cause-effect in the sonata movement's (primarily the *allegro* movement's) development.

From my perspective, the prerequisites for an interpretation of the kind that Adorno and Subotnik make, lack an ethno-sociological empiricism. Dialectical explanations can hardly be an eternal and all-encompassing descriptive system for the intricate network of relationships that affect society's blind process of development. The fundamental concept of thesis—antithesis—synthesis is partly too easy, and as Adorno paints it, and in Adorno's virtuosic use of language, too expanded until it fills a seemingly endless dialectical landscape for which the reader is equipped with no readable map.[109] It is as if Adorno is trying to avoid the simple model of thesis—antithesis—synthesis by juggling several oppositions in the air, at the same time. He throws differing levels of dialectical clarity at the reader, which in the end react negatively to one another. Although the autonomy of art music presents a distorted picture, it does, at least, create a certain space for an independent art. The *bourgeois* listeners rarely understood this when they were exposed to the capitalist system's negative influences, but at the same time they carry the dream of freedom—equality—fraternity (Williams, 2001).[110]

Why did Beethoven's second period music *retreat* from society? Is there an explanatory value in the idea that the only way out that Beethoven's *music* had during *its* second period—presupposing that *it* still *wants to be* authentic and maintain its autonomy—was to *retreat* from society (note my subjectivizing italics). And how did the music itself figure all of this out? The problem is only exacerbated by the fact that music has substantially fewer referential possibilities than, for example, literature, or visual art. It is as difficult to accept that music itself could take the decision to keep its autonomy as it would be to accept that Beethoven's *unconsciousness* made this self-reliant decision and took on responsibility for the compositional process.

Adorno felt that nineteenth century composers became more and more dependent upon market mechanisms in society, and thus wrote music that could not help become an independent agent critical of the society within which it was created. Two negative positions meet here within this maneuvering space. One, an autonomous music that apparently always takes a negative position in relationship to the surrounding society, and another, a left-leaning ideological

---

[109]Cf. Eagleton: "Dialectical thinking seeks to grasp whatever is heterogeneous to thought as a moment of thought itself, 'reproduces in thought itself as its immanent contradiction'. But since one risks eradication that heterogeneity in the very act of thinking upon it, this enterprise is always to the brink of blowing itself up. Adorno has a kind of running solution to this dilemma, and that is style... Every sentence of his texts is thus forced to work overtime; each phrase must become a little masterpiece of miracle of dialectics" (Eagleton 1990, 341ff).

[110]Cf. also Williams' formulation: "One of Adorno's main themes is that all aspects of our lives are increasingly dominated by... instrumental reason ... The consequence is that subjects become alienated of the human goals... In the light of such tendencies, he values music's claim to autonomy because the lack of social purpose it gains is not immediately compatible with instrumental aims. And the distance, however illusory it may be, enables music to pursue social codes in directions blocked by the prevailing imperative" (Williams 2001, 11f).

critical tradition with a negative attitude to society. According to the sociologist Nigel Dodd, Adorno is incapable of defining autonomous music in anything but extremely relative terms:

> We are left with no clear sense of the aesthetic criteria which must be met for a work of art to be autonomous. It seems that to a large extent we must rely on our own judgement ... Adorno insists that autonomous art must combine elements of mimesis, constructiveness, sensuality and rationalism. He writes that the autonomous work of art will outlive the moment of its reception... One might as well add that the work of art should be accompanied by a critical philosophy in order to be appreciated to its fullest extent (Dodd 1999, 80).

Would it not be more fruitful—the question is rhetorical—to begin with the assumption that the collected factors in a mutual relationship affect the development of music, and lead to changes? And do these changes necessarily need to be dialectical in a Hegelian sense? Does the idea of the juxtaposition between the freedom of the individual and the coercion of the collective always form a necessary background factor? In other words, an antagonism that erases everything and is, therefore, inescapable? Or is this antagonism a straightjacket that should never have been manufactured, because the point of departure itself should be the group or the group-individual rather than the *individual subject*? The people who obstinately repeat this thesis about the *individual* person, seem to have always been the individuals who stuck out conspicuously from their groups. Likewise, they were and are like everything else, a "cumulative cultural project." The individual has never been solitary, nor had total freedom.[111]

I prefer, therefore to look at the social processes on the basis of Elias's figuration model:

(a) starting from the (group)individuals, who are in a complex, branching and dependent relationship with one another, the more complex and branching the society, the longer and more complex become these chains of dependency;

(b) that these figurations will always change at different speeds, but that these changes will have unplanned patterns;

(c) that the cumulative accretion of knowledge that occurs within these figurations is a key to the understanding of their process of development.[112]

---

[111] Robinson was not abandoned on his island at age one to grow up later completely alone and in full freedom. Had this been the case, he probably wouldn't even have survived four workdays, let us say, to a Friday.

[112] Elias himself gives an interesting metaphor, "social dance," in order to explain his ideas about figurations: "The picture of moving figurations of interdependent people on a dance floor makes it easier to imagine states, cities, families or capitalist, communist and feudal systems as figurations... no one will imagine a dance as a formation apart from the individuals, or as a complete abstraction" (Elias 1989, 71). One can dance with different partners, one can relate to others on the dance floor, partners chane, dance styles chane over time as do people.

THE AGE OF ENLIGHTENMENT

We also cannot forget that a majority of farmers, simple laborers and a slowly growing working class struggled daily with metaphors like *freedom-coercion*, mainly outside of this bourgeois world.[113] One must, in fact, ask oneself if there even *was* a sufficiently large homogenous *bourgeoisie* during the early nineteenth century to hear the music and tones that unmasked the ever more compromised promises of enlightenment visions.

Like many of the early theoreticians at the beginning of the nineteenth century, Adorno also saw, one hundred years later, an autonomous art form within instrumental music. But where those before him saw developments steering toward an independent spiritual country, Adorno saw this development as art music's logical analysis of social developments.[114] We will return to Adorno's thoughts in connection with our discussion of modernism during the twentieth century. In this context it is only left for us to illuminate his understanding of the harmonic coincidence between Beethoven's music during the so-called middle period and the contemporary bourgeois society. We shall now turn to the sociologist Tia DeNora's empirically constructed study (DeNora 1995).

Beethoven's Public

Beethoven, was raised in Bonn under an enlightened Lord and the student of the enlightenment-minded composer, Christian Gottlob Neefe. He found himself, despite his background, fairly well able to cope with a Vienna dominated by a noble class that, naturally, had little time for the Enlightenment's ideas about equality.[115] DeNora, based on the thought that there is a close relationship between "musical forms and social life," wants to understand the world Beethoven worked in:

> Culture is constitutive of the reality we perceive and take for granted. But these categories are themselves created and recreated by socially located individuals and groups (DeNora 1995, 14).

---

[113]Here a number of other "metaphors" which also engaged, assertive pairs of antonyms such as work-unemployment, food-famine, cold-warmth, life-death, but also more encouraging ones like man-woman, and son-daughter. Life for people within different layers of society was, as we know, incredibly varied during the nineteenth century.

[114]Cf. the philosopher Heino Ewers (1978, 2) who discusses the time span from Hegel to Marcuse and the thesis of art as a particular realm for itself within the *bourgeoisie*. According to Marcuse, one turned one's critical-political power inwards towards art and beauty. There are also many examples of the correlation between the belief in art and religion in Huray and Day 1981.

[115]Beethoven not only wrote music for Royal ballrooms, "an unparalleled way of getting further exposure to an aristocratic audience" (DeNora 1995, 140), but also celebratory songs to the Kaiser in 1796 that remain an irritation to Beethoven researchers (Geck and Schleuning 1989, 50).

In her attempt to understand how Beethoven's artistic status was constructed, DeNora first concentrates on how within a concert culture, people wanted things that were easily digested. Gradually, musicians began presenting longer concerts and symphonies. There is no doubt that Beethoven was a key person in this transformation. But, unlike Adorno's accounts, DeNora shows that the *bourgeoisie* did not make much of Beethoven's music. Instead, she says, it was the nobility who supported and attended concerts and who wanted more demanding content:

> This view runs counter to what Arnold Hauser (1962), Henry Raynor (1976), Theodor Adorno (1976), and a host of other scholars have said, on the basis of scant evidence, about the origins of serious music ideology, and, as such, it challenges received sociological wisdom and Beethoven mythology concerning the origin of the musical canon (DeNora 1995, 36).[116]

DeNora shows how Beethoven had the ability to put his musical powers to use in a social context. She does this from a sociological perspective of what role Haydn played for Beethoven, as well as Beethoven's connections to and commissions from the nobility. For example, Beethoven was the guest of Prince Lichnowsky for a period in 1795. His compositions were performed regularly for Lichnowsky, who also financially supported some of Beethoven's publications.

Trendsetting groups within the high nobility could, in other words, more easily maintain their leading status within musical culture by substantially supporting the dynamic Beethoven. DeNora carefully maps out from primary contemporary sources, an argument showing that Beethoven's original music was *not* a favorite among the *bourgeoisie*, but rather that it was first the nobility weighted down by privilege that paved the way for the bourgeois "genius." DeNora makes the point that there were no clear-cut cases of status or taste and many different factors cooperated to preserve the nobility's advantage as taste-makers. And it was all unplanned. Many different factors cooperated in this (unplanned) process that played into the nobility's hands, allowing them to keep their advantage as taste-makers As DeNora expresses it, Beethoven could take artistic risks that other musicians couldn't, or wouldn't, because it was not worth the trouble (DeNora 1995, 71).

DeNora also argues that the normal public as early as the 1790s experienced Beethoven's music as different.[117] Beethoven both played, improvised,

---

[116] I found a formulation in Williams of the kind that DeNora criticizes: "Much of the modernist impulse in music can be traced back to Beethoven… His middle period, in particular, offers a model of the integrated bourgeois subject that could be only an ideal in everyday life. But at the same time the specificity and sensuality of Beethoven's music also alerts the same subject to what its need for totality excludes" (Williams 2001, 125).

[117] DeNora recalls again and again the sociologist's mantra, that music's meaning for the people of that time was socially constructed. She takes the opportunity at the same time to give a dig to

and composed in a way that attracted attention; his music deviated from the general expectations of the listeners.[118]

In conclusion, DeNora shows the difficulties one meets if one is extracting abstract thoughts about the connection between music structure and society from a theoretical model. Her results seriously undermine Adorno and Subotnik's thesis about Beethoven music's *bourgeois* balance between the outer poles of freedom and coercion.

A benevolent synthesis between the different approaches might show that the nobility's actions (continuing feudal coersion) were compensated for by the *bourgeois* public's presence (newly won freedom). In fact, Beethoven's music did not come to be appreciated by a wide swathe of the *bourgeois* class until long after the composer's death.

One probable and equally valid explanation is that in Beethoven, the genius's freely created new ideas (newly-won freedom) were unified with the persevering working composer's handcraft skill (the feudal society). This thought can be found in Geck and Schleuning's 1989 work on Beethoven's *Eroica*, where they show how one writer and musician at the time, Johann Friedrich Rochlitz, defined a successful work. In the *Allgemeine Musikalische Zeitung* Rochlitz said that the aesthetically successful work balances the *art*istically irrational with the rational and thorough *handcraft* work. This was typical for the bourgeois musical understanding of the time (Geck and Schleuning 1989, 215). Great art, then, should be both correct handcraft and genius (cf. Morrow, above). *Eroica* met these standards. It was twice as long as any previous symphony, and had a larger orchestration than any earlier Beethoven symphony. Like more and more works that became a topic of conversation, it was not limited to only those who were fortunate enough to live in the largest cities. It was also published in piano versions and other arrangements,[119] as well as in published score form for those who wanted

---

current musicology operating from a sloppily under-substantiated historical sketch, that analyzes music's structure as if it were "waiting to be read": "This analytic discourse reifies the relationship between music and extra-musical phenomena in a way that bypasses exploration of how musical texts come to possess connotations and how these connotations are initially established, elaborated, and consolidated over time" (DeNora 1995, 127).

[118] DeNora warns against assuming that the audience of the day experienced a minimal stylistic difference between the late works of Mozart and Beethoven's works from the beginning of his middle period (normally set at about 1803). This opinion probably has more to do with the idea of "style" and time perspective with which we contemplate this period today. While it is a well-known fact that Beethoven's music is often met with skepticism, it is not equally well known—and today more difficult to understand—that even Mozart's music could be judged as far too advanced around 1800 (cf. for example two contemporary French writers, the music theoretician Momigny's opinion on Mozart's 40th symphony [Stockfelt 1988, 69f] and the music critic and rhetorician Geoffroy's opinion of Mozart's opera *Don Juan* [Ellis 2001, 51f]).

[119] For an illumination of how even organists during the nineteenth century could transcribe and perform appropriately long movements from well-known symphonies, etc., see Walter 2000.

to *study it*.[120] As always, it is important to add that *only a small* percentage of the population took part in this process, thus it was neither a quickly growing nor a widespread phenomenon.

New Structures

The structure of Baroque instrumental music was dependent on the way that music was used in courtly society. In looking at all the new music that was written from the later part of the eighteenth century and onwards, it's clear that during the Enlightenment there was also a close relationship between the structure of music and how it was used. But some things did fall by the wayside: the requirement that a movement should have a basic expression, that the voices should be introduced imperceptibly and braided in individually, and that there should be *one* controlled affect, for example. Instead, new musical structures arose. These new structures were suitable for performing and listening to in different contexts and they responded to different functions and needs. They grew out of the same socio-cultural process—which thus both affected the society at a macro level (the burgeoning music market, concert activities, educational institutions, etc.), and as well as on a micro level (peoples' ways of thinking and acting, etc.).

The matrix of society-music-people changes at the same time. As has been shown, the English public, for example, all appreciated and seemed to understand the Haydnesque symphony's "tendency towards trick, artifice, surprise and difficulty." On the other hand the audience couldn't always follow Beethoven in his musical aspirations.

The thoughtful listener could focus on beautiful and *natural* melodies, but also detect something more. In the sonatas and symphonies, they could recognize different themes that in a process-oriented chain of events, worked themselves out with and against one another. After some minutes, they returned in a recognizable form. Listeners could also experience different sections where the harmonic content alternated between tension and relaxation. It was worthwhile to use a rational way of listening if one wanted to follow along with the flow of the music.

As Neitzert formulates it, one understood that music was written for a private artistic enjoyment ["Kunstgenuss wird Privatsache"]. He added:

> Those who as an audience of assembled private persons (i.e. the bourgeois general public) negotiated statements about an author's products. The composer no longer arranges conventional motivic material... Music's content was therefore

---

[120] Cf. Geck and Schleuning who write that the impossibly long duration of the symphony, and its riddle-like title, together with its new stylistic traits was an audible attack on contemporary listeners that forced them to take a stand, for or against arguably the first work of instrumental music that was based on an idea (Geck and Schleuning 1989, 175).

in some sense, more important than its shape. The originality of the melody determined henceforth music's quality (Neitzert 1990, 110).[121]

Within the sonata, harmony's ability to create form, especially the tension between dominant and tonic, was used as a medium in the multi- movement process that gradually became the norm to listen to. While in the beginning of the nineteenth century one could perform some single movements from a symphony along with other works in concert, at the end of the century this concert behavior became more rare. Entire symphonies were performed.[122]

The fact that one saw every piece as a product of an individual composer also added to the idea of pieces of music as Works. The composer's ability to present a work that should be listened to, conveyed a clearer focus on the communication between producer and consumer, and at the same time the composer's personality became more and more identified with the music.

Another important emerging structural principle was the idea of a musical conversation between equal voices, as for example in Mozart's duet for violins or in Beethoven's string quartets. An analogy can be drawn between society's complicated structure and the structure of Beethoven's music. Here we can make a connection to the discussion conducted above of how the complicated relationship between society and structure of Beethoven's music can be understood (DeNora⇔Adorno). Beethoven's musical development gradually led him to write movements with unforeseen length and with a complicated musical language. Amateurs who, at the beginning of the nineteenth century performed his string quartet Opus 18, found great difficulty playing, as well as musically understanding his Opus 135 only a quarter of a century later.[123] But it was the listening public

---

[121] ["Die 'zum Publikum versammelten Privatleute' (d.h. die ‚bürgerliche Öffentlichkeit') verhandeln Äusserungen, Produkte eines Autors. Der Komponist ordnet nicht mehr länger konventionelles motivisches Material nach vorgegebenen Mustern... Der Gehalt einer Musik wird so in gewissem Sinne wichtiger als ihre Gestalt. Die Originalität einer Melodie bestimmt deren Qualität."]

[122] Symphonies also became longer and longer. Weber reminds us that the overtures and symphonies during the eighteenth century were often placed first in the program. They were music pieces that were written with the purpose "to bring the audience to attention as people settled into the hall, or as finales to long performances which listeners often left early" (Weber 1999, 348). As a watershed point, *Eroica* was played in 1807 by the Gewandhausorchester after the intermission and after that, and opera aria: "A drastic break with convention... and subsequently gave a kind of canonic status to this and a few other works that were played in this spot" (Weber 1999, 348).

[123] Looking at the quartet literature that was played during the twentieth century, one finds the same relationship. If the Sundberg quartet society in Göteborg is taken as a typical example, between 1884 and 1934 Beethoven's opus 135 was played only once, and up to 1984, only five additional times. Between 1884-1934 the six Opus 18 quarters were played 5-24 times and thereafter another 10-15 times. The Opus 59 quartets show a similar picture as the Opus 18. One can assume that even professional musicians rarely played Beethoven's later quartets (Cf. Ander 2000, 187).

who were most crucial in deciding whether or not innovative stylistic elements would be accepted.

Aesthetic II: A Summary Discussion

Our discourse about the growth of the aesthetic involved a prolongation of the discussion on taste, where new sensory tools came to be used. Peoples' sense and reason related to and were affected by changes in society. We have also touched upon the fact that new forms of song and instrumental music were played and listened to. People often heard this music in new contexts and their reflection led to the development of different values and evaluation processes. A partly new song tradition with its roots in *Sturm und Drang* and a developing *Lied*-tradition became important elements in a *bourgeois* music culture, along with contemporary instrumental music. As time passed, people within the *bourgeoisie* came to make music, to sing or play—or listen to music themselves, often in the privacy of their homes. "Common people" even engaged in this music alongside their primary professions.

Analogous to the eighteenth-century Christian person's belief in a delayed reward in heaven, they looked forward to reaping rewards in their leisure time.[124] At the same time, these forms of musical compensation added to the experience of solidarity of a particular group and delineated that group from others. In contrast to earlier generations, these groups experienced song and music more as personally motivated and voluntary acts than as a part of "etiquette" as compared with life at court.

Somewhere in this evolving process an aesthetic discourse developed. A majority of people within the upper nobility and the bourgeois class, began to notice this change because they could *name it with words*. For a small minority of musically-interested people within this class "the new" was revealed at the very end of the eighteenth century. The large majority of the people outside of these circles neither experienced nor thought about the emerging concept of the aesthetic. They continued to use traditional music and song for normal days and Sundays in a traditional manner; at the same time as new dances and song- and music-styles gradually became fashionable even among the country folk and somewhat more quickly for the city working classes.

---

[124] The advantages of a delayed reward can even be found within music theory. Most well-known is Meyer's so called "implication" theory that is built upon an assumption about how a musically familiar listener reacts, and how a musical structure (shorter or longer sections) fulfill or does not fulfill the listener's expectations (Meyer 1973, 110ff). The theory smacks of behaviorism. Sparshott points out that this theory has some debatable normative elements: "Leonard Meyer offered the suggestions that musical forms work by the building and release of symbolic tension. On this view great music is that in which the release is postponed, thus calling forth our moral faculty of postponing gratification" (Sparshott 1987, 76).

How should the aesthetic be understood, then, as woven into the complicated tapestry of new cultural connections? These connections generated new understandings and experiences, which in turn introduced people to new ways of valuing song and music. This dimension that Lydia Goehr called an "aesthetic remainder," was experienced as something that remained after the actual function of the music and song was subtracted. I would prefer to call it an "aesthetic addition." As Goehr also states, people began to recognize that the concept of Works was something new, as well as the way the *bourgeoisie* began singing and making music was also something new. For both vocal and instrumental music the expansion of the concept of the concert involved change. Instrumental music's forward march meant that as the previously doubtful semantic status of tones began to increase, listeners in a salon or concert audience could ideally experience that music. Its close subjective power could move them to a cognitively arrived, super-sensual musical world.[125] This contributed not only to an interest in the structure of music, but also played a role in what Dahlhaus called an "aesthetic reflection" (Dahlhaus 1988, 74).

The people who witnessed this development were all educated and most likely very familiar with their contemporary music. From the travel commentaries we learn of social pressures that led to one being expected to be quiet during concerts and operas. This should, in turn have meant that concentration on the music itself increased, and also that the structure of the music stood out clearly, all of which could have conveyed a new way of listening to music. This way of listening, which I have discussed thoroughly in an earlier article (Edström 1989), is known by many names, such as "autonomous" or "structural listening," "active hearing," or "formal hearing" (see below, p. 155). Dahlhaus assumes that listeners were forced to apply a formal listening regimen in order to bring order to longer and longer movements. Among other things, as they listened for longer periods, they began to hear motive added to motive and were able to meditate on the movement's symmetry. If they had not learned to do this, music would have created an unpleasant amorphous sounding muddle, Dahlhaus explains. One could increase the likelihood of reducing the "muddle" by returning again and again to listen to the same work, an option that was, however, generally more theoretical than practical.

As I also earlier have pointed out (Edström 1986), this type of listening could *be understood as work.* We find these listeners had good taste and were able to apply a structural/autonomous way of listening. Most held intellectual professions– academics, lawyers, doctors, teachers, priests, higher bureaucrats, music writers, and so forth (see further below). In opposition to what earlier musicologists seem to have thought, there were without a doubt, many more

---

[125]There is, thus, an elitist streak in this experience, "reserved" for a small group of people.

women than men who were equipped with the requisites for this kind of listening. For these people *a musical text was just as readable as literature*. One could *read* a musical movement and to varying degrees, *hear* it mentally as sounding music.[126]

It is therefore possible that in these contexts the experience of an added aesthetic dimension could have been workable. Above the basic human experience of music as "making special" and thereby an impression of a "special experience," æI, added an extra part and dimension that these people could identify with the "new-old" word *aesthetic*. It is labeled from here on in this text as aesthetic II (æII). This experience was not an *external* one, such as an extra rule of etiquette dictated by courtly society's experience of music, but rather an experience that could take place in the *internal*, in connection to the experience of listening to *art* music.[127] Among the interdependent factors that generated opportunities for an "aesthetic addition" were the idea that music was like art, that music was autonomous, that instrumental music expressed the inexpressible, and that one could also apply a new way of listening in the social contexts in which this music was performed. These factors, to the best of our knowledge, were never found in classical Greek culture nor did they have any relevance in the musical contexts where the great majority of people met song and music, or played or sang themselves.

The *bourgeois* poetry that was sung in different intimate contexts such as in church, was also something new. To a great extent people also listened to songs in operas, oratorios, the performance of *Lieder*, orchestra works with song, etc. Even these forms of music left the arena of pure handcraft during the eighteenth century and entered another arena where *art* was practiced. Although people in these contexts surely could listen very carefully to a execution of a vocal performance, it is less likely they noticed an "aesthetic addition." This was partially because by consciously listening to the texts, the listener was tethered to the earth. And most likely, the content itself was less conducive to transcendent flights. We cannot, of course, rule out an æII experience, particularly if they listened to vocal music figuratively, as they would have listened to instrumental music. Besides, the song texts in most cases had a content that probably complicated a similar journey to a transcendent world. The semantically graspable in the text, as it were, held the listener in place on the earth. That an "aesthetic addition," æII, presented

---

[126] Cf. music historian Owe Ander (2000, 70) who poses the hypothesis that women were possibly more familiar with the "symphonic repertoire than the majority of men," because the female part of the audience at theater performances during the nineteenth century heard music in the intervals, while the men went to the restaurant to refresh themselves.

[127] From a psycho-physiological point of view, all experiences that humans have are both cognitive and emotional. This "aesthetic addition" or "aesthetic reflection" is made up in the same way of two parts melded together, one emotional and the other cognitive. I have earlier discussed how these two different experiences can be understood from a psycho-physiological point of view (Edström 1986).

itself can, of course, not be ruled out, if one listened to vocal music figuratively *as* instrumental music.

Vocal music as the primary musical form was kept alive throughout the eighteenth century, and likely engendered deeper emotions than earlier generations experienced from their secular vocal context. The reason for this speculation lies in the fact that vocal texts concretely resonated with people's life experiences. A basic experience of "making special" æI was (and is) felt by all involved in song and the act of singing (folk songs, psalms, hymns, *Lieder*, arias etc.)

The conditions that Kant formulated concerning "functionlessness," "disinterestedness" and "purposelessness" are applicable to the strong cognitive/emotional aesthetic experience that the above mentioned (small) minority of people felt. Another point is that this conviction is built upon the idea of an inaccessible and true and eternal world. Seen in this way, æII seems to be built upon a *socialized illusion*. But that is, in fact, a false conclusion, because æII was as real as æI. The aesthetic æII, just as æI, should be understood as a social function. There is, however, hardly any possibility for an individual to guarantee that he or she listens disinterestedly to music, something that Kant made a presupposition for considering *the beautiful* as an aesthetic experience. Social functions and purposes always exist, if people do not imagine themselves to be "autonomous," which would render an "autonomous" art impossible. To speak of music in and of itself, as if it existed without people, is always meaningless.

Kant's idea of *a priori* (the thought that the individual and aesthetic experience of beauty was universal) could perhaps equally be understood as a dream that all bourgeois people could share a fundamental spirit of community and feeling of solidarity. But, as Plumpe argued, just because one person says a tulip is beautiful does not mean everyone else would agree. This statement stands in opposition to our experience. Not everybody agrees even if value judgments are clearly made based on the same preconditions (Plumpe 1993, 59f).

My opinion of structural listening as work, and as a precondition that could result in the experience of an aesthetic dimension, stands in opposition to Kant's idea that the aesthetic could not be reconciled with art that had a purpose, for example writing music in order to make money. Even if music can transfer and release emotional reactions, it must be interpreted within a cultural code. Music can never unambiguously speak a simple sentence. Music is made up of tones that are heard in real time. Therefore *the art that is most difficult to maintain a cognitive distance from may also be the easiest one to stand emotionally close to.* If tones and music are to be experienced on music's own terms, so to speak, it may be impossible to translate it to speech at all, or to any other form of communication, for that matter. Perhaps for this very reason, people found it important to dress their musical experiences in transcendental discourse.

It was during this period that we are studying, practically the same people from within the higher social classes had the ability and training to verbally express their aesthetic experiences. They formulated them in written form and in verbal discourses that were built up around art music. As a result, within their social environments, they created, preserved and transformed their values and attitudes toward music. They were, in other words, one of the most important agents, or factors, within the social process to create, preserve and transform valuations and attitudes to music.[128] But, as has been noted, this discourse had very little attachment to the word "*aesthetic*" itself. Of the 440 concepts that Tadday found that were used for judgments of taste, Tadday found *aesthetic* was included only in compounds like "ästhetisch wertvoll" (aesthetically valuable) and "ästhetisch wenig wert" (aesthetically of little worth) (Tadday 1993, 168).

The discussion of *the aesthetic* was, by and large, a public rather than private one. Liedman acknowledges all fields have their "hard" and "soft" sides. He called the area where the *bourgeois* arts were at home, "the soft" side of Enlightenment. But the Enlightenment also had a hard side, where rational decisions and calculations applied. On one hand we have science, technology, administration and economy; on the other hand, ethics, art and religion. I would also add the humanities and social sciences:

> The "soft" without doubt has to do with the ideal, the "hard" with thoroughly worked-out and proven techniques. In the soft, various human values play a role, and because values both involve and are tied to lifestyles and social relationships, dissonance will be generated in the soft fields as long as there are conflicts among people (Liedman 1997, 39).

The "soft" concept of the aesthetic was used albeit indirectly for demarcating purposes. One closed out the others, or in the best case, as a number of writers, musicians and pedagogues came to do from the nineteenth century onwards, one raised the others so that they could experience the "highest" level. As one raised ones' children among the upper classes, one could also in principle "raise" the lower classes.[129] Against the background of the word's (aesthete*) relative rarity in public discourse there is little reason to believe that it had ever crossed the lips of the large multitudes of the *bourgeoisie*. When one gave one's judgment of taste about a piece of music, rather than using forms of the word *aesthete*, one used instead words like beautiful (*schön*) and the remaining hundreds of words that Tadday found. Hopping around in the alphabet and citing some

---

[128] Observe yet again that the basic analytical-philosophical problem remained unexplained: in a Kantian sense everyone could express themselves about the beauty of music, without being able to ground these value judgments in anything other than a metaphysical belief. Thanks to this philosophical democratizing of concepts of taste, critics could come forward as spokespeople for the general public. Cf. Lezle 1984, 23.

[129] Concerning this later educational project see p. 201.

of Tadday's positive words we find: "angenehm, ausdrucksvoll, ausgesucht schön, ausserordentlich, delikat, denkfähig, deutsch, gefühlvoll, geistreich, geistvoll, himmlische Töne, kunstgerecht, kunstreich, kunstvoll, schön, schöngeistig, sehr schön, stellenweis schön, unvergleichlich schön, wahrhaft genial, wohltönend, wunderbar" (Tadday 1993, 172-82).[130]

The public discourse was built through upbringing, education, interaction, and so forth, by people interested in navigating the shoals between lack of knowledge and ignorance of current events. One conversed, Tadday also writes, less about musical understanding as such, but rather informed oneself more about music through a form of conversation, that admitted that every educated bourgeois person contributed to the maintenance of his position (Tadday 1993, 105).

If a general enculturation or education of the bourgeois culture happened in this way, it must also be added that from the eighteenth century the circles of professional musicians, music writers, reviewers, and, above all music lovers grew slowly but steadily.[131] These music lovers often read the new trade journals of the time. This difference between the common person and the one who worked within the developing music-system (Luhmann), or for that matter, the music field (Bourdieu), corresponded to the growing number of divisions within music culture. While those in the large majority who were interested in music and culture, at the very least read about music in the journals that Tadday (and earlier, Morrow) studied, the latter were happy to read a trade journal, such as the *Allgemeine Musikalische Zeitung*:

> Both media are separated "tendentially" through their different relationships to bourgeois society, which since the early nineteenth century, cultivated two different forms of communication about music, which by the end of the twentieth century will become more diverse and radicalized (Tadday 1993, 209).[132]

Finally: at the end of the eighteenth century '*estet**' is defined in Swedish as the science of the philosophy of the beautiful (*Swedish Encyclopedia* 1781) and further that as an "aesthetic thought, aesthetic picture, and so forth, describes

---

[130] One can perhaps object that the use of the word "schön" in itself was an aesthetic expression, i.e., that many of the other three hundred and thirty eight words and phrases themselves were part of an aesthetic discourse. What speaks against this is the understanding that it is only first when a word exists, and its meaning has stabilized within the semantic field that other words can begin relating to the new word. It is only then that one can speak about a discourse developing around the word aesthetic as a central and driving concept. As we soon shall see, the number of people that control this word game grows slowly.

[131] "Enculturation" is defined by Merriam as the general process "by which the individual learns his culture, and it must be emphasized that this is a never-ending process" (Merriam 1964, 146).

[132] ["Beide Medien unterschieden sich tendenziell in ihrem besonderen Verhältnis zur (bürgerlichen) Gesellschaft, welche seit dem frühen 19. Jahrhundert zwei Redeweisen über Musik pflegt, die sich bis zu Ende des 20. Jahrhunderts potenzierten und radikalisierten."]

those thoughts, those pictures that comfortably could be included in a Work of taste" (*Swedish Encyclopedia* 1781). Some years later, in 1811, the hope was aired in a periodical called *Polyfem*—a short-lived literary magazine with a Romantic concentration—that there would be "a revolution in the general public's aesthetic way of thinking."[133]

As this work has shown, it is difficult to invest any great belief in this thought. From our research thus far, it is apparent that the aesthetic was slowly on its way to becoming a kind of meta-concept, which with the help of the printing press was spread within a small cultural elite. But for everyone else in the general public, the concept of aesthetics was unknown and therefore was not apt to cause any major revolutions.

---

[133]SAOL [The Swedish Academy's Dictionary] aesthetic – paragraph [E742]. *Polyfem* III. 20: 2 (1811). Leux-Henschen (1958) writes concerning "the musical aesthetical debate in Stockholms Posten 1779, "an aesthetic debate thus far had been about whose taste was going to prevail. In the debate that also concerned positions of power (within the developing Gustavian cultural politics), a progressive direction was taken by the educated composer Joseph Martin Kraus and others, and a more conservative phalanx was led by Count von Barnekow (Chair of the Musikaliska Akademien, and director of the Royal Opera).

> *Since the truth becomes a fable, the philosopher must give way to the artist: Incipit aesthetica!*
> Luc Ferry

CHAPTER 4: A TIME OF CONSOLIDATION

Introduction

Seen from a qualitative perspective, when it came to the way music was used during the nineteenth century, very little happened that was new, but in society in general a great deal took place. The so-called industrial revolution began in England, and spread at different speeds throughout Europe. This evolving capitalistic market system had manifold and deep consequences: the development of a working class, the mechanized production of different types of goods, the process of urbanization, the building of political parties, the founding of folk movements, free churches, and temperance societies, and the growth of knowledge within the natural sciences. The bourgeoisie now became the social class that above all supported the official culture with both means and motivation. Within the class society that developed, art and music came to function in similarly delineating ways as before. The nineteenth century was, as we have said, rich in advances in the natural sciences and technology. There was also an increase in knowledge under way. As in earlier centuries, philosophers discussed the place and meaning of music. The English historian Eric Hobsbawm suggests that the qualitatively best work within art and philosophy is created during revolutionary times, as for instance in the first half of the nineteenth century. Even then it was the German philosophers who came to exercise the greatest influence.[1] Arthur Schopenhauer, for example, saw himself as Kant's true heir. Like Kant, he thought that the true world, the *noumenal*, was inaccessible. He understood this true world metaphorically as a kind of universal cosmic Will. Schopenhauer emphasized that when we experience something as beautiful, this reaction is a result of a subjective aesthetic contemplation (Dickie 1997, 25). The true instrumental music did not represent something in our daily world, but was rather a *direct* manifestation of the *noumenal* according to Schopenhauer. In the words of the philosopher Bryan Magee:

---

[1] Broad overviews of writings on music by central German philosophers can be found in Huray and Day 1981; Bujić 1988; and Benestad 1978, 218-227.

Just as the phenomenal world is the self-manifestation of the noumenal in experience, so is music. It is the voice of the metaphysical will... Music exhibits to us the insides of everything... Far from being a depiction of anything in the world, it is itself an alternative world, and one that reveals to us the profoundest metaphysical truths that human beings are capable of articulating or apprehending; though of course we are not capable of apprehending them conceptually (Dickie 1997, 417).[2]

In Schopenhauer's own words, music is "a picture of Will itself... music communicates its own essence."[3] Wilhelm Friedrich Hegel also valued music highly as the art of the soul. Within his grandiose philosophical system music outplaced even poetry. It was Hegel who first coupled aesthetics with art.[4] This produced results of great consequence for the development of the aesthetic project:

This was quite a momentous step... identification of aesthetics with art and the philosophy of art... with this, 'aesthetic' has increasingly come to be used as a synonym for art... To the identification of art and the aesthetic we may, I think, trace the following contemporary usage of 'aesthetic' as a synonym for 'artistic' (Diffey 1995, 64).

But Friedrich Nietzsche unlike those named already, did not develop a philosophical system within which music's place was clear; rather his writing during the latter half of the nineteenth century was influenced by many artists, although there were many more writers than composers among them. His positive and later negative ideas about Richard Wagner's operas have been taken up in a considerable number of musicological writings.[5] But Nietzsche is also special

---

[2] Magee points out that Schopenhauer himself was careful to show that there exists a contradiction in his assertion that composers could express the deepest truths and the world's "innermost being" through their music, but in a speech that we cannot understand. Schopenhauer could not demonstrate this and claimed that it must be experienced (as Magee comments, this is an argument that is rejected by analytical philosophers). It is well known that Schopenhauer's thoughts had a great influence on a number of composers, among them Richard Wagner and Gustav Mahler (Magee 1998, 486, 492 [see also the following note]).

[3] Musicologists Huray and Day (1981, 322-330) have a longer quotation of Schopenhauer's *The World as Will and Idea* [*Die Welt as Wille und Vorstellung*] that came out in three versions, the first in 1819. Schopenhauer's ideas gained a new currency when Wagner appropriated them as his own. Dahlhaus proves this emphatically using Wagner quotations that repeat Schopenhauer's theses sometimes word for word (Dahlhaus 1988, 468f). But music was now no longer the servant of the text, rather the reverse.

[4] Even if Hegel thought that the "philsophy of the beautiful arts"was a better description than aesthetics, Hegel came to use the concept of aethetics because it was already established (Åhlberg 2000, 61).

[5] It is perhaps a less well-known fact that Nietzsche also wrote music (for a short example see Scruton 1997, 380). Nietzsche's critical appraisal of Wagner begins with the commentary: "Yesterday I heard—believe it or not, Bizet's masterpiece [Carmen] for the twentieth time" (Bujić, 1988, 103). For the background and reasoning behind this complicated patricide see Köhler 1998. [6] We find here a contemporary parallel in Foucault's last work where he tested a positive synthesis between aesthetics and ethics: "What strikes me is the fact that in our society, art has become something

in the sense that there are many fractures and oppositions in his thoughts, and that his opinions both point to the aesthetic project's sweeping importance and its contingency. This meant that, on one hand, the life of a strong and active individual (Nietzsche's *Übermensch*) optimally should be experienced as an artwork in itself,[6] and on the other hand, it was no longer possible to maintain any communal definition of the *beautiful*, of what was beautiful in and of itself. Nothing is more conditional than our sense of beauty. In stark opposition to the philosophers at the beginning of the century, Nietzsche's philosophy destroyed all hope that art could integrate humanity and bridge the increasingly more obvious social divisions at the end of the century.[7] At the same time he politicized art.

As has been mentioned earlier, philosophical ideas were slowly being disseminated but they were too complicated to become everyone's property. They were presented in contexts in which few could take part. What's more, not even within professional circles were these utterances always completely understood.

Hobsbawm's writings also touch upon art's general meaning during the nineteenth century. He points out that within bourgeois culture, until the middle of the nineteenth century, one generally built up one's fortune rather than spending it. He also maintains that during this time music was the art form that was most tolerated by the *bourgeoisie* (Hobsbawm 1979, 353f). After the revolutionary period, from the 1850s and on, one had the chance within the bourgeoisie to demonstrated one's newly won power and authority in artistic form:

> Few cultures have been so ready to freely invest money in the arts and culture, and from a purely quantitative perspective, no society has so willingly and happily bought such masses of old and new books, *objects d'art,* paintings and sculptures, abundantly decorated brick houses and theater and concert tickets (Hobsbawm 1981, 380).

Hobsbawm sees that the period before the 1848 revolution was artistically more productive than the period after. Music compared to other arts survived relatively well even afterwards. It was in part, more difficult to judge music's advances, especially compared with the understanding and actual progress within the natural sciences. Moreover, the paralyzing demand for realism was felt less by music than by art (witness the effect of photography) and literature, because music as an art form is much less pictorial than the others. Hobsbawm

---

which is related only to objects and not to individuals, or to life. That art is something which is specialized or which is done by experts who are artists. But couldn't everyone's life become a work of art? ... *we have to create ourselves as a work of art*" (cited in Wolin 1992, 191).

[6] We find here a contemporary parallel in Foucault's last work where he tested a positive synthesis between aesthetics and ethics: "What strikes me is the fact that in our society, art has become something which is related only to objects and not to individuals, or to life. That art is something which is specialized or which is done by experts who are artists. But couldn't everyone's life become a work of art? ... *we have to create ourselves as a work of art*" (cited in Wolin 1992, 191).

[7] See Plumpe 1993, II:86.

sees realism as a consequence of the disappointment over the French Revolution's major concepts of freedom, equality, and brotherhood, which were finally crushed by the *bourgeoisie* itself in the revolutionary movements around 1848:

> The vision in its turn transformed into art for art's own sake or an intensive concentration on the formal details of speech, style, the artistic technique (Hobsbawm 1981, 298).

This was, however, not something that reduced the value of music. Quite the opposite, according to Hobsbawm, who sees music like operettas and operas (he mentions a number of Verdi operas) as the only art form that experienced a golden age during this period. The other direction, *l'art pour l'art*, had not become fashionable before the late 1880s, and, he maintains, came at the price of relinquishing "joy and pleasure." He adds: "The beautiful arts were part of the *higher* human aspiration. They were even the crown of the work" (Hobsbawm 1981, 391).

It is clear from Hobsbawm's sweeping formulations that when the *bourgeoisie* decorated their homes with visual and sounding art, art was both directed outward and inward . At the same time public music life was changing: concert activities continued to develop, music groups began to play in restaurants and cafés, song and music was taken up by folk movements of different kinds, and the music market s grew,

The span within the bourgeois culture *was* great. Many wealthy homes had salons that, depending on the circumstances, could function as semi-public as well as private venues, while the majority within the *bourgeois* class lived on limited means, making it difficult to live up to the expectation of educating oneself and to both produce and consume the art that was permeating nineteenth-century society.

We will soon enter into the *bourgeois* salons and pose the question of how music was used and listened to in this context. But first, we'll examine how Hobsbawm's earlier observations drew attention to the division of music culture between a more "serious-minded" and a more "entertainment-oriented sphere."

The Difference Becomes Set in Stone

According to the collection of reviews that Morrow studied, in the fight between the "correct" German music on the one hand, and the light Italian on the other, the former music won. As has been mentioned, a similar struggle, the so-called Beethoven-Rossini debate played out in the 1820s and 30s. The musicologist Bernd Sponheuer shows in this context how different authors used metaphors like "the German Eagle" and the "Butterfly from the South" to describe the differences they experienced (Sponheuer 1987). Hegel compared the lark with the butterfly and heard in the lark's melody, which he not only connected to the Italian, but saw there, according to his dialectical system, that melody generally stood on a higher plane than rhythm and harmony.[8] Many German writers were thought to have denied their own personal experience, for instance, when they were enchanted by Italian opera, but felt they shouldn't be enjoying it. Alongside the metaphors of Eagle and Butterfly, stood others like spirit and enjoyment, or pairs of opposites like timeless and time-bound, and lyric and dramatic, not to mention Higher and Lower. Philosophers, musicologists and many others felt it necessary to defend the "higher" music against the "lower."

Sponheuer sees these conceptual pairs as symptoms of what philosophers and musicologists experienced— a deeply felt pressure for legitimacy manifesting in an urge to both demarcate themselves from the "lower music" and defend themselves against it. This was in itself a consequence of having taken over the classic-romantic art concept and art music's autonomy as a central idea. It also seemed necessary to react against the commercialization of musical life and the spread of entertainment music after the Napoleonic wars (Sponheuer 1987, 33).

Sponheuer quite convincingly shows that the outer pressure for legitimacy led to a rigorous inner selection. An "aesthetically highly placed" music was saved at the same time as the "lower" music was offered up on the altar of the impure. Sponheuer described this cleansing process at some length. Art music was seen as having the ability to erase and reconcile the dualism between culture and nature. In Hegel's eyes, art was, above all, a happy middle point (*glückliche Mitte*) within human ambition. Art that functioned as a goal as well as a means therefore had a key place in the educated person's development and provided the solution for the eternal opposition between sense and sensibility. According to Sponheuer, this was all about a universal program for the "aesthetic principle" within which art was raised aloft to the rank of humanity's Savior.

Through a theoretical aesthetic construction within which thoughts about art's purity, its autonomy, Kantian ideas about its purposelessness, about artistic beauty and natural beauty, the true and real art was separated from the lower forms. It was particularly important to describe music's beauty and to come

---

[8] Hegel writes for example: "Like the bird in the branches, the lark in the bright air, sings movingly, in order to sing, as a pure product of Nature, without any further purpose and specific content, so it is with human singing...This is also how it is with Italian music, in which this principal is particularly present...common in the melodic sound...because even by the enjoyment of art for art's sake, the melodic sound of their Soul is released" ["Wie der Vogel in den Zweigen, die Lerche in der Luft heiter, rührend singt, um zu singen, als reine Naturproduktion, ohne weiteren Zweck und bestimmten Inhalt, so ist es mit dem menschlichen Gesang... Daher geht auch die italienische Musik, in welcher dies Prinzip insbesondere vorwaltet... häufig in das melodische Klingen als solches über... weil sie eben auf den Genuss der Kunst als Kunst, auf der Wohllaut der Seele in ihrer Selbstbefriedigung geht"] (as cited after Sponheuer 1987, 15).

to terms with music's limited ability to signify. The aesthetic process that Goehr described earlier, continues, and becomes consolidated.[9] As before, the listener mainly encountered music in the concert hall and the salon. During this period, the process can therefore be understood as a demarcating project, but it was seldom directed *upwards* toward the feudal class's hegemony of taste, but rather *downward*, partly toward the flowering market of popular and entertainment music, and partly toward the great *bourgeois* public's fascination with the experience of virtuoso music.[10] This final relationship will have an important influence on the aesthetic project's future fate.

Four Thousand Wandering Virtuosi

The castrati of the seventeenth and eighteenth centuries were often described as having an enhanced *technical* ability, a concept that came to be more and more connected to instrumental musicians by the end of the eighteenth century. Reichardt complained that increasingly musicians were practicing their instruments excessively, a development that he thought did not lead to better music making (Reichardt 1976, 195).[11] The number of virtuosi rose to 4000 by the middle of the nineteenth century. Just as the nobility at court in Vienna were amazed at the *wunderkind* Mozart's achievements, *bourgeois* and noble audiences now sunned themselves in the glow of virtuoso performances. They were entertained by their finger dexterity and took pleasure in the beautiful melodies interspersed between the technically demanding passages. Virtuosi demonstrated and reaffirmed the musical-ideological plan of the *bourgeoisie's* power and position. During this time a parallel had already been established between their technical proficiency and

---

[9] Sponheuer discusses among other things how a) the power of music was formulated: "The other Arts pursuade us, Music assails us" ["Die anderen Künste überreden, die Musik überfällt uns"], b) music's sensual characteristics became more prominent, c) music's abstract qualities were seen as something positive, as well as d) how art music's status was raised through the spiritualising and formalising of different categories of beauty (a telling expression can be found here in Richard Wagner's confession "I believe in God, Mozart and Beethoven"] (Sponheuer 1987, 74-127).

[10] Elias comments concerning the difference between Germany and France regarding 'Bildung' and 'Kultur.' In the Swedish edition (part 1) of "Processes of Civilization" he says: "In Goethe's Germany "Bildung und Kultur" in themselves describe a thin intervening layer that has been raised above the people. Not just the small royal social stratum above them but also the broader layer under them fairly shows a small understanding for their own elitist strivings" (Elias 1989, 113). William Weber who mainly treats the time period during the nineteenth century until the revolutionary year of 1848, writes that the relationship between the upper middle class and the aristocracy was different in Vienna, Paris and London (Weber 1975, 12-15).

[11] Reichardt suggested that true art and virtuosic skill were two completely separate things (Reichardt 1976, 229f). He also accused the violinist Louis Spohr of changing tempi like a virtuoso "so that such an Allegro has three or four different Tempi" ["so dass ein solches Allegro drei, vier verschiedene Tempi bekommt"] (Reichardt 1976, 247), something that pulled apart the music and destroyed its beauty. Compare also with Bowen 1999 where it is suggested that tempo changes were apparently very common.

the beginning of the industrial revolution. Heinrich Heine describes in 1840 in a letter from Paris:

> Piano playing's dominance like the triumphal procession of the piano virtuosi is characteristic for our time and shows simply the triumph of the machine over the spirit. Technical proficiency, an automaton's precision... that people have become sounding instruments, is today something that is celebrated and prized to the highest degree (as cited in Ballstaedt and Widmaier 1989, 47f.).

The technically advanced instrumentalists, not least the pianists, continued the earlier tradition of performing variation works, where equilibristic reprises were never lacking. Within opera the castrati tradition disappeared, but the virtuoso tradition took over, especially among talented sopranos. As musicologists Ballstaedt and Widmaier (1989) pointed out, the technical arsenal gradually increased with trills, octave leaps, fast runs, and so forth, and appeared in more and more musical forms. Franz Liszt, the foremost piano virtuoso, and before him the violinist Nicolo Paganini, were cult figures who entranced a great deal of the contemporary musical public. As virtuosos they both gave regular concerts and also appeared in untold numbers of salons around Europe. Their virtuosic skills are, however, not ascribed to any higher spiritual worth and neither was the music described as autonomous. The virtuoso's technical bravura fascinated listeners and held them in a kind of tension. Critics for their part said that virtuoso playing was soulless and empty (Ballstaedt and Widmaier 1989, 44-59). Liszt understood this problem himself. Consequently, he saw himself not as an entertainer, but as a creator, as an *artist*. He viewed his musician colleagues mostly as handcraft workers and only a few as artists (Ballstaedt and Widmaier 1989, 39)![12]

If we look at the programs that were performed by orchestras in Vienna, Paris and London, we find they too contained music with popular content and were not dominated by concerts and symphonies of Mozart and Beethoven, even in the middle of the century.. The musicologist William Weber writes:

---

[12] Liszt was thought of clearly as the greatest piano virtuoso, but by an insightful colleague like Clara Schumann, also an artist. She comments in her journal that she had no desire to compete with the sympathetic Liszt "If he did not delight them through his art, then he entranced them with his Personality—most often though both took place" ["Wenn er nicht durch seine Kunst entzückt, den bezaubert er durch seine Persönlichkeit—gewöhnlich findet aber beides statt"] (Schumann and Schumann 1987, 121). This picture can be compared with Heine's description of a concert with Liszt: "The electrical force of a demonic Nature on a compressed Mass, the contagious force of Exstacy, and perhaps the magnetism of the music itself, the spiritualistic fad of the time, which vibrates in almost all of us—these phenomena are never so apparent to me ... as in a concert by Liszt" ["Die elektrische Wirkung einer dämonischen Natur auf eine zusammengepresste Menge, die ansteckende Gewalt der Ekstase, und vieleicht der Magnetismus der Musik selbst, die spiritualistischen Zeitkrankheit, welche fast in uns allen vibriert—diese Phänomene sind mir noch nie so deutlich... wie in dem Concert von Liszt"] (as cited in Ballstaedt and Widmaier 1989, 46).

In all three cities popular-music concerts considerably outnumbered classical-music concerts. During the season 1845/46 presentations which had a strict classical-music orientation accounted for eight per cent of all high-status concerts in Paris, thirteen per cent in Vienna, and twenty per cent in London (Weber 1975, 21).

It is only during the latter half of the century that the (Viennese) classical symphonies became common in programs. This happened at the same time as the piano virtuosi began to perform works of Beethoven. Upwardly striving musicians had not only musical reasons for performing more "serious" works but also social ones. Classical music's greatest supporters were, as before, those among the educated and style-setting layer of the *bourgeoisie*. Weber points out that the definition of classical music changed. More of Liszt's piano works were experienced as classical during the latter half of the century:

> We can speculate that the lofty ideals of the classical-music scene replaced the giddy mood of before because they were more compatible with the greater stability and seriousness which came about in musical life. After all, one can push novelty only so far. More specifically, classical values suited the needs of virtuosi to glorify their new social standing and provided a solid standard of taste for the elite public that was now firmly established (Weber 1975, 51).

One can therefore ask to which degree the movement toward a more classical repertoire also included the gradual development of a reaction to stylistic renewal, or as Weber describes it: novelty. Dahlhaus (1983, 95) stresses that the development of a musical canon during the nineteenth century happened at the same time as the dissemination of an historical awareness. As he formulates it, even though the idea of originality was a sign of aesthetics during this period of historical awareness, there also existed another sense of composers as authors trained in the handcraft of the classical tradition. Haydn as the father of the string quartet, Mozart as opera buffa's father and Beethoven as the father of the symphony were all *classicus auctor*. Value judgments of this kind are both aesthetically normative and historically descriptive. That which Dahlhaus points to, describes a tension between the concert public's reception of music and the composer's wish through his handicraft to also renew his personal and stylistic palette. We see a parallel tension between the wishes of the publisher to sell as many tickets and scores as possible and the composer's wish to write an art as exclusive as possible, creating a conflict that becomes more pronounced as time goes on. Weber shows that the so-called "low-status concerts," popular concert forms for both the middle class and the working class, became more common during the nineteenth century. We find a large number of different types of concerts offered to the public. Some cities had more intensive concert series than others. Among these concert forms Weber counts the performance of a) amateur orchestras and choirs b) newly created professional orchestras, c) with orchestra with soloists ("professional instrumental concerts") and d) promenade concerts that were held in parks and dance venues. This last type was held in locations where refreshments could be served.[13]

Weber mentions that the music at promenade concerts was far from the main attraction. People wandered about talking, eating and drinking. It was reminiscent of a similar "soundscape" when the nobility was surrounded by representative music entertainments.

Weber, who suggested that the professional concert life of the 1870s developed its modern form in Paris, Vienna and London, sees a connection between music listening/understanding and music habits among the different social classes. The *bourgeois* mind valued among other qualities diligence, endurance and enterprise. Families in business and finance constituted the main part of the public that listened to virtuoso concerts and concerts with mixed programs and shorter pieces, while people from the free professions and bureaucrats preferred chamber music and symphony concerts (Weber 1975, 124).[14] It is here among these latter groups, that the idea of the "aesthetic addition" becomes applicable. Moreover this idea was most relevant for the music-making women of the *bourgeoisie*.

A Swedish Example from Göteborg

Weber's conclusions can also be illustrated from a Swedish perspective. The politics of concert programming and orchestra organizations differed little from continental practice in Göteborg from 1840 to 1870. The music historian Anders Carlsson (1996) describes the social schedule of the wealthy bourgeoisie: balls, parties and feasts at home and in places around the city. These events had

---

[13] The most well-known representative for this form of concerts in Vienna was Johann Strauss the younger, who not only played waltzes and waltz potpourris, but, according to the musicologist Martin Tegen, "included fantasies and potpourris of his repertoire, built on melodies of current composers like Auber, Bellini, Dalayrac, Ernst, Hérold, Mozart, Müller, Rossini, Weber and others. And was not satisfied to stop there. He took up opera arias, symphony movements and ouvertures, as well as song transcriptions, virtuoso pieces... often in the Kapellmeister's own arrangements... [Strauss was] one of those who created the 'popular concert' " (Tegen 1986, 49).

[14] Tegen 1986 presents Weber's two different categories of the "entertainment bourgeoisie" and the "educated bourgeoisie." Dave Russel (1987) shows, in part in reaction to Weber, that the popular music in England during the period between 1840 and 1914 was based very little on class. Brass bands among the working class and the middle class played the same repertoire of popular music. Tegen suggests, in the same spirit, that even if the music that he discusses was mainly composed for the bourgeoisie, people from other classes also enjoyed it. Dahlhaus, on the other hand, suggests that opinions like Tegen's are based on wishful thinking: "Musical classlessness is a phantom, an upside down Utopia" ["Die musikalische Klassenlosigkeit ist ein Phantom, eine rückwärts gewandte Utopie"] (Dahlhaus 1988, 199). Compare also with Carlsson 1996, 141ff. In Edström 1996 different choirs, for instanse *Götaverkens arbetares sångkör* (the Wharf Workers' Singing Choir) and *Akademikernas Sångkör* (The Academics' Choir) apparently had the same repertoire of "middle music," but that its meaning must be seen as a function of the person's references, music's use and the context in which it is played. Even if within *Götaverkens arbetares sångkör* one knew that music had it's origins in the "wrong" class one could still like it.

music as entertainment as well as dance music. One could hear military music on the city's streets and in its parks. When the sharp shooters (a voluntary defense force) marched out for their shooting drills, their small music corps sometimes played a march. There was also entertainment music in some of the city's larger establishments. Travelling virtuosi occasionally gave concerts programmed along continental European lines. Even though there was no opera in the city at this time, vaudeville as well as theater performances often had live music between acts. In 1859 the new little opera house and theater, Nya Teatern opened its doors. This theater also had a small permanent orchestra. If we study the programs that were printed for orchestra concerts from the 1840s to the 1870s, we find as on the continent, a distinction made between seriously oriented concerts and lighter ones. Earlier, Göteborg had mainly relied on the city's few professional musicians as well as some good amateurs, but, by the middle of the century, a number of foreign musicians were drawn to the city. Under the direction of the Czech musician Joseph Czapek, then resident in Göteborg, a number of concerts were given during the 1850s with a classical symphonic program.[15] Through funds provided by the city's wealthy bourgeoisie, Göteborg could boast a permanent orchestra with mainly foreign musicians between 1862 and 1866, and a new orchestra between 1872-1878.

If we take the latter orchestra's repertoire as an example, we find that there was a difference between subscription concerts, popular Sunday concerts, and outdoor concerts. Originally it was thought that the professional orchestra of about 30 musicians would play subscription concerts with (a) an overture; (b) some solo pieces either sung solos or instrumental solos with orchestral accompaniment; and (c) conclude with a symphony. The public, however, was apparently interested in a lighter program. The orchestra, writes Carlsson, was forced to follow prevailing taste and play more short and popular pieces. There were also subscription concerts that were made up of up to ten different works but no symphonies (Carlsson 1996, 358f).

Even in Göteborg, the public eventually learned to sit still and be quiet. The city's music critics tried to raise the public taste by propagandizing for the subscription concerts—concerts that now included not only music of the Viennese classics, but also works of Schumann and Wagner—and ignoring lighter music. But audience interest for these subscription concerts never materialized. When it came to popular concerts and summer concerts, programs were made up of a great many pieces. In both cases refreshments were served both during and before concerts. The Summer concerts, writes Carlsson, were obviously popular and drew very large audiences "at least to the buffet tables set up close by," which from

---

[15] In the beginning of January 1856 a symphony of Mozart was performed and one of Beethoven, as well as an overture of Mendelssohn and two piano pieces arranged for orchestra (Carlsson 1996, 203).

the perspective of the restaurant owners was not inconsequential because music for them was a great expense (Carlsson 1996, 386; cf. Weber 1997, 690).

Carlsson mirrors Weber, in noting a similar movement towards a more classical repertoire of larger symphonic concerts. If half of the works that were played at subscription concerts were written by dead composers, then 34% and 37% was written by dead composers for the popular concerts and summer concerts, respectively. The number of works by unidentified composers (in practical terms these were the shorter pieces of a lighter character) was 4% of symphonic concert programs, 22% of the popular concerts and 13% of the summer concerts (Carlsson 1996, 395). The "unidentified" were thus best represented at the "light" popular concerts.

The less well-to-do parts of the *bourgeoisie* and the working class in Vienna, Paris and London could in some cases listen to popular concerts from stages in the public parks, and probably had the means occasionally to get tickets to one of the musical events that Weber labeled "low status concerts." This was also true of Göteborg, even if the city's working class was small in the 1870s due to the late beginning of industrialization in Sweden (Carlsson 1996, 441).

* * *

As in other cities, investing in public concerts meant the professionalizing, commercializing and democratizing of music life. But concert forms maintained to a great degree the social differences that were present earlier and mirrored those that developed within the increasingly industrialized societies. Social differences, differences in material and nonmaterial prosperity—in living conditions, family size, education, cultural and literary education, career, etc.—had, in other words, equivalences in musical life. The differences were obvious, even in the use of language, in the way one labeled and assigned value to different forms of song and music. Those who went to the subscription concerts where the "higher" music was performed, were mainly members of society's highest class. Thereby the music's worth, both artistic and aesthetic, was associated with this class.

This had, in and of itself, nothing to do with how music was used in listener situations, for instance, whether it was listened to at all, casually, now and then, or in a concentrated manner (and all variations in between). That one did nothing during the performance except sit still and listen was a clear sign that this music belonged in a different league than the music that was played at summer concerts and popular concerts. During these latter concerts, different activities to varying degrees limited music's acoustical precedence. Music was connected to more worldly things like food and drink.

Music and song was also found at home, not just in the *bourgeois* salons. Even in these contexts we can observe the distinctions between different forms of music that became a part of the culture from the nineteenth century on, distinctions that led to music being assigned different value, different artistic ranks, and aesthetic weight. Music's place and use defined, to a great degree, music's worth.[16] For instance, the context in which Beethoven's music was played and who supported it, as we have seen, had a great deal of meaning for the worth of this music. As Bourdieu formulated it: "Internal struggles are to an extent arbitrated by external sanctions" (Carlsson 1996, 252). Art music's position within the social and economic power structure closely coincides, in other words, with its position within the music field.

One musician and composer at this time spent a great deal of his five-year period in Göteborg in musical salons, even though posterity rarely connects him with either salons or Göteborg. He embodied the bifurcation of music culture that could be observed within the home. We will soon return to Bedrich Smetana, and to Göteborg, but first we will sketch how Swedish musical life in general was affected by the new philosophical currents on the continent.

Swedish Music Journalists

When the new philosophical ideas washed up on Sweden's beaches, they were first picked up by the Swedish academic world, and afterwards, at a leisurely pace, filtered into the *bourgeois* sensibility. As had happened earlier, the concept of "aesthetic" was already written about at the end of the eighteenth century, and as the musicologist Sten Dahlstedt has mentioned, Kantian philosophy had already found a foothold in both the University cities of Lund and Uppsala (Dahlstedt 1986, 28). My interpretation of this statement is that probably a few dozen people in these towns had read some of Kant's works.

During the nineteenth century Swedish musicologists and music journalists also stood very close to the German tradition. The few Swedish music journalists active during the nineteenth century worked almost exclusively in and near Stockholm. The opera was there, the Musical Academy was there, and above all, there was a larger audience for concerts, lectures and cultural activities than in other places in Sweden.[17]

Also in Sweden at the time, a small group of musically educated persons, gradually emerged as interpreters of the past and present schools of philosophy. One such example is Abraham Mankell who in the middle of the century was a diligent and engaged music journalist and lecturer. Mankell, who worked as a singing teacher and organist in Stockholm, adopted Rousseauian ideas about

---

[16]Note again that overtures and symphonies far into the nineteenth century were played at the beginning or end of a concert program: Cf. Weber 1999, 349.

[17]As can be seen in Ander 2000 there was a respectable bourgeois-noble music life in Stockholm already during the first half of the nineteenth century.

melody's origins and naturalness. He further considered that knowledge was not helpful to the process of assimilating music and that music became superficial if it was not integrated, simply and naturally, with feelings. Similar lines of thought can be found in the writings of the influential Carl Jonas Love Almqvist. Both highlighted folksongs and other simple songs as the true music instead of music in larger formats and forms.[18]

This conception came under harsh criticism by the middle of the century from another school that considered the followers of Mankell uneducated dilettantes. Among those who wrote in the larger forms are the composers Franz Berwald and Ludvig Norman. Of much greater importance for the music-interested *bourgeoisie* later in the century was Adolf Lindgren, thanks to his music articles in the *Nordisk Familjebok* (*Nordic Family Encyclopedia*), as well as his work as a reviewer, and his articles (including many years of contributions to the *Svensk Musiktidning* [*Swedish Music Journal*], as well as essays and books. Lindgren was equally well educated in German music history and other humanistic disciplines.[19]

Against the background of this sketch we can now return for a closer look at the everyday situation in a Göteborg home at the middle of the century. When we left the city at the end of the eighteenth century we found both a rich *bourgeois* music-making tradition at home and saw that the public musical life also produced an occasional concert. Even though Göteborg had a comparatively small population of nobility, city officials, and academics, and therefore did not have the same social structure as Stockholm, nevertheless, there was a genuine musical interest in the city. With Smetana's help, we will now have a look at the music in Göteborg salons.

---

[18]Compare with the musicologist Norlind's judgment: "Mankell loved the simple, folk music so much, that he not only ignored the higher art music, but even intensely fought against it" (*Allmänt Musiklexikon* 1916, 611).

[19]We can therefore depart from the idea that around the end of the century Lindgren's articles in the *Nordisk Familjebok* [*The Nordic Family Encyclopedia*], the foremost Swedish encyclopedia of the age, was the period's most important resource for knowledge on music in Scandinavia. Articles, for instance on music, are long (ten columns) and deserve to be read in their entirety. Lindgren notes that 1) from the music one can hear if there is an agitated condition that's being described, but cannot say with any certainty which condition: "one hears that, but not what;" 2) that music that only wants to awake "passions and sensations," without "ennobling them through" a harmonic musical form, are "unhealthy and objectionable" on moral and aesthetic grounds; and 3) that music's non-definition and "non-expressivity in conceptual terms" makes it more ideal than the other fine arts and gives it a particular position among them. Dahlstedt discusses Lindgren's importance for the development of musicology and suggests that Lindgren should "be seen as a clever music critic who is well-read, has a good stylistic sense and, in some cases, an independent understanding of questions of aesthetics" (Dahlstedt 1986, 57).

Music in the Salons—Intimate Scenes of Home

When Smetana came to Göteborg there was an announcement in the press that "an artist on the piano" had landed. His activity in the city became extensive: lessons in piano, song, theory, and composition, choir directing, concertizing and arrangements. He also composed during his visit to the city, and on several occasions, played his violin in the city's *bourgeois* salons. Smetana, most well-known for his virtuoso piano technique, had both a Viennese classical and a modern repertoire. He composed art music but also pieces in popular forms like the waltz and the polka. He also arranged well-known classical works for multiple pianists like Beethoven's overture from *Egmont* (for eight hands) and Spontini's overture to *Ferdinand Cortez* (for sixteen hands!). Concerning the repertoire Smetana used for lessons it is mentioned that:

> Smetana was thought to have had a varied repertoire that he chose for his students with salon music as well as works of Beethoven, Mendelssohn, Schumann and other composers considered Classical today. There is no evidence therefore that Smetana entertained any kind of purist attitude that salon music was inappropriate. Quite the opposite, salon repertoire was ... *a lubricant for a great deal of private musical life*... thus it was natural for Smetana then to also give lessons in this music to the women of Göteborg (Carlsson 1996, 225 [my italics]).

According to Carlsson, music like this was performed at parties and gatherings in the home. Everyone performed according to their own ability and skills with songs, piano music, duets, trios, quartets, or different combinations of instruments.

In other words, in the salons of Göteborg, like those in Germany, England, France, and so on, *all* forms of music were performed by professionals and amateurs alike: sonatas, string quartets, and eight-hand arrangements of Beethoven symphonies, opera arrangements played by virtuosi. Opera melodies, *Lieder*, and folk song arrangements were sung by sons and daughters. Solo pieces for different instruments were performed in a steady stream.

Ballstaedt and Widmaier show that what was considered salon music was not completely unambiguous. A common general definition was *Unterhaltungsmusik für Klavier*, music for entertainment at the piano. Often this meant shorter pieces with a limited grade of difficulty. From the middle of the century, salon music included "Fantasien, Lieder ohne Worte, Potpurris, Impromptus, Bagatellen, Etuden, Nocturnos, Scherzos, Transcriptionen, Charakterstücke, Variationen, Balladen, Polonaise, Walzer, Mazurkas, Boleros u.s.w." (Ballstaedt and Widmaier 1989, 17). Also pieces and arrangements for other instruments, as well as songs within these forms and styles were reckoned as salon music.

A TIME OF CONSOLIDATION

Salon music naturally presupposes that there was a need for this kind of music. Children, especially girls, learned to play as a part of their education.[20] The purpose was not that they should become professional musicians. By practicing and planning ahead the students learned discipline and that practice created skill. Parents could be proud of their childrens' accomplishments and maybe even give them some concrete reward. When guests visited or were invited home, they could hear the family's musical children. Apart from entertaining with music—the guests were pleased (in the best case scenario) and would gladly visit again—one could also dance waltzes and polkas. Those who, contrary to expectations, didn't like salon music, could leave the room on some errand. Because music competed with social discourse, serving and eating and drinking, one could only rarely concentrate fully on the song or music being performed.

The demand for this repertoire had steadily risen from the beginning of the nineteenth century. At the same time the production quality of pianos and other instruments was slowly rising.[21] The production of pianos was being industrialized and music publishing became more effective. From the 1860s, a new printing technique for music made production cheaper at the same time as the copyrights expired for composers like Beethoven and Schubert:

> The fact that one owned an edition of Beethoven's sonatas showed good taste, in the same way as having a fine edition of Goethe's poems on the salon table, without actually needing to have read them (Ballstaedt and Widmaier 1989, 108).[22]

---

[20] The role of music in childrearing was an area that was often explored in the books of the day. Martin Tegen gives an example from Sweden: Mathilda Langlet's all-encompassing *Housemothers in the cities and in the country* [*Husmodern i staden och på landet*], also takes up childrearing. In one chapter she warns about the dangerous effects of pleasures and amusements outside the home. Only music was permitted (Tegen 1955, 89).

[21] Ballstaedt and Widmaier name a typical example in the piano firm of Blüthner which had, in the 1850s only had a handful of workers, while fifty years later, they had 650 employees. Thanks to the industrialization of the process, the number of pianos produced in 1870 and 1910 respectively were, 25,000 and 75,000 in England, 21,000 and 25,000 in France, 15,000 and 120,000 in Germany and 24,000 and 370,000 in the United States (Ballstaedt and Widmaier 1989, 66).

[22] Copyright protection lapsed at about the same time as German Nationalism—depending on the German successes in the Franco-Prussian War and Bismark's declaration of the German Reich in 1871—reached its first high point. Geck and Schleuning show how Beethoven's *Eroica* has been reinterpreted through the ages and that during this period, in the 1870s, the well-known director Hans von Bülow not only connected this work with Prometheus and Napoleon, but also with Bismark. In the song text that Bülow set to one of the symphony's most well-known melodies (he crossed out the title Napoleon and replaced it with Bismark) it says: "Hear ye Peoples, Hail the Hero, proclaim your Word, the new German World. Until it find's its heart's mark, henceforth against every enemy, strongly armed, you have unified us." ["Das Volkes hört, Heil Dir o Held, Es schuf Dein Wort, Die neue Deutsche Welt. Bis in des Herzens Mark, Fortan gen jeden Feind, Gewappnet stark, Hast Du uns geeint"] (Geck and Schleuning 1989, 306).

Music schools and institutes were also started in the large cities. The demand rose for instrument teachers.

Different salons offered music of varying degrees of excellence and ambition. On the one hand there were musical salons within which the cream of the current artists could give chamber music concerts. On the other hand there were also many modest performances given by the daughter of the house in front or a few relatives and friends singing to her own accompaniment on the guitar.[23] William Weber believes he has found a pattern among the different occupational groups concerning how these salons were arranged and points out the role women also played as organizers. He suggests that businessmen enjoyed a passive role in both political life and in the organization of musical life, where they let their wives organize charity concerts and arrange musical salons. Within the educated *bourgeoisie*, it was the reverse. Within this group men saw:

> [s]o much to be gained from social activism in musical life that women achieved no such power in classical-music life. Males imposed upon this world a lofty intellectual definition through which—thanks to the traditional conception that men were more serious that women—they excluded the other sex from leadership, even though women attended classical-music concerts just as much as men (Weber 1975, 126).

Use and Status

The range of music varied within the home and the salons, as did the use to which the music was put. It is obvious that music was tailored for the salon in a way reminiscent of earlier feudal and noble cultures where music was viewed as functional. Publishing companies advertised in musical and cultural periodicals for composers who understood the market's need for appropriate music. These advertisements sometimes urged unknown composers to write elegant but not too difficult "Original Salon Compositions." For both the publisher and the composer it must have therefore been clear that the musical product being discussed could be of interest to the market for printed music. The gap widened between what a publisher usually paid a composer and what a composition generated for the publisher if it became a success. On the other hand most pieces were sold only in

---

[23]Compare with the musicologist Eva Öhrström 1987, 131f who gives an example of the "large city's musical salons" in Stockholm and Göteborg. In Josef Holecek's rich work on the guitar we see that far into the nineteenth century the guitar was seen as a woman's instrument. One played salon music and sang to one's own accompaniment (Holecek 1996, 91-98). In Tegen we see that also in Sweden music-making in salons could also become regular concert events in the richer homes of the *bourgeoisie* (Tegen 1955, 90). He mentions, for example, that in one Stockholm home at the end of the century, all seven children played. When the dining room was changed into a concert hall, the home filled with music-lovers to hear performances of "oratorios, cantatas, solid works for mixed choir, while the orchestra was represented by some clever and attentive pianist" (Tegen 1955, 88). For an example of music's place within a noble family, see Andersson 1998.

smaller print runs, indicating that most printed pieces did not generate profit for the publisher. The demand was high and the composers and the publishing houses were hunting for the piece that would bring big success, so it was not unlikely that a salon composer had an opus list that ran to more than 500 pieces (Ballstaedt and Widmaier 1989, 79ff). They used opus numbers to show that their pieces were Works (which of course wasn't the case).

Mass production on this scale led to the development of simple musical patterns that made the composition process easier and speedier. Pieces often had a musical structure that corresponded to their vivid titles. Ballstaedt and Widmaier found that:

a) about 10% of the pieces had titles like "The Well," "By the Seashore," "Embers," and that the music in these pieces had correspondingly pictorial passages;

b) about 25% of the pieces followed well-known styles like marches, Venetian gondola songs, lullabies, and so forth; and

c) a large group of about 65% had titles that referred to feelings, moods, religious thoughts, or had titles after girl's names, etc.[24]

Within this last group it can be difficult or almost impossible to find a clear correlation between the title and the music, but there is a prevailing musical affect describing a sentimental tone, an atmosphere, that is brought about using various musical materials. Ballstaedt and Widmaier see this sentimental tone both as a musical correlation to peoples' social situation and as a distinction between the bourgeois person's everyday reality (toil and competition) and their daydreams (represented in the titles and contents of salon music).

One could drift away into fantasy both as a listener and as a performer practicing these pieces, thanks to their structure and evocative titles. Ballstaedt and Widmaier argue that this music's structure was well suited to a non-concentrated way of listening: one could alternate between thinking about something else and really listening to the music. One was not likely to miss anything too important if one didn't follow the piece's formal structure. Within the art music tradition the ability to follow a formal structure was valued highly, but within salon music it was of secondary significance. The forms were simple and there were not more than a few thematic ideas to keep track of, Musical ideas were clearly repeated but were never "exposed" to the metamorphosis of compositional handcraft, or

---

[24]Ballstaedt and Widmaier also touch on the special connection between the sentimental and emotional salon music and the female gender. A circular logic developed: women were seen by their nature to be more emotional, therefore this music suited them better (Ballstaedt and Widmaier 1989, 210f). It was not a new idea that composers wrote music that in different ways related to the outer world. If we go back in music history we find for example, Beethoven's *Victory of Wellington*, Haydn's *Creation*, Biber's *Biblical Sonatas* and so forth, until we meet the instrumental works of program music of the classical Greeks.

formed a part of the exposition of a sonata form. The pieces simply met peoples' expectations, and corresponded to multiple functions including the human need for music.[25] The pieces' titles helped both the listeners and the players to maintain a mainly emotional and associative way of listening with variable levels of concentration. The experience of music was characterized above all by the social situation and the social interplay that prevailed in upper and middle-class salon culture.

If we depart from the perspective of the composer, we see that, when they wrote salon music they were aware of the social situations in which the music would be used. They adapted the structure of the music from the very beginning of composition to these expectations. The point was that the music should be *used*. This was also a general point of departure for composers of the eighteenth century and earlier. They didn't compose cantatas, divertimenti or sonatas for "eternity"; instead, they wrote just like the later composers of salon music in the nineteenth century, music whose styles and ideas were similar to their other compositions and the pieces of their contemporaries. If we steal a look into the future, we see that the same rules apply for all the commercial popular music of the twentieth-century. For example, a *schlager* (or Tin-Pan-Alley Song) composer who wrote a seaman's waltz in the 1930s had to write a melody that was neither too similar nor too different from all the other seaman's waltzes. As we shall see, Arnold Schönberg broke with this functional tradition when he wrote his songs *Das Buch der hängenden Gärten* (see page 185).

The Schumanns and Salon Music

Musicians also held musical salons themselves where they performed with other musicians, and where amateurs could also present songs or instrumental music. These events were often quite informal gatherings of friends. Unexpected visitors were also not uncommon, mainly musically interested people from the *bourgeoisie*. Clara and Robert Schumann's diaries give a clear picture of music's place in the home of the successful music couple. When Robert wasn't writing articles, when they were not giving lectures, practicing, composing, attending or giving concerts, they were socializing with visitors. They also visited friends

---

[25]Carlsson (1996, 224) analyzes a piece of salon music by Smetana that in all its parts corresponds to the criteria that Ballstaedt and Widmaier (1989, 255-345) identify for salon music. The latter carry out an analysis of the once popular "The Virgin's Prayer" of the Polish composer Thekla Badarzweska. Here one finds again what one sought: simple accompanimental figures in the left hand (that also worked for a large number of other melodies, if one learned these figures once then that "was enough"), virtuoso figures and singable melodies in the right hand, clear periodicitiy as well as simple large forms, and rich piano sound. Music should as a general rule be varied. See especially Ballstaedt and Widmaier 1989, 262-90. Compare also with Keldany-Mohr's analysis of the same work (Keldany-Mohr 1977, 104f).

themselves, took part in or arranged salons themselves, as the following four examples describe:

> A Mrs. Moody has written to me to ask if I can give her lessons… From her name she might be judged to be English, whereby I fear that she may actually not want lessons to study the piano, but rather because it is a la mode to take lessons (October, 1849 Clara Schumann) [Moody later did take lessons and proved to be a terrible pianist].

> Tuesday… the first soirée at the home of Mrs. Schumann … twenty guests, also a count. Clara played in two trios [of Mendelssohn and Moscheles], Emilie List sang a few of my songs and one of Mendelssohn, but not terribly well… (October, 1840, Robert Schumann).

> Yesterday, finally Saturday we were at David's [and made music] with the same company. Octet of Mendelssohn, written in the most beautiful youthful style. Septet of Moscheles, which, after [the octet] seemed a lesser work. Mrs. Schloss also sang (October, 1840 R. S. [both Ferdinand David and Ignaz Moscheles were contemporary and well-known musicians]).

> Kraegen is a good man but major Serre is spoiled… His touch at the piano is fine, but his playing is ugly and lacks fantasy. It is too bad for him! I played several sonatas of Beethoven, but neither Becker nor Kreagen found any satisfaction in them…their education is more concentrated toward the virtuoso [music] than toward the true music (August, 1841 C.S.).

A reading of the couple's dairies shows, as far as I could see, that the word "aesthetic" does not appear, but that they often describe artistic value judgments of their own and others' compositions and how the compositions were performed.[26] It is not a bold proposition that to suggest that this was a rule. Aesthetics were rarely if ever mentioned in other contexts than in public cultural and philosophical discourse. But within this sphere we find, on the other hand aesthetic ideas and expositions in in Huray and Day's anthology (1981). In the musicologist Bojan Bujić's similar anthology for the period between 1851 and 1912 there is also a flood of discussion around aesthetics.[27] The word also appears

---

[26]It is often more rewarding to cite negative value judgments than positive ones. Here are longer examples of both. Clara Schumann writes: "Sunday the 12th David held a dinner for Liszt…Liszt played, as soulfully as ever, even if it was sometimes tasteless, which one can especially accuse his own compositions of… a chaos of dissonances, the flamboyance, an endlessly present murmuring in the deepest Bass and the highest discant together, boring introductions, etc. …as a player however he astonished me in the extreme in his concert on the 13th, and especially in the Don Juan Fantasie." ["Sonntag d.12 gab David dem Liszt ein Dinée… Liszt mag spielen wie er will, geistvoll ist es immer, wenn auch manchmal geschmacklos, was man aber ganz besonders seinen Compositionen vorwerfen kann… ein Caos von Dissonanzen, die grellsten, ein immerwährendes Gemurmel im tiefsten Bass und höchsten Diskant zusammen, langweilige Introductionen etc.… als Spieler hat er mich aber in seinem Concerte am 13sten in das höchste Erstaunen gesetzt, und ganz besonders in der Don Juan Fantasie"] (Schumann and Schumann 1987, 197).

[27]Among the excerpts in Huray and Day 1981 can be mentioned Francois Joseph Fetis's 1838

naturally in the writings of Swedish music journalists. In the previously mentioned work of Abraham Mankell, *aesthetics* appears in the title of his 1849 book *Blickar i musikens inre helgedom. Ett bidrag till tonkonstens Ästhetik* [*Glimpses into the Inner Sanctum of Music: a contribution to the Aesthetics of Tonal Art*], and in his music history from 1864, for example:

> With considerable success, Swedes have worked within the symphonic style. A. Lindblad has also allowed us to hear symphonies of quite different stylistic traits. In one he is reminiscent of Beethoven's famous *Eroica*. Thoughts are presented without plagiarism, an aesthetic reminiscence of Beethoven's smoldering brushstrokes (as cited after Ander 2000, 510).

The word also appeared in the music reviews of the large daily papers. The question is—and it is a question to which we shall soon return—to what degree did the contents of these performances in general play a role for how music was used and understood.

The music that was performed in salons was, as we have seen, not just instrumental. People sang a great deal and from a broad *bourgeois* repertoire that consisted of arranged folk songs, newly composed tunes in folk music style, *Lieder* of various levels of complexity, popular songs, arias from musicals, vaudeville, operettas and operas.[28] All of this music lay generally close to the instrumental salon music's structure and content. The song tradition that we studied earlier with the help of Stoljar, *remains, in other words, just as beloved and meaningful during the nineteenth century.*

Suspicion and devaluation of salon music from those who stood on the side of true art music, was therefore based on salon music's structure and content

---

review of music aesthetic's actual state as well as Eduard Krüger's 1842 discussion on Hegel's music philosophy. In Bujić 1988 we find again the work of Eduard Hanslick, August Wilhelm Ambros, Richard Wagner and Hermann Kretschmar among others. There are naturally many other important works that could be mentioned again because of their *general* importance for aesthetics: Friedrich von Schiller's *Über die ästhetische Erziehung des Menschen (1790)*, Arthur Schopenhauer's *Die Welt als Wille und Vorstellung (1819)*, and Hegel's *Vorlesungen über die Aesthetik* held in the 1820s.

[28] Concerning folk music it seems at first glance strange that in some bourgeois circles there was an early interest in genuine folk music, which should by rights have found its place even farther down the aesthetic scale. This music, on the other hand, was not threatening to the "higher" music. It was different and "original" and it could be refined and arranged. It was also a musical source that was appropriated in the construction of a national identity. The search for an original national folk music was carried out with similar motives from the end of the eighteenth century onward. This process began earlier in German speaking areas than, for example, in Norway, and created different results depending on the situations that prevailed in respective nations. For example, were there German composers who wrote music as German as Edvard Grieg's music was Norwegian? The search for a national identity was as a rule, both directed *inwards, toward* the culture in question, and *outwards, at* another culture or land. For an overview over nationalism and folk music in music history writings, see Allen 1962, 208-13.

and was seen as an entirely too mundane commodity often played in contexts that worked against a full concentration on the music. It had doubtful educational value and was much less worthy and perhaps even harmful to play and to listen to. Few granted it any measure of aesthetic value. Sponheuer also claimed that the contemporary players commented from different points of departure on the way music was dichotomizing:

> Nägeli sees a double development, "upwards towards ideal music" and "downwards toward a popular music"… Schumann thought that he saw in Meyerbeer's *Hugonots*… and in Mendelssohn's *Paulus* the contemporary paradigmatic personification of the Poetic and the Non-Poetic, at the same time as Liszt characterized Tone Poets and Music Producers as opposites of one another (Sponheuer 1989, 178f).[29]

Sponheuer also piles up the invective that originated from the pens of important and respected music journalists. They wrote among other things, about salon music as "fusel oil," a smelly byproduct of home-made alcohol production, "a plague," "weeds," "sounding boredom," "non-music," or like the "licentious Parisian and Italian Opera music" (Sponheuer 1989, 180). Despite their opinions, as we have seen, salon music was very popular and respected. It was music that few if any claimed would contain an 'aesthetic addition" (æII), rather more likely a music that among other things, decorated and functioned as recreation. Listening was therefore better described as *entertainment rather than as work* in this context. And this was true of a great deal of music by composers who could be found within the temples of art music. Music of Mozart, Beethoven, Schubert, Schumann, Brahms, and others was *also regularly* performed in salons.[30]

---

[29] Nägeli sieht eine doppelte Entwicklung der Instrumentalmusik „aufwärts zur Idealitet" und "abwärts zur Popularität des Divertissementsstyls"… Schumann glaubt in Meyerbeers "Hugenotten"… und Mendelsohns "Paulus"… die paradigmatischen Verkörperungen des Poetischen und Nicht-Poetischen seiner Zeit zu erkennen, die Liszt in allgemeiner Weise durch Entgegensetzung des "Tondichters" und des Musik-Fabrikanten… zur charakterisieren versucht.

[30] Neitzert believes that it was in the interest of composers who wanted to show their works' autonomy not to write music that was too simple:—"The conventional now develops the stigma of the trivial, the dillitantesque connected to the dishonorable" ["Dem Konventionellen wurde nun das Stigma der Trivialen, dem Dilletantischen das der Unwürdigen angehängt"] (Sponheuer 1989, 169). Here one can also suspect the thought that if a large number of people liked a simple piece then it must be qualitatively inferior (the composers of the twentieth century went in an opposite direction: that in a modernist spirit, Schönberg, Webern, Boulez, etc., wrote music whose complexity has seldom been matched). On the other hand, as Adorno noted, not even an uncompromising composer like Wagner in the nineteenth century could some prevent parts of his grandiosly conceived opera works from becoming popular: "Already in Wagner's lifetime, in flagrant contradiction to his own Program, flashy numbers were taken out of the context of the total work like the Feuerzauber and Wotan's farewell, the Ride of The Valkyries, Liebestod and Karfreitagszauber (Good Friday Sorcerer) were chiseled out, arranged and popularized, showing the idea that the Music drama's equilibrium and distribution depending on the prudent placement of every piece, is not extrinsic; the collapse into fractured pieces witnessed the fractured nature of the Whole. It is readable in style categories that describe the conflict of their Romantic and positivistic

The works that were chosen of course were not long and complicated, but rather manageable songs and shorter instrumental pieces of the "type" of Beethoven's *Menuett*, Schubert's *Marche militaire*, and so forth. This music could be used in a similar way to the rest of the salon music

There was thus a problem for those who wanted to slander salon music. Composers who populated the highest Parnassus of art music also wrote pieces performed in the salon. On February 24th, 1838, when Robert Schuman wrote he had "composed the little 'Traümerei' thing" he intended to place his small pieces in *Kinderszenen* (Op.15) high above the sphere of normal salon music, but he surely could never have imagined that these very pieces would be some of the most popular music in salons, cafés and restaurants and at pianos in private homes.[31] Schumann chose the title, *Träumerei*, to show how he wanted the listener to experience the piece. For instance the first chord comes on the second beat and lasts a dotted half note thus minimizing the effect of the energetic quarter-note upbeat (c-f), and the main phrase's highest note is reached on the unstressed beat two in the next measure. It sounds like a dream.[32]

At the same time that Schumann wrote music that could be adapted for different groups and social situations, he also wrote an equal amount of music that was seen as of the highest level, such as his symphonies and string quartets.[33] In

---

Elements." ["Daß schon zu Wagners Lebzeiten, in flagrantem Widerspruch zu seinem Programm, aus den Totalwerken Glanznummern wie Feuerzauber und Wotans Abschied, Walkürenritt, Liebestod und Karfreitagszauber herausgebrochen, arrangiert und populär wurden, ist den Musikdramen, deren Gleichgewichtsverteilung jene Abschnitte klug einschätzt, nicht äußerlich; der Zerfall in Bruchstücke bezeugt die Brüchigkeit der Totalität. Sie ließe in Stilkategorien sich aussprechen als der Konflikt des romantischen und des positivistischen Elements" (Adorno 1952, 68). It was just these pieces that also were played in restaurants and were repeated in volumes that decorated pianos, or as Huyssen commented: "The logic of this disintegration lead to Schönberg's modernism on the one hand and to the Best of Wagner on the other. Where high art itself is sucked into the commodification, modernism is born as a reaction and a defense" (Huyssen 1986, 41).

[31] Apparently few pieces have been so often analyzed as this one. The structure, 24 bars, is visually simple but at the same time throughgly worked out. The elegaic theme, a rising bow movement, is repeated six times. Apart from places in some sections where the middle voices imitate the theme, the whole piece's effect is built on repetition and variation. One main idea is the variation of the pivotal notes at the same time as the harmony increases in complexity.

[32] Edward Lippman has thoroughly discussed the titles that Schumann gave his pieces. On the one hand Schumann suggested that the titles of the pieces, the story and the ideas that the music wants to tell, came after the pieces were composed. On the other hand, Lippman shows that also the non-musical sources of inspiration could change for one and the same work (Lippman 1964, 313). The first movement of Schumann's F sharp minor Sonata was originally conceived as a *Fandango* (Lippman 1964, 314).

[33] Schumann's opus list shows a large socially affected realm of variation that was not untypical for other contemporary composers. Here we have education music for children and youth, songs for different kinds of choirs. We find for example opus 29 "Three poems...for multiple-voiced Song," opus. 55 Five Songs ...for mixed Choir," opus 65 "Ritornelle... for four-voiced Mens' choir," opus 69 "Romance for Womens' Voices" ["Drei Gedichte... für mehrstimmigen Gesang," op. 55

the public discourse *Träumerei* of Schumann was and is, however, an example of a piece that could be defended as art music, while *The Virgin's Prayer* by Badazewska is not (see Ch. 3, footnote 25). But however one argued, whatever value system one employed, it was not possible to place an *objective* stamp like "art music"/ "aesthetic music" or "non-art music" / "non-aesthetic music" on any piece. Music's meaning in the final analysis *is* subjective; the individual's background, education and judgments about how the music was played, used, and in what context it appeared, always guarantee the existence of a subjective experience.

And because it wasn't possible to set up any universally applicable structural dividing lines between art and non-art, it became necessary to preach purely moral judgments and to use positive or negative judgments.[34] Put another way, ethical judgments were more stable than aesthetic ones. For those who stood on the side of "high music" (theorists and critics, philosophers, composers, trained musicians and amateurs, and others,) it was problematic that music was partly seen as something sensual and earthy, partly something eternal and heavenly. On the one hand they had entertaining salon music suitable for a varying listening processes, and on the other, a classic-romantic symphony appropriate for concentrated and structural listening.[35] This tension between the everyday and the eternal can be illustrated with the following nineteenth century example from a cloister:

> A five-year-old child sang an aria that was thoroughly woven with emotional cadences, sighs and trills more or less in a style between Meyerbeer and Verdi, and the nun's surging accompaniment on the piano with diminished seventh chords in tremulando, so that the contrast between this worldly way of listening, demonic lascivious music and the nun's world-rejecting facial expression and clothing, as well as the singer's childhood purity rattled me to my very bones (Sponheuer 1989, 181f).

Fünf Lieder…für gemischten Chor", Op. 65 "Ritornelle… für vierstimmigen Männergesang", op. 69 "Romanzen für Frauenstimmen"] and so forth. We also find music that was perfect for salons like the *Fantasiestücke*—originally called *Soiréestücke* [sic!]—for clarinet and piano (Op.73) and *Fünf Stücke im Volkston* for cello and piano (Op.102). It is clear that one often had a problem in assigning a *Lied*'s place within this hierarchy. If, for example, as late as 1839 Schumann wrote that until that point he had always placed song compositions as lower than instrumental music, and never seen them as great art, would soon begin to write a number of *Lieder* of his own. As Edler (1982, 213) writes one saw by this period that this was a continuation of his instrumental music.

[34]Sponheuer judges Wagner's opinions about French opera as a high point: "Perhaps among this type of unsurpassed formulations by Wagner the "great Parisian Opera Whore" can be considered the culmination." ["Vielleicht darf die in ihrer Art unübertreffende Formulierung Wagners von der 'grossen pariser Opernhure' hier als Gipfelpunkt gelten"] (Sponheuer 1989, 182). As the reader will notice, the question of music's influence on a person's morality continuously appears. It was not only relevant in the nineteenth century but even in classical Greece. And who has not run into it concerning the music of the young in the twentieth century?

[35]See also the discussions on different ways of listening in Edström 1987 as well as in Stockfelt 1988, who discusses different "listener modes" during the late eighteenth and nineteenth centuries.

As before, one cannot exclude that people who were educated to experience the 'aesthetic addition' æII, could listen to and use selected salon music in such a way that something aesthetic appeared. There was also salon music and similar entertainment music that looked toward the "high" music, and was described as uplifted entertainment music [*gehobene Unterhaltungsmusik*]. The pieces that did not reach so far remained in the inferior category of *Kapellmeistermusik*.[36]

The "highest" and "truest" instrumental and vocal music was made up of Works in a league of their own, a music that therefore was to have an inner, eternal super-cultural quality. It existed, therefore, for itself—almost apart from all social contexts.

From 1850 Towards the Twentieth Century

Even though both Schumanns were musicians and composed music, it was only Robert Schumann who played an important role as a music journalist and critic. In these roles he exerted his influence on his readers, an audience that included many writers and composers. Robert Schumann grew up in a literary home and in his youth was strongly affected by the new romantic literature. His reading included Johann Wackenroder's novel about the romantic composer Berlinger and E.T.A. Hoffmann's stories about musicians and composers, and, above all, the works of Jean Paul[37] whose 1804 "Vorschule der Ästhetik" had a strong effect on Schumann.[38]

Schumann was a member, in other words, of the first *bourgeois* generation familiar with the word *aesthetic*. The word, as we have seen, seldom appeared in newspapers or magazines. It formed part of a general philosophical and a higher cultural discourse. In an early study of why people are so sensitive to critique concerning questions of taste, Schumann writes that when it comes to "aesthetic objects," differing viewpoints are most painful and personal. This means that if one criticizes a work, *one indirectly criticizes the author personally.*

---

[36] Observe that art music composers now and then wrote music outside the "pure" art music frame. To give three examples of differing grades of debatablity: *Valse triste* of Jean Sibelius (restaurant music?), "Att älska i vårens tid" of Gösta Nystroem (Tin Pan Alley?), Anders Hillborg compositions on texts of Eva Dahlgrens (pop?).

[37] See further in the literary historian Christian Brantner's work (1991) concerning how Schumann was influenced by the contemporary literature and also on the similarities between him and the fictional musicians and composers in contemporary novels.

[38] In Schumann's youth, Hegel held much-discussed lectures on aesthetics, and different publications appeared in whose titles the word aesthetic appeared, like Weisse's 1830 *System of Aesthetics as a Science of the Idea of Beauty* [*System der Ästhetik als Wissenschaft von der Idee der Schönheit*] and Müller's *Ästhetisch-Historische Einleitung in der Wissenschaft der Tonkunst* and many others. Of the last, Edler writes: "A great deal of Schumann's music-historical knowledge is based on this Work." ["Auf diesem Werk beruhen im wesentlichen Schumanns musikhistorische Kenntnisse"] (Edler 1982, 19).

Here we have a problematic question that needs to be examined before we can study the twentieth-century attitude toward aesthetics. Do we not see a picture emerging of what we could call an "aesthetic sphere," a group within the *bourgeoisie* that began to change their way of listening? Formulated a different way: were conditions within music culture gradually developing so that the "aesthetic addition" began to expand? And, one wonders, how large *was* the group for which this increased "addition" may have been valid? For Schumann naturally was not alone as a "literary" composer. There were many similarly multifaceted persons such as Berlioz, Liszt and Wagner, for example. To this list we can add hundreds of nineteenth-century composers who also wrote reviews and articles, and taught. This large collective of nineteenth-century composers and writers created from then on both a music that aimed for the highest Parnassus and a music that was gauged to be nearer or even placed within the world of the lower salon music. As every western music history describes in detail, an enormous amount of music was written during the nineteenth century. Materially, the *bourgeois* class was on the rise and the range of concerts and operas in the larger cities improved. Instrument building and publishing industries enjoyed continued success. The composers of art music entered as Lady Music's high priests into a capitalist production of goods, where many different cogs were needed to keep the wheels of production turning. Composers seldom managed to live on the proceeds of their compositions, but also worked as teachers, musicians, directors and music journalists. Those who succeeded with the public and the critics could hope that their works were printed and given out in different settings and arrangements. They hoped, also, that their musical capital would translate into a higher social status, raising their chances for a better standard of living. The music world in relation to other systems in Luhmann's sense became a more expanded system.

The language of music also expanded to include new stylistic (rhythmical, melodic, harmonic, sounding, etc.) solutions which were tried, rejected or accepted according to the time, place and public. While the musically educated connected music's style with its function during the previous century, now one could, more clearly than before, identify individual composers through their background and personal music style. A *Nocturne* by Frederic Chopin *sounded* different from an *Intermezzo* of Johannes Brahms. Richard Wagner's Introduction to *Tristan und Isolde* was not mistaken for the Overture to *The Masked Ball* of Giuseppe Verdi, and so on. These composers competed in a Bourdieuian sense for the spiritual resources that were available to the art music field. Personal style was a new element to use in this struggle.

As the art music field expanded and more could be included within it, it was also integrated with other artistic fields. These other fields experienced parallel developments and had their own influence. It can therefore be enriching to explore Pierre Bourdieu's (1996) analysis of how literature developed a relatively autonomous field during the same period. We will find striking similarities in our narrative.

It is not just the fact that the public did not buy the literature that it "should," but also that one assumed that the true literature (like music) was written for Art's sake—not for the immediate needs of the market, or to support oneself. Although "higher" and "lower" music were both written for the market, and one can in principle treat them both as goods (compare below p. 188). Bourdieu shows that *at the same time* that the literary field's economy expanded, a new generation of writers around the middle of the nineteenth century challenged traditional values. Originality and opposition to the old way became tools with whose help the *avant garde* established themselves within the literary field. Even if this process did not always directly generate economic possibilities for them, they were compensated with a greater cultural and literary capital, which could be spent in the newly established areas within this literary field:

> Some writers go as far as to see in immediate success 'the mark of intellectual inferiority'... the artist cannot triumph on the symbolic terrain except by losing on the economic terrain (at least in the short run), and vice versa (at least in the long run) (Bourdieu 1996, 83).

Built into the same process, as Bourdieu writes, there is also the thought that an artist, writer, composer, etc., should provide something different—an idea that can be seen as a propagation of the image of the genius. These thoughts coupled themselves with a general belief in progress during the nineteenth century, perhaps most noticeably in the field of natural sciences. New theories and techniques were applied directly in community life. Discoveries were made both in technique and art. The important thing was to never stand still.[39]

Bourdieu writes that Gustave Flaubert within the art of the novel and Charles Baudelaire within poetry could create a different literary experience for the time, a world where form, style and content came closer to one another. Poetry, wrote Baudelaire, has no other goal than itself (Bourdieu 1996, 106).

Statements like these were also made by instrumental music's promoters, and with greater believability, because instrumental music's problematical semantic status made it more "suitable" to transport people outside of the everyday. "Suitable" should be understood here in the sense that a culture's structural forces could socialize people to understand music as a bearer of the inexpressible or of "eternal beauty" as Jean Paul formulated it in Romantic terms (Tadday 1999, 21).

---

[39]Compare with Allen 1962, 245-260 for a description of the various ideas that led to the view that development and progress were interchangeable concepts. Allen writes that the French philosopher Fontanelle "[was] one of the first writers... to use the word progress in the modern sense" (Allen 1962, 245).

From Bourdieu's analysis it follows that the literary field, within which individual literary judgments and methods of reception flourished, grew up earlier than similar fields in music culture. When one read a poem of Baudelaire or the prose of Flaubert, the reader could place these experiences within an aesthetic field. The different fields of art consolidated one another and had a *general and recurring effect for the vision of all cultural activities and their value*. Art (literature, music, painting, etc.), could supply something over and above the everyday. But as has just been mentioned, instrumental music could be experienced as an autonomous world for itself to a *higher degree* than literature. Music's structure initially did not supply any more exact message or meaning, but one could sink into it or rise up into it in experiences that were difficult to describe. Listening to music this way could be seen as a work in itself. It follows therefore that even if the process that is described by Bourdieu is similar, the "aesthetic addition" can hardly be exactly the same within literature and music.[40]

Different Ways of Listening

The speed of development of the process that has been described here was naturally different in different places in Europe. It is a given that a proportionately larger number of people in cities like Vienna, Paris, London, Leipzig, etc, developed the habit of going to concerts and generally taking part in cultural life.[41] Though it came later, there was a similar general change in cultural life in nordic cities such as Oslo, Göteborg, and Helsingfors. We have seen, within music culture, including art music, that some forms of music did be higher, others lower. At the same time, these differentiations were seen to not correspond to purely artistic differentiations that could be expressed with an aesthetic choice of words, but taste and opinion had also a moral and ethical dimension in that *the higher music*

---

[40]Bujić (1988, 13) comments that Schumann "has caused a lot of trouble by his observation that 'the aesthetics of one art is the same as that of another, only in a different medium'." Bujić also gives a long quotation from Grillparzer that describes the differences in experience between different artforms and comments: "Grillparzer's opinion is very different and much nearer the truth" (Bujić 1988, 13). Note that this process which Bourdieu describes unfolds at different speeds in different countries. At the end of the century in Sweden authors like Strindberg and Heidenstam appear not infrequently in aesthetic arguments in writings of different kinds. Concerning Strindberg see for example the nine articles from the 1880s that are collected under the title *Estetiskt i Likt och Olikt [Aesthetics in Similarity and Difference]* (Strindberg 1913). This is not to say that the concept for them was unambiguous, but readers at any rate eventually became familiar with the word. Heidenstam introduces for example the essay "Inbillingens logik" from 1892 with the words: "Because I am speaking of imagination, you could perhaps call the example aesthetic. I do not completely understand this foreign adjective, in fact it has never succeeded in giving me anything of serious significance."

[41]Apparently Leipzig had, in relation to its size, the richest bourgeois musical offerings among these cities. The city's conservatory contributed to this, as well as the symphony orchestra, and the Gewandhaus orchestra. Leipzig was visited by a stream of music students from the Nordic countries (compare with Ander 2000, 193ff).

was represented by social groups that stood for economic, political, and moral-religious power. It also emphasized the interplay between the way in which one should use or listen to music and music's structure.

Even within the world of higher music clear differences in valuation existed. In the German speaking areas one talked about the composers that represented the old and the new.[42] Johannes Brahms, according to Robert Schumann, belonged to the future (it was apparently self-evident for Schumann—and has long remained so—that all great masters spoke German as their mother tongue).[43] Even to the influential music critic Eduard Hanslick, Brahms was a composer who created new paths. Brahms' music supported Hanslick's main argument in his aesthetic manifesto *Vom Musikalisch-Schönen (1854)* (Hanslick 2003). The book has a subtitle that is seldom given: *Ein Beitrag zur Revision der Ästhetik der Tonkunst* [*A contribution to the revision of the aesthetics of composition*], and it goes without saying that this is an attack on the romantic way of interpreting music as the language of feeling.[44]

Hanslick's famous statement that the contents of music are sounding, moving forms did not mean that he closed his ears to music's ability to call forth feelings, but that he ignored the importance of feelings for the experience of music. He stated that different generations of musicians had reacted in different ways to the same music (examples are given from Haydn, Mozart and Beethoven), but he contended that this had no effect on the value of the music or "on the aesthetic enjoyment that was caused by these works' beauty and originality." Hanslick believed therefore that music's effect on feelings had neither necessity, constancy, nor exclusivity, which was characteristic of every phenomenon that could lay the foundation for an aesthetic principle (compare with Bujić 1988, 17). A Beethoven sonata should therefore not be listened to using an emotional listening mode.

---

[42]Groups do not always follow the lines of division that we find natural today. Compare with Dahlhaus's discussion of Franz Brendler's contemporary classification, "the rare combination of Wagner, Liszt and Berlioz in one "New German School" ["der seltsamen Koppelung von Wagner, Liszt und Berlioz zu einer 'Neudeutschen Schule'"] (Dahlhaus 1988, 208f).

[43]Schumann wrote for example, concerning Niels Gade's overture *Nachklänge von Ossian* that the surrounding countries were in the process of freeing themselves from German influence ("ausgeprägter Nordischer Character"), but that no land yet had masters that could compare to "our greats" (Edler 1982, 34).

[44]The work was published in seven editions during the nineteenth century and was translated for the first time into English in 1891 (Bujić 1988, 12 [first Swedish translation was in 1955]). As can be seen in Bujić, there were already many contemporary contrary accounts to Hanslick's version, among them A.W. Ambros's *Die Grenzen der Musik und Poesie* from 1855 and Franz Brendel's *Die Ästhetik der Tonkunst* from 1857. The latter argued for an empirical point of departure: " Our first concern is not with philosophical investigations; on the contrary, musical practice must provide the point of departure from which we embark on our search for more exact knowledge. This is the path trodden by all sciences today. A similar method in the aesthetics of music promises that problems will be given their proper solution, one which we have been seeking for a long time" (as cited in Bujić 1988, 131).

A TIME OF CONSOLIDATION

Hanslick's opinions fall in line and march behind the art music column: music means itself, its ideas are musical, music's form is its content, and so forth.[45] The highest instrumental music was that which did not entice its listeners to any non-musical thoughts, but was rather—as it had been formulated regularly since the early nineteenth century—absolute. And we could conclude that music that apparently did generate non-musical associations (salon music, for example) could not pretend to have an aesthetic status. But Hanslick and his followers' Papal Bull struck down even Wagner's operas on similar stylistic grounds. They saw this music as too emotional and formless.[46] In the heat of battle, they automatically were suspicious of art music that was driven by a non-musical program, for example Franz Liszt's programmatic orchestra works, or—as they saw it—entirely too melodic and pompously orchestrated symphonic music of Tchaikovsky (as in *Romeo and Juliet*).

The fight between these two teams continued but did not lead to the banishment of Wagner's, Liszt's, and Tchaikovsky's music from the art music and aesthetic fellowship, even though their music often landed on the lowest rungs of the ladder.[47]

---

[45] Even for another very influential music writer and theorist like Adolf Bernhard Marx form and content were one and the same. Marx who contrary to Hanslick, tied himself to Hegel's great theoretical structure, had to struggle, therefore, with Hegel's thoughts about history as a dialectical process. Hegel was skeptical of much of the music after Beethoven and thought that art music was doomed to an substantial decline. One can hope, Hegel writes, that art increasingly rises and perfects itself, but its form has ceased to answer the spirit's greatest needs (cf. Dahlhaus 1988, 238). Thus, it was this fact that resulted in the difficulty for the subsequent Hegelians (like A. B. Marx) to reconcile their own belief in art's gradual progress with Hegel's conviction that art's greatest period *had already taken place*. The result was, therefore, writes Dahlhaus, that "the passion of progress and the delusion of imitation" are so entangled with one another that they cannot be sorted out (Dahlhaus 1988, 356).

[46] Hanslick wriggles his way out of the problem of the clearly semantic content in vocal music: "However firmly we must insist, in our investigation of 'content' in music, that all works with literary texts in fact contradict the pure concept of music, we must never overlook the fact that the masterpieces of vocal music are indispensable in appreciating the substance [*Gehalt*] of music" (as cited in Bujić 1988, 38).

[47] In Edström 1993 it is reported for example that the leading music critic in Goteborg from the end of the 1910s, Julius Rabe, propagandized for Mozart and Beethoven but also for Carl Nielsen's music as absolute. Music of Berlioz, Richard Strauss, Wilhelm Peterson-Berger were made suspect in different ways. Of Wagner's Prelude to *Tristan and Isolde,* Rabe could comment "A type like Richard Wagner belongs to the helpless past... his music is supported only by purely sensual emotional dynamics, and when as in *Tristan*, he finds himself in an erotic atmosphere, one cannot completely separate his music from being a *kind of musical pornography*, and our moral fanatics should be glad that the great majority of the audience's listening to Tristan enjoys only the acoustical sensuousness" (Göteborgs Handels- och Sjöfartstidning 27/2 1919 [my italics]). For a fine description of the relationship between newly written art music and the existing musical perspectives in Sweden during the 1920s see Broman 2000.

Exactly as it did in the literary field, though later, an *avantgarde* emerged within the art music field. This modernist movement with Arnold Schönberg at its head felt Brahms was a progressive compared with the emotional Tchaikowsky.

Hanslick's way of listening to and contemplating music inspired those who were interested in the structure of music to develop their musical theoretical tools further. Music was understood through the process of describing more and more refined technical, especially harmonic methods (for example Riemann's functional analysis), that were seen to be value neutral. These different methods (especially form analysis, and melodic and rhythmical analysis systems) fit like a hand in a glove with the opinion that music was a self-contained, autonomous language. It was not at all about analyzing music's structure from a "contextual perspective" where one primarily relied on the music's intended use. Earlier centuries' functional perspectives had now been exchanged for an aesthetic-analytical perspective. Music theoreticians and music historians were interested more and more in the piece's formal development and its organic structure.[48] These methods loaned the analysis of music's structure an *aura of objectivity, at the same time as the aesthetic judgments that were passed on music in and of itself were experienced as objective.* It is likely that this fact has generated an acceptance among the general public that "professional" music analyses and opinions about a particular piece's value are more objective and reliable than, for example, an art critic's analysis and opinion of a painting (compare with footnote 3).

On the other hand music was explained—and here naturally we are talking about music that one knew or suspected to have non-musical content—with the help of verbal "translations." But, as we have seen, even supposed absolute music could be described in the same way by adding a program afterwards, a poem or even an illustrative title or by interpreting the important thematic ideas metaphorically as representing feelings, abstract or concrete phenomena, etc. This last-mentioned method of description became a "business idea" near the end of the nineteenth century in the form of Concert Guides that described music in a hermeneutic spirit and had one or two important themes written out in notation.[49]

---

[48]Compare with the musicologist Jim Samson who writes how music theory's development supported the aesthetic project: "Music analysis was instituted at the turn of the nineteenth and twentieth centuries, its 'historical moment' arriving rather more than a century after the 'historical moment' of aesthetic theory" (Samson 1999, 42). Allen writes in detail about the relationship between a) evolutionary theory, b) theories about biological development and c) theories about societal change in different stages, theories like those from the nineteenth century all came to play a very great role for the writing of music history and the understanding of the value of different forms of music (Allen 1962, 91-129).

[49]The hermeneutic school of thought is associated today mostly with Hermann Kretschmar who in 1887 published his first *Konzertführer* or Concert Guides. Similar works were published by many different writers and came out in very large editions (I see in the *Konzertführer* that I happen to own, "Knauers Konzertführer" by Gerhart von Westman [1951], that my copy is from the thirteenth edition!).

This of course was partly motivated by the idea that a concert public needed to be educated in the right way. William Weber wrote:

> One of the most basic presumptions established in the classical music tradition by the middle of the nineteenth century was that listeners needed to learn about great works and great composers—indeed, be educated in the subject (Weber 1999, 353).

This way of listening to music's developing form and concentrating on music's structure has sometimes been called an autonomous mode of reception. It was principally easier to apply such a listening mode if one often had the chance to hear similar music and even the same piece several times. The greater the musical competence, the more likely it was that the person could apply this mode of listening, as well as an emotional mode of listening —if he or she wished and the musical structure allowed. The reverse did not happen automatically, however. The perception of form was made easier through a gradual development of a standard repertoire. One became familiar with the music and could better follow the music's development because one did not need to spend all of one's concentration on every new musical idea or shape, when one already had many of them "chunked" in ones' memory. It was especially possible for those who, for example, had played a Beethoven symphony in a four-hand arrangement or maybe studied it from a pocket score. The most common technical forms for a movement: ABA form and its variations, sonata form, rondo, etc., rewarded this way of formal listening.[50]

In all of this discussion of the various ways of listening it is sometimes forgotten that the *soundscape* of a large orchestra was a new phenomenon in and of itself that few had experienced. The sounding experience of a church organ was something else. It can therefore be difficult to understand how befuddling it could have been for a nineteenth-century person to listen to orchestral music. The sound milieu was completely different from the daily sound world. The public— listeners—began with no point of reference when meeting the orchestral. The Swedish composer Gunnar Wennerberg said that at this time when an orchestra began to play, he didn't know where he was.[51]

As has been mentioned before it was almost an obligation for bourgeois women to play music. Women were as diligent concertgoers as men and participated equally in salons. It is therefore reasonable to assume that they had as good a chance of developing a mode of formal listening as men. But at the

---

[50] As can be seen in this study, we have, however, strong grounds to doubt that formal listening quickly became a more normal way to listen (see below p. 169).

[51] Ander 2000, 342. Compare with Edström 1996, 589 for similar comments at the beginning of the twentieth century. Oberve that organs in churches could be experienced as substitutes for orchestras. Already in the middle of the nineteenth century, however, there were only organs in about 40% of Swedish churches.

same time they were regarded by men—and some probably also played out this culturally proscribed role—to be more emotional and easily moved. This suggests therefore that the musically interested women could both apply a structural and an emotional mode of listening. This means that both as music producers and listeners, they could have used music in a richer way than men (male musicians, critics and musicologists/historians notwithstanding).

These observations point to a contradictory cultural message about womens' musical potential that the generations growing up after the eighteenth century were forced to relate to. Music's domain *was* Lady Music. Music was a feminine word. But at the same time a woman had only a narrow entrance into the male working world and was seen as less well-favored even when it came to having compositional talents The exceptions that society accepted during the nineteenth century were unmarried instrumental virtuosi, singers, and piano teachers.[52] The career categories to which women were denied access for the longest were as conductors, and within the world of humanities, as philosophers. This clearly shows that the official aesthetic project's world was male and continued to be so even during most of the following century.

It is, however, difficult to ignore that a piece could be listened to in different ways. It was *possible* to apply a purely intellectual/cognitive mode of listening to a happy short waltz, whose first part was built around *one* musical idea (a descending chord with an upbeat and a concluding phrase) that is repeated with small variations (like *Edelweiss* of Vanderbeck).

It was also possible to apply an emotional mode of listening to an organ fugue by a Baroque composer, a form that tends to promote structural listening. If these similar cases are possible to consider, then in a discussion of how people normally listened to music one cannot begin from these unusual scenarios, but rather from the modes of listening that people most *likely* were engaged in. It

---

[52]Concerning piano teachers see Öhrström 1987 as well as singers' social position in the Opera in Stockholm during the nineteenth century's first half, see Ingeborg Nordin Hennel 1997.

becomes necessary to have a discussion of different modes of listening that a) depart from the music's structure and length; b) note in what context the music is performed; and c) how and by whom; as well as d) take into account the listener's background and competence. These are the collaborative factors that contribute to a *reasonable judgment of how music was listened to and used.*

From this discussion one can, on the one hand, conclude that the above-mentioned melody "Edelweiss" is not terribly well-suited to a formal listening mode. The melody functions well as dance and entertainment music that does not lose much of its content with an inattentive listening mode. The melodic and rhythmic material are easily followed and the thematic ideas are repeated a number of times, so it makes very little difference if one is occasionally interrupted in the listening process. On the other hand, to take an example from Brahms, Hanslick's favorite composer, his Cello Sonata in E minor is a perfect example for a formal listening mode:

It becomes clear that every pair of measures creates a musical phrase. Each phrase that follows has at least one rhythmical form in common with the first phrase and thereafter with each other (a dotted quarter plus an eighth). Every measure leads melodically on: mm. 3 - 4 are a retrograde variant of mm. 1 - 2, while the F# in m. 4 functions as a bridge to mm. 5 - 6 after which two intervals of a ninth increase the melodic tension before the F#, in an upbeat quarter note motion, landing on B (where a sharp functions as a leading tone to B). At the same time, of course, on the harmonic plane, Brahms moves from the minor tonic via the double dominant to the dominant, which matches the respective melody notes E, F#, B. Thereafter the basic rhythm is repeated in two similar stepwise upward moving gestures, after which the motion is rhythmically condensed in mm. 13 -15 before the highpoint is reached in m. 16 (then four more measures follow before the piano overtakes the cello's leading role).

It follows therefore that it paid (and pays) for a listener of Hanslick's type to follow along in the process that musically is thought to have its "own inner" development, which did not hinder another listener from bathing in his own feelings, despite Hanslick's words of warning. For Hanslick, the structural/formal/autonomous mode of listening could also be described as an aesthetic way of listening. He apparently placed the immediate/emotional reception mode on a "lower" level.

The musically competent listener has a greater choice having to do with his or her background, education, and habits: he or she can change between different ways of listening. It is then a different matter that all modes of listening are a result of socio-cultural processes that also assigned different music various worldly values. That the highest art, whether we talk of music or literature, etc., had both a higher moralistic and artistic content than the lower art, was a socially inculcated truth. The higher was found within an aesthetic sphere, and was described therefore with words like "true, real, honest, eternal, beautiful, sublime" in relationship to the others and to lower arts. But from a sociological point of view it is not which came first, the chicken (art's structure) or the egg (human reception and understanding of it), but that an aesthetic mode of thinking and way of speaking is taking place within the same complicated socio-cultural process.[53] Bourdieu formulates it this way:

> The experience of the work of art as immediately endowed with meaning and value is an effect of the harmony between the two aspects of the same historical institution, the cultivated habitus and the artistic field, which mutually ground

[53] As a part of the creation of a particular aesthetic sphere for different arts, one must include also the different educational and general cultural projects that were begun so that the majority would have access to the music that was played within the aesthetic field. Those who acted in favor of this could be both liberal bourgeois organizations that organized lectures, concerts and so forth for the growing working class, and gradually also socialist parties and organizations, that with their sights set on the take-over of the socio-political power in society, wanted to insure that they had people within their leadership that would be able to manage this task. Within the bourgeois lecture organization *Arbetareinstitut i Göteborg* [*The Workers'* [sic!] *Institute in Göteborg*] an initiative begun in the 1890s to organize so called "peoples' concerts." The concert organization's purpose was not seen as completely idologically neutral, as can be seen from the fact that two plain clothes' police detectives were sent to make sure that nothing unforseen happened during the first concert (Edström 1997, 88). Compare with the section below "education and/or entertainment" on p. 205.

each other. Given that the work of art does not exist as such, meaning as an object symbolically endowed with meaning and value, unless it is apprehended by spectators possessing the *aesthetic disposition* and competence which it tacitly requires, one could say that it is in the eye of the aesthete which constitutes the work of art–but only… to the extent that it is itself the product of a long collective history (Bourdieu 1996, 289 [my italics]).[54]

If Dahlhaus talked earlier about aesthetic reflection, Bourdieu speaks in the quotation above of aesthetic disposition. Against this background and with the development described during the period of consolidation throughout the nineteenth century, we will now take a look at a new variant of aesthetic experience.

A Common Bourgeois Form

We have now combined different factors that came together to form the aesthetic field, and moreover discussed the different forms of music that were assigned different values, as well as the interplay between music's structure and its modes of reception, etc. It is clear that the conditions for the "aesthetic addition" (æII) still remain in place. But now there was a sense of an ongoing paradigmatic shift to call *all* forms of listening to music—at least those that were considered *artistically valuable* and of high musical value—as a *general aesthetic experience*, æIII. An important component of this music's meaning and value came to be seen as aesthetic. We understand now, also in keeping with Elias's ideas about the connection between socio- and psychogenesis, that the aesthetic disposition to which artistically interested people were dedicated, became a part of their personality, their social habitus.[55]

From this point on we will concern ourselves with three aesthetic experiences:

a) æI, the form described as a "special experience";

b) æII, the "aesthetic addition"; and

c) æIII, a general form of aesthetic experience.

---

[54]Bourdieu has been criticized for presenting this idea as original and as his own (compare with Tom Huhn's review of the article: "The Pure Gaze: Essays on Art" in *The Journal of Aesthetics and Art Criticism* 1994, 88).

[55]Elias uses this term in his book from 1939 (*Über den Process der Zivilisation* [*The Civilizing Process*]). Mennell comments: "By 'social habitus,' Elias means the level of personality characteristic which individuals share in common with fellow members of their social group. Since then, Pierre Bourdieu has used the word habitus extensively in his works" (Mennel 1989, 30). The concept, that actually goes back to Aristotle, is used, as mentioned, in Bourdieu as a sign for an individual's socialized way of thinking, interpreting and reacting, but can in the figurative sense also be used for occupational groups, social classes, etc. For a detailed discussion see Bourdieu 1984, 169-226.

The difficulty of differentiating between æII and æIII is due mainly to our obvious inability to experience other peoples' mental representations of æII and æIII except by analyzing the cultural processes that formed them. I depart admittedly from the prior assumption that people had an experience that they described. But this experience, using the language of music psychology, presupposes that the neurological is first registered and thereafter actively cognitively represented. One *has an experience of something that one understands as something.* This "something" is in our case the aesthetic, in all of its variants are representations that are difficult to unambiguously circumscribe and describe. The music psychologist Edwin Gordon uses the general notion *audiation* for the musical perceptual process:

> Audiation is to music what thought is to speech... Sound is not comprehended as music until it is audiated after it is heard (as cited in Gruhn 1998, 95).

Audiation is a mental process that happens when something "musical" is experienced as *something*, and only applies, of course, when we hear a recognizable musical theme like Beethoven's "destiny theme," or when we give a name to a chord like a diminished seventh, or when we hear internally, with our mental ears, how a clarinet sounds. In all of these cases we must have an inner representation of what should be described. To be able to explain how a clarinet sounds we must have an aural memory of it. It is therefore not unlike the music psychologist's point of departure in discussing the neurological-cognitive process of aesthetic experiences. The phenomena themselves, experienced as aesthetic, are nevertheless, as this book bears witness, a more complicated concept to circumscribe experientially. It is, simply put, easier to recognize the main motive of Beethoven's fifth symphony and describe it than to recognize æII (æIII etc.) and describe them.[56]

It is possible to read something similar in Dahlhaus's discussion where he writes that "aesthetic autonomy" is not the same as "the principle of art for art's sake" (Dahlhaus 1983, 146). The first concept he sees as connected to the forward-looking educated *bourgeoisie* and the latter with an artistic, bohemian subculture. The former seems therefore to be closest to our more general concept of æIII, and the latter is more exclusively æII. If this seems reasonable, Dahlhaus also believes that a general form of aesthetic contemplation eventually became standard behavior at concerts, and even at the opera. The amount of truth in this statement is, as this work has shown, problematical. That people learned to sit still

---

[56]The music psychologist Wilfried Gruhn points out that the more musical experiences one has anchored in consciousness and that are a part of the brain's neural network, the more successful one is in building new combinations and expressive forms, which are experienced as musically meaningful units placed in the musical context in which they belong. He adds: "Musical understanding means then, to be able to understand something as something; to understand an acoustical event as a Signal, a series of Tones as a Symbol (for instance: notated rests) or Structure (for instance, a triad)" ["Musikalisches Verstehen bedeutet dann, etwas als etwas erkennen zu können, ein akustisches Ereignis als Signal, eine Tonfolge als Zeichen (z.B: Pausenzeichen) oder Struktur (z.B. einen Dreiklang) aufzufassen"] (Gruhn 1998, 232).

at concerts when music was played, created a more likely environment for, but not a guarantee that a general "æII-standard" was present. On the other hand, the terms aesthetics and aesthetic gradually began to appear more often even outside the strict philosophical and art-critical discourse during the nineteenth century.

When "the aesthetic" was discussed there was a tendency, for cultural reasons, to deny any social interference. The experiences, it was believed, were caused by the music itself. In this simultaneously ongoing socio-cultural process, what culturally informed people labeled as aesthetic grew out of a network of thoughts and ideas. These ideas were in a symbiotic relationship with the preconditions (concentration on the piece of music as a Work, the expectation of attentive listening, etc.) whose presence in themselves were needed to reach an aesthetic experience. In these cases one could describe musical experiences as true, real, noble, artistic, emotionally deeply charged, etc. Gradually these experiences also came to be thought of as aesthetic. As both a condition for, and a consequence of, this was the contemporary development of the concept of the "aesthetic attitude" and one could also describe someone as having an "aesthetic disposition." People also spoke naturally of "aesthetic enjoyment" and "aesthetic experience," caught up in a language use that itself was a part of the same sociocultural process. As a part of this, philosophers tried to define and analyze how this multitude of aesthetic constructions could be understood and set in correct order.

But it is problematic to clearly delineate æIII from æII. It is already clear from the contemporary divisions in, let us say, a cognitive aesthetic area: *formal listening/autonomous aesthetic/absolute music*; and an emotional aesthetic area: *associative-emotional listening/heteronomous aesthetic/program music*. Today we know that an experience never is only cognitive or emotional but rather both, or more accurately as Damasio (1994) points out, even our feelings are driven of subcortical and cortical areas in the brain.[57]

---

[57] I have, in an earlier work, similarly tried to separate the aesthetic experience into two parts. I presuppose that the experience's "quality and depth" could be of a particular kind. I assumed that the "feeling-aesthetic" part could be more "limbic" in its nature and that the other, the 'cognitive-aesthetic" was more "corticodal." It was established also that it "has not been possible to find in the neurological literature any direct psycho physiological correlations to both of these types" (Edström 1986, 34). For a summary of the aesthetic experience from a broad art perspective see also the work of the idea historian Sören Kjørup (2000, 43-56). Aesthetic experience is difficult to describe because we have trouble measuring its duration in time. For even if we have assumed that it not only occurred when people listened to "attractively beautiful" music, but also when they heard "fear-inducingly violent" music, there is nothing to suggest that it is a state that lasted, so to say, from the first to the last measure. As a confirmation or a commentary to the difficulty of coming closer to a definition of æIII, the following quotation from Carl Dahlhaus may be of some use: "To expect from a basic understanding of Aesthetics of the nineteenth century, that it is easy to gasp, has a hard shell, and is clearly delineated, would be a sign of a lack of philosophical experience. And to try to fence in this very difficult concept in a structure of definitions, would, if it succeeded, lead to the suspicion that aesthetic categories, if they really existed in historical reality,

This is not only because it is difficult, perhaps impossible, to find a structural definition of what was art music and what was, for example, salon music, but above all, that those who were socialized in an aesthetic thought and experiential world probably also could experience an aesthetic dimension when listening to salon music. One example could be when one listened to the instrumental version of *Ave Maria* by Bach and Gounod, the aesthetic experience in this case, could be transferred from one field of art to the next, and within the field of music from one music style or genre to the next.

Time, of course, always brings change, which is why *sub specie æternitatis* has never been valid. We see therefore that the experience of æIII in no way was dependent on the individual piece of music. Even if all of this salon music was regarded as a "pure" commodity, and many of these of pleasant melodies were admittedly practically mass produced for the bourgeois music market, this does not necessarily reduce the melodies' individuality for a single listener. It was possible to experience æIII in Schumann's *Träumerei* as well as in the more commodified melody in Bach/Gounod.

In a similar way, learning to play an instrument was part of the aesthetic process. One learned to approach different music in different aesthetic ways. The active pursuit of playing music was another important factor, that was intimately interwoven with the general aesthetic process. Thus, in the middle of the century one probably played a "serious" Beethoven sonata in comparison with an "entertaining" popular waltz with different attitudes. Moreover, following Weber's conclusions, the former was probably more often likely to be played by academics, and the latter more often by a merchant's wife.

If we see history from a nineteenth-century perspective, it is conclusive therefore that æIII became a culturally socialized form of experience that could occur when the above discussed conditions (combinations of person-background-music-performance-place) were met. It was a form that gradually became possible and desirable to strive after for those who sought and wanted to display their well-rounded bourgeois education.

Eagleton, as we have seen, regards the aesthetic project as a *bourgeois* compensatory and dialectical *social* process. As the following quotation shows it is also possible to regard this process in a similar way from the *individual* (group

---

had collected a confusing abundance of thoughts and expectations, and would thus shrink into a systematization of banalities." ["Vom einem Grundbegriff der Ästhetik des 19. Jahrhunderts zu erwarten, dass er eindeutig, fest umrissen und genau begrenzt sei, wäre Zeichen einen Mangels an philosophischer Erfahrung. Und der Versuch, das schwer Greifbare in das Gehäuse einer Definition einzusperren, würde sich, wenn er gelänge, dadurch rächen, (dass ästhetische Kategorien, um die sich in der geschichtlichen Wirklichkeit ein verwirrender Reichtum an Gedanken und Vorstellungen gesammelt hat, in der Systematik zu unansehnlichen Banalitäten schrumpfen" (Dahlhaus 1988, 219).

individual) perspective, in that a pronounced and active interest in art can have had a similar individual function:

> In economic life, individuals are structurally isolated and antagonistic; at the political level there would seem nothing but abstract rights to link one subject to another. This is one reason why the 'aesthetic' realm of sentiments, affections and spontaneous bodily habits comes to assume the significance it does. Custom piety, intuition and opinion must now cohere an otherwise abstract, atomized social order (Eagleton 1990, 23).

For a considerable number this sought-after aesthetic experience became a form of compensation for an unsatisfying daily life.

There were naturally many other individual variations of motive for an "aesthetic" interest. On one hand some people completely lacked an interest in culture, but because of their socio-economic position, acted as if they were actively engaged in and appreciated the socio-cultural play. Then there were also those who were genuinely interested in music, which is why their way of using music was widely different from what it had been.

It can also be added that not only the professional musicians increased in number. The degree of specialization within the music corps also increased as well. While earlier it was expected that a prominent musician could also compose, we see during the nineteenth century examples of musicians like Richard Wagner or Johannes Brahms who begin to come close to the role of exclusively professional composers. This process gradually brings about not only a finer division among musicians, but also, as we shall see, a similar change among audiences.

More on Song's Underrated Importance

The great majority of the people met music mainly in the same ways that they had always met it. The way music was used also changed very slowly. One had ones' traditional music in parishes and on holidays. Folksongs were sung in Sweden, and some chapbook songs, psalms, melodies both German and Anglo-American (especially within different folk movements).[58] One could hear and learn popular melodies from vaudeville, operettas, well loved salon pieces, individual popular pieces of Beethoven, Brahms, Grieg, and others, marches, Strauss waltzes, and so on, that were performed in parks and concert halls. This music was spread not only among the bourgeoisie, but became more commonly heard among the

---

[58]See Bernskiöld 1986 and 1992. Studies of music in the Swedish Mission Society, *Svenska Missionsförbundet* show how a large group of people (and this holds true generally for all free churches including the Salvation Army) comes to develop a substantially broad musical competence thanks to their participation in these communities. Within the Mission Society this meant not only songs where music was a vehicle for the message of the text, but also gradually involved instrumental performances of the "masters of the classics" (Bernskiöld 1986).

artisans and working classes.[59] Operas, romances, chamber music, symphonies, works for soloists and orchestra, i.e., the higher music, could be heard in some public social situations played by professional musicians—and by professional musicians or advanced amateurs in more or less private situations. Obviously, the working class and artisans in the cities also gradually took up melodies from the latest hits from the popular operas operettas and musicals of the day.[60]

Instrumental music grew in social importance from the second half of the eighteenth century and in the music philosophical discourse, until it took over as the leading musical form. Instrumental music has the advantage that it can be re-interpreted to a greater extent than vocal music that seldom, if ever, can be rid of its text. The text is a parameter that is understood more easily than tones, but also becomes dated and thereby more quickly goes out of fashion. He holds that the way of listening to music gradually at first, and especially in the twentieth century, changed so that vocal music was listened to like instrumental music (Dahlhaus 1988, 304f). Dahlhaus touches thus on the continuous discussion since the nineteenth century about how texts in vocal music should be understood. The basic question was, of course, whether or not the text was a part of the aesthetic experience (æII) that one presumed a *Lied* of Schumann, for example, could convey. If one answered yes to this question, then the text must be understood as a part of the absolute, pure instrumental music. As we have seen, all program music had to wrestle with the same basic problem. If one answered no, then one must explain how the text, i.e., the semantically comprehensible poetry, could lose much of its meaning when it was set to music. As Dahlhaus also points out, however, the poem was sometimes read by the public while it was being performed by the singer (Dahlhaus 1988, 302).

Of course, the question of whether song could be regarded as belonging *at all* to the same category as music is also involved. Clearly in our cultural sphere we use different words for these phenomena of music and song. The term of music's supremacy is clear when we can say of an unusually beautiful song "Now that was music!" but the opposite cannot be said of a symphony: "Now there was a song!" A Lied composer began in the vast majority of cases from a finished poem, but the music thereafter came to be considered the important part of the *Lied*, and could, as Schubert's most famous songs, become material for other instrumental transcriptions.[61]

---

[59]For complete repertoire lists of the music that was performed by the orchestras in Göteborg in the middle of the century see Carlsson 1996.

[60]For a study of how salon music and popular music was spread among the English working and middle classes during the nineteenth century see Scott 1989. Compare also with Tegen 1986.

[61]The opposite, if it is really an opposite, occurred when the same poem became the material for several settings. In these cases we consider, however, the respective compositions as *new* independent works. This is true, of course, even of different settings of the same opera libretto.

Dahlhaus's "solution" is to suggest that at the beginning of the nineteenth century, people tended to hear instrumental music as text (like vocal music), and then a hundred years later, the opposite occurred and people listened to vocal music instrumentally., Therefore vocal music (like programmatic music) could be experienced as aesthetically autonomous music. Dahlhaus adds though, that this conclusion built more on the aesthetic postulate, than on an "psychologically apprehended" reality. Thus it follows that Hanslick's musical vision of a structural formal listening seemed to be built more on a hope than on a praxis. But Dahlhaus has apparently not come to this conclusion completely. Dahlhaus says, in his normal dialectical manner, that no one disputes the fact that formal listening was undeveloped, unless they mistake aesthetic daydreaming for psychological reality. The Sonata form, which clearly had a large scale form, and was not just a potpourri, should ideally be listened to in a formalistic manner, although whether it was listened to this way is impossible to prove empirically.[62] In my understanding it was only a minority—composed mainly of musicians (both women and men) as well as music journalists—who had the ability to listen to vocal music *as* instrumental music. The others surely listened to the text of the *Lied* in an aria, or for that matter in a folk song, and understood at least part of the text's message, which negatively affected their ability to enter into the "highest aesthetic condition" (æII).[63] Besides that, there is the fact that *vocal music in no way became something unusual during the nineteenth century.* Quite the opposite. People continued to listen to and sing songs in "earlier" contexts (opera, sacred contexts, within the family, at work, etc.) and in new contexts (concerts of different kinds, gradually in choir concerts and romance concerts as well as musicals, vaudeville, etc.). A person always has a voice wherever that person goes—it is always nearest to song.

This also means that we must take with a *large grain of salt* the statement, common in traditional music histories, about instrumental music's rising importance for the majority of people. As we have seen, song was regarded as something more natural than instrumental music,[64] because most people heard more vocal music in their lives than instrumental music. For example, we might ask how many Göteborg residents heard Beethoven's Ninth Symphony, Berlioz's

[62]"Dass das 'Formhören' in der Regel schwach entwickelt ist, leugnet niemand, der nicht den ästhetischen Wachtraum eines Zeitalters mit der psychologischen Wirklichkeit verwechselt. Die Forderung aber, dass ein Sonatensatz als grosse Form und nicht als blosses Potpourri aufgefasst werden müsse, bleibt von den Mängeln, die der Realität des musikalischen Hörens, anhaften, prinzipiell unangefochten" (Dahlhaus 1988, 306 [my italics]).

[63]If this can be seen as a valid general argument, then it follows that there are an unending number of variations that have to do with a) to which degree one understood the text b) how large a part of the text one remembered, and c) which type of text it concerned (lyrical, narrative, news, etc.). As is well-known, chapbook songs were sung as a rule to a limited number of melodies, i.e., the same melody can be used as a neutral medium to communicate the contents of many different texts.

[64]For the parallel vision within the religious revival during the nineteenth century see Bernskiöld 1992, 71.

Symfonie fantastique, or Schubert's great C-Major Symphony performed by a symphony orchestra during the nineteenth century? Apparently at most a hundred people—and then only on visits to one of the larger music cities.

Vocal music's great importance even during the nineteenth century does not emerge if we study the traditional music histories like Grout 1960 or GAD's *History of Music* 1990. Here accounts of eighteenth- and nineteenth-century large symphonies, solo concerts, chamber-, and piano music histories dominate over vocal music in all of its forms.

This insight *has a double effect, however*. If vocal music has always been the normal everyday music to a greater degree than we have tended to think, and instrumental music, was, as it were, music for Sundays and Feast Days, the importance of the earlier discussion of how music is divided into high and lower pales in comparison. It suggests an interpretation that this division probably did not have quite the extensive and sweeping importance that is portrayed in the literature. Again, and in yet another question, we come to the suspicion that even the division into higher and lower was a distinction that only affected a very small part of the population.

We seem to need a concept that focuses more closely on that which truly does differentiate, a word for the music that most people shared from the middle of the nineteenth century onward.

Autonomous Discussion

Before our discussion about the twentieth century it is important to take up a further discussion of some of autonomy's most central uses as they have appeared in our discussion of the history of western music. We have seen that the concept has been used to suggest that song/music was freed from its immediate functionality in the eighteenth century. Music developed in general a freer and more independent role, or a *social autonomy*. I understand this meaning as autonomy I (aI).

This understanding is, however, still problematic. As music came to be offered in the market it was, thus, principally available to all. This is not to say that the social connections to a particular song/music were arbitrary. Far from it: no one used the second movement of Beethoven's *Eroica* as dance music, and Wagner did not rearrange and insert "The Virgin's Prayer" in his opera *Tristan and Isolde*. On the other hand, Beethoven's Overture to *Egmont* could be played as restaurant music, and a simple folksong could be material for an extensive art music reworking for a large symphony orchestra. The possibilities are, however, not limitless. There is in other words, a connection between music's structure and the use intended by its composer.

Subotnik's analysis of the balance that was found in Viennese classic music depends on a form of agreement between an intra-musical stylistic autonomy and a musical meaning-autonomy. Mozart's music is described as having an autonomous, intra-structural element. Music has, on one hand, a structure that itself generates an inner harmonic balance in a musically self-reflective way. On the other hand, music also has an inner musical *meaning* (Subotnik 1991, 196). In another context Subotnik speaks of "the loss of autonomy after Beethoven." In a longer citation she summarizes her thoughts:

> Hence, whereas Beethoven had seemed able to render autonomy of styles identical with meaningful autonomy of structure in his music, the stylistic autonomy of his successors tended to vitiate the meaningful structural autonomy of their individual works (Subotnik 1991, 185).

Against the background of Morrow and Tadday's work, however, it is difficult to understand the relevance of this inner-musical autonomic function within music. The presence of an intra-musical autonomy in Viennese classic music was not even obvious for nineteenth century listeners. And furthermore, how should this intra-musical autonomy have entered music *by itself*?[65] As a matter of fact, music's structure was discussed in a continuously critical light as a forward moving social discursive process.

Instrumental music around 1800 could be considered an almost independent agent. It was thought that music could lift itself to its own metaphysical autonomous sphere and from there declaim the truth that speech could not formulate. This autonomous sphere lay high above the social, everyday life and can therefore be considered an *inner autonomy* (aII).

The highest instrumental music therefore lived an autonomous life, and must be interpreted by an autonomous way of listening to understand it. It was here that we met the aesthetic addition (æII). This way of understanding the concept of autonomy was not unusual within the "higher" *bourgeois* cultural discourse. Within this sphere the thought was entertained that art generally was a goal in itself (*l'art pour l'art*). As Liedman has pointed out, the artwork served no foreign lords. It had not only an aesthetic meaning, but also, as we have seen, an *ethical* one. It was something good in itself:

---

[65]Compare with the musicologist Marcia Citron who discusses music and autonomy from a feminist perspective. Her perspective is clear in the following introductory sentence: "In the early part of the nineteenth century, particularly in Germany, writers and literati constructed the *myth of autonomous music*" (Citron 1993, 142 [my italics]). A number of other musicologists have also argued for the abolishment of the concept of autonomy. In the noteworthy debate between Lawrence Kramer and Gary Tomlinson, Kramer writes that musical autonomy, yes, even Dahlhaus's relative autonomy is a chimera: "Neither music nor anything else can be other than wordly through and through" (Kramer 1992, 9).

The artwork has an ethical meaning through the form it gives to the concept of autonomy; in an artwork, people can see their own independence made visible. The artwork is free from outer necessity but shows instead an inner necessity, an inner stringency and formal clarity (Liedman 1997, 379).

In connection with the discussion of the stylistic changes of Beethoven's music during his second period—a discussion that concludes in a criticism of Adorno's/Subotnik's analysis of the underlying, empirical relationship to this changing process—the thought emerged that art music had a *critically autonomous potential*, aIII. My interpretation of this line of thought is that the *music in itself*, in order to be an independent force, must also criticize the bourgeois society of which it was a part in order to continue to be autonomous in the two meanings that I have described (aI and aII). This, writes Subotnik, led to an prolongation further and further into the nineteenth century that

> [m]usic, especially instrumental and nonfunctional music, began to depend for its acceptance outside the composer's own circles on an irrational and uninformed faith in the importance... of the composer's manner of utterance (Subotnik 1991, 183).

When Lydia Goehr discusses music's autonomy in relation to society, she calls the last relation "the critical solution":[66]

> Music is connected to society by an 'and' as well as a 'versus'... music can be purely musical *and* political committed without contradiction... Adorno captures this dialectic well when he writes: '[p]recisely that which is not social in art should become its social aspect'... Music responds to its conditions of production by resisting them. Music's freedom is essentially a form of resistance... Of all the arts, music is the most able... to serve fine art's political function. Why? Because it completely lacks representational and conceptual content (Goehr 1994, 106).

As Goehr adds, the critical solution to the problem of autonomy stands in the ability to see the relationship that autonomous music is free from the political-ideological in society, and at the same time, that music can be experienced as an abstract sounding medium in the fight to realize the promise of human freedom. Goehr summarizes:

> At the core of the critical solution lie two desires that must always go together: first, the desire to maintain the autonomous development of musical composition by *not* conceiving it as mere consequence of social developments at large; second, the desire to find within that autonomous development the source of music's

---

[66]Goehr writes that this "critical (or political) solution" has been discussed since Plato's days, but especially during the last two hundred years. She adds to this with the following soporific roll call: "Thus it emanated out of romantic aesthetics, Hegelianism, Marxism and critical theory, phenomenological existentialism, as well as the liberal traditions of political philosophy. All these traditions... have tried to articulate satisfactory conceptions of autonomy" (Goehr 1994, 104).

freedom to manifest the political. It helps to characterize the first form... as 'freedom from' and the second as 'freedom to' (Goehr 1994, 108).[67]

But it was clear for Goehr that the critical solution did not reach the heart of the problem. She writes that it is impossible to escape the thought that "the internal relation that connects the purely political function of music to autonomous musical form *cannot adequately be described*" (Goehr 1994, 110 [my italics]). There is therefore no sense in asserting either that music has no ideological or political meaning or significance, or its opposite. Both ways rob music of its meaning:[68]

> The fact, however, that musicians have so consistently been able to get away with the extreme separability response still tells us something important about music, namely that the description of music's relation to the extra-musical always falls short of being convincing. The failure might... perhaps be metaphysical (Goehr 1994, 111).

I find—exactly as Goehr, indirectly admits—that the thought of a critical autonomy, æIII, does not lead to an understanding of *how* instrumental music's structure, developed by the composer, can function as a political/ideological critique, more than on a conditionally abstract plane. One can turn the conventional in music upside down just as one can write music within culturally accepted norms. In the preceding examples music can stand out from the normal and accepted forms, in the second case they can strengthen accepted ideology.

But for a stream of instrumental music to function as an effective ideological critique, something else must be demanded: placement in a social context, by setting a political/ideological text, by bearing a dedication to a political person, through a program music description, and so forth. In all of these cases, there was little room for the aesthetic addition (æII) but a believable possibility for æIII. On the other hand, the most pronounced examples of political/ideological

---

[67] Goehr also tries to add the perspective of "freedom within," and goes into a long digression. She comes to the question of art's truth, the "best" music as well as a discussion of Isaiah Berlin's "non-Utopian pluralism" etc. The discussion however adds nothing definitive. The article concludes, rather, closer to form and content in the following rumination: "The critical solution also suggests many elements of the Tractarian [Goehr refers to Wittgenstein's Tractatus...] metaphysics. But since, at a crucial point, it ignores the consequences of that metaphysics and tries to say what cannot be said, it leaves us, as philosophers are often left, able to say much more about the problem than we can say about the solution... and at a certain point... the best thing we can do is just stop talking" (1994, 111 [the last words are of course also in reference to Wittgenstein's last paragraph in Tractatus]).

[68] It should be mentioned that Goehr's point of departure in the article is Hanns Eisler's denial before the McCarthy Commission in 1947 (The Committee on Un-American Activities) that his music had a political content. He took no responsibility for the possibly political texts that he had composed apolitical instrumental music to, but opportunistically declared that "this is poetry!" (Goehr 1994, 99).

music, like the famous Marseillaise, can be (or are always) something more than the everyday, and can therefore bear æI.

Those who believe in the idea of autonomy begin to project the concept into reality sooner or later. It is therefore important that one *not accept the concept of autonomy* literally. Nothing is independent. A considerable number of authors, however, have tried to correct this unavoidable fact. In connection with natural sciences' greater value-neutrality in relation to the humanities, Elias even talks about a limited and relative autonomy.[69]

Musicologist Richard Middleton, with a point of departure in the Frankfurt school, presents his own theory of relative autonomy—"a theory of articulation"—for the connection between art and society:

> A theory of articulation... preserves a relative autonomy for cultural and ideological elements (musical structures and song lyrics, for example) but also insists that those combinatory patterns that are actually constructed do mediate deep, objective patterns in the socio-economic formation, and that the mediation takes place *in struggle*: the classes fight to articulate together constituents of the cultural repertoire in particular ways so that they are organized in terms of principles or sets of values determined by the position and interests of the class in the prevailing mode of production (Middleton 1990, 9).

Middleton clearly sees the cultural and ideological elements as relatively independent, but also upholds that these elements act as an intermediary for deep objective patterns "in the socio-economic formation," a mediation that involves a fight. There is an antagonism between these factors. I understand this process more from the perspective that either the cultural or the ideological elements are independent and that the person feels deep, *subjective* experiences out of the respective (group)individual's cultural and socio-economic position.

Autonomy as a concept is appropriated apparently as some kind of emergency solution. It is naturally possible that it helps in the short term, but the ethnomusicologist's problem is, as Donald Broady puts it in another context, that it functions like a "rhetorical trick" to veil what cannot be explained (Middleton 1990, 287).[70]

The question is therefore, if the explanatory power that "autonomous explanations" promise is actually nothing more than mental mirages or glittering

---

[69] For a discussion, see Mennell 1989, 160-66.

[70] Broady discusses the problem with "the relative autonomy of the superstructure," and observes in following Bourdieu that Marxists earlier often wrote "as a last resort" when their definitions began to ebb away (Middleton 1990, 287). Broady points out that the contemporary Marxist discussion could not untie the knot of how culture could both be dependent on economics and separated from it. In talking about relative autonomy, Broady writes that it functions in this case only as a way to *name that which is left over,* as it were, that which the available tools have left unexplained.

promises in watery reflection, is it not better to say that the tools and methods at hand were not able to solve the problems or dichotomies, than to support analyses that ascribe to music with some form of autonomy?[71]

In a comparison between the beginning of the eighteenth century and the end of the nineteenth century it is fairly reasonable to suggest that music's structure governed music's social placement and its social functions were reduced later in this time period. But, at the same time, new places and new social functions appeared. We now know that a considerable number of people imagined that a certain kind of musical experience transcended the everyday and maybe even crossed the borders between the experienced subject and the sounding object. We also looked with skepticism on the concept of music as a full-blooded living agent that took upon itself the assignment of critiquing society.

It follows from our analysis of the concept of autonomy that it is tempting but not very meaningful to see *autonomy* as an independent concept. The use of the word during the nineteenth century was without any doubt *closely connected* to the aesthetic project. What I have chosen to label the aesthetic addition, æII, is more closely connected to the idea of an inner autonomy (aII). The project spread out physically and psychologically within a growing middle class and within the working class's intellectual *avant garde*. But as a witness, Karl Marx, stated: the time that they had left over for artistic activities was severely limited.[72]

* * *

We began this chapter with thoughts about what the nineteenth century meant generally for the use of music. We have seen that there are different answers to this question. Without a doubt, more and more people within communities became acquainted with the music that all of the makers of taste counted as the highest–music that possessed aesthetic conditions. As the process has been understood here, the aesthetic project expanded so far that it was generally spoken about and it was presupposed that the aesthetic experience (æIII) took place within the world of art, provided that those who listened had enough insight and knowledge.

---

[71] There exists however a form of relative autonomy within musical life; the independence that for example different social concert institutions have thanks to taxes and or contributions. These funds create a space for independent action. One can invest in art that the decision makers judge to be autonomous! If the music that is performed does not meet public expectations, however, the institution will lose in the long run or even go under. Clearly an exclusive culture can survive with a high status longer in communities where power is held by the party and/or the social classes that stand behind this art. The lower the economic support a community gives to a form of music, the more important it becomes to play a repertoire that fulfills the wishes of the audience. It is a problem that becomes more and more clear the closer we come to our own time.

[72] After Eagleton 1990, 99. Compare with Gronow 1997, 15.

In the greater picture, however, the prerequisites for the aesthetic project did not change. The Enlightenment promise of a future for all where freedom, brotherhood and justice would reign had not been fulfilled by the end of the century. The capitalist system and the industrialization of Europe's countries did not bring with it conditions that increased the chances of people within the working class experiencing, as it was formulated, "aesthetic enjoyment." For the vast majority, the way music was used changed only marginally. Very little happened along the road. æI endured.

Eagleton argued that the aesthetic project, and the Enlightenment in general had a truly liberating power within a social fellowship, but at the same time there was also a negative effect. Max Horkheimer called it a kind of "internalized repression" (Eagleton 1990, 28). Eagleton pessimistically concludes that one cannot assert that a reconciliation between these two really took place. He formulates it this way:

> From one viewpoint, the aesthetic *is* ideological. But to claim that reconciliation of freedom and necessity, self and others, spirit and Nature lies in the aesthetic is tantamount to confessing, gloomily enough, that it is hardly anywhere to be found (Eagleton 1990, 99).

The search for an autonomous aesthetic refuge did not cease, however. The dream of an aesthetic reconciliation continued and the illusion of development endured. History's blind developments can be difficult to anticipate.

> *It was the culture industry, not the avantgarde,
> which suceeded in transforming
> everyday life in the 20th century.*
> Andreas Huyssen

CHAPTER 5: A PERIOD OF EXPANSION

Introduction

As we turn our attention to the twentieth century, a period that has only recently ended, we slowly approach our own time. We are used to thinking that it is more difficult to understand our own time than the past. That which we understand or think we understand is, strictly speaking, that the past. but at the same time, assertions about tthe past are always problematical. I can hardly *experience* and *understand* anything more completely than my present—if present is taken to mean, let us say, a decade. It is when everything is real and simultaneous that people *both know most and feel most intensely about what is happening*. As soon as we leave the experienced present, or the now, and look back, something different appears unbidden: we see things from an increasing distance, we forget, reflect, see other contexts, change our minds, change the order of events and so forth–a process that continues until we die.

Thanks to writing and notation, music and musical experiences have been preserved on paper as in earlier centuries, but new media like the record player, radio, film and TV have also made it possible that the *musical performance* itself can be preserved. Long after the music sounded we can experience it fresh in recordings. We believe perhaps that we hear or see the same as those who originally recorded the music and those who listened to it when it was performed.

When it comes to music history, especially of performed music, we can have, for the first time, "direct contact" with the past through these media. At the same time we have the advantage of knowing how history turned out, even if the knowledge is compromised and distorted. Distorted, because we have—as always in historical research—drawn conclusions about the changes that have happened over longer time periods and observed the events from a distance with a good overview and little emotional attachment. We often manifest a desire to objectivize peoples' earlier, subjective contemporaneous experiences. Even more so, the history of individual pieces has also affected us, which is in part due to how the each piece's destiny has been understood from its first performance onwards, and partly how a piece's structure would come to be related to music that followed.

Although people today also experience temporal demarcations (we know well when we were born, left school, etc.) we tend to divide the *historical* time stream according to the more important world events. It is rarely when one was born, but rather when World War II ended, 1945, that becomes an historical point of departure. Likewise we find often that one interprets the "objective" history from *different* criteria. When did modernism really begin, we can ask ourselves, and when did it end, if it has ended? The sociologist Fred Ingles sees modernism's period as between 1914 and 1989:

> The heavy machine guns of August 1914 ended one epoch; the enormous, peaceable and irresistible crowds in Leipzig, Prague, Budapest, Berlin and elsewhere throughout the course of 1989 ended the next (Ingles 1993, 3).[1]

The work of sociologist Alain Tourraine makes it clear that the roots of modernity can be followed right back to the time of classical Greece.[2] In his large work he paints a scenario that is similar to many of the earlier great theoretical constructions. Tourraine focuses on the relation between the senses and the subject, between the objective sensory-driven world and the individual's subjective world, as well as between science and freedom:

> Modernity… is the result of a dialogue… Without Reason, the Subject is trapped into an obsession with identity; without the Subject, Reason becomes an instrument of might. In this century, we have seen both the dictatorship of reason and totalitarian perversions of the subject. Is it at last possible for both figures of modernity, which have either fought or ignored one another, to begin to speak to one another and to learn to live together? (Tourraine 1995, 6).

Liedman, also inspired by Tourraine's writings, goes far back in time and writes that modernity, like the European process, begins during the late Middle Ages or sixteenth century, "and becomes expressed in trade, urbanization, the life of the state, scientific and political thought, technique, art, philosophy, and so forth" (Liedman 1997, 591). Modernism is used as a symbol for the process under which artists gradually departed from earlier "classical models and thereby achieve an increasing freedom in their creations" (Liedman 1997, 18).

---

[1] Other writers, for example the sociologist John Docker will place the beginning of modernism in the 1890s (Docker 1994, xviii), which Hobsbawm also does. He establishes that when the *bourgeois*-liberal society broke apart at the beginning of World War I in 1914, the disintegration had already been anticipated by the modernist changes within the arts (Hobsbawm 1994, 178). For a definition of musical modernism, see below p. 184.

[2] Tourraine believes that the Greek view of people has many more similarities with modernism than with earlier Christianity. He summarizes the decisive changes that occur during the eighteenth century: "The new industrial societies acquired… a capacity for transforming themselves… There was no longer such a thing as human nature, and man no longer had natural rights: he was no more than he did, and his rights were social rights. Reason was no longer thought as the discovery of an order; it became a force that could transform history, and the idea of society, which had been mechanical, now became organic. As a result, the divorce between subject and society disappeared. Man became a truly social and historical being" (Tourraine 1995, 59f).

One can also problematize the concepts of modernity and modernism from a post-colonial scientific perspective, which researchers like the literary scholar Edward Said, the socio-anthropologist Veit Erlmann, and others, have done. Erlmann suggests that focusing on the period from World War I to the end of the 1980s as a part of modernity is in many respects a Eurocentric problem that unfairly sets up Europe "as a given referent of historical knowledge":

> And as a corollary of this, while Europe is comfortably imagined as the cradle of modernity, its crisis stems from beyond its borders and much less often from within them (Erlmann 1999, 174).

Erlmann also points out one of these crowning ideas: the idea that a crisis of modernity in the twentieth century is dependent upon the concept that modernity was *a solid undertaking from the beginning* (Erlmann 1999, 174).

There are as always different ideas about time delineations and labels for them. There is nothing odd about this. This present work has just come through the Romantic period, a classification of a time that the majority of people during this period, had no idea they were living in.[3] We also soon come to what modernism conveyed for art music, and will take up the continued modernistic renewal. We will also touch on art, according to Hegel the happy middle ground in society, now capable of reconciling the Enlightenment's many diverse wishes.

As we have noted, Nietzsche, a generation later, during the end of the nineteenth century, was scornful of Hegel's work. We have also met many contemporary researchers who, from different epistemological points of view, analyze modernism's history and explain the aesthetic project. Apart from Tourraine's viewpoint we have touched on Luhmann's thesis on increasingly self-regulated systems as well as Habermas's thoughts on the instrumental rationalism's invasion of all of our realities, Adorno's belief that the Enlightenment imploded in a descending spiral toward a black hole, and not least, Elias's composite theories within which his civilization theories have a central place.

Here is not the place, however, to make a basic analysis and comparison of these authors' different theories. (Readers know by now that I am most inspired by Elias's scientific view).

At the same time it is, in my opinion and luckily enough for this current work's overarching purpose, other developments than those that primarily form the material of most philosophers' and even some sociologists' interests–that have a decisive meaning for peoples' use of music during the twentieth century. It is obviously very important to discuss how general processes of change in society have formed peoples' lives during the twentieth century. There is, however, a

---

[3]Sweden, compared for example with England, was late to industrialize. At the end of the nineteenth century about 66% of the Swedish population were farmers with secondary occupations, while in England, the corresponding figure was about 10% [sic].

specific process that has had a truly decisive effect on the development of the aesthetic project: the creation of recording and reproducing technology for music and the dissemination of mass media.

The leading light for our continued thinking is as before that new ways of using music have added functions and meanings that have influenced the role and place that aesthetic music experiences have played. While these, and similar thoughts are common among researchers inspired by sociological theory, we find them also formulated by some philosophers. When, for example, the philosopher Francis Sparshott considers musical behavior, he writes:

> It is in principle true that musical behavior could be identified by the purpose served… or by the means employed. This being so, in any culturally unstable situation either could be used to change the other: the achieving of musical ends by new means and the putting of musical procedures to new uses could (and often does) change the understanding of what music is (Sparshott 1987, 44).

The most relevant from an ethnological standpoint is that changes within society and individual cultural areas lead to a faster dissemination of ideas, ideologies, paradigms, and material objects between different layers of society than was possible in earlier centuries. If a musical work, for example a revue melody, became popular when it was performed at a New Years' revue in Stockholm in 1900, it took perhaps six months before it was even known in the town of Kiruna in the far north of Sweden. Forty years later about 66% of Sweden's population could listen to the radio when a similar piece of music made a hit at a New Years' revue in Stockholm. Today, into the next century, a majority of the world's population can simultaneously see and hear a hit melody performed on TV. The focus on what percent of the population that could have known and used a certain music gradually develops a completely different significance. At the same time we know that this has not led to a uniform taste in contemporary music or that everyone likes the same music—which brings us to our next topic.

Changes in Art Music

We noted earlier that composers of art music were divided into A and B camps. Those composers whose music could be thought of as having a programmatic point of departure and those who wrote a music that had a too sensual character and varied instrumentation easily risked landing in the B camp (especially if they were not German). Added to this, the non-German composers who were inspired by their own national folk music, for example Sibelius or Stravinsky, further risked B camp status (as also happened with these composers' music).[4] Adorno pointed out time and again, from his modernist point of view,

---

[4] Adorno's parsimoniousness against these composers has often been commented open, perhaps most amusngly by Francs Sparsott: "Careful readers of Adorno will observe that Stravinsky's

the danger that art music had become a cultural commodity. The literary historian Andreas Huyssen writes this explanation:

> I think it is significant to point out that Adorno's modernism relies on certain strategies of exclusion which relegate realism, naturalism, reportage literature and political art to an inferior realm. All forms of representation fall under the verdict of reification (Huyssen 1986, 25).[5]

For Adorno this development also meant, as suggested, that art music which claimed to continue to be autonomous must stand apart from all representation of reality, even though music was "thoroughly socialized," ["*durch und durch gesellschaftlich.*"] Two Adorno quotations cast light on this in different ways: "Art's double properties, that it is autonomous and that it is a social fact, spread unbroken through this autonomous zone" (Adorno 1970, 16), as well as: "The contents of Art can be defined as well as undefinable. Therefore we need a philosophy of art as an interpreter of art in order to express that which art cannot express, even though the art alone can express it, in that it cannot say it" (Adorno 1970, 113).

If we fall into a clinch again with these Adornean ideas, it might be well to remember that, within a capitalistic material system, a form of aesthetically advanced art music developed, and this form should be understood as a social reflection of its contemporary culture, to which it was autonomously related, but at the same time also critically related through its (negative) sounding message.

The difficulty of understanding how this could happen in reality is not reduced if we add Goehr's earlier observation about the problem of picking out the political-critical part within the musical flow from the form of the music. It *is* difficult to combine the above thoughts into a single understandable synthesis. My critique of Adorno, thus, always develops from the position that music is an object that is used (something that is heard, listened to, sung, played) and that whatever it meant, how it functioned, what role it played in everyday life must be understood from this perspective. I find it difficult to accept that music that was seldom performed–the last works of Beethoven, for example, or the works of Schoenberg–could have had the societal importance implied by the sheer volume of writings devoted to these works (probably hundreds of yards of literature). It

---

deepest offense, which he shares with all too many contemporary composers, is that he is not Viennese" (Sparshott 1987, 43). Cf. Allen's discussion of different national variants of chauvinistic music history writing from the nineteenth century onwards (Allen 1962, 122f, 159-74 and 208-13). The reader meets examples of an outlook of German glorification that one can also find in the products of many non-German writers. Here we find repeated also an early critical review of German publications during the twentieth century that glorified German music history influenced directly from Nazi propoganda (Allen 1962, 162f).

[5] Huyssen comments sarcastically that it is odd that modern realism's most receptive critic, Adorno, reinforces, thus, albeit from a negative perspective, that language's representations, and we can add music's as well, represent reality, namely that they can recreate a referent (Huyssen 1986, 25).

doesn't help much that the theories built up around this tradition, for instance, Adorno's, seem to have covered all aspects of reality by developing a long chain of concepts that in an infinite dialectical regress are interdependent and interact with another. However one tries to see his pessimistic points there seems to be no possibility whatsoever of using a cultural object in a positive way for mankind. The dialectical process fools us in the end. The developmental path doesn't take us to the supposed goal. It is as if life either is just going downhill in an eternal slalom race, or is going cross-country in a circle, hoping to connect to the starting point, but always upon arriving there, finding it has been transformed into a different track.

In this context one cannot ignore Nietzsche's similarly pessimistic analysis: if everything is only an endless stream of illusions, it is difficult to restrain the thought that art is perhaps not capable of speaking the unspeakable as promised. Or as Nietzsche poetically "formatted" it:

> Very early in my life I took the question
>
> Of the relation of *art* and *truth* seriously:
>
> Even now I stand in holy dread in the face
>
> of this discordance (from *Nachlass* as cited in Bernstein 1992, 1).[6]

The philosopher Jay Bernstein reformulated this "holy dread": if our experience of art as art only has to do with taste, both art and aesthetics land outside of eternity, right and truth. We land rather in a state that he suggests is typical for modernism:

> If art is taken as lying outside truth and reason then if art speaks in its own voice it does not speak truthfully or rationally; while if one defends art from within the confines of the language of truth-only cognition one belies the claim that art is more truthful than that truth-only cognition (Bernstein 1992, 2).

One way of escape out of this securely locked opposition is to regard (a) modern science/technology, (b) ethics and law, and (c) modern art as all having taken different paths, but then one must give up on the idea of art's social truth, and therefore, Bernstein says, autonomous art stands in an independent relationship to truth and morality. Herein lies the main cause of Nietzsche's fear:

---

[6] Nietzsche also writes: "We cannot look around our own corner." As Ferry points out, we already find ourselves having arrived at Nietzsche's thoughts about the subconscious, which are similar to those that Schönberg (influenced by Freud) would later express in his correspondence with Kandinsky: "Every search that tends to produce a traditional effect is more or less marked by the intervention of consciousness. But art belongs to the unconscious" (as cited in Ferry 1993, 233).

The experience of art *as aesthetical* is the experience of art as having lost or been deprived of its power to speak the truth—whatever truth will mean when no longer defined in exclusive ways. This loss, no matter how theorized or explained, I shall call 'aesthetic alienation'; it denominates art's alienation from truth which is caused by art's *becoming* aesthetical, a becoming that has been fully consummated only in modern societies (Bernstein 1992, 4).[7]

The entire discussion above departs from Nietzsche's idea of the illusory nature of believing in a true and eternal relationship between art and life, a thesis that undermines the thought of art's possibility of criticizing society in an Adornean sense, namely to function as a negative corollary to the *bourgeois* enlightenment project. If art stands outside of truth, then it cannot make any demands on truth from any part of society other than itself. However, if one adds that the whole enlightenment project and our trust in our ability to think rationally has capsized, it is perhaps possible to logically combine these opposites. But I see this solution as a capitulation, and it seems therefore that Habermas's ideas about the rational discourse provide a better way forward.[8] However, as the cultural sociologist Johan Fornäs has pointed out, one must observe that for Habermas, the arts are "non-propositional systems of symbolic actions" (Fornäs 1995, 160) and are thus exempt from rational discourse. Fornäs summarizes:

> [W]hereas mutual agreement may be reached in cognitive, normative or explicative discourses, the discussants cannot be expected to reach the same conclusions in aesthetical or subjectively expressive matters, while tied to subjective and personal experiences (Fornäs 1995, 161).[9]

Nevertheless, there was a way out of this widespread negative and pessimistic quagmire. And despite what the quotation above expresses, it involved the way that one supported oneself with like-minded people who also had true knowledge of which music was right, whatever everyone else might say.

---

[7] It is in the nature of things that great art axiomatically was described as having aesthetic content. If, however, we apply Luhmans' idea that art as a completely separate and parallel system in relation to other systems, art has no pretensions to truth. "Truth" is part of a scientific system. If Luhmann's "art solution" is a separated system, there are others that have suggested exactly the opposite, namely that everythings humans produce is art (cf. footnote 183 concerning Croce).

[8] Cf. the philosopher Wolfgang Welsh who writes that Habermas criticizes Nietzsche for his thoughts about "[the] universalization of the aesthetic and censured subsequent forms of this strategy." About this last comment ("censured subsequent forms") Welsh proposes the following: "It's precisely because Nietzsche stands in the background of the *Dialectic of Enlightenment* that Horkheimer and Adorno, in Habermas's view, have arrived at 'an uninhibited scepticism regarding reason'" (Welsh 1997, 38).

[9] Fornäs 1995 is a tremendously comprehensive review of current theories of culture and a personal attempt at a multi-dimensional synthesis. If there is any problem with this work it is this: Fornäs's encyclopedic ambition conveys in the end that the reader with Fornäs's help has taken a position on everything, but remains uncertain about what has been said. Even so, the way in which Fornäs proceeds must be tested again and again…

Some Knew

A key idea in the elitist and modernist art history at the beginning of the twentieth century was that some *knew* what was artistic truth and that modernist truth stood on a higher plane than other truths. This was true not only of Arnold Schönberg, but a number of other composers.[10] One way for us to tackle these questions about truth and art lies in analyzing it once again and then trying to write the problem away. In reality, namely, the vast majority of listeners interested in art music came to a crossroads at the beginning of the twentieth century where they chose to turn aside from the progressive art music road that lay straight ahead.[11]

We are as always interested in when this modernist process began that led to this prolonged crossroads in time. Were Beethoven's works during the middle part the starting point? Was it accelerated through Wagner's thoroughly worked out break with traditional forms, eternal melodies and the negation of common cadences in the introduction to *Tristan and Isolde*? Or was the process first taken seriously with Schönberg's twelve-tone pieces?

The answers to all of these questions is, of course, *yes*, but at the same time partly uninteresting, because this process naturally integrated with all the other artistic processes and changes in society that have meaning for the use of music and its function. Elias always warns about the belief that one can find a single unambiguous inspiration at a particular moment in time that marks the beginning of a social process. What we can establish is that art music undergoes a stylistic and structural change over time and that it neither begins with Beethoven nor ends with Schönberg.

Especially within German-Austrian related art music a well-known process of development was underway that was closely related to the activities of the Viennese Arnold Schönberg. From a Schönbergian perspective, 1907-08 was a decisive year because it was then that he took a conscious step away from the traditional tonal system, as every singer who has tried to perform from *Das Buch der hängenden Gärten* (Opus 15) has already noticed, and as the contemporary public who listened to his second string quartet (Opus 9) strongly experienced (Morgan 1991, 67-73).[12] Barely a decade later, 1923, Schönberg published his

---

[10]Cf. Ferry 1993, 198. Cf. also with my analysis of the latest—perhaps the last—modernist debate in Sweden in *Svenska Dagbladet [The Swedish Daily]* in 1995 (Edström 1997).

[11]Depending on the different conditions of the political-cultural art that developed in respective countries in the West from the 1920s onward, this turning aside from the main road was a very drawn-out process. It continued apparently at least until the 1970s. According to a survey, the total number of London audience members that go to concerts of new art music faithfully does not exceed more than 400 (Nielsen 1999, 18).

[12] During my student years at the Göteborg Conservatory of Music (1966-69) vocal lines with frequent intervals of tritones, sevenths, ninths, and so on were regarded as extremely difficult to

first pieces with a predetermined series of twelve tones that returned in an orderly way in different guises, suitable for a talented composer of Schönberg's caliber to manipulate. This type of art music has come to be related to modernism more than any other music. Music, as it is formulated in the Danish musicologist Jan Maegaard's book *Musikalisk modernism* [*Musical Modernism*] (Maegaard 1967), is distinguished by its tendency in one way or another to "deviate from the usual formal language and shows tendencies toward a challenging of the tradition (Maegaard 1967, 9). This included music whose melodies often had a large range and a large number of wide intervals. Rhythm was often complex with varying time signatures.[13] The music was less built up of clearly defined motives and phrases. The works were often chamber music, the most highly respected musical form.

This form of modernism lay far from the contemporary movement that we most closely associate with Francesco Pratella and his futuristic music manifesto, which prescribed intervals of less than a half tone, polyrhythms and, not least, that one should take inspiration from "the crowd, of great factories, of trains, of transatlantic lines, of battleships, of motor-cars and aeroplanes" (as cited in Morgan 1991, 115). A number of new sound resources were discovered that were used in works like *A Meeting of Motorcars and Aeroplanes* (Morgan 1991, 116). In contrast to the music of the second Viennese school, this music died away quickly and still belongs to the future, or if you like, completely in the past. For even if it was an important concern for Futurism to bridge the gap between the social oppositions that were built up between the "normal" taste and the accelerated stylistic development within *bourgeois* art, it failed.[14] Art was not only used to criticize early art, but also to criticize *art institutions* themselves (museums, concert associations, etc.). Art's traditional institutions, however, did not change, nor did people's everyday taste. As has been pointed out, radio, gramophones, film and after the Second World War, television, did bring decisive changes. Even

---

sing. The songs in *Das Buch der hängenden Gärten* were seen as best suited for those with perfect pitch even if they had poor voices. —The musicologist Brian Etter has recently pointed out some partially overlooked reasons why Schönberg came to push the limits of tonality in those years. It was not only Schönberg's own personal crisis, but also his interest in theosophy and gnosticisim (Etter 2001, 144-204).

[13] Luc Ferry comes to the same conclusion and writes that painters and musicians sought "dissonance, atonality, illogicality, rupture, difference" (Ferry 1993, 229). Similar ideas can also be found in Swingewood, who in the first place sees modernism within art as an aesthetic movement within modernity. He also emphasizes that art within the *bourgeois*-capitalist society developed a unique position within society as a free zone, and yes, he also mentions the difficulties inherent in the word "autonomy" (Swingewood 1998, 137).

[14] One should observe that this direction, that Huyssen named as the "historical avante garde" that is to say "Italian futurism, Dada, Russian constructivism, and productivism as well as surrealism," was not discussed by Adorno. He discussed modernism.

though new technology and new instruments were used by the futurists, the new technologies were quickly taken over by other more market-friendly forces.

The second Viennese school's modernist music (Schönberg, Alban Berg, Anton Webern, and others) lived on, even though from the beginning its wings were clipped by the demands made on listeners. If they were to achieve æII through listening to instrumental music, the same prerequisites as before still applied. If the broad variant of æIII was involved, it meant that that the listener succeeded in penetrating the music structure's unusual surface and found in meaning its different syntax in order to create space for an emotional-cognitive process to take place.

The philosopher Arthur Danto claims that fine art reached an end point at the beginning of the twentieth century.[15] A corresponding claim for art music would be to say that with *avant garde* music and 12-tone music something similar happened within music culture. It is obvious that this branch of development within modernist art music (12-tone music and its later developments) to a great extent made it more difficult for the musically interested public to follow the music's flow. It was hardly music that one could hum after the concert.

Departing from the mechanical way that 12-tone music and subsequently serial music was composed, one could perhaps see this development as an example of Habermas's thesis about how a goal-oriented instrumental rationalism invaded the *Lebenswelt* of music.

Earlier, it had been possible to play a simplified version of a Mozart minuet, or an arrangement for violin and piano of Puccini's *Tosca* and later listen to the original; now there were no simplified editions, or arrangements for violin and piano of 12-tone music.[16] This did not mean, however, that much moderate newly composed and innovative art music did not have a large public during the twentieth century (see below). A similar thesis, that art music's time is already over by the 1920s, therefore, only can be seen as partially true (Davies 1994).[17] Seen

---

[15] Danto has recently also assured us that the traditional art historical story has been broken because now: "Anything can be art... Because the present situation is essentially unstructured, one can no longer fit a master narrative to it" (Danto 1997, 114). The title of his book is appropriate enough: *After the End of Art: Contemporary Art and the Pale of History*.

[16] The conductor and composer Wilhelm Stenhammar was one of many in the inter-war period to argue that the concert and music offerings did not have positive consequences for musicmaking in the home (article in the evening newspaper *Stockholms Aftonblad*, 5/1 1924). In his grandparents' generation there was a different interest in music, but now he sees that "Musicians have become a music delivery service for people, who as a rule, do not have time to make music for themselves at home. In this way the public gets a more elegant product, but values it less. Is it not a sign of music culture that a group of people run about listening to concert music that goes in one ear and out the other." When asked what he thought about modern music he replied that he began to count the beginning of "decadence from Beethoven." His contribution attracted attention within music circles in Sweden (cf. an open letter in the journal *Musikern* 1924, 33ff).

[17] Cf. the philosopher Stig Brostrøm who discusses the reasons why late-twentieth-century art (installatons and the like) that its only purpose is to have none. It is frequently demonstrated,

from a large time perspective, 12-tone music was perhaps more a turning point than an end point.

Schönberg's music was, understandably, criticized very early on. Ten years after 12-tone music's birth, the Swedish musicologist Gunnar Jeanson summarized his experiences on the occasion of Schönberg's sixtieth birthday, and came to a discussion of the differences between Schönberg and Stravinsky. He asked why Stravinsky had become "relatively popular while Schönberg only succeeded in winning a small circle of admirers," and answered:

> [with] Stravinsky, a living contact with the Russian folk music is created, providing a stimulating counterbalance to all of the experimental tendencies, Schönberg, on the other hand, with no connection to a folk ethos, has driven abstraction to its ultimate end (Göteborgs Handels- och Sjöfartstidning 13/10 1934).

Many Disembark

The fact that many listeners got off the train along the art musical journey is not only related to the stylistic developments of the second Viennese school. The wider public had general problems in understanding and thereby different musical styles acquired changes within twentieth-century art music. For example, if you name composers like Stravinsky, Bartok and Hindemith, they first attracted larger audiences during the later part of the twentieth century. In other words, moderate art music as a consequence of a culturally cumulative process has become acceptable.[18] If Stravinsky's *Rite of Spring* was a bewildering experience for its premiere audience in 1913, three generations later it was met with benevolent

---

he notes, that Adorno considered the second Viennese school to be the end of art music. This idea corresponds thus to Danto's view. Brostrøm comments: "in this process Adorno stands, as I see it, as a bridge… In some contexts Adorno uses the latest art to show that art no longer is possible in the traditional sense, at the same time as has just been seen, it constitutes a prelude to a new aesthetic art. It is this risky game that makes Adorno difficult to understand, and why he is quoted so often and understood so little."(Brostrøm 1994, 27). Which "art" Brostrøm is referring to is not defined; it can be the serial art music after the Second World War that Adorno saw as old and ossified, rather than new. The saving grace that someone is being misunderstood does not, however, solve the problem: is modernist art's function to show us that it does not have one, is it no longer art, but something else, which is not seen or heard, even though it is still firmly attached within the institutional world, in whose own interest it lies to consecrate it as art. Adorno's problem was rather that for reasons that were either musical or ideological or both, he could not hear Stravinsky, as well as many other composers, or jazz music as art. Furthermore, he could not see that contemporary popular music could also have a critical potential, even though by his own definition both were 'completely commercial' and not at all autonomous.

[18]Cf. with the musicologist Gunnar Valkare's dissertation, where he operates on the thesis that an auditive recapturing mechanism gradually slows and mellows art music's technological development (Valkare 1997).

curiosity when *Göteborgs Symfoniker* (Sweden's National Orchestra) performed the work outdoors in front of an audience of thousands at the Göteborg city festival in August of 1998. From famous scandal in Paris to domestic bacchanal in Göteborg.

That the *Göteborgs Symfoniker* can make creative and independent decisions to perform works that earlier, from a public standpoint, were almost experienced as non-music, is largely attributable to the fact that the orchestra as an institution is primarily publicly funded (compare with the discussion of autonomy on page 170). The forms of independent institutions that developed within modernism could therefore use the power of their positions to see that the general public is exposed to different forms of modernist art. In other words, institutions can, to return to Luhmann's ideas about autonomous systems, develop a limited autonomy as regards the surrounding social process. The thought that all culture is dependent on market forces is thus not entirely correct: there are still opportunities to write commissioned pieces for concert institutions primarily supported by public funds.[19]

In a democratically controlled country, the parties that want to take power have to take into account the views and values of the voters. Put simply, those entitled to vote change their attitudes faster than their basic values. Those who want to win by producing goods and services in a market must take economic considerations into account.[20] Whether the form of autonomy that a Swedish orchestra has today to make decisions about programming will increase or decrease is at best an open question…[21]

---

[19] Art music during the twentieth century has also been the music form that has generated the most royalties per minute from STIM, the Swedish performing rights society (Edström 1998). Because the period of copyright protection gradually was increased to 70 years after the death of the author, music and texts whose authors died before 1937 are free—provided that the work has not been altered by someone since. In Sweden (and many West European countries) this means in turn that for a record company, radio company, or concert organization, in fact for everyone who uses music in public, it is acceptable to use this music without paying STIM (although SAMI, a society for performers, protects recordings and most recordings/performances are from more recent dates). The least commercial recording project a record company can undertake should therefore be to record a newly composed, extremely difficult long work for symphony orchestra. The cheapest is probably to engage a single violinist to play traditional polskas from the nineteenth century.

[20] Also the music that is played by symphony orchestras, with or without support of the general public, naturally is included as an object in the market economy. The majority of symphony orchestras play music that, with or without public support, are sold as recordings. For a concert—subsidized or not— one has to get a ticket which involves buying an experience, that can be valued in relation to other needs and experiences.

[21] Cf. Björnberg who writes that the cultural climate during the 1980s and 90s developed negative repercussions for the public music institution's legitimacy and that "art music's ideological aura tends to become even more pale" (Björnberg 1996, 15).

It is impossible to tell whether a structural mode of listening was employed by many at the outdoor concert in Götaplatsen in 1998. Most likely æI dominated among the listeners. The prerequisites for æIII were present, but probably not æII due to the context. In this case, at the end of the 1990s, the role of music, its function and meaning in society, was very different from the beginning of the century. As the literary historian Frederic Jameson has pointed out, it is ironic, therefore, that Adorno's prophetic diagnosis has been fulfilled albeit in a negative way:

> Not Schönberg, but Stravinsky is the true precursor of postmodern cultural production. For with the collapse of the high-modernist ideology of style, the producers of culture have nowhere to turn but to the past: the imitation of dead styles stored up in the imaginary museum of a now global culture (Jameson 1991, 18).

The question is whether Jameson's conclusion not only shows that Adorno's prophecy went wrong, but also that Adorno's methods misfired. We can, of course, also speculate whether Stravinsky should be seen as a forerunner of postmodernism or as a representative of modernism. For, without a doubt, many different stylistic directions and artistic approaches developed at the beginning of the twentieth century during modernism's youth, a time that not only saw a breadth and depth of newly composed art music, but also had a parallel stylistic development within popular music.

Music Spreads Out

During the nineteenth century, it gradually became possible for more people to hear music at restaurants, cafés and in parks. In Sweden the soundscape of the larger cities changed only slowly at the end of the century, but during the first decades of the twentieth century more and more musicians found work in restaurants and larger cafés. During these decades silent films also contributed, producing work not only for pianists, but also other instrumentalists. The largest movie theaters had small salon orchestras. In great cities like London and Berlin the largest silent film orchestras were comparable to small symphony orchestras.

In Göteborg during the winter months in the 1920s, up to 200 musicians worked in the restaurants, cafés and movie theaters. At the end of the 1920s two million movie tickets were sold in Göteborg (pop. 200,000) and double as many in Stockholm. How many people heard music in restaurants and cafés is difficult to calculate. Statistics are hard to come by, but it is known that among the *bourgeoisie* it was normal for both men and women to go to restaurants. In Göteborg the famous department stores like Meeths and Gillblads had café restaurants where well known orchestras entertained (Edström 1996, 378-400). Within the working classes it was mainly men who visited cafés of different kinds and heard music like duets for accordion and violin.

I have earlier described much of the repertoire that was played at movie theaters, symphony orchestra's popular concerts, or wind bands that played in parks and squares, as *middle music* (Edström 1992, 1996).[22]

This music dominated in most contexts where music had an accompanying and entertainment role. Overtures, salon music, solo pieces, fantasies, potpourris, character pieces, waltzes, marches, and so forth, can therefore be considered as "middle music." A description of middle music's characteristic qualities cannot be done with any exactness. Middle music has a structure and form that can be compared with simplified classical romantic music. The melody is often tonally oriented and singable. Harmonies are adapted to the melody, are "functional," and seldom multifaceted. The general structure is not predictable: inner voices accompany and support rather than enjoy a life of their own (polyphony is unusual). The music's level of technical difficulty can vary. What can be described as middle music in 1910 is, however, not the same as in 1950. New generations of people have new experiences. New music develops. The stylistic breakup within popular music from the 1960s: pop, rock, punk, etc., as well as the accelerating stylistical changes within art music during these decades gradually undermined the conditions for middle music. At the outer borders of this term we find, therefore, a musical no-man's land that geographically dislocates with time, and that is dependent on who is listening, and to what use the music is being put. Perhaps I should immediately stress that my point of departure concerning the concept of middle music is structural and not functional. This does not mean that there is not a connection between a music's structural and functional qualities, but only that it seems better and safer to discuss middle music according to its concrete structure (cf. Edström 1992, 51f).[23]

---

[22]Dahlhaus occasionally called music in salons and on boardwalks "die Mittlere Musik" (quotation marks are from the original). He regarded these as both concert and background music, but neither as "really functional" ["eigentlich funktional"] nor "as objects suitable for aesthetic contemplation" ["als Gegenstand ästhetischer Kontemplation für sich bestimmt"] (Dahlhaus 1988, 199). During the late 1700s, writes Dahlhaus, art and non-art music were divided "durch einen qualitativen Sprung." He continues: "He who considers the dichotomy to be a prejudice that we as historians should not take to our hearts, finds himself in embarrassment as he at the same time must give up the nineteenth-century concept of art." ["Wer also die Dichotomie als Vorurteil verwirft, das sich ein Historiker nicht zu eigen machen dürfte, gerät in die Verlegenheit, zugleich den Kunstbegriff des 19. Jahrhunderts preisgeben zu müssen"] (Dahlhaus 1988, 202).

[23]Cf. Björnberg's discussion about different definitions or delimitations of the term "popular music." The terms that lie closest to middle music and that were in common use then were "entertainment music" and "popular music (Björnberg 1991). All music that during the period up until about 1960 was described as entertainment music or popular music is considered here to be middle music. From Björnberg's discussion a definition of popular music is developed which departs from the current situation; it is music conceived and created for distribution through mass media (which was not the case with middle music), that spread both via live music (from scores) and new mass media and gramophone and radio (see below).

A very great deal of middle music had text: *schlager* (popular songs in the style of the Tin-Pan-Alley tradition like Irving Berlin, George Gershwin, etc.), folk song, romances, *Lieder*, choir songs, and so forth, which meant that one seldom could escape from the fact that the text conveyed a clear semantic content. As before, people during the twentieth century continued to sing at home, at school, at work, in religious and secular societies, at festive occasions, and so on. This meant at the same time that the musical mother tongue, from a structural standpoint, had changed very little. So, for example, a melody in a major key for a chapbook song from the beginning of the nineteenth century, a religious revival song from the end of the nineteenth century, a *schlager* from the 1930s, or a current dance band hit are all structurally similar s a rule. The winning songs at the Eurovision Song Contest, at least up to the 1970s, could be characterized as middle music with very few exceptions. The same can be said about the majority of the songs by the Beatles.[24]

Mass Media — New Ways to Use Music

Mechanical musical instruments like music boxes were not regarded kindly by piano manufacturers at the end of the nineteenth century. It was much harder to learn to play the piano than the music box. There were larger and smaller music boxes—some contained in beautiful wooden boxes—in which one could put different disks or cylinders with popular pieces: waltzes, marches, polkas, and so forth. Both music boxes and during the last decades of the nineteenth century, player pianos soon developed competition from both the cylinder-playing phonograph, and especially of the disc-playing gramophone at the beginning of the twentieth century. All of these machines could play music when one wished. Young and old, musical and unmusical, whether one could play oneself or not—it made no difference. If the machine worked then the music came out.

While simple music boxes were cheap, player pianos and phonographs were expensive. One phonograph could cost about as much as an industrial worker earned in three months. A gramophone cost about a month's salary. The most expensive mechanical instruments, the player pianos, could only be bought by the well-to-do families and were, therefore, uncommon.[25] On every occasion

---

[24]If we look at the current situation, it could perhaps be said that within the broad popular music category of rock, there is also a kind of middle music that can be described as 'Middle of the road' (MOR) and that on either side of this lane there are many other styles like punk, heavy metal, and rap.

[25]Cf. musicologist Greger Andersson's enlightening article on the noble Gyllenstierna family's musical life around the turn of the twentieth century. Here one found many of the latest fashions: player pianos, symphoniums, phonographs, and so forth. As Andersson writes, it was "a milieu

that one listened to music from these machines something new was encountered: one was not dependent on oneself or other people in order to hear music. The machine played itself. During the first decades of the twentieth century, double-sided gramophone records became more common. The number of recordings and production of records rapidly increased. While in the beginning, a large amount of art music had been recorded, the new medium came to quickly be dominated by popular music: *schlager*, marches, character pieces, melodies from operas and operettas, popular and shorter passages of art music from the baroque to the romantic, and so forth—that is to say, the same middle music that one heard at restaurants.

The music that was recorded and broadcast by mass media (gramophone, radio, film, television and today, the internet) came gradually to be completely dominated by non-instrumental popular music, that is to say, accompanied song. We find here the solution to our earlier doubts about instrumental music's dominance during the nineteenth century (cf. above p. 94 and 167). When the "common man" from the interwar period thought about music, he thought *most often about song*. Music researchers thoughts about the hegemony of instrumental music, therefore ought to have quieted down during the first half of the twentieth century (but it has taken some time…).

These observed divisions between recorded music and popular music, and art music respectively, mirrors a general change that concerns all forms of products that could be mass produced and that changed everyone's everyday experience. An observation that the sociologist Paul Willis makes of the 1990s can also easily be applied to the beginning of that century:

> Commercial cultural forms have helped to produce a historical present from which we cannot escape and in which there are many more materials—no matter what we think of them—available for necessary symbolic work than ever there were in the past. Out of these come forms not dreamt of in the commercial imagination and certainly not in the official one—forms which make up common culture (Willis 1990, 19).

It is these "forms" that dominate everyday culture.

After World War I the recording business started up again on a large scale and became an industry. In the middle of the 1920s about 25 million records were produced in Germany, of which about 20 million were exported! The English export business reached 12 million records and the North American about 10 million records (Haas 1957, 59).

---

rich in resources that was not afraid of new music—and sound reproducing machines" (Andersson 1998, 133).

A PERIOD OF EXPANSION

During the 1920s recording and playback technology improved considerably. In an announcement from 1926 the violist Barthold Lundén in Göteborg wrote about the sound quality of HMV's new gramophone:

> Such fullness in the sound, such a euphony, it was no longer a gramophone. It truly defies every description, how wonderfully well everything is replayed the different choir voices, the orchestra and in the end the great roar of the organ! One should never say never, but in this case, I can hardly believe that I would be prophesying falsely, if I say that we cannot expect any appreciable improvement over what the "new gramophone" has produced (as cited in Edström 1996, 253).

We know that Lundén was wrong: recording and playback technique has substantially improved since the 1920s.

At the same time the reviewer for the daily *Göteborgs Morgonpost* [*Göteborg Morning Post*], Herman Hamnquist, reports that he had walked the streets of Göteborg and heard how the sounds streamed out of the open windows. Sometimes they came from a musical instrument, but also from a gramophone, and in ninety-nine of a hundred cases, the syncopated measures stumbled forth to the incomparable enjoyment of the assembled listeners. But, Hamnquist continues, there are luckily other spiritual nourishments, and then goes on to talk about the Swedish composer Emil Sjögren. Had Hamnquist promenaded farther into the park and perhaps journeyed out into the archipelago, he perhaps could have heard music from portable gramophones. Even though they were more expensive than simple gramophones, they were very popular. Advertisements offered tips about the new environments in which one could listen to one's own music. In camping tents, on the beach, and on the sailboat, Columbia's gramophone raised its voice with its pure, colorful tones, and assured us that the machine was already in "millions of homes."

The gramophone, though, was a rather expensive machine that required records, which, of course, also cost money.[26] Most of the records contained about three minutes of music o a side. Shorter symphonic pieces could just be squeezed onto the somewhat larger records with a playing time of four minutes. For the first time it became possible for a single individual to listen alone or with friends of family at home—or with a travel gramophone in another suitable place—to a symphony movement performed by a large symphony orchestra or a well-known tango with a German dance orchestra. Earlier, very few could even imagine listening to music in the home's *intimate sphere* that was designed to be performed in a *public context*.

---

[26] At the end of the decade one could buy a portable gramophone for about 110 kronor, which was roughly half of a monthly salary for an industrial worker. A radio could be had for more reasonable prices.

To the value ascribed to the gramophone and its music, we can also add the value of a new social activity; listening to favorite records *together with people of the same age*. This was something that did not quickly spread in the 1910s, but it enjoyed a very wide spread by the end of the 1960s, when practically every young person in Sweden, for instance, to that of their own music system, or had access to their parents or siblings.

In musically-interested homes where music had earlier been a rarity, the gramophone had already created major change by the inter-war period. In homes where sounding music was a daily occurrence, perhaps the gramophone did not create the same revolution, but may have spurred an increase in music-making. Alternately there were fewer occasions when the children played for family gatherings, etc., and their music was replaced by the latest gramophone record. One extremely important activity for which the gramophone (and the radio) were unusually well suited was dance. One testimony from the 1920s reads:

> We put a little candle wax on the kitchen floor and wound up the gramophone. It was "A Galaxy of Stars" and all the other old tunes and then we danced (Stigsdotter 1985, 276).[27]

***

In connection with the access that one had earlier with music, and the fact that one could play a record many times, the use of the gramophone brought about a larger change than anything earlier. The music sounds exactly the same every time it was played. We can therefore assume that *much changed concerning the way people listened*. As the historian Cyril Ehrlich expressed it:

> [P]laying-time restrictions influenced repertory; the three minute jazz or dance number; the four minute popular classic... The manner of hearing was *concentrated*, far more commonly, perhaps than any time before, and certainly since; both because the brief duration of each side discouraged daydreaming or alternative pursuits, and because the high cost of discs encouraged intensive use of a small collection. During the 1930s and '40s record owners of every taste...*knew* their chosen music with a thoroughness previously only achieved by trained musicians (Ehrlich 1991, 333).

Ehrlich's approach suggests, therefore, that especially during a few decades from the 1920s onward, there were different ways of listening to the gramophone at home. On one hand there was a concentrated listening to the few records that one had (where one surely had memorized not only the music but also every skip and scratch). The more compact the living quarters, the more members there were in the family, the noisier it was in the apartment, and the number of distracting moments increased when one played gramophone records. The situation at home

---

[27]Observe that in most cases *schlager* also functioned as well-loved dance music (Edström 1989).

encouraged a background mode of listening. But one can, on the other hand, also imagine that gramophone music sometimes took the foreground even though one was occasionally reminded of where one was.

After the end of the World War I, radio waves began to spread out over Europe. This happened, by the way, during a period when sweeping changes were taking place in European societies. In Sweden, this included the great voting rights reform, the great democratic breakthrough. During these years, women's social rights formally became the same as men's.

Listening to Music on the Radio

In the early 1920s there were only a few radios mostly built by amateur enthusiasts. By 1937, a little over a decade after its official beginning in 1925, there were over a million license owners, which is to say that there were at least that many radios. Ten years later another million had received licenses (Björnberg 1998, 42f).[28] From the 1920s another change begins in earnest that can first be traced to cafés. While one or another café owner had already bought a phonograph at the beginning of the century to attract more guests, it was now usual to find a large radio taking pride of place. At the beginning of the 1930s there were over 80 radio cafés in Göteborg delighting guests and owners alike, but with obvious consequences for musicians and composers.[29] In these milieus one probably often heard music in the background.

The possibility of listening to radio music at home is in principal not different from what has already been described. There is only one, and not a very large difference that involves personal choice: when someone placed a record on the gramophone the music and the time of listening are chosen, when someone turned the radio dial one heard what was playing on the radio at the time. Sometimes one knew of course what was being played if one looked in the program list, but more often one simply turned on the radio. But one could also try to dial in some other music than what was being played on Swedish Radio, or turn it off. Other people

---

[28] The expansion of the radio can also be measured in money: while in 1927 "electronic special devices" were sold for 4.8 million kronor, in 1932, the figure is 12.6 and in 1937, 24.7 million kronor. Today there are many more radios than people in Sweden. Concerning the amount of time music is heard on the radio, Björnberg shows that up until Sveriges Radio (The Swedish Broadcast Corporation) increased the number of channels, between 45 and 50%, and a number of years from 1961, up to 70% of broadcasting time was given over to music and thereafter a variable amount returning to between 50 and 60% (Björnberg 1998, appendices 1-5).

[29] That recorded music had a negative effect on musicians' job prospects was a fact that the Swedish musicians' union mentioned already at the end of the 1920s (see Edström 1982, 142f). The copyright organization STIM carried out a long battle from the 1920s with the restaurant and café owners who illegally used copyrighted music in their places of business (see also Edström 1998, 88f).

in the room who could not affect the choice of music, were in both the case of the gramophone and the radio passive listeners from this perspective.

A great difference between radio and gramophone was also that in the radio one could hear whole symphonies and operas presented in complete live broadcasts. It was only at the end of the 1930s that the radio began to record whole broadcasts on tape that could later be rebroadcast. Before this, of course, parts of broadcasts could be recorded on 78 rpm records.

Radio listeners could hear radio music as background music but also concentrate on it, as if they were at a concert. Communication with the gramophone and the radio was always one-way. While it was possible to play a record and repeat it many times, on the radio, the only change possible was to regulate the volume. In none of these cases was there a possibility for a two-way and direct communication between musician and listener.

In the inter-war period, several personalities connected to the so-called Frankfurt School issued warnings about this aspect and other negative consequences that were seen as connected to the use of the new media. The cultural sociologist Martin Jay in his thorough study of the Frankfurt School also takes up how Adorno was affected by his friend the composer Ernst Krenek's ideas about the negative role of the radio. Krenek believed that the musical content in the offerings on the radio were stamped by conventionality and that music was reduced to an everyday ornament. Radio broadcasts of music could, according to Krenek, express music's simultaneousness, *nunc*, but not its presentness, *hic* (Jay 1973, 191). Jay introduces a third thinker, the literary sociologist Walter Benjamin, into the circle and writes in summary:

> [R]adio brought about a crucial change in the aesthetic experience of the listener... Instead of experiencing the music with its 'auratic' qualities intact, the radio listener heard it in a depersonalized, collective, objectivized form, which robbed it of its negative function. Adorno's own study of radio music agreed with Krenek's conclusions (Jay 1973, 191).

It was thus said that music's "aura," or its "auratic qualities" could be lost through the process of mass production. Those who bought a painting that was mass produced or a record, thought, however, very little about whether the work's authenticity had been compromised, but rather enjoyed more the possibility of contemplating and owning the reproduction. The situation was naturally different between a painting and a composition, where perhaps there was an "original manuscript," but the interpretation of the notes always generated the possibility of different performances.

Some futurists and painters, however, had already stood up for this development. When Marcel Duchamp showed a mass produced urinal as art, he succeeded in destroying the artworks' aura (Huyssen 1986, 10).[30] As has been pointed out, the musical futurists and the musical avant garde did not have the same success. Their music was very seldom recorded or heard outside the walls of the initiated.

At the end of the 1920s the problem of the radio becoming a danger for our musical society was discussed. The theme was even debated on the radio. Newspapers published letters to the editor and mirrored the debate. The music reviewer and director of music at the Swedish Broadcasting Corporation Julius Rabe maintained that like the art of painting where modern reproduction techniques made "it possible to spread awareness of and knowledge about works of sculpture and art," the experience of a musical work could be "richer and deeper." When, after hearing the work on the radio or on the gramophone, one then visited a concert where the same work was played:

> Then concerts become the festival days in our musical life, delivering gripping experiences of longing and shared love to music that is organically united to a congregation of listening audience members (*Göteborgs Morgonpost* 28/2 1927).

Statements in the Radio's tenth anniversary publication from 1934 show clearly that at a very early stage "normal" radio listeners also thought about the new relationships that the radio generated. We find also a clear example of æII and æIII in an essay by the high school teacher Sven Olof Molin:

> How common is it not, that one listens to Beethoven symphony, for example, during a noisy conversation or even with the splashing of the water tap and the noise of the dishwashing as an extra accompaniment! Such listeners use the radio completely negatively, in my opinion, where it comes to function as a way to blunt the senses and awareness. I also have a rich experience of the opposite, in fact many, nay an uncountable number of times, that at home… a whole coterie has sat and experienced Haydn or Beethoven in absolute silence, with the lights dimmed or replaced with the illumination from the radio. We then found ourselves not merely in the concert house…but rather completely removed. *Removed from the present—from the kitchen table and the dishwashing!* (Henriksson 1934, 243 [my italics]).

In this jubilee publication from 1934, we find different kinds of evidence for the radio's powerful impact and its meaning, even though it is impossible to know how representative the answers are for the population as a whole. The composer Gösta Nystroem warned, as only one of many musicians during this time, that mechanical music laid too much of a damper on living music. Nystroem thought mainly from the perspective of a large city. In country villages one had fairly little access to live music in general, at least of the type that Nystroem was mainly

---

[30]See also Huyssen's chapter "The Cultural Politics of Pop," where differences between Adorno's and Benjamin's (and others') views are discussed (Huyssen 1986, 141-59).

concerned with. For country people the radio meant the opposite: the cultural isolation, which many experienced could be reduced to a great extent, and not that one stopped attending concerts that didn't exist. The radio had a particular large influence for those with limited finances and also generally for women.[31]

The editor Alf Henriksson preached his passion for general education and saw that both Beethoven and the popular accordionist Jularbo should be offered, but warned anyway about too much "thoughtless listening." In fact he wrote that "to be able to have the brain deafened with silly noise is not an inalienable right of humanity" (Henriksson 1934, 238).

Beethoven's name shows up in some other contexts: a listener, growing up with the Free Church songs of Ahnfeldt and Sankey, confesses that he has difficulty in understanding Beethoven, while another listener writes, that on first hearing the seventh symphony, he was able to maintain concentration for a few minutes, but on the third listening he "was transported in ecstasy" and has since then never neglected Beethoven (Henriksson 1934, 249). The content of the personal commentaries varies, but even though they were chosen by the Swedish Broadcasting Corporation, clearly shows us the essentials: *the use of song/music changed and thereby also music's function and meaning.* As a letter carrier in Göteborg expressed it, he could now from his own home "enjoy varying things, but have access to lighter music, cabarets and real concerts," and he states that:

> For me the radio is indispensable. It has like nothing else *changed the shape of my home life* (cited after Edström 1996, 242).

Ethereal Music and Aesthetics

While middle music had completely dominated the silent movie theaters, even from the start, it also constituted the main part of the music played by the Swedish Broadcasting Corporation in their programs. "The Gramophone Hour" was the sounding definition of middle music. Only during the second half of the twentieth century did gramophone music gradually begin to be dominated by a narrower section of middle music, and songs, while at the end of the century, the radio offerings were almost completely dominated by the music forms that have too long been described as youth music: rock'n'roll, pop, rock, dance band music, "world music," etc. Many of those who first encountered rock and roll in the 1950s are now retired.

---

[31] Hobsbawm comments that the radio coverage was greatest in English-speaking countries: "It is perhaps not surprising that the radio audience doubled in the years of the Great Depression, when its rate of growth was faster than before or later. For radio transformed the life of the poor, and especially of housebound poor women, as nothing else had ever done before" (Hobsbawm 1994, 195).

Middle music dominated people's everyday musical world long into the twentieth century. Middle music, therefore, was a foundation on which people built all of their personally felt musical values. But the starting points varied: for some, middle music was a structurally more simple form of music than that heard during a symphony concert. For another small group of people it was a more evocative music than the melodies and old dance songs that one listened to and enjoyed dancing to.

From the large survey that the Swedish Broadcasting Corporation sponsored around 1930 we see that women in relation to men generally wanted more "higher" music on the radio.[32] This development shows thus that the misgivings that Krenek and Adorno during the 1930s gave voice to—concerning the radio's totally conventionalizing function as an impersonal and collective music medium—were far from fulfilled. Quite the opposite, more people than ever before in history came in contact with art music thanks to radio and film.

Concerning what is possible to say about middle music generally, it is, however, not as easy to define music's functions unambiguously, because these naturally enough depend upon how music is performed, each (group)individual's references, as well as the context. The premier mode of listening, like the context as a rule was rather an emotional-associative than a "Hanslickian" one.

The situation for listeners at the movies was principally different. Here one learned to a great extent to listen *with the eyes*. The music's function as an accompaniment and supportive medium undergirded above all an associative listening mode.[33] Also later, when talking pictures replaced the silent film musicians, music became a very important part of the contents of the film. The first Swedish talking picture in 1929 was called *Säg det i toner* ["Say it in Tones".][34] Film producers during the 1930s staked very large sums of money so that almost every talking picture had at least one big popular hit number that could be linked to the film, while at the same time the song could be a sounding symbol for the film. The film's contents also had much background music of different kinds. Middle music in the form of operettas was also often heard from the screen. During the latter half of the century stage musicals were also produced as films launching new music- and dance-styles packaged in a long film format.

---

[32]For a thorough discussion of this large survey see Edström 1992.

[33]For an introduction to and discussion of music for silent films and music in the succeeding talking films in Sweden during the interwar period see Edström 1996, 345-78.

[34]The melody was released December 14, 1928, a day that was proclaimed as "Say it in Music Day." It instantly became a great success, thus it was printed in large numbers and came out in many gramophone recordings. Thanks to the fact that the melody was an important song in Colin Nutley's successful 1992 film *Änglagård* [*House of Angels*] it is still a part of our shared melodic culture.

One paradigmatic example of the difference in attitude toward the period's contemporary music (that is to say dance music and *schlager*) and art music is played out in the 1942 Swedish film *Det är min musik* ["That's My Music,"]. Here we meet the poor, young genius violinist who is about to give his debut concert and some normal "Stockholm Lads" who play dance music. The former is admired by a lady from the upper class. Her husband supports the violinist financially. Higher music and the educated *bourgeoisie* world are connected. At one point, the violinist is a substitute in a dance orchestra, but fails miserably when he cannot improvise a "hot solo" in a foxtrot. He takes his revenge immediately by playing a solo piece of typical middle music, Brahms's Hungarian Dance No. 5. When the dance-happy girls stop and stare dreamily at the violinist, his music is shown to belong to a "higher aesthetic plane." The good Swedish welfare state feeling that prevails in the Swedish films during the War years demanded an establishment of good musical relations: in the final scene we see the classical violinist giving a celebrated concert and then the plucky dance orchestra plays their well-arranged *schlager* in notated form—that is to say middle music—at the party following the concert.

Form an aesthetic standpoint, æI can pertain to all the cases where music is experienced consciously to a great extent: at home, on the streets and in the squares, at cafés and restaurants and movie theaters, and so forth. A cultural displacement toward æIII only found room if the context allowed and if people were socialized to understand the overarching aesthetic discourse. At this time the *bourgeois* aesthetic project had over a hundred years under its belt. The likelihood that æIII could be experienced was greatest in the context where music was performed in restaurants and movie theaters as well as in *bourgeois* homes. As in the later cosy and probably relatively silent sound milieus, it was at least possible to concentrate on the music itself and forget the food and the clinking forks, while in the movie theaters one could also close one's eyes and forget about the moving pictures. In a time relatively poor in terms of live and mechanical music, probably both the pleasant restaurant locales and the dark movie theaters could both be reshaped into a kind of concert hall for more people than we normally realize and with æII and æIII as helping spirits to bring them to a higher transcendental world.

Middle music can be compared to a sounding cement that functioned structurally as a collectively binding musical power in the developing belief of the creation of a conflict-free Swedish socialist state. Middle music, whereever it was performed, did not hinder an aesthetic experience, but it was obvious that one could approach structural listening from two different directions. The listeners also had a socialized aesthetic preparedness came to this dominant music from a higher perspective. But as has been pointed out, even with good knowledge about the art music tradition *gehobene mittlere Musik* [higher forms of middle music], could certainly make æIII possible, especially if the contextual relationships were conducive, likewise for those who came to this music from contrary perspectives. So even if music was structurally the same, it did not necessarily mean the same things to different people, especially if they had different references.

As we have seen, the high school teacher Molin commented that he and his friends experienced a sense of removal from the present when they listened to Haydn and Beethoven at home. We can, of course, see from his profession that he was a cog in the wheel of the *bourgeois* education project. It continued to be an important task within this project to nurture, form, and educate people. Because this has a direct effect on the experience of art, we will further explore the discussion of the educational and social conditions for the aesthetic experience.

Education and—or—Enjoyment

During the twentieth century, the word pair enjoyment/education became a common tool for describing the differences in the use of art. Against the background of the contexts and the social connections that music had that could convey æII and æIII, the connection between aesthetics and education lie close at hand. Entertainment music and dance music stood for enjoyment.[35] But obviously it was also pleasant, fun, enjoyable, etc. to visit a concert, or a musical salon, and it was fun to listen to a wind band in the city park or a street musician in the square. Listening to music was also a social activity. One met people—if one was not only sitting alone and playing gramophone records or listening to the radio. It was a break in the daily routine.[36] But there were, or course, many exceptions to the rule: depending upon individual people's references and tastes in music it might have been just as much work to listen to a long Bruckner symphony, not to mention the string quartets of Schönberg. And the opposite could also occur, that someone really thought it was beneath ones dignity to be exposed to the latest top hits.

---

[35]Björnberg remarks that Swedish Radio had one channel its offerings were dominated by general education. With two stations, from 1955, "enjoyment" also began to take a larger place. The Swedish Broadcasting Service's mandate to "raise" the musical taste was, as one might expect, a project that clearly stretched far into the future. Björnberg also gives an example of how, as late as the 1959/60 season, music radio's general program was formulated, with popular concerts' place described as: "This type of higher entertainment music is bordered below by *schlager* music and its heaviest offerings are pieces by the likes of Liszt, Grieg and Saint-Saëns." As Björnberg comments, there was an ambition "to raise the musical quality—from an unquestioned though seldom explicitly formulated concept of quality"(Björnberg 1996, 12).

[36]It can be seen in my work on the musical life of Göteborg during the interwar period that musical interludes during the work day were very much appreciated. Street musicians were a welcome addition to "the proletarian cultural life, where there was a lack of entertainment other than the movies and the Salvation Army concerts" (Edström 1996, 271).

To listen to music that one looked down upon must be understood as a bad point of departure for the aesthetic experience. There was also a general *bourgeois*, or perhaps better described as a Protestant Christian, understanding that too much enjoyment also spoiled the possibility of an aesthetic experience. This idea is a *bourdon* that drones throughout the *bourgeois* culture. As the writer Alf Henriksson expressed it, it was not an inalienable right to have one's brain deafened with silly noise.

In a sense, we have already met this way of thinking in Kant. Perhaps the most important aesthetic criterion for Kant was "disinterestedness" (cf. Kant 1951, §2-4). This idea becomes ideally a part of the aesthetic experience that has been described as æII. And, as we saw, this was an impossible precondition from Nietzsche's perspective. This assurance has been repeated by many later philosophers. Arnold Berleant writes, for example :

> Theoretical developments since the Enlightenment have pressed the theory of disinterestedness quite out of its shape. The Romantic attraction to the emotional and expressive dimensions of aesthetic experience, and the sharing of such experience through artistic communication, have definitively incorporated the personal contribution into the artistic and receptive processes (Berleant 1994, 243).

"Disinterestedness" requires, as we have seen, that there exists a "disinterested" state among those who are listening, and that what is being listened to is something self contained and separate. Thus the doctrine misses the essential point according to Berleant. The listener and the music are dependent upon one another: "No aesthetic perceiver without a perceptual object; no perceptual object without a perceiver who activates the experience" (Berleant 1994, 250). Even Dissanayake comes straight out and says that this ability is highly specialized and beyond the reach of the untrained person (Dissanayake 1993, 130). In a summarizing passage, she adds:

> As the subject of aesthetics developed… a startling and influential idea took hold… a 'disinterested' attitude that disregards any consideration of one's own personal interest in the object, its utility, or its social or religious ramifications. This unprecedented idea led to still another: the work of art is a world-in-itself. 'Disinterest' implied that one could transcend the limitations of time, place and temperament… [and] that works of art were vehicles for a special kind of knowledge… had no purpose… Enjoying an aesthetic experience was its own reward (Dissanayake 1993, 197).[37]

---

[37] For similar critiques Cf. Shusterman 1992, 45. One can therefore think that by the beginning of the nineteenth century it should have been obvious that there existed a kind of opposition between the idea of "disinterestedness' and the documented interest that more and more *bourgeois* people showed in art.

It is clear that within the *bourgeois* society and within trend-setting socialist organizations during these decades there was a fear that modern society, and not least the new media, would be able to change the parameters of the *bourgeois* education project. They were afraid that listening to music would become an all too physical enjoyment and the idea of an autonomous cognitive listening could give way to the purely emotional. It was feared that this change might hinder the formation of responsible citizens and good workers.

This was expressed in several ways in a well-respected and very typical lecture for the time that the educated composer Ture Rangström held at the end of the 1920s.[38] His rhetoric comes out of the German Romantic-Idealistic tradition. We meet again the thought of the close connection between aesthetics and ethics: music's educational value lies, he says, in its ability "to bring forth fruit in the wastelands within us the sprit's and the senses' knowledge about themselves, with the power of knowledge to expand, broaden and govern." Rangström, in passing, raises a warning finger for "the chapels of jazz, that with heart and soul seek to deafen the harmony of the masters, the angels and the spheres." He summarizes:

> Music gives us, like educational material, many weapons in hand against loneliness, the darkness of ignorance, the soul's raw materials and the weight of the physical. Music's sound gives wings to the senses and song makes it easy to be good. It is not without cause that music in poetry and life is always named: the reconciler. Reconciliation is education, it is the victory over the lowest tendencies toward conflict and selfishness. The education that music gives and tones always aim for, is thus at the core of man's character (*Göteborgs Morgonpost* 11/10-27).[39]

What Rangström expressed lies in line with the idea of giving education to the working and farming classes. Even if the *bourgeois* educational organizations and the social democratic party did not act out of the same ideological motives, they both propagandized that the "lower" classes should be able to take part in *bourgeois* education: art, literature, music, and so forth.[40] Earlier, we have met this "domesticating" process by way of the special worker concerts that were started in

---

[38] The lecture took place in conjunction with a concert in Stockholm, and was cited in the daily papers. My citation is taken from *Göteborgs Morgonpost* 11/10 1927.

[39] In an interview with the well-known director Armas Järnefeldt (*Göteborgs Handels – och Sjöfartstidning* 11/2 1927) there is also a description of music's noble influence, that it creates better character, which can be read in books on aesthetics. Järnefelt, however, was doubtful: "I cannot help that I believe this is just a saying. No one becomes a better person simply by listening to a symphony... but it does broaden a person's horizons. It gives one a larger front on life, if I can put it that way. One becomes richer, one's emotional life more full and more multifaceted. Goethe says... when one hears a piece of music, one bounces back and wonders, what was that...that was beautiful...[one] wants to experience that again."

[40] If, as has been seen from a socialist perspective, one's goal was to create educated and wise citizens before the coming shift in power, the great value for the *bourgeoisie* lay in the transfer of their own values to the upper calls so that imagined conflicts would not develop.

Sweden in the 1890s. In Göteborg these concerts continued right up to the last decades of the twentieth century. Concert number 1000 was held in 1937 and number 1600 in 1983.

Elementary school songs and Church hymns had, of course, long served this socializing function. Teaching songs and music education in elementary schools mirror also the same double function of education and enjoyment. One was not to only enjoy singing and playing. It was also part of the student's upbringing, under the guidance of a musical master.[41] One sang psalms, school songs folk songs and other songs, often with pedagogical, educationally correct and patriotic texts.

This meant that the music teacher who, during the interwar period, tried to use *schlager* as school songs soon landed in hot water (Edström 1989, 303). Schlager songs didn't have any higher value among musicologists either. When, for example, Adorno discussed the contents of *schlager* and their significance at the end of the 1920s, it probably didn't cross his mind that *schlager* might have any aesthetic value.[42]

Folk music and folk songs had, on the other hand, a stable position among both high and low culture, as a part of the Swedish cultural legacy. Folk music as a true and ancient form of national music, as well as its use as a source of inspiration for works of art music, meant that this music partly found its place within the aesthetic field. But even here there was a clear hierarchy within which modal *polskas* were placed higher than waltzes in the major mode. As can be seen from the following review of Julius Rabe from the summer of 1923, he could describe a fiddle player's tune as if he were writing a review about art music. Here we find many artful formulations, even if the word aesthetic is not overtly used:

> From an artistic perspective it was, however, the Dalecarlia musicians that came to be seen as the highpoint [fiddle players'] music could create astonishment. The introductory wedding march in the dorian mode on d had a power and logic in its harmony and a respectfulness in its internal consistency, with which they managed to make myself and a few other musicians present, completely flattened with surprise, not least the characteristic change between f and f# created a lustrous and overwhelming effect [...] Such experiences could not be

---

[41] *From Studyplans for Teachers* [*Läroplan för läroverken*] from 1929, we learn that the study of music theory and music history were important elements. We also learn that one could increase students' "treasure of valuable songs" (Edström 1996, 53).

[42] Adorno is probably the musicologist who became known earliest for his antipathy toward *schlager* music. In the Swedish magazine *Våra Nöjen* [*Our Entertainment*] there is a 1929 reference to Adorno's views on some famous German *schlager* artists. The paper wrote that "this undoubtedly colossally well educated and colossally reliable author has—apparently with the help of a pair of tongs—plucked out three *schlager*." Concerning a *schlager* of Oscar Strauss it is said that Strauss is not capable of handling material: "If he finds a beautiful chord that fits the text well, then he cannot resolve it. So he finds help in the pedal—when the danger is greatest it is the pedal that's nearest" (*Våra Nöjen* 1929, 21:30).

daily food, but even if one takes into account a good deal of the individual genius involved in the creation of similar works of art, it is impossible not to experience a living sense of the artistic value available in the old fiddleplayer's culture, in the service of which this tune so successfully played its part (*Göteborgs Handels- och Sjöfartstidning* 1923, 8:8).

It is thought-provoking that the status and the close relationship the Swedes had to their own folk music meant that school children even up to the 1960s often sang "*Jag vet en dejlig rosa*" and other folk songs in the class times set aside for music.[43] This was at a time when more than forty years had already passed since *schlager* in all of its forms had begun to take over the role as the most popular kind of music in Sweden. Put simply, Swedish folk music stood for the rural culture and older times, while *schlager* as the music that one sang most, listened to and danced to belonged to urban culture and the new modern times.

We find, thus, that within the conceptual pair of education/enjoyment there was a well developed sense of what kinds of music were generally appropriate for enculturation and childrens' education. When the ethnologists Jonas Frykman and Orvar Löfgren discuss this process they come to similar conclusions:

> [The] culture that the *bourgeoisie* supports becomes the normative for other groups in the society—also for the working class. It is during the era of Oscar II [from the 1870s] that the *bourgeois* culture becomes the *victorious* culture. It is now that a new cultural hegemony is established, a hegemony that still is recognizable in today's society (Löfgren 1979, 222).

If art within the *bourgeois* culture has long been seen as a compensatory factor, we now find the same thought expressed generally for the entire industrial society, which splintered people into different social spheres: "opposites like home—outer world, work—leisure, production and reproduction" (Löfgren 1979, 65).[44]

Another Swedish ethnological work, the 1985 collection of articles titled *Modärna tider* [Modern Times], concerns just the time when broadcast media make the big breakthrough.[45] Here the criticism is that the same ideals as

---

[43]For a depiction of the power that stood behind Swedish folk music at the beginning of the century, see Ling 1979. Cf. also Burke 1994, 270ff. During the rest of the twentieth century it is apparently at school, at the folk high schools and the academic institutions where Swedish folk music kept its status. Through this process, which is very little documented, Swedish folk music was able to hang on to its reputation as the music of the Swedish people, even though in reality since at least the middle of the twentieth century it was probably was near and dear to only a small minority of the population.

[44]They add that at the same time there was being created a "new ideology about the possibility of become a new person." As we have seen this possibility had already been a fact for a long time: culture as a compensatory way out can be seen as a part of the Enlightenment project (cf. Eagleton 1990, 59f).

[45]It can be illuminating to compare this with films like Chaplin's Modern Times and the 1932 Swedish film Modärna fruar [Modern Women]. The latter, written by film scholar Olle Sjögren, is a story of bourgeois women in Stockholm who are tempted by jazz and drawn into dance

permeated nineteenth-century's *bourgeois* childrearing—discipline, a strong work ethic, satisfaction with limited means, thriftiness—were still valid in the interwar period (Frykman and Löfgren 1985, 272f). These were the ideals that also stood as signposts for the working class and the developing middle class.[46] But on the other hand, it also emerged that the education project did not draw as many as one had hoped. In a report from a lecture society struggling for survival, it is said that in the 1920s if the topic of the lecture wasn't of interest and there wasn't some "jazz happening nearby, one could expect 30 listeners, otherwise it would be more like 10-12 people" (Frykman and Löfgren 1985, 341). The difficulty of convincing people to take advantage of the educational opportunities that were on offer was discussed also from the perspective of the radio. Those who were already interested listened happily to lectures on the radio, while others "waited for the accordion music and the cabaret." He adds:

> Many educators were skeptical of radio's ability to "spread light in the darkness." Some experienced it even as a danger to culture, something that used up time that could be spent reading and making music (Frykman and Löfgren 1985, 343).[47]

In other words, the educational and cultural agenda from the 1920s that could take advantage of the radio medium did not always have the success that was expected. Partly there was a lack of awareness among many educators that meant that they did not experience their message as class- and culture-specific. In many cases the target group partly defended itself against the cultural pressure, "that continuously stuck its face behind every speech about objective value and classlessness" (Frykman and Löfgren 1985, 350). And as we have seen, even though the time was marked by optimism about future developments and a belief in new technology, from the *bourgeoisie* quarter there was also an apprehension that above all the working class and the farmers (the rural population) would "misuse" the new media.

If the contents of many lectures had an all too clear ideological bent, there was, however, very little awareness—if any at all—among popular concert goers that the music they heard could be sounding examples of *bourgeois* value

---

restaurants: "A housewife who has tired of her professor, can flirt with a younger man, but is expected to see that in the long run it is better to exercise the mind than 'jazz' with the legs" (Boëthius et al 1998, 300).

[46] The article by the ethnologist Margareta Stigsdotter, *Den långa vägens män / The Long Road of Man*, is mostly about the lives of people in service. Observe that if at the beginning of the century there were about 80,000 privately employed white collar workers, this number had risen to about 500,000 by the beginning of the 1950s. There were as many state and community employed white collar workers.

[47] The idea that education and knowledge can have negative influences for those who hold power is an old one. Woodmansee writes, for example, how conservative forces in the eighteenth century saw a danger in the way literacy was spreading: "Readers who had glimpsed another, better world in books will rise up and forcibly attempt to impose their vision on the real world" (Woodmansee 1994, 91).

judgments. Added to this, with relatively few exceptions, more middle music was played at these concerts than "higher" art music—and naturally older modernistic music. Instrumental music's affiliation with class and ideological messages have always been difficult—perhaps impossible—to distinguish from the value judgments and filters that we already have as bearers of culture. One and the same piece of instrumental music, Beethoven's *Eroica* for example, can, as has been shown, be thought to stand for a widely diverse number of ideological messages (cf. chapter 4, footnote 22).

This can also be seen in the ethnologist Alf Arvidsson's study about musical life in a small town in northern Sweden during the twentieth century. The music that one heard and made within this industrial community was almost always middle music. Here we also meet the same discussion between benefit and enjoyment: without enjoyment it was difficult to arrange the meeting. Even when a company sponsored the development of a wind orchestra the motivation was both education and enjoyment. On one side we find that in the background there was often a clear educational concept: that musicians and their listeners would be able to take part in the "higher" music, but on the other hand, the same wind band could also play dance music. One made a distinction therefore between more and less *educational* enjoyment. As Arvidsson formulates it, the latter was favored in contrast to "meaningless" enjoyment (Arvidsson 1991, 79).[48]

It is possible that the workers at the factory also met a form of courses whose basic goal was self-improvement. Within the Arbetarnas Bildningsförbund, [the Workers' Educational League] and other study societies, courses were arranged in instrument playing, orchestral playing and musical knowledge. The Swedish Broadcast Service also had different lecture series on the topic of musical masters.[49]

***

The tension between what people generally experienced as pleasure and what was counted as education is thereafter preserved. The difference in Swedish

---

[48] Arvidsson shows that music's capacity to entertain—that, for example, it was fun to sing to, listen to and dance to music—is a problematic dimension that is included in most of the situations where music occurs: within political parties, other kinds of folk movements, churches, etc. This process happens also later in the century when the Farmers' Party [*Bondeförbundet*] and the SKP (Swedish Communist Party), faced the same problem as both parties used folk music to create their respective images. One of those that played folk music within the last-named groups witness, for example, the conflict between enjoyment and Marxist indoctrination: "We had started with [folk music] because we thought it was fun," but "after a while those people that looked upon folk music as more theoretically and ideologically [acceptable] began to enlist" (Arvidsson 1991, 107).

[49] For more information about course activites and radio programming see further in Edström 1982, 170f; 1989, 300f; 1996, 213f as well as—especially concerning the radio—in Björnberg 1998, 29, 49, 58, 213.

between the word *bildning* (*bourgeoisie* education in general) and *utbildning* (education/schooling) is just the prefix *ut*, but it is clear that in child rearing and all school situations there is an element that is often experienced as less fun than playing and playing games. It was (and is) easier to get people to take pleasure in something when the reward comes quickly than when one needs to wait for it for a long time. Song was excellent from this standpoint. Most children liked to sing. It is more difficult to learn to play the violin.

The result of this argument is, as we have seen, that general education and general *bourgeois* knowledge of the arts lay very close to one another. Everyone should acquaint themselves with the *bourgeois* cultural legacy within which there was an aesthetic discourse. Both liberal and socialist educational organizations therefore had for some time organized concerts and lectures in order to satisfy the "great masses need for aesthetic enjoyment," as it is called when the "Workers' Institute in Göteborg" began to arrange its concerts in the 1890s (Edström 1996, 336).

When Bourdieu in the middle of the 1960s studied how the connection between education and enjoyment could be understood from the perspective of how different social groups experienced art and culture at French museums, many observations were made that we can apply to the interwar period. It is suggested that the higher the level of education and thereby also general knowledge of the visitors to the museums, the more varied and the great the exchange these visitors had with the exhibited objects (mainly art). But Bourdieu also believes that the agenda of education and child rearing that the *bourgeois* and socialist education providers had worked for since the nineteenth century, was successful to a large extent. Art's aesthetic value was so deeply ingrained in the minds of common people that their reactions to it (whether they could decode it or understand it) did not challenge art's position. The same social process conveyed that an accepted *bourgeois* taste not only was experienced as generally applicable, but also as self-evident and naturally endowed:

> The deliberate neglect of the social conditions which make possible culture and culture to become nature, a cultivated nature with all the appearances of grace and talent but nevertheless learned and therefore 'deserved', is the condition for the existence of the charismatic ideology, which allows culture and especially 'the love of art' to be given the central place they occupy in the *bourgeois* 'sociodicy' (Bourdieu 1991, 110).

Bourdieu finds also that the code of a work of art and its readability were most difficult to understand for those with the least education the more it deviated from the normal representative and narrative in art (Bourdieu 1991, 41). As we have earlier established, the stylistic difference between modernist art music and popular music from the same period increased drastically after the turn of the twentieth century, a difference that led to a great majority of people to say that they did not understand this art music.

***

If we, on the one hand have decided that instrumental music's semantic vagueness can lend music a non-ideological air, we have, on the other hand, also seen that vocal music was both more common and had an (understandable) text. It has also been shown that music through broadcast media could be a part of everyday life. These observations are grounds for the particular circumstances that are specialy inherent in the musical-aesthetic education project. Of course, we cannot forget that modernistic music did not make this educational project easier. On the other hand, there was generally a large amount of earlier western art music that could be played and listened to if one wanted to educate oneself in the world of music. Conversely, there was also music that was seen to have a low status and thereby had little aesthetic potential.

Education and aesthetics have, therefore, close points of contact. In the contexts where different movements and organizations arranged courses and lectures, musical offerings often played an important role in attracting people. Educational music programs were also regular features in the Swedish Radio's broadcasts. Through study circles and radio courses knowledge about composers and musical forms augmented the member's understanding. Those who arranged these courses had apparently firm ideas about which kind of music contained the most value and which music was only enjoyment. Also, one surely also had opinions about which music had the highest aesthetic value. How these values could be defined and what constituted the aesthetic experience were also questions that philosophers wrestled with.

Is it possible to define art or the aesthetic experience?

No philosopher during the eighteenth century found complete satisfaction in their predecessors' attempts to define good taste. The creation and word play surrounding an aesthetic faculty which began with Baumgarten did not lead to a generally accepted or lasting definition of what the aesthetic was or what aesthetic experience included. A generally accepted definition of good taste or an aesthetic experience did not guarantee either. But one could always discuss which qualities that were necessary so that something within a given culture could be experienced as *beautiful* (Hogan 1994).[50]

---

[50]The philosopher Patrick C. Hogan points out that two important tasks within aesthetics are often integrated: a) to give individual value judgments concerning the beautiful, and b) to isolate systematic qualities of the beautiful (Hogan 1994, 337). He tries in the article—and according

As we have seen, it came close to being self-evident that aesthetic experience was a presupposition of art music. Thus, it became important for philosophers to try to analyze and define what was art and what was non-art. From an ethnological point of view this seems, of course, to be an impossible project, because it assumes that the reason for the affect lies within the object, the music itself! If we follow some of the philosophical paths that were tried we also find many different attempts. What follows here, however, should not be seen as *eine kurze Einführung* into philosophical music aesthetics. Rather, I account for some of the more important stations along a changing philosophical process. At the same time the reader, through my choice, can share how I have understood this change: that is to say I try to illuminate

a) if it is possible to identify structural qualities that make it possible for art to call forth aesthetic feelings;

b) if art is perhaps a completely open concept;

c) if the content of art is constructed by an art world; and

d) if we—as a variant of a)—should focus on what is demanded by art for aesthetic experience of a certain intensity and quality to be experienced.

At the end of the day, the question is whether it is at all possible to define what art is or, for that matter, if it is meaningful to find a definition of the aesthetic experience (attitude, feeling, judgment, interpretation, etc.).

The philosopher George Dickie holds that even before we begin to discuss this field of inquiry, we must be clear that the way we define art can be classification, and also evaluation. He assumes that if we say that something is, for example, art music (a classification) that means that it is not necessarily good art music (an evaluation) (Dickie 1997, 50). The question is whether this external method manages to effectively repress the assertion, as well as the fact, that the process of differentiating art music from non-art music taking place within a culture depends upon a number of factors that are decided by anything but value-neutral people. Defining what can be counted as art music already presupposes a judgment from the beginning.

As we have just seen in "a", above, one can look for structural qualities within a culture that make and object "objectively" a bearer of an aesthetic experience, and in this way try to define art from non-art. The theory that Clive

---

to my understanding, succeeds—to show that: "(1) There are no principles of taste. (2) Singular judgments of taste can be true or false if there are principles of taste or a sensus communis. (3) There is no sensus communis and thus singular judgments of taste are neither false or true. However, (4) judgments of taste are open to rational debate in terms of understanding and idiosyncracy... and (5) the systematic study of beauty is viable because there are laws of taste or, equivalently, aesthetic universals" (Hogan 1994, 338). What Hogan refers to in the two last points are in the two certain forms of patterns and sounds. When we seek out realism within literature, our short-term memory creates limits for the length of lines in poems, etc. (Hogan 1994, 342-8).

Bell introduced in 1914 departed from the point that there existed certain objects that had a structure/form that called forth a special and personally experienced feeling:

> All sensitive people agree that there is a peculiar emotion produced by works of art… This emotion is called the aesthetic emotion (as cited after Dickie 1997, 54).

That which caused these feelings in different objects was, above all "significant form." The circularity in this definition precludes its usefulness. On the other hand, and this can later be seen in Dahlhaus, one can naturally make a comparison between Bachs/Gounod's "Ave Maria" and Schumann's "Träumerei," and come to the conclusion that the former can be analyzed as a work of art, but isn't one. "The difference," writes Dahlhaus, "between art and kitsch lies in the details" (Dahlhaus 1988, 210). He states also that the difference lies in the structure and not in the collected relations between context–structure–use of music, a statement that is clearly problematic.

It did not help, according to Dickie, that from the 1920s onwards, this formalistic theory was continuously patched and repaired. The obvious problem lay always in the fact that one was forced to show a structure that was presupposed to have the content or the individual *essence* that called forth the aesthetic emotion.[51]

Different authors have different views on which theory followed. Shusterman, for example takes up the philosopher Morris Weitz idea that the concept of art is an *open* one[52] (see "b," above) and that, in line with Wittgenstein's thought about family similarity, there is an endless number of different sports that are all called play, but when taken together do not have totally similar qualities, but some overlapping ones (for example chess and football). But this theory does not help if one tries to define art in relationship to *non-art*, that from the starting point are two different categories. That Weitz's theory involved in part a classification, and in part an evaluation, made the trial unsuccessful.[53]

---

[51] Bell believed that his theory also could be applicable to music. Shusterman writes, however, that the circular theory was not only based upon "a mysterious aesthetic emotion itself identified only through significant form, it also clearly could not cover those arts where representational content was crucial" (Shusterman 1992, 37). Dissanayake comments that Bell's and others' theories presupposed an increasingly elitist view of art (Dissanayake 1991, 197f).

[52] Dickie's exposition is more thorough than Shusterman's. Before he takes up Weitz, he passes by Susan Langer and R. G. Collingwood. These are passed over by Shusterman's short review.

[53] Cf. Shusterman 1992, 37 and Dickie 1997, 71f. Surprisingly enough, neither Shusterman or Dickie takes up the philosopher Benodeto Croce's aesthetic work from the beginning of the twentieth century. Perhaps Croce was too radical. The philosopher Colin Lyas (1997, 103f) points out that Croce avoided the whole of what art was by defining all objects made by humans as art. Lyas writes after Croce that there are only degrees of difference between different objects (art) and not an artistic different, that is to say, art and not-art. In this way "the unending and futile search of a way of distinguishing in kind between those things we make that are art and those

As we have seen, these theories did not do well when they met reality, and it was (and is) therefore not surprising, writes Dissanayake, that Danto and Dickie later laid out theories that placed the consecration of art within a network of agents, artists, buyers, sellers, art institutions (including musicological institutions) etc., which together created an *institutional art* (according to point "c" above). It was this combined art world that, could define a certain material or phenomenon as art.[54]

This theory seems, naturally enough, sympathetic to an ethnomusicologist, especially as later philosophers also added that what is experienced as art has a social history. There is much in this theory of art as a praxis, but Shusterman also suggests that it is not enough:

> In defining art as a practice defined by art-historical narrative, all substantive decisions as to what counts as art or in art are left to the internal decisions of the practice as recorded by art history. Philosophy of art collapses into art history (Shusterman 1992, 44).

The way out of this dilemma for Shusterman is to give up all attempts to define art from non-art, and instead, after the philosopher and sociologist John Dewey, focus on art as experience, that is to say, as an aesthetic experience (see point "d" above). There is simply something of independent value in art, something, writes Shusterman, "about its own goods for which we pursue them as ends in themselves rather than means to other goods in other practices" (Shusterman 1992, 46 [we recognize here Dissanayake's anthropological idea, æI]).

However, it is apparently difficult within the philosophical tradition to nail down what this should be. Added to this, it is still left to solve how music can express something that people can experience. Shusterman is forced to state that Dewey writes a great deal about the "aesthetic experience," which he saw as a part of our life and that was (and is) a quality that could be found within art, as well as sports, cooking and science, etc. But, writes Shusterman, Dewey unfortunately also suggested aesthetic experience as a theoretical definition of art: "By standard philosophical criteria, this definition is hopelessly inadequate,

---

that are not" disappears (Lyas 1997, 104). But because people now for many hundreds of years have differentiated and still daily differentiate between art and non-art, it is difficult to see how a philosophical attempt to redefine the word's content will change how it is experienced in reality.

[54]Danto's theory is described neither by Shusterman (1992, 40) nor Dickie (1997, 79-81) as an institutional theory. For a thorough description of Dickie's own theory, as found in an early and later version see Dickie 1997, 83-93. Dickie wrestles with how his own theory (in the new version) can escape from being experienced as circular. In the end he takes a back swing at his theory and confesses, lying on his back, that there is a chain of dependence between his five (sectional) definitions (Dickie 1997, 92), which is why the theory is not perfect. The hope for a supercultural definition or even a just a definition completely free of connection to culture is tenacious within philosophy.

grossly misrepresenting our current concept of art" (1999, 33).[55] Shusterman also lets slip the criticism that Dewey is "unhelpfully inconsistent" when it comes to really working out what aesthetic experience consists of (Shusterman 1992, 55).

Neither do we find any help in Dickie. He apparently starts from the point that even if art cannot be defined in terms of emotional experience, "it is certainly true that in some sense art frequently expresses emotion" (Dickie 1997, 120). In the end Dickie states, after he has discussed what art (and music) can actually express, that whatever it is, it is not enough grounds to make a definition between art and non-art. His argument departs from the idea that there is nothing necessarily connected between music that is experienced as sad and whether or not the composer was sad when she or he wrote it. The listener doesn't need to be sad either—even if one thinks that the music sounds sad—when one hears the piece. The result becomes:

> If sad music does not necessarily stand in relation to some particular instance of sad feelings, then it is unnecessary and misleading to use the verb 'expresses'... consequently the word 'express' should be avoided in favour of locutions such as 'the music is sad' or 'the music has a sad quality' (Dickie 1997, 123).[56]

One solution could lie, therefore, in that music, as Dickie formulates it, can be seen to have a qualitative sadness. This way has been well-worn by previous attempts. In a discussion between the philosopher Peter Kivy and Colin Radford, Kivy writes that music's character has a tendency to affect us, that is to say "that the expressive properties of music have a tendency to arouse the same emotions in listeners" (Kivy 1993, 5). That Kivy expresses it with the formulation "the expressive properties of [sad] music," can be seen to lie very near Dickie's own formulation that "music has a sad quality." These philosophical definitions were supported by the opinions of the music psychologist Harold Fiske. Fiske shows that when it comes to understanding how music can communicate meaning, there is essentially one possibility: Music's influence lies not in its structure, and is not dependent on the listener's ability to decode the composer's possible intentions from the sounding structure itself. Fiske finds, therefore, that the expression lies in what he terms as music's "appearance-value":

> - [i.e. that] specific expressive reference originates with the listener in response to some life experience affect finding association with some particular realized

---

[55] Mentioned among the problems that arise are: a) how one can delineate between good and bad art, and b) if sunsets—an aesthetic example often cited by philosophers—can be seen as art.
[56] This could be accused of being a pseudodiscussion, but from a philosophical standpoint is not seen to be. If one does not understand the connection/communication between art (music) and people, no theories about art and aesthetics can be guaranteed. If philosophy cannot show us the causes for art and music, and thereby also how aesthetic experiences develop as art and music express something, another way must be sought altogether.

tonal-rhythmic structure or some multi-structural relationship (Fiske 1990, 125).

This "appearance value" has a connotative character and can vary for the listener from "a sense of emotional-tonal equivalence to a metaphorical", which, according to Fiske, can never completely be the same from one individual to the next. Fiske draws the conclusion:

> Similar appearance-value seems to be a more likely possibility, particularly between individuals from similar environments who *have experienced the same musical language under similar conditions.* The result is an illusion of communication created by a co-incident event (Fiske 1990, 127 [my italics]).

It appears, therefore, that the different formulations that are used by Dickie, Kivy, and Fiske point toward the same insight: by listening/playing music, people can have the experiences that are described with concepts associated with feelings, abstract and concrete associations etc.[57] This might be an unassailable fact for an ethnomusicologist, but at the same time contains a philosophical problem. The philosopher Monroe Beardsley was, however, more optimistic (Beardsley 1981, 527f). For him the "aesthetic experience" as a point of departure was an experience that came from an object that controlled the experience, gave it intensity and a kind of overall dimension. Beardsley presupposed that it concerned a detached experience (we find ourselves, in other words, deported to thoughts that we met with Kant and his followers). Both Dickie and Shusterman invite a detailed critique of Beardsley's opinions. Both express the same main point that Beardsley's view does not distinguish between different forms of aesthetic experience or between good and bad art. Dickie and Shusterman go on, therefore, to a description of the philosopher Nelson Goodman's theory, whose insistence that the aesthetic experience, in every important detail is a cognitive process (thus, in an aesthetic context even feelings can be regarded as cognitive) and also seems to have a number of trapdoors,[58] which is why thereafter both writers introduce their own theories.

Dickie suggests, for his part, that both Beardsley and Goodman are correct in that evaluation of that which we experience as art has been seen to generate useful experiences—which Dickie, in an addition, suggests can be both positive and negative. He departs from the rhetorical question of why people set value on art if they do not convey meaningful experiences, but steps away from the idea that aesthetic experiences must be objective or distancing. Dickie discusses a number of different qualities, both traditionally aesthetic and non-aesthetic, and also contextual qualities.[59] He suggests that one starting point is that the aesthetic

---

[57] For a thorough study see Davies 1994 and Sparshott 1987, 62-6.
[58] See Dickie 1997, 152-6 and Shusterman 1997, 36f.
[59] Dickie writes: "Valuable experience cannot be aesthetic experience as traditionally conceived,

A PERIOD OF EXPANSION 215

experience is valuable in itself whether it leads to anything else or not. They are "intrinsically valuable" (Dickie 1997, 158). Dickie does not give any concrete examples of this, but I can imagine one example within Western culture could be that listening to Beethoven's *Fifth Symphony* is somehow a worthy aesthetic experience in and of itself. He then suggests different qualities that in different degrees give the possibility of an aesthetic experience, such as totality, splendor, elegance, and complexity. Dickie also includes cognitive qualities. The example that he gives is that when we read a realistic novel, for example Mark Twain's "The Adventures of Huckleberry Finn," correct and true information add to the experience that the novel's *inner* qualities are strengthened:

> Such cognitive properties are instrumentally valuable because they produce aesthetic qualities that themselves are instrumentally valuable for producing the intrinsically valuable experience of aesthetic properties (Dickie 1997, 160).[60]

Dickie establishes that there are a number of different prerequisites for different types of art. But he believes that each art form has its own properties and the evaluation of these properties leads to an aesthetic experiences of different intensity for different people (Dickie assigns these properties different values from one to five—and can add them up to give a final score).[61]

Shusterman says on the other hand, that the thought that it is possible to analytically define aesthetic experience must be given up in its current form. His resignation has to do with:

> The *anaesthetic* thrust of this century's artistic avant-garde, itself symptomatic of much larger transformations in our basic sensibility as we move increasingly from an experiential to an informational culture (Dickie 1997, 29).

The current situation can be traced to causes that lie in the past, not least in the time period we have recently discussed, between the World Wars. Shusterman holds up Walter Benjamin's analysis of the difference between *Erfahrung* and

---

that is, as a detached experience… there is no specific kind of highly structured experience of art that is produced by *all* artworks. It seems more promising to focus on the valuable experience of various valuable aspects of artworlds such as unity, intensity, and other aesthetic qualities as well as nonaesthetic, referential aspects" (Dickie 1997, 157).

[60] A possible equivalent example for music could be a listener who experiences a cognitive strengthening of the experience of music's structure in itself. This could be due to a good correspondence between, for example, the contents of the text and the music in a *Lied* or between the contents of the program and the music in a programmatic work.

[61] Levinson has a similar, fairly traditional "catalogue" of philosophical preconditions when he tries to find criteria "for a characterization of aesthetic pleasure to be accounted a success" (Levinson 1996, 3). He names five conditions: a) illuminates the relation between aesthetic pleasure and the aesthetic attitude to artwork; b) takes note of the difference in aesthetic pleasure between artistic and natural objects; c) distinguishes the aesthetic pleasure from normal sensual pleasure, as well as from intellectual pleasure; d) illuminates how aesthetic pleasure is immediate and does not appeal to external qualities or rewards; as well as e) should be able to contain non-aesthetic aspects (cognitive content, political messages, and so forth) without losing the aesthetic pleasure.

Erlebnis as a key to this changed use and understanding of art. For Benjamin the latter included a changed experiential process, a consequence of modernism and technology, which taken together, conveyed that the aesthetic experience's connection to the autonomous artwork was broken down (Dickie 1997, 31). The earlier experience of great art, thus, gave rise to *Erfahrung*:

> Such experiences once had what Benjamin called *aura*, a cultic quality resulting from the artwork's uniqueness and distance from the ordinary world. But with the advent of mechanical modes of production... aesthetic experience comes to pervade the everyday world of popular culture and even politics. Aesthetic experience can no longer be used to define and delimit the realm of high art (Dickie 1997, 31).[62]

If this change was already noticeable in the 1920s, Shusterman suggests that developments since then have been rapid and that today we live in a world that is overloaded with impressions and information. This has, he says, led to a weakening of our experiences and means that the future of the aesthetic experience and its ability to be defined must be set in question.[63]

These philosophical expositions show in summary how one:

a) focused on art for itself as an aesthetic object and tried to find the structural qualities that led to it being experienced as art;

b) also—or perhaps instead—tried to show the prerequisites for an artistic experience and clearly define the inner aesthetic experiences that art can communicate; as well as

c) analyzed which qualities art must have—including their value—in order for an aesthetic experience can develop (cf. Dickie's own theory).

---

[62]Martin Jay writes about this process in a similar way: "Faced with an increasingly overwhelming surplus of often threatening stimuli, the individual was forced to rely on the short-term devices of *Erlebnis* to survive and thus lacked the ability to integrate the shocks of daily life into meaningful *Erfahrung*. The result, as the critic Peter Bürger has put it, has been the 'shrinkage of experience'" (Jay 1998, 45). For a musicological treatment of *Erlebins*, and *Erfahrung*, as well as other concepts like *Verstehen* and *Erklären*, that all have their home in a hermeneutic and later also in a phenomenological tradition, see Dahlhaus 1983, 71-85 as well as the music historian K. G. Jernhake (1999, chapter 1).

[63]Shusterman takes the idea of "the waning of affect" from Jameson who—in his analyses of fine art, for example of how the work of Warhol is related to van Gogh etc.—introduces this concept. What Jameson gets out of this is difficult to grasp. It is thought to be about "all affect, all learning or emotion, all subjectivity has vanished from the newer image," that is to say, from late art like Warhol. He says later that postmodernism which signals "the end of the *bourgeois* ego, or monad, no doubt brings with it the end of the psychopathologies of that ego - what I have been calling the waning of affect" (Jameson 1991, 15), and besides that it can be characterized as "the waning of the great high modernist thematics of time and temporality, the elegiac mysteries of *durée* and memory" (Jameson 1991, 15). Whether these citations clarify something for the reader is doubtful: to read Jameson is sometimes like casting oneself into a modernist labyrinth without Ariadne's thread. Cf. also the discussion of surface aestheticization below p. 272.

Philosophers know that none of their definitions and analysis can escape criticism if they uphold their own rigorous analytical requirements in their work.[64] That I, therefore, concluded this review with Dickie's and Shusterman's thoughts, respectively, is because I regard *both of their theories seem most plausible*. The prerequisites that Dickie (in his own theory) set up for the aesthetic experience are without doubt relevant for the aesthetic experience that I have defined as æII and æIII.

Shusterman believed, on the other hand, that the idea of philosophically differentiating what aesthetic experience can mean has been seen to be impossible—even if desirable. For him the reason for this lay in the development of the information society bringing with it different ways of experiencing art.

Shusterman was also pessimistic when it came to the successful creation of a lasting definition of art and non-art. In my opinion, the institutional explanatory model (Danto/Dickie) with its historical additions do provide a possible way of defining art music from non-art music, as long as we keep in mind that changing power relationships within society can alter the *value judgments* that divide art from non-art, if such a definition was once sustainable. To give a concrete example: during the 1930s Beethoven's music was described overwhelmingly as *serious, classical,* or *art music*. Schönberg's music was also regarded as art music. If, however, we travel into the realm that I labeled middle music, we come upon a socialized uncertainty. Music's structure, its performance and the place where it occurred, the composer's nationality, if he or she was well-known or unknown as an art music composer, and so forth, were all important factors that contributed to the status of the composer's music

What is experienced as art, in other words, is a social story, which is why it is completely possible that a social development leads to a situation where a concept loses its meaning and slowly other general keys for evaluation become tools that lock out the earlier terms of evaluation. If this happens, the three hundred year old marriage between art and aesthetics is weakened at the same time. At the very least they are set in a new relationship with one another.

This last argument makes it necessary to return to the inter-war period in order to continue our discussion of how music's use has changed since this time. We must look for answers to the questions of what was seen to be art music at the end of the last century. The answer can principally vary between "all of it and none

---

[64]Whether or not this is always a healthy sign, this review revealed that the two concepts of art and aesthetics, braided together, seem impossible to define or encircle and will continue to be controversial (I am reminded of the different examples from current newpapers that were cited as an introduction to this work). An optimistic working out of the philosophers' discussions is that eventually everything will become clearer. A pessimistic understanding is that the door to their ivory tower is stuck ajar and the full reality cannot make its way in. The discussion of how and what music expresses continues, of course.

of it," meaning that one can also assume that aesthetic experience can act as an intermediary with "all of it and none of it." In this case it can be assumed that the concept of aesthetics has imploded, but that the word lives on with a completely different meaning. We shall see....

Consumption and Aesthetics

The historian Christer Ahlberger has shown in a creative way how one can understand the changes in consumption that occurred between the age of Enlightenment and the last century. Consumption is divided according to three aspects: an economic, ethnological, and anthropological. The economic aspect is divided between a modern dimension, that is to say, the goods are made for a market where they have an exchange value, and a traditional dimension. The traditional dimension means that the household was self-subsistent, that is to say that the goods had a local market. Within the ethnological aspect there is a division between modernization, in the sense of a willingness to accept the new, and its opposite, that everything must be preserved (tradition). Finally, the anthropological aspect also has a modern pole, the way in which consumption is carried out for daily use including the owning of and access to different goods and materials in the home. Traditional consumption was characterized by abstemiousness with short periods of extravagance, for example celebrating weddings. What Ahlberger shows is that it was rather the population that did not own land for instance salaried workers on farms that bought the new consumption goods, especially ready made goods. It was, as one source described it, "railroad builders that first began to use ready made clothes." Then came the people in service and last the farm owners. Another source reports:

> It was without a doubt the working class that played the largest role in the spread of industrially made clothes. Through the industrial revolution a new consumer group was formed. An important circumstance was that salaried workers had cash (cited from Ahlberger 1996, 150).

It was those without land and the salaried workers rather than the richer and more tradition-bound farmers that consumed the mass-produced goods. The former group was, we can say, *more modern*, in its buying habits: they accepted new goods that were produced for a market and used them in daily life.

It seems possible to apply Ahlberger's argument when we turn our discussion to which groups most diligently consumed music at the beginning of the twentieth century. The musical market that expanded most during the first half of the century was, of course, the gramophone industry. The hypothesis is that mainly young people and unmarried people were the largest percentage of consumers of broadcast media's offerings, and therefore the group that in larger numbers than others also came to use music in a new way.

When the ethnologist Johan Söderberg discussed the changing habits of consumers in Sweden between 1920 and 1965, he began by saying that leisure time consumption was one of the fastest expanding sectors. By the 1930s research showed that young people had relatively large incomes. The fact that entertainment culture was focused toward the needs of youth was discussed both in the press and in the Parliament.[65] Full minimum wage was awarded at age 18. Because young people often lived at home, but seldom paid for their lodgings in full, they had "more money at their disposal when they were young than later in life" (Söderberg 1997, 210).[66] As we have seen, it was difficult to motivate youth to attend educational lectures organized by the different organizations and societies. The increased number of choices in every area that attracted youth: books, films, *schlager* and dance, sports, etc., appeared in every field where different viewpoints clashed with one another: put simply, a conservative and collective adult world was set up against an individualistic youth culture.[67]

The five authors of the book *Från flygdröm till swingscen* [*From Dreams of Flight to the Swinging Scene*] (Boëthius et al 1998) in their first article explore similar ideas, but state that there was an ideological symbolic struggle around youth in the interwar period. The fact that adolescence now began to stretch over a longer time period as a consequence of longer education and training periods, brought attention to the situation of young people and their choices:

To summarize in brief, the debate concerned the future of young people: should they live out their needs in an irresponsible way or should they practice self-discipline… in order to participate in the development of modern society (Boëthius et al 1998, 45).

In addition, if the United States stood for "individualism and free market forces" a German tradition stood for "authoritarian leadership" (Boëthius et al 1998, 45).

At the same time that broadcast media were making their appearance, a developmental process was taking place in society where different approaches clashed with one another, an older, autocratic and undemocratic, and a younger, where the opposite had begun to happen: "This created chaos in the traditional

---

[65]A motion in the Parliament from 1932 cites: "The public entertainment culture in our country has in recent times increased in extent and intensity in a way that creates the most dangerous worries with regards to both the moral and economic welfare of our youth" (cited from Boëthius et al 1998, 54).

[66]For a thorough historical and ethnological analysis of youth culture in Sweden from the seventeenth century and onwards, see Wennhall 1994.

[67]Different movements with the same goal of protecting youth developed during the first half off the twentieth century: propaganda against "smut" literature, that is to say, a campaign against Nick Carter detective novels, and from the 1920s, campaigns against the evils of visiting open-air dance floors and dance halls. Even the youth interest in football their "leather ball culture," was attacked. All of these—and similar groups would follow—can be gathered under the umbrella of "moral panic."

values systems" (Boëthius et al 1998, 46). While the word pair 'education—enjoyment' was used earlier as a description of the process, we can now add *responsibility—irresponsibility*, and *permissiveness—discipline*.

The ethnologist Johan Wennhall writes that dance was at the center of 1920s youth culture. Music, as he sees it, had "a subordinate role as accompaniment or as background" (Wennhall 1994, 119). This commentary is frankly curious. Without broadcast media and the new music (foxtrot, shimmy, Charleston, tango, carioca, etc.) no dance culture would have developed. The new composers stood both for a new music culture and a new dance culture. This can be seen as a clear result of Wennhall's description of theSyncopation Supper Club that was founded in the early 1930s. As in other similar clubs in Sweden, the main motivation for gathering was to listen to the new music. But one was also inspired to play, to dance, or to go to music events together. Popular culture and mass medias forms became a part of youth culture and a step in the emancipation process for these youth:

> The Syncopation Club, together with all the other conscious contemporary experimentation, revolution, unrest and alternatives developed, however, at the wrong time... war stood in the way (Wennhall 1994, 121).

The development of youth culture that was observed earlier could grow strong again only after the Second World War: at the beginning of the 1960s the teen market represented 25% of consumption of beauty products (of which probably 90% where girls), 75% of moped sales (of which probably 90% were boys) and 90 % of record player sales (Söderberg 1997, 211).[68]

The observed development implied, therefore, that youth, by the early 1920s were socialized to use music in a new way. Consumption took place according to market conditions (the modern aspect described by Ahlberger, above), youth sought out the new (the ethnological aspect) and there were no misgivings about listening to as much popular music as possible (the anthropological aspect). They played records and listened to the radio, but also started bands and played together.

What did this consumption mean on a deeper level and–something that is not often expressed–what did the "production" of new music mean?[69] And

---

[68]On a personal note, this completely agrees with events during my own schooldays; I bought a moped in 1960 and got an amplifier when I graduated in 1965 (a Philips, 2x2 watt)!

[69]The large number of boys and younger men (and a few girls) that tried out for different dance orchestras from the end of the 1920s onward, constituted an important prerequisite for the development of dance music sections within the Swedish Musicians' Union. Already at the beginning of the 1940s, a few years after the start of a so-called B section, the music union organized more than 10,000 part time musicians in the so-called B section. The latter played swing, as a rule, the youth music of the day. In 1955 the Union had 1,365 members in full-time positions (including more than 110 women), as well as 16,165 (2,145 of them women) part-time employed within the category of "musicians, choir and ballet personel" (Edström 1982, 230). The

what significance does it have for the aesthetic project? We will soon seek out the answer in the sociologist Tia DeNora's work on music in daily life. We are well-acquainted with her basic position: "To understand how music works as a device of social ordering, how its effects are reflexively achieved, we need to look at musical practice" (DeNora 2000, 45). But at the same time it is perhaps surprising that in this sociological discourse the word "aesthetic" actually appears on almost every page of her work. Let us, therefore, make a first acquaintance with how her ideas about aesthetics and our modern consumption of music can be formulated. For, as many have pointed out, there is an inbuilt paradox in modern consumption. While industry seeks maximum standardization in order to create cheaper and cheaper products, the message being projected is that every person should strive to become more individualized.

If the main focus during the nineteenth century was the development of personal character, the twentieth century paradigm fixated on the development of individual personality, to stand out from the crowd (Frith and Horne 1987, 17). In the discussions of these writers about the relationship between consumption, clothes and fashion (cf. Ahlberger concerning the consumption of ready-made goods [see above p. 218]) and current popular music (pop/rock), we find a usable argument that looks both forward and backward in time. Frith and Horne state namely that fashion and clothes cannot be divorced from pop and rock.[70] Youth music's history is as much "a history of image as well as sound":

> Fashion is a branch of aesthetics, of the art of modern society. It is also a mass pastime, a form of group entertainment of popular culture related as it is to both fine and popular art, it is a kind of performance art (Wilson, cited in Frith and Horne 1987, 18).

Personal Use

This chapter's final section will look at a summary of how the personal use of music changed during the first half of the twentieth century, but we will, as has just been seen, also take into account the research that has been carried out about our own situation at the end of the twentieth century. This last-mentioned serves as an overture to the coming discussion of how the aesthetic project has changed during the second half of the twentieth century and how its development can be understood in relationship to the use of music, the transformation for society in general, and how people's modes of thought and action have changed.

---

present-day idea that music-making among youth started with the communal music schools of the 1950s and 60s and with African-American youth music during the same time, is misleading (Cf. Persson 2001).

[70]The music that falls within these two categories of pop and rock is much discussed and differs, apparently, from country to country (see further p. 233 as well as in Lilliestam 1998, 20f).

Neither gramophones nor gramophone records were cheap during the interwar period. One record cost about the same as a mid-priced CD today. But the music lasted no more than six minutes. We can well imagine that within the gramophone industry they were aware early on that some genres and artists sold better to some groups in society than others. The actual proof we have that this is true, however, is very small. A great deal of the population bought neither gramophones nor records. It was, as we have seen, much more common to have radios. Music both spread through mass media and was apparently also its most important content.

At the end of the 1920s, in connection with the improved sound reproduction capabilities of better electro-magnetic techniques, it is clear that some male record stars had their largest listening audience among women. Jack Smith, "the whispering baritone," was perhaps the first who was introduced as a ladies' man. In an advertisement, the text claims that "female fans have not seen him, they have only heard him." But he sings so that "even the guys will be fond of him." The ad goes on to say:

> He sings as if he were sitting in front of the fireplace in your own home and sang only for you. Come in to our gramophone store and listen to one of his melodies, and then we cannot be responsible if your pin-money gets spent (cited from Edström 1996, 252).

A new youth music culture developed. Young people gathered together in groups to listen together to gramophone recordings. They called it "dining on records." During the 1920s this group was apparently very small and only increased in size slowly during the depression and the beginning of the 30s. Those who were interested in American dance music and jazz could only buy these records during the 1930s in the larger cities, and during World War II, imports were very limited. On the other hand, the range of Swedish recordings of swing music was quite large. One could also always listen to English radio stations where the latest music was played by well-known orchestras or on records. Swing music became associated with youth culture when people saw zoot suiters and films targeted at young audiences featuring jazz and swing music (cf. Boëthius et al 1998, 300).

However, young people and youth culture do not appear in contemporary advertisements for gramophones and radios in newspapers and magazines. Youth still had comparatively little buying power. The large consumer groups were among adults and especially among the well-to-do. But, as mentioned earlier: the number of radios rose quickly to one million in 1937 and crossed the two million mark in 1947.

By the beginning of the 1950s few could avoid radio music. Recording machines had begun to be sold after the war, but they were expensive. They were followed in the end of the 1950s by tape recorders that came to be generally available. At the same time, vinyl records made their entrance, making it possible to listen to recorded music that lasted up to 40 minutes in stereo reproduction.

The availability of different kinds of music increased constantly from the interwar period as the number of channels within which *music reached into the home* also increased. If this development began in earnest with the gramophone and the radio, and from the 1930s with talking films, and from 1950 one could also see and hear music via TV. The number of radio stations increased during the 1960s and thereafter has grown continuously. From the 1990s, music has also been downloaded from the Internet. Concurrently with this process, there has been more music in locations where people have very little control in *choosing what they listen to*: waiting rooms, elevators, stores, restaurants, etc.[71]

If we consider the first category, music in the home, to be "voluntary," the others are public categories that can be seen as "involuntary." But it is also still true that a family member in her own home could be involuntarily forced to listen to music that she had not chosen, and, on the other hand, that today one can voluntarily choose a store or a restaurant where one's favorite kind of music is played. During this process it is well known that more and more styles of music have been born, music styles that often are designed for different youth audiences. If youth music comes under a constant process of differentiation, we meet, however, within public music, for example in airports, the opposite, a similar and "global" instrumental music designed to have a desired affect upon as many people as possible within the milieu that it is played.

On one hand, therefore, during the twentieth century the stylistic diversity within contemporary music, as well as in art music and popular music, has grown, giving rise to a development of musical taste and subgroups. At the same time, this has led to an increased possibility for every individual to use one or many music styles to confirm or change their own social place. This, however, meant an increase in musical possibilities for differentiating oneself from others (according to one's status as social-individual, gender-specific, generation, social-group, and/or ethnicity). On the other hand, as we have already seen, the opposite also has taken place: we encounter the same functional music at "all" the world's airports. As Frith and Horne have formulated it, what they call "pop songs" have become a part of daily life in the West. This music is "inescapable in lifts and airports, pubs and restaurants, streets and shopping centers and sports grounds" (Frith and Horne 1987, 5).

---

[71]While during the 1950s there were great possibilities for restaurant guests to experience musical standards served with dinner (guests asked the musicians if they could play their favorite melodies), guests in today's restaurants have little to no possibility of affecting the mechanical musical offerings that are part of the milieu (cf. Edström 1989). It is often difficult enough to get the staff to turn down the volume.

The possibility of differentiating oneself from other generations and groups through music is naturally not a phenomenon that appears only with the advent of broadcast media. What was new was the increased access to mechanically reproduced music, which gave this process of demarcation a broader content and more refined spectrum. People no longer need to be able to play or sing themselves. As before, people knew their favorite music intimately well, but now, in a way that was not possible for earlier generations, one could also use music as a companion and design element in daily life. In a dialog with music's structural qualities people could create a relationship that could be used consciously or unconsciously to reach social or psychological goals and effects.

These perspectives can be seen in DeNora's study of music in daily life. The consistent sociological perspective that she presents will undergo a fairly detailed review as the antithesis of the philosophical musings that we have met earlier in this book. DeNora's perspective of the music that we consume and are surrounded by, is at the same time an overview of how music interacts with people and what significance it has. Her empirical material is admittedly taken from the 1990s, but her reasoning is generally applicable for other parts of the century. The following citation from *Music in Everyday Life* is given so that we as musicologists can raise our "level of attunement":

> It is possible to speak of the content or effects of musical works, but never to speak of those matters in relation to (that standard phrase within arts sociology) 'the works themselves' (De Nora 2000, 31).

DeNora sees the use of music in daily life as a self-technology. When she studies music's role in daily life she asks, among other things, how one should understand music's working power related to the quest for self-identity, as well as:

> How music's power in relation to the self and to subjectivity [may] be seen in the private, aesthetically [sic!] reflexive musical practices of individuals? (DeNora 2000, 48 [I will return to DeNora's use of the word aesthetics]).

From her empirical material she draws a conclusion that music has became an ordering factor on a personal plane. Similar ideas recur also in the work of the Norwegian musicologist Even Ruud, who from the perspective of a music therapist, shows that our social identity can be formed through the use of music to mark out positions in the everyday social environment, where our individuality and independence, gender identity and social connections, ethnicity, and so forth, can be given form, and content through our experience of music (Ruud 1997, 208). DeNora also comments that people can function as their own disc jockeys, where music in daily life functions as a medium for creating, maintaining and improving "cognitive, bodily and self-conceptual states".[72] This lies near the

---

[72] Among the examples that DeNora gives, is that of a woman who programs her music radio alarm to correspond with how the coming workday will be. If the workday is going to be difficult she chooses one station, if it is going to be calm, she chooses another (DeNora 2000, 50).

behavior of using music as a tool for changing moods or creating the right mood during the course of the day. Among other areas of use that are mentioned, music is used for blocking out distracting sound, increasing concentration, memory, for projecting or strengthening identity, and so forth.[73] DeNora argues strongly that music should not be seen solely as a stimulus:

> Rather, music's 'effects' come from the ways in which individuals orient to it, how they interpret it and how they place it within their personal musical maps, within the semiotic web of music and extra-musical associations. Moreover—and this would be a grave disappointment for Adorno—the concept of the musical 'work', the total work as a, or indeed *the*, meaningful unit, is mostly irrelevant (DeNora 2000, 61).

This means at the same time that music is an important medium in the creation and maintenance of every person's identity. Music becomes a sounding reminder of who one is, a social and cultural memory activity. Ruud makes a similar point: one sees oneself more clearly in music's reflection. Through our understanding of what music means for us we create and reinforce ourselves at the same time (Ruud 1997, 199). The fact that music can have a summing-up function for our own identities is reflected in our deep provocation when our musical taste is attacked by others (cf. Schumann's reaction earlier, p. 153). Words simply no longer are enough:

> The choice of aesthetic [sic!] expressions, whether it is Whitney Houston or Duke Ellington, can be sounding symbols for the yearnings, values and belongings that strengthen us as human beings (Ruud 1997, 208).

Music and the use of music appears, through the methodology in which DeNora grounds her analysis, an important co-creative agent, that one interacts with voluntarily. People make and listen to music. Music forms and strengthens people.

Regarding the opposite, that is to say music that reaches us involuntarily as we move through the public sphere, the processes remain partly the same, but partly these processes occur on the unconscious plane because music in these cases can be experienced but not listened to. Music in this case as in other cases, can be strongly foregrounded or background. We learn in DeNora's book that people closely integrate music in their daily lives. This happens through processes that DeNora describes as "musical entrainment"[74] where music contributes to the

---

[73] For those who have acquainted themselves with the music habits and uses of youth, her analysis of how people can set their day to music will not come as any surprise. Cf. Erling Bjurström 1997, Doris Axelsen 1997, and Lars Lilliestam 2002.

[74] DeNoras methodological material is variable, including a) music from *Placenta Music Inc.*, styled for prematurely born babies to allow them to "appear to create, with minimal cost or effort, a modified and regularized environment, b) music that is used for work outs, at the gym or

regulation and modification of "physiological states... behavior... the temporal patterns of mood and feeling... social role and action styles" (DeNora 2000, 79). DeNora summarizes in conclusion:

> [F]or particular listeners and perhaps types of listeners, certain musical figures, devices, genres, forms or works may serve as triggers or latches into particular modes of agency... Tuning in to music also involves a kind of identification, a recognition, at a sympathetic and embodied level of the various shapes and textures of 'happening', of, as discussed above, the body in music... and of the ways in which music handles itself... Perhaps music... allows us, should we latch on to it, to engage in a kind of visceral communion with its perceived properties (DeNora 2000, 161).

It emerges, however, that older people who were interviewed have a more difficult time listening to music in all of the situations in which they meet it. These "older people" are people who were children and adolescents in the interwar period, reminding us that the course of events DeNora describes begins in the mass media during this period, and the quick changes that have taken place since then, have different affects on these age groups and succeeding generations. Since the interwar period, thanks to the necessity for private and public dance, access to broadcast media and society's general evolution, music has played a role as an important socializing agent especially for youth and younger adults. These possibilities have gradually accelerated. Ruud states, therefore, like many other contemporary researchers, that music is extremely important during youth, because it adds to the construction of an individual cultural platform, "an alternative draft of an identity marked by one's own experiences of life" (Ruud 1997, 201), or in Frith's and Horne's words:

> Pop culture describes the peculiar way in which our most intense experience of ourselves as ourselves (active, special) is lived out on the fantastic site of consumption. Pop music is a crucial source of imagined identities (Frith and Horne 1987, 181).

One of DeNora's citations above showed that the concept of aesthetics recurs regularly in her work.[75] The question we must ask is how the concept of aesthetics can be understood when music's use has changed since the interwar period, and how this transformation relates especially to the socio-cultural changes that occurred during the second half of the century. These now await further illumination.

---

similar fitness centers, c) music in different kinds of stores, and d) music that is used for romantic situations, that is, "music and intimate culture."

[75] The same is true of authors like Ruud, Bjurström and Axelsen. Axelsen adds the "Aesthetic" category as an introduction to her description of highschool students listening to music. Other categories—according to McGuire—are: a) existential motives, b) stimulation, c) relaxation, d) expressive and e) affiliation motives (Axelsen 1997, 122).

*The work "itself" cannot be specified;
it is anything, everything, nothing.*
Tia DeNora

CHAPTER 6: THE PRESENT

The use of music—the transformation of aesthetics

Introduction

In a 1997 article I tried to make a diagnosis of the post-war Swedish music culture, an analysis that to a great extent can be applied to most industrialized countries in the West. It is clear that, because of the outcome of the Second World War, new paths were developed. In Sweden, artists turned toward the rest of Europe looking for new inspiration. Cultural questions were given a higher priority in the programs of political parties than earlier. The educational system was to be reformed with the mission of creating democratically-thinking people.[1] Society's continued imbalances would be fought through new forms of education and new study plans. More and more parents became acquainted with ideas about giving their children a new and less strict upbringing.

Artists, for their part, had already been in search of new modern methods of expression. The difference was that from the middle of the 1940s, modernist modes of expression became part of the construction for anew society. In Sweden the breeding ground was ideal for the development of a symbiosis between the earlier (*bourgeois*) modernist belief in development within cultural fields and the ideology of the ruling Social Democratic Party. Since, in every essential, even the leadership of the Social Democrats (as well as the *bourgeois* parties) were bearers of *bourgeois* value systems, it was now possible of a *cultural* elite to transfer and combine their belief in a true and autonomous art with the Social Democratic party's desire to come to grips with music culture. Two processes, one "autonomous," elitist and delimiting, and the other populist, open and democratic, joined forces along the way. For the first time it also became possible for those who wrote modernist contemporary art music to see an economic dividend on their social and cultural capital (to make a connection to Bourdieu). On the continent this concerned composers like Olivier Messiaen, Pierre Boulez, Karlheinz Stockhausen, Luigi

---

[1] Everyone saw what raising children within the fascist system in Germany and Italy had led to. All political parties in Sweden, apart from the Communists, recognized that the Soviet system was also an ideological straight jacket for people.

Nono, and others, who enjoyed a great acceptance within the world of art music subsequent to their appearances at the summer course in Darmstadt which in turn raised their social status and symbolic capital.[2] In Sweden there were similar composers around the so-called Monday Group: Karl-Birger Blomdahl, Sven-Erik Bäck, Ingvar Lidholm, and others, and in England, where traditionalists held power longest, a similar phenomenon could be found in the "Manchester School" with composers like Alexander Goehr, Peter Maxwell Davies and Harrison Birtwistle (Nielsen 1999, 32f).

The composers within these modernistic directions later captured the most important positions in the art-music field. These composers and their "stylistic colleagues" in other Western European countries found themselves thus—consciously or unconsciously—within the higher artistic areas of the art-music field.[3] Some of them, like Stockhausen, Boulez and Maxwell Davies, have apparently already moved on to the highest Parnassus.

This music generally enjoyed prestige as high as art music earlier had done; it was a part of the same aesthetic project as it had been earlier (æII and æIII). It was music for listeners that met the expectations of the contemporary public interested in modernism.[4] If we see the development from the perspective of Luhmann, the autopoietic system continued to develop. The rationally thought-out serial music went its own way without references to the rest of human systems. Adorno on one hand saw this art music as a dialectical recoil, music was no longer a free work but rather an ossified formula:

> Adorno had foreseen the decline of the avant-garde quite early on. There are indications of his recognition of the precariousness of the modernist venture as early as 1932... and in 1954 he took the bold step of giving a lecture... entitled 'Das Altern der neuen Musik' (Paddison 1993, 272, cf. Hobsbawm 1994, 518).

---

[2] For an overview of the significance of the Darmstadt courses see Valkare 1997, 167-79. In Valkare we also find the idea that the size of the *partitura* score and the visual presentation of the manuscript are a few of the many items in the toolbox of the Modernist composer that could be used to achieve a position within this field.

[3] Relationships varied from land to land. Poland was, during the 1950s to the 80s, something of an exception within the Eastern Block. Here Modernist composers could become famous and with Poland as a base, could make international careers for themselves, which was not possible in the same way for Soviet composers. Depending on what perspective one had, perhaps one could just as well describe the different groupings as circles of friends than as homogeneous compositional schools. Cf. the Swedish composer Bengt Hambræus's communication to Per F. Broman (Broman 1999, 253 footnote 70) on the Darmstadt courses as "a meeting point for 'a bunch of friends'."

[4] I described the results of the battle in the field as follows: "Simply put one can say that the Modernists won. Less simply put, one can say that Modernism, within which music can be seen as an autonomous art, a sounding medium with an unusual ability to express people's inexpressible existential situation in an increasingly capitalist and thoroughly commercialized society, won (this presupposed that the composers were true to themselves and took advantage of the latest, rationally well-worked out composition methods). Those who wrote music that had a broad anchoring among musicians and the general public lost the battle" (Edström 1997, 14).

But there were probably few, perhaps no one among the true believing modernists that understood the old in this new music, but for other people this music was practically non-music. We stand by with a witty lecture formula ("The aging of new music"), or as the musicologist Max Paddison formulated it, with the knowledge that Adorno once again has left us with an unsolved antagonism (Paddison 1993, 273).[5]

This modernist direction, in relation to its quantitative importance, to generate attention within the art music field.[6] Then it is another thing, as cited in Nielsen 1999, that the faithful public for this music, for example in a great city like London, is probably no more than about 400 people.

Apart from art music, certain types of jazz moved closer to the aesthetic field. This process, which will not be looked into further in the present work, can be traced back to the 1920s where certain popular works within art and entertainment music got jazzed up in arrangements for the jazz orchestras like Paul Whiteman's Orchestra (in the United States) and Jack Hylton's Orchestra (in England). A number of pieces for the piano by composers like Zez Confrey, Clemens Doucet, George Gershwin, Billy Mayerl and Lee Sims had stylistic elements from both the jazz music and art music of the time. Other important influences in this process were the writers and jazz enthusiasts who initiated writings about jazz like Hughes Panassié (1934) and not least the jazz music itself that arrangers and composers like Duke Elllington wrote. During the big band jazz period of the 1930s and 40s both musicians and listeners were taught to accept a jazz music that bridges gaps between different styles, a change that after World War II continued in directions like cool jazz and third stream.

Before World War II jazz had often functioned as dance music and was also seen that way. The word jazz in Sweden in the 1920s was a synonym for modern American dance music. Jazz was a music form that generally attracted youth and that was listened to alone or together with others at home and in cafés and similar locales. Jazz was also performed in club milieus with their special atmosphere for a public that varied in their attentiveness as listeners.[7]

[5]Dodd comments in his work on the Frankfurt school on its lack of empirical material and analytical precision (Dodd 1999, 77-85). On the Frankfurt school's use of the concept of "culture industry" Dodd writes: "Their characterization of the culture industry itself is so generalized that virtually anything can be described as coming under its auspices… nothing can escape the logic of commodification. When translated into an empirical context and adressed to specific instances, there seems to be little in this approach that can prevent the individual tastes of the interpreter from shaping the analysis" (Dodd 1999, 81).
[6]It was also the predecessors of the Modernists that in Sweden in the 1950s and later in the middle of the 1990s initiated well-known debates on the role of Modernist art music (cf. Edström 1997).
[7]See also Wennhall on the "Syncopation club" that during the 1930s arranged record dinner parties in cafés, organized trips to jazz events and inspired people to play themselves (Wennhall 1994, 119). For a more thorough description of the changes in jazz during the interwar period see Edström 1996, 409-444.

The process of how jazz as a form of art music accrued aesthetic value can also, with a few reservations, be followed within Sweden's borders. The jazz music that could be taken into the aesthetic field earliest was probably the kind that lay closest to earlier art music structurally, for example an artful arrangement performed by Jack Hylton's orchestra.[8] At the same time, among a less literary and culturally interested group of people, an aesthetic sense of jazz was developing that lay near the form of interest for primitivism described at the time by writers like Artur Lundquist, among others.[9] A similar disparity recurs in the 1930s debate between the proponents of "sweet" jazz and those who favored more "real" forms of "hot' jazz. It was the latter that came to be thought of as real jazz.

Bebop, an especially important phase in jazz history from dance and entertainment music to listener music appears in the 1940s. Musicologist Scot DeVeaux, in a fascinating description of the external and internal reasons for the development of bebop in the 1940s in the United States, shows how important it is to not reduce bebop to a development that is either described as "a social upheaval expressed through music" or as an example of "stylistic evolution" (DeVeaux 1997, 27). In a way reminiscent of DeNora's descriptive style, DeVeaux describes a number of factors that explain why bebop developed, but also why it did not last. Among the factors he mentions are the situation of African Americans in the United States and especially those among them who were professional musicians during the war, the two-year ban on record production, the upsurge of new smaller record companies, professional musicians' jam sessions after work, interest in the small group of jazz aficionados, the high level of engagement with music during the war—and not least how the white commercial music industry functioned.[10]

Since the end of the 1930s there has been a clear distinction between stratification within jazz reminiscent of the one that developed between "higher" and "lower" music during the nineteenth century. One can, therefore, speak about a unique jazz aesthetic where, among other factors, a great deal of emphasis was laid on the "sound" that musicians had and their improvisation skills.

In 1940s Sweden bebop was in a tug of war with an established competitor, New Orleans jazz that college youth identified themselves with. One was expected to listen to the former type of jazz, and dance to the latter one.

---

[8]In the largest entertainment magazine of the time, *Våra Nöjen* [*Our Enjoyment*] 1929:19, there is a long article about Jack Hylton. It says: "Who is this man, whose name is on everyone's lips, who understands how to appreciate jazz music in its most noble and refined form.".

[9]Cf. Edström 1996, 418-11, where the conflict between a conservative sense of culture and the youth "wild dancing" to jazz as well as "The Young Ones" views on literature are discussed. How traditional views break up when met with the younger writers' views on entertainment can also be followed in *Våra Nöjen* (cf. the previous note).

[10]Cf. Scott DeVeaux who also describes bebop as an "autonomous modernism" or as "politically engaged avant-garde" (DeVeaux 1997, 23).

It was not until the 1960s that bebop and other forms of jazz were placed definitively within the aesthetic field and thereby, for the larger public, became differentiated from other forms of music. When, for example within STIM (the Swedish performing rights society) at the beginning of the 1960s, discussions took place about which composers could receive stipends, there was debate about whether a jazz musician could receive one. Composer and bassist Georg Riedel, it was decided, could receive a stipend because the kind of jazz that he wrote was not commercial:

> We generally use an expression that may sound paradoxical, that is, serious jazz music. This type has nothing to do with *schlager*, dance music and even less with the rock and twist music of the day—the distance is just as large as between Alfvén's and Jularbo's music. Riedel's activity as a composer of this jazz music generates very little income. A relatively large stipend sum would therefore be desirable (as cited in Edström 1998, 178).[11]

Now only a few years passed before jazz musicians developed the status of cultural personalities in the eyes of the public and received state stipends and artist's salaries.[12] The forms of jazz that these musicians played had as a rule, however, a very small listener's circle.[13]

This was also true of free jazz, a radical modernist form of jazz that even those who liked bebop, cool and third stream often had difficulty understanding. Those who wanted to dance hardly bothered with it at all. The structural—musical—distance between contemporary art music and free form could sometimes be very small. By the time this new form developed, New Orleans and Dixieland jazz were no longer viable alternatives for youth culture. By then, a new wave of Anglo-American youth music had already rolled over Sweden.

Youth Music and Aesthetics

I remember my persistent attempts to convert my cousin in the spring of 1958 failed as we sat in her room listening to records when we were teenagers. She loved Elvis Presley and I was a fan of Tommy Steele. Tommy disappeared relatively

---

[11] This description can be contrasted with what the Swedish Composer's Society considered at the end of the 1920s. Because many well-known "classical" melodies were dressed up in *schlager* clothes, the society requested the introduction of protections for art music in jazz or waltz form. One characterized "jazz –maker's pranks…like barbarism, misleading tastes and spiritually heinous deeds" (Edström 1998).

[12] Cf. also Bruér and Westin 1974, 145f.

[13] For a thorough account and analysis of music preferences and musical activity during the 1960s, see the work of the sociologist Göran Nylöf. Here we learn that a) the higher the education level, the greater the interest for jazz, classical music and songs and ballads; b) farmers and workers thought least of jazz, opera and contemporary music; and c) about 60% of the population between 16 and 70 years old had never been to a jazz concert "and did not want to judge jazz music positively… about the same percent [opposed] to classical music" (Nylöf 1967, 256).

quickly from my life. Elvis remained, disregarding his changed repertoire and body size, uninteresting, not only as a person and a symbol, but from a musical standpoint as well. At the beginning of the 1960s there were an incredible number of other artists to choose from. My interest for this music and the fact that I both played art music and jazz, left me rather neutral toward the youth music of the day. The changes that were observed earlier–youth *could* choose and identify itself with different forms of music–was obvious to my 40s generation. My school classmates listened to everything, and from the end of the 60s I did too, that is to say I had my ears opened to groups and artists like the Beatles, Blood, Sweat and Tears, Frank Zappa, Emerson, Lake and Palmer, Yes, and others. The stylistic breadth has only increased since then. Exactly as we have seen before, there was a need to label different forms of contemporary popular music. The differences between what was called rock and what was called pop have, since the 1960s, been a twisted and tangled field among popular music researchers. How the differences should be defined, what musical structures and what social factors different authors have pointed to has varied depending on what generation they belonged to, and on time period and place. As the musicologist Lars Lilliestam's survey shows, rock has often been experienced as angular, that within rock the lyrics means something, rock is socially engaged, it is authentic, it is non commercial, and so forth, while pop is round, the texts have little meaning, it isolates individuals, is not authentic, it is commercial, and so forth. Lilliestam writes that the great problem with the concepts of rock and pop are that their meanings change and that they are used in different ways and often without consistency (Lilliestam 1998, 25). In the 1990s, Lilliestam adds, the concept of rock was so broad that it became almost meaningless, if one did not define more closely what type of rock.

Without carrying more hay to this stack, it is difficult to resist noting that early on, value judgments crept in that were similar to those used to describe the "higher" worth of Beethoven's music and the "lower" worth of Badarzerska's *Virgin's Prayer*. For even though one seldom expressly stated things in this way, journalists, critics and musicologists (that as a rule, were leftists on the ideological-political scale) judged that music which was seen to be authentic, non-commercial, or whose message was expressed in socially critical lyrics had a higher value. How a particular canon was developed within popular music from the 1960s is, in other words, an extremely interesting but fairly unresearched field. Rock (= "a higher form of music") and pop (= "a lower form of music") is precisely like "aesthetics," "subjective," "objective,"—and according to the philosopher W. B. Gallie's formulation—"essentially contested concepts" (cf. footnote 1).[14]

---

[14]For an illuminating discussion of the constructed differences between pop and rock see Williams 2001, 75-97 who shows how thoughts about the authentic in folk music were transferred to working class music, and were later an important part of rock's "authenticity," that is to say, a music form that, one thought, was not "dominated by the market" (Williams 2001, 88).

The musical resistance that the different music styles within youth music generated from the 1950s led to a gradual reduction in the forward speed of the ongoing *bourgeois* education project. The daily use of personal music encapsulated young people's musical habits, which changed with greater speed than their parents' had in relationship to their grandparents'.

During this time there were also changes in the general access that young people had to activities with people their own age. Young people also had a greater buying power than before. They were in school longer than before. The process of individualization changed. It became more important to choose and navigate between different life styles that were marketed more aggressively in a more youth-oriented marketplace.

Sharp music teachers now asked their students to bring along their favorite records to school in a vain attempt to make students' music—the same music that they listened to with their friends in their free time—into school music. But the contexts were too different. Equally clever instrumental and ensemble leaders had a little more success when they allowed students to make tame arrangements of rock and pop songs. For many students the structural distance between communal school music and youth music became too large.

Curious young musicians constantly tested the usefulness of technical improvements: stereo sound, better microphones, speakers, mixers, new instruments, spot lights, etc. Music's "sound," length and form changed. Listeners as well as practitioners were required to keep up with the changes.

Through the mass media distribution of music during the postwar period, changes to further develop individualization exploded. Today, more and more people automatically turn on the radio or TV (MTV!) when they come home. People cook to music, eat to music, read assignments to music, etc. Now people don't just listen to music alone, with family or "dined on records" with their friends as they did before the war, nor do they find themselves in social situations where one can listen to or be aware of music. We can also listen to music when we drive cars, through earphones to recorded music on cassettes or CDs when we bicycle through traffic, walk around the city or take a walk in the woods. This increased listening *encapsulates both earlier and new situations which affect music's meaning and function.*[15] This new kind of use, listening to music with

---

[15]Cf. Baacke 1998. Under the rubric of "Die Zukünfte analoger Wahrnehmungen" ["The Future Analogous Perceptions"] music, pictures, clothes, and other cultural codes today stand in a mutual analogous relationship to one another and affect our experience of our environment: "Audiation and Visualization lead, of necessity, to a need to consider more strongly than before the rules and processes of analogous perception... [it] is precisely why global perception changed in the long run." ["Auditisierung und Visualisierung der Welt führen zu Notwendigkeit, die Regeln und Abläufe analogen Wahrnehmens stärker zu beachten als bisher... Weltwahrnehmung verändert sich langfriestig gerade deswegen"] (Baacke 1998, 56). It was not only within music fields that this "encapsulation" change could be observed. Within visual art, artists like Rauschenberg and

stereo headphones and portable players, has become very important, as can be seen in sociologist Michael Bull's fascinating study of how sixty people in London listened to music in their daily lives.

This is a new picture, at least in part. One main hypothesis is that people's relation to their environment, time and place is changed by the music that they listen to, and that this process creates other conditions for the function of music and thereby, also its meaning. Encapsulated in their own music world these people behaved in different ways. Many put on their earphones as soon as they woke up, put in a special tape when they rode the subway to their work, but also listened with their earphones even when they went out to the pub. Some quotations can cast light on the kinds of conclusions that Bull draws:

> Left to themselves with no distractions, users often experience feelings of anxiety. This is apparent in the many users who… put their personal stereos on to go to sleep (Bull 2000, 33).

> Switching off becomes tantamount to killing off their private world and returning them to the diminished space and duration of the disenchanted and mundane outside world (Bull 2000, 36).

> This continuation of mood [maintenance] from home to street is achieved by bridging these spaces with music (Bull 2000, 48).

Music contributes, therefore, to a mental cleansing that allows the user to control time and place in a different way than before. They can create their own sound story and score their days in a way that they do not have to share with anyone else. This use counteracts the chance-based aspects of daily life and erases the differences between people's inner and outer lives, between the private and the public (Bull 2000, 153).

Bull also discusses this new use in relation to the concepts of *Erfahrung/Erlebnis* (although Bull's terms are "integrated experience" and "fragmentary experience"). He emphasizes, in opposition to a number of earlier sociologists, that the new forms of use are to be understood as active and describes them as "utopian moments of resistance in the everyday life of personal-stereo users through their management of space, place and time" (Bull 2000, 130). In summary he says:

> The *aestheticization* practices of personal-stereo users are best understood dialectically as strategies of retreating into pleasurable and managed modes of habitation (Bull 2000, 180 [my italics]).

Music's function and meaning changes continually. Seen from a quantitative standpoint, music today is probably more a dimension of "everyday life"—the daily routine, the daily work, the social relationships—than a private meeting.

Andy Warhol had used the everyday visual language that had long been a part of advertising and packaging Cf. Hobsbawm 1994, 514.

This is, of course, not completely easy. Many listeners, as we have seen, listen to their personal music players with earphones in social contexts where there are other people present. But many also go to concerts and clubs with live music.[16] At the same time it is clear that youth music for the postwar generations is, from a *qualitative* standpoint a very important dimension of life. And, yes, for many of those that wrote about this music, it has also become important to defend it from an aesthetic point of view. This was true, for example, of Richard Meltzer in the 1960s.

"The Aesthetics of Rock"

If we look back at popular music's use before World War II and think about the interest music and cultural researchers had for these music forms, we find few that had a larger understanding for this music from an artistic or aesthetic perspective. Before the Beatles success in the beginning of the 1960s, there were few musicologists who took rock and pop seriously.[17] Shortly thereafter, in 1970, the young American student Richard Meltzer published his book, *The Aesthetics of Rock*. In the introduction to a later edition (Meltzer 1987) he describes his writing process:

> I'd get up in the morning, smoke some dope, put on an LP, enter its, uh, *universe*, take profuse notes, play another album, jump from cut to cut, make the weirdest of plausible connections (no professors—whee!—to monitor the hidebound topicality of my thoughts anymore) (Meltzer 1987, x).

From this quotation, one could believe that the book is one long rambling collection of accidental associations. And it is that—but, it also contains an appreciable amount of humanistic knowledge that passes review just as quickly as most of the value judgments about rock and pop that drift by. He can, for example, write as if in passing that "rock is the only possible future for philosophy and art," then describe something about Andy Warhol's art, followed by a citation from a bit of a Beatles text and then a criticism of the philosopher John Dewey, followed by a statement that neither aestheticians, art philosophers or art critics can do justice to art from an art theoretical standpoint if they stand outside it. Art,

---

[16]The number of people within the total population who go to concerts in a concert hall and sit quietly and listen, has become a small proportion of the total population. The difference in the amount of time that these particular concert-goers spend on this activity, and the time that people *generally* listen to music in the course of the day in different social and private contexts, is quite large. The amount of music available has become so enormous that those who have difficulty shutting out music approach places that play the 'wrong music" or music through loudspeakers with great hesitation. As many earlier campaigned for smoking bans, today people call for music bans.

[17]The musicologist Willfred Mellers became well known at the beginning of the 1970s for his book on the Beatles, *Twilight of the gods: the Beatles in retrospect* (Mellers 1973).

writes Meltzer, must be understood "*from* and *within* being" (Meltzer 1987, 7). His prose is at once anti-intellectual and intellectual. He sees his own writing of his total world, "the rock'n'roll world" as an aesthetic discourse.

To describe what Meltzer means by "aesthetics" in all of its variations included in the book is actually a subject worthy of a philosophical dissertation. One simple way to avoid this problem of definitions is to say that *everything has an aesthetic potential*. He points to an article of the philosopher J. L. Austin who suggests that one way to reconstruct what "aesthetics" involves would be to collect all the words that are used to assign value to art. Meltzer contributes with a first list:

> Incongruous, trivial, mediocre, banal, insipid, maudlin, abominable, trite, redundant, repulsive, ugly, innocuous, crass, incoherent, vulgar, tasteless, sour, boring (Meltzer 1987, 13).

Popular music researcher Greil Marcus comments in an introduction to Meltzer 1987 that this indicates that anything could be expressed in the 1970s. A number of negative words were transformed into positive ones thanks to their ability to delineate a space in opposition to the conventional outside world. Anything could happen: *rock was the world.*

Even though, naturally, Meltzer's broad register was not representative of the way in which a "typical" Swedish group or individual listened to and used pop and rock during the 1950s and 60s, his book shows the power and multifaceted nature of the youth culture in these decades.[18]

The word *aesthetic* is used an uncountable number of times in his book. But Meltzer was not alone. Many of the must influential young researchers who wrote about rock and pop during these years and afterwards, were often interested in posing the question: what is the rock-pop aesthetic? Among these, we will turn our attention to Peter Wicke's and Simon Frith's understanding of the rock pop aesthetic.

---

[18] In Robert Pattison's book, *The Triumph of Vulgarity* (Pattison 1987) patterns of thought are soon to recur that have clear parallels to Meltzer's work. Rock is in the end "crude, loud, and tasteless." In a chapter with the heading "A Rock Aesthetic" he also says: "The artistic virtues of rock and Romanticism are originality, primal, energy, honesty, and integrity" (Pattison 1987, 188). Rock is simply a form of vulgarized romantic, but now it is no longer about joy but about everything that can be fun. In the end the reader is left with the impression that rock can be what Pattison says, but it gradually has become much more. Under the rock umbrella there are a number of different stylistic trends with widely differing expressions, everything from "art rock" to "fun rock" to "death metal." (In reading Pattison and Meltzer one is reminded of the Russian literary scholar Michael Bachtin's thoughts the carnival of folk culture. Ideas borrowed from Bachtin recur often in musicological literature of the "new musicology" sort, cf, for example, Kevin Korsyn's article in *Rethinking Music* (Cook and Everist 1999) or Lawrence Kramer's *Musical Meaning – Toward a Critical History* (Kramer 2002). But Bachtin is also referenced regularly by researchers within popular music, for example Hawkins 2002. Cf. also the website http://www.popcultures.com/theorists/bakhtin.html!.

Wicke — East Germany

Musicologist Peter Wicke is interesting, not least because he was active as a musicologist in East Germany,[19] one who mainly wrote about the development of rock and pop in the West. In articles like "Rock music: A Musical-Aesthetic Study' (Wicke 1982) and later in the book *Rock Music: Culture, aesthetics and sociology* (Wicke 1990), Wicke tried to show, from his theoretical point of departure, how rock and pop were used in reality. He wanted to understand the contemporary mass culture's role in society and how new music forms were related to the mass media music culture:

> These kinds of music function in connection with systems of electronic mass communication that create historically altogether novel forms of artistic production, distribution and assimilation, which cannot be validated in terms of individual self-expression in 'the work of art' (Wicke 1982, 221).

From Wicke's starting point that there was a collective movement where individual's roles were small, it was interesting for him to write about how this contributed to new or other aesthetically mediated values and value relationships. Wicke continued in a classic Marxist tradition to discuss the difference between a goods—music—use value and its buying value. He also made a distinction of a special aesthetic dimension between "the practical/functional aspects of use-value (music for dancing, music as background, compensation, distraction)" and "the aesthetic aspects of use-value (the perceptual experience of musical products)." (Wicke 1982, 226).

Wicke saw that the meaning of the former increased at the expense of the latter, and at the same time that an "aesthetic value abstraction process" occurred. The interest within disco, for example, was directed more and more towards records, artist appearances and image. Disco stood, therefore, in contrast to "the Mersey beat," that is to say the Beatles. In this form of rock he found, despite that fact that it concerned dance music, that it once again became possible to experience music as socially meaningful thanks to its particular form (Wicke 1982, 227).

As I understand this (and the following) discussion, Wicke repeated here the earlier idealistic and romantic-philosophic argument of a particular type of music's artistic-aesthetic superiority:

> Given this independent aesthetic valuation of the sound-shape in its own right [sic!], socially produced in a practical, functional context and once again experienced as significant by virtue of the spontaneous, unmediated [sic!], direct relation between musicians and public, a relationship towards music was

---

[19] ALmost two decades after the reunion with West Germany in 1990, it is perhaps necessary for "new readers" to point out that East Germany's official name was the German Democratic Republic (which naturally, in reality was a Communist one-party state).

established out of which the crucial internal musical dynamic principle of rock music arose (Wicke 1982, 227; cf. Wicke 1990, 35).

It is also here that he found aesthetically valuable concepts like "feeling," "drive," "involvement," and "power" which mirrored music's qualitative content. He concludes that rock's aesthetic had from the beginning nothing to do with the individual's experience, but rather with the collective experience.

From this Hegelian-Marxist view of contemporary history, it becomes understandable that Wicke seemed to regard the Western youth's struggle within the capitalist values system, in a way that is reminiscent of how Hegel had earlier described the function of art music. While Hegel saw art as the happy middle for the *bourgeois* person, Wicke saw youth devotion to and interest in rock in a similar way.[20]

Despite Wicke's assurances, he seems to be using the concept of aesthetics in a way very close to the early romantic theoreticians. It is a concept that is used *against* other forms of music in a delimiting way and where music's *inner* structure has a large importance. We find as well the type of argument that Adorno represented, that is to say, one that did not go the way it was supposed to. Wicke writes that it did not take long before "rock music itself [was] integrated into the circuit of exploitation of capital," something that, in turn, began a large artistic productivity, but: "Rock music is not rational, like music in the European art tradition" (Wicke 1982, 231).[21] He even went so far as to say that in contrast to our art music, collectivity is an integral part of African American music and rock—and therefore a decisive social and aesthetic factor.[22] Rock was a music form

---

[20] Cf. Wicke's formulation: "Young people react to such conflicts from within a social space in which aesthetic practice can still become a counter-project" (Wicke 1982, 230).

[21] In Wicke 1990 the ideological rhetoric is toned down. The arguments from 1982, however, can be found. Compare, for example, the section about the *Beatles* song "Love me Do," a chapter (Wicke 1990, 48-72) that begins and ends with the classic romantic idea of music as a sensual language, that is to say that rock "is performed according to an aesthetic of sensuousness" (Wicke 1990, 72). At the same time as Wicke's point of departure is that rock creates new experiences and that "a totally altered relationship between art producer and recipient has asserted itself; that everyday life and creativity, art and media have been brought together in a new context", and states also that "the illusions which once assigned to rock music the power to undermine social relations, to explode them… have since long faded away (Wicke 1990, 74). This does not stop Wicke from writing in the book's last paragraph that "the aesthetic nature of rock music is of far-reaching importance," and that, therefore, a different understanding of culture's progressive and democratic possibilities needs to be created for rock to give rise to a new ideology: "But for this an 'alternative *politics* of culture' is required, and this can hardly be developed in books, but only in revolutionary praxis" (Wicke 1990, 182f). The question is, of course, which form of revolution Wicke was thinking about. During the years between 1987 when Wicke's book was published in German in the DDR and came out in an English translation (Wicke 1990), the DDR imploded in a friendly way.

[22] Cf. Wicke 1982, 235 with Wicke 1990, 18f.

within which one clearly can see the opposition between a capitalistic production system and music's own social form. The basic opposition within capitalism is reproduced directly in musical practice:

> The attempt to bridge this contradiction aesthetically—to reconcile the socially antagonistic polarities of the music of constantly new formal modalities in, and through, the process of creation of musical objects—has been a crucial distinguishing and motivating factor in rock (Wicke 1982, 237).

If we ignore the ideological rhetoric that it was necessary to insert into a text of this kind at the time (Wicke 1982), we find in summary that the concept of aesthetics is almost used as a delineating and stylistically valuing term for music's inherent qualities, as well as a concept for a physical dimension within a collective social process.

If Meltzer based his work to a great extent on his own experiences, Wicke built more on the reading of the literature in traditional academic fashion, but also on personal contacts within the international community studying contemporary pop music (IASPM) that was founded in 1980. Both Wicke and the sociologist Simon Frith were, from the beginning, a part of the leadership within this organization. Frith is perhaps the only popular music researcher who through his countless articles, many books and participation in a number of anthologies, has had a large international impact. It is, therefore, also interesting to look at works in which he problematizes the concept of the aesthetic. But because an idea spread through the 1970s that modernism was over, it is necessary first to assess ways in which this understanding affected views in society and culture. Frith and Horne write, for example:

> The historical moment of *postmodernism* is also the moment of the birth of rock culture, which is... implicated in many postmodern themes: the role of the multinational communication industry; the development of techno-logically based leisure activities; the integration of different media forms; the significance of the imaginary, the fusion of art theory and sales technique. Pop songs are the soundtrack of postmodern daily life, inescapable in lifts and airports, pubs and restaurants, streets and shopping centers and sports grounds (Frith and Horne 1987, 5).

Postmodern Times

In an earlier essay (Edström 1997) I discussed, among other things, musicology's slow process of gradually accepting new scientific directions that were developed in the post modern era—when ever that can be said to have started.[23]

---

[23] From Swingewood 1998, 162f it is understood that the concept of postmodernism first showed up within literature and architecture during the 1940s, that is to say, at least 30 years later than the time Jameson tends to place the discussion.

As has been already glimpsed, Fredric Jameson, for example, considered Igor Stravinsky as a post-modern forerunner. Which Stravinsky—the earlier, interwar period or the late Stravinsky—he does not say.

In the article on Postmodernism in the *Swedish National Encyclopedia* (1994) musicologist Tore Eriksson writes that post Modernism in art music is a definition of a technique "where widely differing styles become the musical building blocks without necessarily leading to pastiche or citations of individual works." As an example, he sites works of Alfred Schnittke. This music is "less abstract" and more listener- friendly (in comparison to what, one might ask, but one answer might be serial art music). Concerning popular culture, Alf Björnberg writes under the same article heading that popular-culture and music has long been marked by "pastiche techniques, eclecticism and blending together of aesthetics and commercialism." Reasonably enough, he adds that this makes it difficult to nail down what the use of the term actually stands for in different style categories (NE 1994, 13:241). Prince's music is given as an example of postmodernism in pop music. In both these cases (art music and rock music) the examples are taken from music from recent decades.[24]

In any case, what is what in "art music," "popular music," "folk music," etc., has gradually become even more difficult to define (Lilliestam 1993). But one cannot understand now the earlier-mentioned breadth of genre and style combinations within respective folk, popular and art music as a consequence of post modernism, nor can one say the opposite either. It is not a chicken-and-egg problem. The social processes that have led to and begun the observed changes lie, as always, long before the discovery of the word. But the question remains: is the categorizing and relativizing of observations a part of modernism and not something that comes later with postmodernism? Like many successful concepts, postmodernism is similarly forward and backward looking, just as much a confirmation that something has recently happened as it is a confirmation of work that is being created right now and will be created. We have also seen that postmodernism at the same time contains a technical handcraft-oriented dimension (cf. the above definitions in the *Swedish National Encyclopedia*).

The question of whether postmodernism also is a *scholarly* category, one that can be characterized as "pastiche technique, eclecticism and the blending

---

[24] Cf. the collection *The Last Post: Music after Modernism* (Miller 1993) that contains eight articles. Postmodernism breaks with the idealistic and formalistic research tradition. Robin Hartwell writes in the article "Postmodernism and art music": "The use of a variety of musical styles within a single work attacks the aesthetic of the unity of the art work... The postmodern work accepts the modernist position of the arbitrary connection between the sign and the signifier... Neither can we force the sign to bear our meaning. On the contrary, we are an inconsistent, incoherent mixture of external forces, absorbed to varying degrees. Postmodernist music is mimetic in that it attempts to present a picture of this incoherence and the play of these forces" (Miller 1993, 50).

together of aesthetics and commercialism" has often been discussed.[25] A theoretical relativism and cultural pluralism is generally favored within postmodernism. Indirectly, then, postmodernism can hardly be seen as a particular method or theoretical structure. To make a connection to the literary scholar Andrew Milner, postmodernism consists of a direction within which artists, critics, writers about culture and academics create, act upon, and write about the contemporary cultural movements that stand in opposition to modernism's Scylla and Charybis: in our case, modernist art music ("High Art") and its antithesis mass culture ("Porno Pop") (Milner 1994, 135-40).[26] But Milner sees nothing positive in Postmodernism as a scholarly method.

Principally criticism against Postmodernism's intellectual property can also be found in the writings of the literary scholar Christopher Norris. Again and again he throws out the idea that rationalist [Enlightenment] concepts cannot, in and of themselves, be the reason for different forms of oppression of people who think differently, other cultures or other classes and subgroups within their own culture, in a word the Others. For Norris it is self-evident that "logic, reason and reflexive autocritique" are the tools within the rationalist thought tradition that postmodernists also need. That it is possible to use and propagandize for anti-rational means with the help of rationalist arguments shows that it has also been possible to betray these values. With Habermas, therefore, Norris sees that Postmodernism:

> [i]s a retrograde cultural phenomenon which unwittingly runs into many of the dead-end antinomies encountered by thinkers in previous phases of anti-enlightenment reaction. Worst of all, it embraces a through-going version of the Nietzschean-relativist creed according to which there is *simply no difference* between truth-claims imposed by sheer, self-authorizing fiat and truths arrived at by process of reasoned debate or open argumentative exchange (Norris 1993, 288).

---

[25]Cf. another early collection *The Anti-Aesthetic* (Foster 1983) where writers like Fredric Jameson, Jean Baudrillard, Jürgen Habermas, Edward Said, Craig Owens, among others, all contributed thoughts on postmodernism (for and against!). With the exception of Habermas, who still departs from a critically scrutinizing theory, the articles generally aim to deconstruct the modernist elitist belief in a preferential right of interpretation. Note that the same basic criticism that is directed toward postmodernism as a method can also be directed toward modernism as well (cf. Dodd 1999, 210ff).

[26]Milner formulates his own and Raymond Williams' view: "Even in the midst of alienation, the vast majority of human beings still live out considerable portions of their lives through face to face, networks of kinship and community, identity and obligation, friendship and love. Indeed, this is what most of us mean by 'life'. The ideal of a common culture that Williams here invokes is, in my view, neither inherently reactionary, nor inherently utopian. Quite the contrary, it represents the only possible alternative, within the space of postmodernity, to a radical commodification which will eventually entail the effective absorption of the cultural into the economic" (Milner 1994, 155f).

The critique of Norris and others is important because it points out that there must always be a balance in the discussion between individual's and group's experience and the community's collective experience.[27]

A valuable discussion of Postmodernism can also be found in the work of the sociologist Alan Swingewood (1998). He focuses first on Jean-Francais Lyotard's influential *The Postmodern Condition* (Lyotard 1984) where gaps in the metanarratives are analyzed from a postmodern perspective.[28] Lyotard wrote his work during a time when thoughts about the death of subjectivity, on the constructed power of language over reality and critique against the Enlightenment project were high on the list. He argued:

> Pluralism and difference arise out of language and aesthetics, and especially through the avant-garde with its commitment to experiment. The postmodern is thus that 'which denies itself the solace of good forms, the consensus of taste.' (Swingewood 1998, 161).

But it is clear that Lyotard took his criticism too far. It is, as Swingewood suggests, difficult to recognize oneself. Apparently there is an elitist modernism within Modernism, but this does not mean that integrating ideas cannot exist side by side. "Wholes," writes Swingewood, "can coexist with difference, diversity and openness, elements made by participants or agents whose actions constitute wholes" (Swingewood 1998, 161). He argues, therefore, for the idea that within the Modernist project, there have more or less always been tendencies that we have begun to call postmodern, among them Erik Satie's ballet *Parade* and Honegger's orchestral work *Pacific 231* are typical examples. For Swingewood, the meaningful difference between the two movements is the idea that Modernism's

---

[27] It is thought-provoking that Norris has just presented Adorno as an example of a researcher who, despite nearly giving up all hope, still did not give up on the Kantian idea that one can both think as an independent, self-aware individual and function as a member of a society, whose importance is greater than the opposition between the individual and the communal. Nothing could, therefore, be more foreign for Adorno, writes Norris, than the irrational and anti-rationalist rhetoric "which currently pass for advanced wisdom in many quarters of the postmodern cultural scene" (Norris 1993, 287). My critical view of Adorno maybe conveys to the reader a too-negative picture of Adorno's importance. He was, without doubt, one of the most important cultural sociologists of the twentieth century. Cf, for example Bull 2000 and Nicholsen 1993. In the latter the reader meets an Adorno who enjoys Schubert, Beethoven, Schönberg, among others, impressions gleaned in part from his radio lectures "Schöne Stellen."

[28] like the marxist metanarrative of emancipation through revolution, or the Enlightenment metanarrative of rational thought leading to moral order (Swingewood 1998, 159f). Norris also discusses Lyotard's work. Lyotard's postmodern idea that one can trace, through philosophers like Nietzsche and Heidegger, the intellectual trails that led to Auschwitz, has to do, therefore, with their anti-rationalist ways of thinking, and not the tradition they attacked as such (1993, 286). The problem: how we should regard the senses, the tools of analysis that we use through our speech to understand the past, is a problem that probably cannot be solved *within the system itself*. Wittgenstein's patent that we can safely dissolve this problem through describing in language information gleaned from our five senses—or perhaps even better, through written analyses—is thus the best proposition, or in any case, a more tempting one.

proponents still believe in its alternative potential. Defense against "the increasing commodification and commercialization of art," is necessary because this process threatens art's 'autonomy" and, he adds:

> Through its imaginary, artistic devices and poetic language, modernism projects an alternative reality, a utopian and subversive aesthetic standing apart from the 'inauthentic' and 'degraded' forms of commercialized mass culture. This is the critical distinction between postmodernism and modernism, for while both may share similar internal elements and forms, it is the postmodern which seeks a rapprochement with contemporary capitalism, eroding the boundaries between culture and society (Swingewood 1998, 166).

In summary, we can say that postmodernism is undoubtedly a contemporary way of processing and understanding the plurality of value norms and styles that surround us today. It shows us that the romantic dream of art as a true and connecting medium in a society characterized by economy and politics, as well as modernism's hope that artworks in a struggle against the increased commercialization could maintain truth and wholeness in itself (autonomy), has been complemented by other processes and value norms. Postmodernism is, simply, a questioning discourse that takes place within modernity. In the market-driven world of postmodernism, many believe that the reification of culture has gone *too* far.[29] The risk is obvious that culture's binding function disappears if the goal of culture is not to continue to give people the opportunity to *cultivate* their own cultural interests themselves. Milner strongly stresses culture's unifying power:

> The problem with any radical commodification of culture, such as entailed in postmodernism, is not simply the perennial failing of all markets, that they confer the vote not on each person but to each dollar and thereby guarantee undemocratic outcomes, but also the much more specific failing that the market undermines precisely what it is that is most cultural with culture, that is, its sociality (Milner 1994, 151).

Postmodernism's stringent methods have, as we have seen, little to recommend themselves. It lies in their nature. Everything becomes "the same."[30] That there are many who think that it represents the triumph of the West over Culture, is one thing; that postmodernism has not yet conquered rationalism's fundamental

---

[29]Cf. Dissanayake's commentary concerning art's separation from everyday life that she considers began with the introduction of written culture in Plato's time: "It has taken 2500 years for postmodern philosophy to finish the job literacy began" (Dissanayake 1992, 220).

[30]Cf. Dodd, who after a review of various postmodernist arguments from Lyotard, Baudrillard, Richard Rorty and Zygmunt Bauman writes in summary: "A fragmented theory has been used to interpret a fragmented society. The use of mimesis in social theory is consistent with the crisis of representation in postmodern aesthetics, and with the pluralism of values that characterizes postmodern culture in general. But for sociological purposes, it is unhelpful and unconstructive" (Dodd 1999, 181).

ideas and patterns of thought is quite another, and more important, thing. Postmodernism is not *the great disparity* but rather *both* the many differences *and* the many similarities of the times. To cite an example for contemporary popular music theory: "Pop music takes its power from the consequent meeting of consumer fantasies of difference and musician's fantasies of collectivity" (Frith and Horne 1987, 21).[31]

That we live in postmodern times does not mean that everything within a culture is seen to have equal value, either. Hobsbawm writes that it is still necessary and possible to have opinions about what is good or bad and differentiate between professional and amateur. Those who are involved in art and production in different ways often deny that it is possible to make these distinctions. Hobsbawm suggests they are made by referring to the fact that (a) sales statistics actually do not say anything about a product's true worth, (b) by referring to the modernistic-elitist argument, or (c) from a postmodernist belief that no objective differentiation can be made. Arguments like these are similarly empty:

> Indeed, only the ideologists and salesmen held such absurd views in public, and in their private capacity even most of these knew that they distinguished between good and bad (Hobsbawm 1994, 521).

There is a postmodern egalitarian message that constant repetition has been a kind of normative sheen. As Hobsbawm points out, however, it is an illusion to believe that relativists do not make judgments.[32]

As we have seen, it is possible to hear postmodernist tendencies in Satie's *Parade* and other works from the 1920s. Since then a number of works have been written with ambitions to art-music status, where elements of pop music, jazz, pop rock, etc., are included. In a similar way, artists and musicians have also tried to widen their professions: a singer incredibly popular in Sweden in the 1930s, Sven-Olof Sandberg, later sang at the opera in Stockholm, the clarinetist Benny Goodman commissioned and played *Contrasts* of Bela Bartok in 1938; and the singer Alice Babs was a soloist in Duke Ellington's *The Majesty of God* in 1973. During the 1990s "the King of Pop," Michael Jackson, sampled and integrated

---

[31] Swingewood has a similar thought: "The constituting role of dialogue in culture cannot be exaggerated: the culture of modernity is decentered and built around differences at all levels of society" (Swingewood 1998, 179).

[32] Cf. also cultural-sociologist McGuigan, who points out as well that we are continuously judging things. He, therefore, wants to study how this process happens from a sociological perspective: "People will value: we make judgements as to quality and worth all the time; and these are not just monetary evaluations... It is the sociality of value, which is of prime interest, then, not the remote aporias of aesthetics. Because the aesthetic move is perpetually in danger of dropping off the edge of the theoretical board game, the sociological and the ethical moves in the value debate provide rather more substantial directions for cultural analysis" (McGuigan 1997, 146).

music of Beethoven, among others in some of his songs, while the Swedish artist Eva Dahlgren sang her own texts to the composer Anders Hillborg's music in 1998, and so forth (cf. Edström 1992).

Thus: a belief in total postmodern relativism only hinders the analysis of the ideologies, structures and agents that in the guise of different forms of power positions exercise influence on the construction of value judgments and people's use of music in different contexts and situations. Modernism's advance has possibly decreased, while modernity, judging by all appearances, is still unfolding.

There is still one unsolved problem: if more and more people begin to see that "everything is the same," then shouldn't "everything" also be experienced as aesthetic?

Simon Frith's "approach to music and society"

If, from the titles of Meltzer and Wicke's works, the relevance of the aesthetic concept can be seen within pop and rock, then Simon Frith in his article "Towards an aesthetic of popular music" (Frith 1987) takes an altogether more careful approach. In 1987, however, Frith was already well-known and had discussed value judgments and the role of aesthetics within pop and rock in the critically acclaimed book *Sound Effects*:

> The problem is to decide the criteria of judgment. High art critics often write as if their terms of evaluation were purely aesthetic, but mass culture critics can't escape the fact that the bases for cultural evaluation are always social: what is at issue is the *effect* of a cultural product. Is it repressive or liberating? The aesthetic question—how does the text achieve its effects?—is secondary (Frith 1981, 54f).

But Frith is not just a sociologist. He was also a fan of rock and pop and a well-known critic. Frith was driven, like most of the other writers on rock born in the 40s and 50s, apparently by both conscious and unconscious desires to legitimize their own youth music and, at the same time, distance themselves from Modernisms elitist ideology. From this perspective it appears completely understandable that he often has given first place to social questions and second place to aesthetic ones.[33]

---

[33]Cf. Rock musicologist (or perhaps, cultural theoretician) Larry Grossberg who writes that he and Frith studied popular music out of their own curiosity, as well as, from a scientific standpoint, to discover what happened/happens within popular music. Most writers on rock and pop probably share this motivation (Grossberg 1999). The question is whether this personal motivation is so very different from the majority of musicological researchers' motives for changing about a particular form of music. Don't musicologists often want to study the music in question because they enjoy it and want to legitimize it? The latter happens as a rule whether one thinks about it consciously or not.

Frith also called attention to the fact that it is very difficult to predict which records or groups will break through, something that has to do with how people apply aesthetic preferences when it comes to music in contrast to how one values normal products (Frith 1983). With "people" even at the beginning of the 1980s, Frith meant teenagers. From his British perspective Frith saw that even "the aesthetic of the teenage market was a working-class aesthetic" (Frith 1983, 182).

Frith states—after the reader has read his solid sociological analysis of the use of music and its significance among teenagers in England—that other sociologists have not equally penetrated the crux of the rock/pop matter:

> If the essence of rock is fun, it is a concept strangely neglected by sociologists. Analysts of high art are obliged to respect the autonomy of aesthetic judgments, but sociologists of popular art... don't confront fun, but describe the 'irrationality' of mass taste with aloof disgust, as if irrationality were irrelevant for popular culture instead of part of it. Marxists, in particular, have interpreted the fact that people *enjoy* mass culture as a reason for gloom... But the power of rock fantasy rests, precisely, on utopianism (Frith 1983, 264).

These conclusions are reminiscent of the philosopher Bruce Baugh's attempt to contemplate what a rock aesthetic includes. Here we meet a similar discussion that takes rock's "difference" as a point of departure, a theme that is often taken up (cf. Willis below). While traditional music aesthetics is about form and composition, rock aesthetics, according to Baugh, is about how music feels and how it affects the listeners physically. He counts rhythms, timing, the voice of the singer and the volume level as more important musical parameters within rock than within European art music. Rock guitarists like Eric Clapton and Jimmy Hendrix play with an intensity that directly affects the body. Like most rock guitarists, therefore, they do not have an intellectual attitude or approach to music (Baugh 1993, 28). The conclusion is that it is possible to define the basic principles for a rock aesthetic by turning "Kantian or formalist aesthetics on its head":

> Where Kant prized free and autonomous judgment of reason, and so found beauty in form... an aesthetics of rock judges the beauty of music by its effect on the body... makes beauty in rock to some extent a subjective and personal matter (Baugh 1993, 26).

There is, however, no reason to believe that those who heard or danced to a polka in the nineteenth century or, for instance, a foxtrot in the 1930s used music in a completely different way than youth today use pop and rock. Even though we cannot hardly expect to find the aesthetic experience of æll in this context, there is, however, nothing that can be interpreted in rock's relationship to the body that is different than for the foxtrot or the polka and all other similar music.[34]

---

[34] Cf. Edström 1987 where the myth of the specialness of African-American music is discussed.

As stated, Frith considered the traditional aesthetic questions always to take second place.[35] But can't words like "fun" and "irrational" be understood as aesthetic expressions within rock and pop? To put it another way, these words—even those found in Meltzer's list—should be regarded in a similar way to the nineteenth-century view of experiential words like sublime or other adjectives that slowly became a part of the network around the aesthetic concept. Don't words like "fun" and "irrational" signal that the aesthetic field has expanded, and that these words are in a close relationship with the words that were already within this field? Much suggests that this is in fact the case, but we are not speaking about æIII, but rather about *a new concept*, æIV. æIV is different from æIII in that æIV experiences concentrate more on giving free reign to the experience and, also that vocal music has now had a *complete breakthrough*. The experience is dominated by the irrational, the fun, the playful, spontaneous, unrestrained, etc.

At the same time, we must ask if this broadening from æIII to æIV didn't begin much earlier. Did this bridge already happen in the nineteenth century when people listened with delight and light-hearted humor to entertainment music? Or perhaps æIV first appeared when dance and jazz music first made its entry in the inter-war period? One argument that it did not already begin in the nineteenth century is that the *bourgeois*, idealistic and romantic cultural tradition had a continuing solid grip on people's imagination. On the other hand, there is much to support the argument that this process (from æIII to æIV) had its roots in the nineteenth century and perhaps can be traced through the roaring 20s where social change was more penetrating, not least within the music world: gramophones, radio, films, public dancing, new music styles, etc. That this process did not blossom out fully until after World War II, has to do with the other changes in society and the expansion of youth culture that we are studying now.

Some years later when Frith together with Horne published their book *Art into Pop* (Frith and Horne 1987), we find a deeper discussion of rock, pop, art and aesthetics. A statement from rock composer Brian Eno also focuses on the changing use of popular music through "Walkmans" (foreshadowing the latest revolution in MP3 players):

> We call it music because it comes in through the ears, but it is very different from, say, Beethoven. *It's made differently, played differently, heard differently* (Frith and Horne 1987, 174 [my italics]; cf. Bull's analysis above).

Through this possibility, one could, as has been touched on earlier, take along one's own music into contexts where music couldn't be heard earlier. Music became contextualized in a new way: one could listen to and use music on the bus, in nature, in drawing lessons, during dinner at home, and so forth.

---

[35]Alan Moore stands out among rock-music researchers who depart from the opposite point that musical structure plays a large, even primary role (Moore 1993).

It is, however, in the above-named article (Frith 1987) that Frith gets into a clinch with the concept of aesthetics, where he states in the introduction that it could be seen as inviting ridicule to ask the question whether ABBA's and Mozart's music can have the same aesthetic weight from a enjoyment and entertainment standpoint.[36] The problems that a sociologist and aesthetician meet are the same according to Frith, who asks: "How do we make value judgments? How do such value judgments articulate the listening experiences involved?" According to Frith, it does not help to say that rock and pop are commercial music forms. Therefore, the most successful rock and pop has fulfilled the function that these music forms are judged to have. The fact remains that people play and listen most to the music that they like. The answer to the questions must, therefore, be sought with help of a traditional sociological analysis.

Frith throws out an earlier argument that rock's aesthetics are intimately related to the concept of 'authenticity." He asks rhetorically: "How do we recognize good sounds in non-rock genres... not described in authentic terms in the first place?" (Frith 1987, 137). Frith finds, however, that questions like these do not lead forward. In the introduction to the article, he has already said that the value of pop (and rock) lies in that pop music, like art-music, transcends its own social value:

> Everyone in the pop world is aware of the social forces that determine 'normal' pop music—a good record, song, or sound is precisely one that transcends those forces (Frith 1987, 136).

In order to substantiate this claim, Frith tests a new methodological way. The main question for him is not what music says about people, but rather how it constructs them. Frith returns therefore to the article's introduction in order to clarify music's social functions and what they mean for aesthetics. Frith summarizes:

> The social functions of popular music are in the creation of identity, in the management of feelings, in the organization of time. Each of these functions depends, in turn, on our experience of music as something which can be possessed (Frith 1987, 144).

Because we are *one* with our music, we often experience, according to Frith, that we are owned by our music. He finds, therefore, that transcendence is equally important within popular music aesthetics as in art music aesthetics, but that within popular music, transcendence does not mean that music is free from social forces *but rather is formed by them*. Frith adds in parentheses, however: "(Of course, in the end the same is true of serious music, too)" (Frith 1987, 144).

---

[36]Cf. the sociologist Gerhard Schulze's commentary: "With the dissemination of cultural criticism at the end of the 1960s, it became possible to view high culture from a distance without being thought a philistine." ["Mit der Verbreitung der linke Kulturkritik Ende der sechziger Jahre war es möglich geworden, zur Hochkultur auf Distanz zu sehen, ohne gleich als Banause zu gelten"] (Schulze 1993, 540).

If we try to describe what Frith means by "the aesthetic of pop/rock," it is about what a person thinks of the musical forms out of everyone's individual taste, the valuations made and what stylistic elements one experiences that the music possesses. We meet, thus, old and well-known formulas.

However, we have not yet turned our attention to the article's last section, entitled "The aesthetics of popular music." But no real clarity emerges. In the end we are left consequently with doubts, that what Frith says is a repetition of the old saw that aesthetics concerns how music is evaluated and the stylistic features that delineate pop/rock from other music, as well the satisfaction we find in listening to music that we value positively and to which we experience an emotional reaction. What the continuous presence of a dialogue between music and the individual means, in turn, for the transcendental dimension Frith never clearly explains. So either we are left standing with a variant of the old insight: "Aesthetics is often classified as a branch of value theory",[37] or we take Frith at his word when he concludes by pointing out that the music we value highest is that which has a kind of collective and subversive effect. How this influence functions, however, cannot be understood, writes Frith, who is forced, therefore, to end the article with the words: "That impact is what we first need to understand" (Frith 1987, 149).[38]

***

These authors went many rounds in the fight between aesthetics and rock/pop, and even though not many blows landed, I maintain that the fact itself that these influential people engaged in the match had an equally consolidating and legitimizing function. That it garnered more points for style than actual points did not affect daily musical life for at least 90% of the younger generation. It is now old knowledge that, as always, aesthetics was a field that interested researchers to the greatest degree, and the general public to a much lesser degree, if at all.[39] That these researchers (Meltzer, Wicke, Baugh and Frith) wrote their texts out of their own experiences with current rock and pop was also clear.

---

[37] The quotation is from the philosopher Kendall Walton. The article's main point is that when someone really appreciates a work one calls out "How marvelous!" (Walton 1993).

[38] Since then, Frith has written an impressive and coherent work (Frith 1998). The book concludes with a chapter called "Toward a Popular Aesthetic" (Frith 1998, 269-78). Here we find most of his earlier arguments concerning aesthetics. For example, he states again: " 'Transcendence' is as much part of popular music as of the serious music aesthetic, but in pop transcendence articulates not music's independence of social forces but a kind of alternative experience to them (Of course, in the end, the same is true of 'serious' music too)" (Frith 1998, 275). I have not been able to find that Frith formulates a clearer description of the concept than in his earlier cited work.

[39] Cf. Grossberg (Wilson-Brown and McClary 1999) who states that there was a clear difference in the English and American popular press's ability to discuss the meaning of rock and pop from a contemporary social-sciences point of view. While those who read the English New Musical

The thought itself that popular music needed legitimacy was naturally related to the question of popular music's general worth. Here there was a rich variety of different positions where, on the one hand, pop and rock were seldom seen as a higher form of culture, thus questions of aesthetics and artistic intention lacked relevance. On the other hand, a common thought among humanists and cultural personalities was also that rock and pop had "negative commercial affects." This kind of music was in the service of capitalism and therefore had a manipulative affect on people's ability to form their own judgments.[40]

Perhaps the opposition between how the worth and function of the arts (and art music) are viewed, and the satisfaction and pleasure that youth experienced when they used their youth culture is most clearly formulated by Paul Willis and his collaborators. Here a concept is also introduced that is of particular interest for us: "grounded aesthetic," that seems more verbose than the extension of the concept of æIII to æIV that was just suggested as a new "hedonistic" aesthetic experience.

Everyday Aesthetics in Youth Culture

Willis's attack is clear and radical. In the first sentences of the book, he says that art music and all traditional (*bourgeois*) art lacks relevance for the lives of most young people:[41]

> Many of the traditional resources of, and inherited bases for, social meaning, membership, security and psychic certainty have lost their legitimacy for a good proportion of young people. There is no longer a sense of a 'whole culture' with allocated places and a shared, universal value system... a result of much-commented wider processes related to late modernization: secularization, consumerism; individualization; decollectivization; weakening respect for authority; new technologies of production and distribution (Willis et al 1990, 13).

Willis grounds his analyses in a large interview with English youth. His point of departure is that symbolic activities are a common human experience, simply a result of the fact that humans are a communicative species. But Willis does not see post-war consumerism as something that has made people passive, rather the

---

Express now and then met the name Derrida, his name did not appear in American rock and pop magazines.

[40] For a glimpse into the debates that happened in Sweden from the 1960s, see Lilliestam 1998, 49ff, 97-115.

[41] Willis's way of writing and his sometimes oversimplified positions against the English establishment make his formulations into boomerangs, despite their intended effect, as when he suggests that "the taste for art is learned" [sic].

reverse, that it is in itself a form of cultural production. All who listen to music, he writes, "do their own symbolic work.... There is a kind of cultural production all within consumption" (Willis et al 1990, 20).

It is these ideas that to all appearances lead to the idea that, exactly as within the framework of "grounded theory," the idea of "grounded aesthetics" must be seen as a theory that is built up through an interaction between preconceptions, earlier methodological views, and collected empirical material, which through a process generates a grounded theoretical framework that is tailored to the reality of the research field itself.[42] Willis identifies his "grounded aesthetic experience' as a creative element in a process where symbols and practice accrue meaning "[and] are selected, reselected, highlighted and recomposed to resonate further appropriated and particularized meanings" (Willis et al 1990, 21). "Grounded aesthetics" is quite simply the driving force of daily culture. The object is never the most important, and therefore *the beautiful* is seen as "living symbolic activity" more than a quality of an object. "Grounded aesthetics" creates a meaning addition that not only reflects or repeats something, but, rather increases the experience (Willis et al 1990, 23).

Willis devotes a great deal of thought to how young people use music. It is not only something that the majority of them spend many hours daily with, it is also an activity: the buying of records, the creating of bands with friends, the discussions with others, reading of magazines and newspapers, as well as listening to, dancing to and gathering to music. And—one of Willis's leit motifs—all of these can be seen as creative cultural activities. Music and text make possible symbolic work in the power of the "sound" of music. When one dances to music this creates a foundation for a "bodily grounded aesthetics." Texts are an especially important factor because they:

> [p]rovide young listeners with a set of public discourses (about emotional or romantic relationships, for example) which both play back to people their own situations and experiences, and provide a means of interpreting those experiences... Pop lyrics help in this way by working in everyday, ordinary language, and giving it a special kind of resonance, power and poetry (Willis et al 1990, 69).

Willis also points out that the technological development that has occurred within music has brought with it "a veritable explosion in musical activities," which is to say that thousand and thousands of young people play and create their own music and their own lyrics.[43]

---

[42] Grounded Theory goes back to B. G. Glaser and A. L. Strauss *The Discovery of grounded theory,* 1967. It has been used in music pedagogical dissertations like Börje Stålhammar (1995, 27) and Christer Bouij (1998). For an introduction from a music pedagogical perspective, see Stålhammar 1999.

[43] Willis takes notice of the prolific musical activities of African-American youth. He suggests that

No reader can doubt that Willis's aesthetic project has considerably expanded the boundaries of the concept. Here we clearly already have the æIV variant. But we also approach the idea that within a society *all activities that can be described as cultural*[44] *can be seen to have aesthetic content*, and therefore besides æIV we now meet a concept whose content both *qualitatively and quantitatively approaches infinity*, æV^n (consider the "postmodern" question that I just posed that if "everything is the same" therefore "everything" also has an aesthetic potential). It logically follows that it will be impossible for philosophers to define this "postmodern" aesthetic experience, and as we have seen earlier, Shusterman has, for similar reasons, postulated that this is what has become the case in our time (see p. 215). I consider, therefore, æV^n to be another expansion of the aesthetic concept.

Simon Frith has pointed out that Willis looks upon all youth activity with a certain amount of romanticizing, a critique that Willis refuted by clarifying the conditions for the "grounded aesthetic process." One condition is that the symbolic object can mediate in a progressive way, that is to say, it can function as a conduit between symbolic and social meanings. Even if this process is open in principle, he adds the following condition:

> There must be some kind of *homology* between the symbolic resources and meanings and values… of the receivers. But mediation of meaning does not, itself, guarantee a creative generation of grounded aesthetics. For this we need to entertain the notion of at least a momentary *integration* between the text and sensibility, between text and process of symbolic work within the receiver, including and involving changes in the meanings… which feed into the work (Willis et al 1990, 154).

Willis sees also that this process does not exclude that people can trigger a creative aesthetic process even if the resulting situation can be socially loaded: "It's possible that aesthetic effects might flow from 'bad' artifacts" (Willis et al 1990, 154). This process can be facilitated if there is an aesthetic tension between different artifacts.

---

the developments in music have "revolutionized potentials for the symbolic creativity of young people in music and greatly increased the possibilities of music-making, particularly around the practices of mixing, sampling, bootlegging and home recording… [and] have enabled a process of the more formal reflection of grounded aesthetics in a 'bottom-end-up' process of promoting the grounded aesthetics of wider groups and collectivities" (Willis et al 1990, 77). A similar parallel change happened during the 1990s among immigrant youth in Sweden.

[44]Since the 1960s, more and more activities have come to be regarded as cultural. Behind this expansion is the thought of seeing culture as an all-encompassing human activity (an anthropological cultural concept), as opposed to an aesthetical cultural concept that only contains the traditional arts, see further in the music pedagogue Bengt Olsson's work (Olsson 1993, 13-15).

For Willis, therefore, the commercial contemporary culture was the sphere within which people, and especially youth, could live out the oppositions that existed within the English society of the 1980s:

> The simple truth is that it must now be recognized that the coming together of coherence and identity in common culture occurs… in leisure not work, through commodities not political parties, privately not collectively (Willis et al 1990, 159).

This radical interpretation naturally stands in stark contrast to most of the earlier Marxist-inspired critics' views on the meaning of popular culture. It also broadens as indicated the view of the concept of aesthetics in a way that seems to be completely new but isn't. The fact is that we can go back a hundred years in time and find that this view was present to a great degree. We shall first meet the sociologist Georg Simmel, and thereafter look for answers to the effect of social development during the latter half of the twentieth century on people's personalities. One of the basic points of departure in our discussion is that there exists a close relationship between society's general changes (sociogenesis) and changes in the ways in which people think and react (psychogenesis).

A Sociological View of Aesthetics

For Simmel, writes the sociologist Jukka Gronow, a social experience or a social object—for example a meal or an item of clothing—can also be an aesthetic experience/artefact. The well-being that follows with the social activity is simultaneously an aesthetic sense of well-being:

> Whoever speaks of forms moves in the field of aesthetics. Society, in the last analysis, is a work of art (as cited in Gronow 1997, 140).[45]

There is a form of idealism in Simmel that is reminiscent of Kant, and that is channeled toward the thought of the human tendency for "sociability" and how in a process ideas and structures tend toward sociation.[46] If Kant saw *the beautiful* as disinterested, etc., Simmel saw the social-aesthetic interaction between people as a bridge between the individual and the collective:

> Simmel intended to show that in the world of sociability the whole antinomy of taste between the subjectivity of feeling and its general communicability in a sense disappears… since we can be assured that, at least as long as the social formation exists or is preserved, as long as the game is played or the sociable gathering goes on, the feeling is shared by all (Gronow 1997, 150).

---

[45] Cf. sociologist David Frisby (1991, 75) as well as Ch. 5, footnote 53 concerning Croce's philosophical attempt to avoid the whole problem.
[46] This description is connected to Lash (1999, 122).

In reaction to those who criticized this Simmelian imperative, Gronow states that the "pure" form of interaction that Simmel intimates includes that all social interaction is reciprocal and built on an engaged understanding between the parties. This possibility of bridging social conflicts that nineteenth-century aestheticians saw in art Simmel saw in "the sociability of cultivated people," or with Gronow's interpretation as the everyday interaction between normal people. Gronow adds:

> This was done by emphasizing and analysing the dimension and possibility of reciprocal and equal aesthetical pleasure and freedom inherent in almost all everyday social intercourse in general, and in fashion in particular (Gronow 1997, 157 [Cf. the earlier discussion on music and fashion on p. 221]).

Simmel saw for himself how culture at the end of the nineteenth century became more and more diversified, and that money, as a value placed on all transactions gave them an aura of objectivity but at the same time created a distance.[47] He also considered the importance of style and style history, an area that was also important to musicologists at the turn of the century (for example Guido Adler's *Der Stil in der Musik* from 1911). In Simmel's formulation the question of style was an attempt to solve one of life's greatest problems in an aesthetic way: how an individual work or an individual's way of being, something that is a singularity, at the same time can be part of something larger, a uniformly encompassing context (Simmel 1995, 160).

There is thus in Simmel an anti-modernist tendency, an aesthetification of the everyday, that in part is reminiscent of Willis's search after a "grounded everyday aesthetic." There is also a post-modernist tendency as well in that he displays a great deal of openness in his views on culture and aesthetics.[48] But Simmel, unlike Elias, Habermas or Luhmann, does not add an overarching social theory to help us further on our musical-historical journey following the concept of aesthetics. A markedly later addition that illuminates much of the changes that we have witnessed during the twentieth century from a new perspective is therefore also necessary. We turn, therefore, to the more important ideas of two important German sociologists, Ulrich Beck and Thomas Ziehe.

---

[47] Cf. Frisby (1991) who discusses Simmel's weaving together of the role of money in modern society and everyday life's all-encompassing aesthetic potential.

[48] The philosopher Erik Edholm has a formulation that clearly points to this feature: "Simmel's clear reluctance toward systematics and closed hierarchical forms, against disciplined order… even his great sociological work is built up as a barely adequate camouflaged collection of essays" (Simmel 1995, 10). Cf. also the sociologist Lars-Erik Berg (1998, 180).

Social Change Leads to New Aesthetic Ground Rules

Not only youth culture changed in the decades after World War II. As Beck points out, the working week became gradually shorter. Life expectancy increased. People—both old and young—developed increased buying power that could be invested in both material and spiritual products (Beck 1992). During this time urbanization increased—in Sweden a population shift also occurred from the north toward the south—which led to many losing their cultural roots. At the same time the generally longer standard education gave the younger generation better tools to use in an increasingly complex society. As Beck points out however increasing numbers of people realized the social development did not always lead to the *Schlaraffenland* (a paradise on earth) that was foreshadowed by increased effectiveness within industry and advances in the natural sciences. It became clear that there were many risks: traffic accidents, dying forests, environmental poisons, and so forth. Modernisation contributed to a risk-filled social development.[49]

What is interesting for us to note is that Beck comes to the conclusion that people from this time find themselves in another phase of modernity, in a *reflexive* phase that affects all of their (our) experiences of the environment around us.[50] This is also an important point for Ziehe:

> Our culture invites us to more and more knowledge that allows us to observe, educate, categorize and comment on ourselves... Increasing numbers of secondary experiences related to ourselves are available... and that always exist before our own primary experiences. Also children and young people now have already been drawn into the possibilities of reflexive knowledge. They all have ... their own media packet about themselves within their own heads (Ziehe 1986, 346).[51]

---

[49] The title of Beck's extremely influential book (published first in German in 1986; 60,000 copies were sold in Germany in the first five years), is *Risikogesellschaft: Auf dem Weg in eine andere Moderne*. [*Risk Society: Towards a New Society.*] The following definition of risk is given in the English edition: "*Risk* may be defined as *a systematic way of dealing with hazards and insecurities induced and introduced by modernization itself*" (Beck 1994, 21). Cf. also Neubauer and Hurrelmann 1995, 1.

[50] People's increased capacity for reflection is already a main concept in Elias's writings in the 1930s. The concept of reflexive/reflexivity appears also from the 1970s in the toolboxes of more and more important sociologists, among them, Anthony Giddens and Habermas. The sociologist Richard Kilminster writes in his superb work from an "Elias perspective" summarizing the changes around 1980: "The changes in behavioural codes, perspective, feeling for life, attitude and orientation begin to stabilize... around a more *ego*-dominated mode of self-regulation... At this point, a type of person best survives who has a developed capacity for self-orientation and self-regulation... what is widely being called in the 1990s the age of 'reflexivity' or the 'risk' society" (Kilminster 1998, 164). Cf. also Fornäs 1995, 5f.

[51] Ziehe was praised for his dissertation on youth and narcissism. Here similar discussions about youth reflections and ways of relating to contemporary German culture recur. If I clip three citations, it is indirectly clear from the use of language that his works come to influence most pedagogues, psychologists and youth researchers: a) In relation to the consumption of

This brings on different forms of structures: political, ideological and personal, that all can be seen as reflexive. During this process, writes Beck, increasing numbers of older social structures will be relegated to the background (class for example) or lose their social meaning for individuals (families, for example). Instead, the individuals themselves, as well as new interest groupings will become more important. People's reflexive thoughts become the most important basis for the individuation:

> We are eye-witnesses to a social transformation within modernity, in the course of which people will be set free from the social forms of industrial society—class, stratification, family, gender status of men and women (Beck 1992, 87).

These older traditional social factors are reduced in importance, while the new, secondary forms grow and make individuals dependent on "fashions, social policy, economic cycles and markets." Beck clarifies:

> Thus it is precisely individualized private existence which becomes more and more obviously and emphatically dependent on situations and conditions that completely escape its reach (Beck 1992, 131).

But even though people to a greater degree than before become the social reproduction units in life, the standardization of the market makes it easy to slot people into prefabricated roles: "The very same media which bring about an individualization also bring about a standardization" (1994, 130). What Beck implies—he takes television as an example—is that media isolates and standardizes. The media dictates that there are other ways to socialize, and at the same time, that these ways become trans-cultural. In an increasing number of nations similar ways of being are developing. Through the media, writes Beck, we live, therefore, a kind of special and temporal double life. People in different contexts see the same concert with Michael Jackson or with the New York Philharmonic.

      The freedom to reflexively take decisions about one's own life path are, therefore, according to Beck, partly illusory:

---

commodities the dichotomy refers to the growing materialistic access to commodities and the simultaneous physical impossibility of using them." ["In Bezug den *Warenkonsum*: hier besteht der Widerspruch zwischen der wachsenden materiellen Möglichkeit zum Erwerb von Waren und der der gleichzeitigen psychischen Unmöglichkeit (deren Aneignung)"] (Ziehe 1975, 103), b) "Self reflexivity is a collective change of the forms of interactivity that makes it possible to lessen the feeling of Angst caused by the perceived powerlessness, at the same time as the knowledge of the perceived powerlessness is dealt with" ["Selbstreflexion ist eine kollektive Veränderung von Interaktionsformen, die es ermöglich, die *Angst* vor erfahrener Ohnmacht abzubauen, um die *Erkenntnis* von Ohnmacht verarbeitbar zu machen"] (Ziehe 1975, 262), as well as, c) "The 'Narcissist' thus, is a reflexive person: with an ability to face the powerlessness and suffer without feeling the neurotic burst inwardly or to place the neurotic burst between the self and the external reality" ["Der 'Narzissmus' ist dann ein reflektierter: als Fähigkeit, an erfahrener Ohnmacht praktisch zu *leiden*, ohne sie als neurotischen Bruch in sich selbst hineinverlegen oder als psychotischen Bruch zwischen sich under die äussere Realität stellen zu müssen"] (Ziehe 1975, 263). The cited article from 1986 is also included in Ziehe 1991.

As people are removed from social ties and privatized through recurrent surges of individualization, a double effect occurs. On the one hand, forms of perception become private, and... *ahistorical... history shrinks to the (eternal) present*, and everything revolves around the axis of one's personal ego and life...On the other hand, those areas where commonly organized action can affect personal life steadily diminish... Individualizations of life situations and processes thus means that biographies become *self-reflexive* (Beck 1992, 135).

To return to song/music and apply that which has been said to music's function and role in Western society, it has been shown that the use of music has changed in similar ways. Mass-media-produced standardized music functions also transnationally and trans-culturally. The choices of musical styles have multiplied keeping pace with an increasingly pluralistic society.[52] One is forced to choose in a different way than earlier generations. Traditions are no longer important. An increased pressure towards individualization happens at the same time under the rules of the market.

Music is always experienced in real time–in the now–and can thereby be said to have an ahistorical dimension. When it comes to art music, jazz and folk music, there are trends within them where older music is performed on historically-relevant instruments and with historically-informed performance practice, at the same time what we hear—the sound—is always in the present, giving the experience both an ahistorical and an historical dimension. One can speak of a dissolving of the time horizons.

Ziehe for his part also emphasizes that reflexive consciousness leads people to take a stand about what they can achieve (what is doable). At the same time, the range of culture compels that a decision be made, which is why more and more is dependent upon the individual. This leads the individual to relate to various horizons of possibility. When the individual will achieve or master these possibilities, Ziehe sees that one chooses certain reaction patterns that he labels (a) subjective; (b) ontological; and (c) potential (Ziehe 1986).

Examples of these reaction patterns can be found in the work of the Swedish youth researchers Johan Fornäs, Ulf Lindberg and Over Sernhede on three music groups. In one section in this study they depart from the typologizing above, and suggest that because choice of lifestyles was so enormous for young people, individuals needed to orient themselves and find a balance. It is in relation to this fund of "doability, reflexivity and individualizing" that youth engage in order to find meaning in the late modern life. The authors find that ontologizing as an attempt at orientating does not appear for the three groups, but subjectivizing and above all potentializing, that is to say:

---

[52]This change can also be dressed in the clothes of postmodern speech (cf. above p. 240).

The charging of the everyday with intensity... 80s-like in its connection to the aesthetification of self-description...affirm... the modern and try to sharpen it to try to hold the feelings of emptiness at bay. This appears in all of our groups (Fornäs et al 1988, 220).

Not least, it relates to one of the groups, where it especially applies to "having fun." The members are "fascinated by surface, stylization, aesthetification" (Fornäs et al 1988, 220).

While Ziehe, to a greater extent than Beck, can be said to have influenced pedagogical and socially-minded youth research, as far as I have been able to discover, it is Beck's writings that are most cited by contemporary sociologists. At the same time as Beck's theory seems to be justified when it comes to overarching social changes and changed patterns of socialization, it has an objective preponderance in as much as he never discusses the individual person's *subjective* experiences.[53] There is, of course, always a reason to question the thought of the "self-created individual." A person is never a *homo clausus*. The opposition that Beck implies between set roles and the self-reflexive taste thus stretches further back in time. By the 1920s labels like "jazzgossar" ["jazz lads"] and "swingpjattar" ["zoot suiters"] suggest that the categorizing of youth in ready-made lifestyles and music styles is not a new thought. Youth modes of thought and action were, however, different in the interwar period. Later, during the postwar period, a number of new youth categories developed–everything from rastafarians to hip-hoppers, youth groups that in most case also had/have their special attributes and are connected to specific music styles.[54]

Late Modern Changes

If the sociologists Heitmeyer and Olk (1995) emphasize that Beck sees the concept of individualization as a mainly socio-cultural term, other researchers have focused more on the subjective side of the concept. Heitmeyer and Ott cite, among others, the sociologist Scott Lash's thoughts about "the end of the individual" and the individual's narcissistic self reflexive expressions and forms.[55]

---

[53] See Heitmeyer and Olk for a summary of the critique that is directed at Beck (Heitmeyer and Olk 1995, 16-33).

[54] See Lilliestam 2002 for a discussion of how the young talk about different groups in society and directly connect them with different popular music styles. Heitmeyer and Olk have pointed out that there is a danger in uncritically using Beck's "risk" concept where there is a tension between the individual's identity and fixed group behavior: "Whether individuals perceive themselves as exchangeable or unique depend on whether they view themselves as being personally responsible for leading their own lives... However, the attempt to present oneself directly and intentionally as unique... is regularly at risk, particularly in the fulfillment of a 'standard existence' or a 'standard identity' (e.g. skinhead, rocker, etc.) (Heitmeyer and Olk 1995, 24).

[55] The introduction to the English edition (Beck 1992) is, by the way, written by Scott, Lash, and Brian Wynne. Cf. also note 1 in Beck's own foreword: "The concept of reflexive modernzaton has

Lash (1999) has developed Beck's ideas in an interesting way, and at the same time introduced a variant of the metanarrative—the last of its kind that we will explore. Lash returns also again and again to Simmel's sociological view, that he places somewhere in the middle between the first and simple modernity and—here the word appears again—the *reflexive* modernity.[56] Within the first modernity Kant's thoughts of the pure judgment still prevail, the individual that is a consequence of the universal and the logical categories. Within the second, reflexive, modernity—Kant spoke not only of the prescribed judgment but also about the reflexive judgment—it is true that even though we can identify a rule, the individual is not ruled by the collective, something that is especially apropos for the judgment of art:

> We judge art not through logic but analogically, through analogy. We judge art not only through cognition but through the much more particular structure of feeling… The reflexive turn in both sociology and cultural theory takes its point of departure effectively from this sort of reflexive judgment (Lash 1999, 3).

These two modernist forms are found, writes Lash, side by side. Under the first one we are weighted by regulations and organizations of different kinds: parties, unions, the welfare state, etc., while through the other, reflexive, we live in uncertainty. We never really come to grips with the object. We are forced within the other modernity therefore into a continuous reflexivity. Within the first modernity the oppositions often sat between subject and object, but within the other, between necessity and freedom.

Perhaps we should not follow the whole journey that Lash takes in order to clarify the second modernity. But what he looks for is its "groundless ground" (cf. Willis et al 1990) in order to understand how this second modernity is threatened by the global information society. The subject has, under the first modernity, a capacity for reflexivity, but this ability is hollowed out more and more today because:

---

recently been broadly discussed and further developed by Anthony Giddens (1990; 1991) and by Scott Lash (1992)" (Beck 1992).

[56]Simmel's position is developed by Lash in his discussion of the concept of allegory. Lash suggests that Nietzsche, Simmel, Benjamin, Adorno, and others all write essays, a style that seems scientific, but isn't. The essay, according to Lash, "emerges in an aesthetic mode: serious, and at the same time superficial, light, ornamental." Concerning Simmel's impressionistic sociology, he adds: "Simmel as allegorist is no different… here we have through Simmel spoken of allegory in terms of sociality, of sociation, of modes of social life which go on outside of the normality of the institutions" (Lash 1999, 133). Cf. also "Thus Simmel… foregrounds the aesthetic. But instead of a focus on a lasting inner subjectivity, this Simmel is at home in the *fugitif*, the *contingent*, the *transitoire* of Baudelaire" (Lash 1999, 124). Note, by the way, that there are clear points of contact between Liedman's idea of historical work (Liedman 1997) and his concept of hard and soft revelations, and Lash's sociological division in to two modernities (Lash 1999). A source of inspiration for both was the work earlier cited of Tourraine.

a) there appears to be a loosening between people and machines, that suggests that in the global information culture "the hierarchy of subjectivity and the object, of subjectivity and technology, is disrupted", and that we will get "things that think" (Lash 1999, 342);

b) a similar process for symbols and objects becomes clear: between earlier symbols, art and speech, constituted a horizon against which objects appeared, Lash suggests that the objects in the information age "tend to take on capacities previously associated with subjects: they take on powers of judgment, of measuring, translating, and interpretation" (Lash 1999, 342). Now the material objects are *both* symbolic—take, for example, an interactive film/text book/game, etc.—*and* actively consciously created, that is to say, "a fusion... of subjects and objects, objects and symbols" (Lash 1999, 343); and

c) network societies break all boundaries between people and non-people, between countries, between the cultural and the material, between those that have access to information and those who are left outside: "The global information age is not a narrative but an *object* culture" (Lash 1999, 345).

But there is hope, writes Lash, in summary: when we follow the virtual and real objects, we weave them into allegories at the same time as we also weave objects together into a web:

> Webs reaching back into long ago and far away. Webs that, at work and play, may link us to other similar subjectivities...Webs that may help to constitute communities of subjects and technologies. Webs that may once again open up the possibility for the retrieval of ontology. That may once again open up the possibility of redemption (Lash 1999, 346).

Lash's analysis is thought-provoking also because it assumes that younger generations already occupy the information world that he speaks of. Actions and interactions are handled in a changed way that affects everyone's experience of reality. And, as always, new ways of use affect culture's and music's function and meaning.

Our assignment becomes to connect Lash's metaphor of webs to the other threads of the argument that *we* followed, partly the liberally-colored ones that we found in Willis and other rock and youth researchers, partly the less decisively-colored one from the previous section, and try to weave together an understanding of how the aesthetic project has changed during the last decades of the twentieth century. We will carry this out from within the current society of experience.

The Thoroughly Aesthetified Society

When Hobsbawm wants to comment on what happens within a whole cultural area in the middle of the nineteenth century, he writes that what was new was that technology "drenched everyday life as well as in public with art. Never had it been harder to avoid aesthetic experience" (Hobsbawm 1994, 520). He adds: "The 'work of art' was lost in the flows of words, of sounds, of images, in the universal environment of what would once have been called art." Hobsbawm asks, however, whether art was no longer art—and answers, that for many this was still the case. In any case, most people still made distinctions between what they thought was good and bad.

We have earlier established that from a philosophical point of view, it is been difficult so far to find criteria for what is art and non-art. We have also seen that since the nineteenth century both the young and the "lower" classes were brought up to understand art and culture in the way the educated *bourgeoisie* understood them. This was true, not least, for the type of music that was asserted to be "higher." It has also been discussed how, among other factors, mass media has contributed to the increase in the number of choices of music, and that this choice has been dominated by entertainment and popular music. Music can be found today in every milieu and in every nook and cranny. While a hundred years ago it was very unusual for the majority of people in Europe to hear popular music played by an orchestra, today it is just as common for people to hear music via loudspeakers. That which a very few could once count on in a month, now happens to everyone almost every day.

During the inter-war period there were few people who did not know the year's biggest *schlager* (popular songs), those that were played in the radio, those that were highlighted in talking pictures, the melodies that one could hear at the cafés and restaurants and that so many hummed during the day and sang at parties. As we have found, many social changes contributed to the situation that popular music after World War II, to a great degree aimed at the younger generations, quickly spread over the West. At the same time, the new European art music's structure continued to change in a pace and extent that led to the majority of the musically-interested public to realize that more and more they rarely "understood" or liked the music.

For the purposes of their survey at the end of the 1920s, the Swedish Broadcasting Service divided music into 12 categories. When the sociologist Göran Nylöf made his important sociological studies 40 years later, he used 11 categories (Nylöf 1967). Another 40 years later, all of this music was still available, either in recorded or live form, but at the same time there has come an almost unimaginable amount of new music, not least within the above-named expanded category of contemporary popular music. It is not difficult to find a dozen subcategories of popular music alone in a large record shop.

The question of what this has meant for this aesthetic project that we have followed over such a long time period cannot be held back. If we earlier studied the relationship between *psychogenesis* and *sociogenesis* within courtly life, now we will discusses what this relation can mean for people's aesthetic experience during the latest decades of the second millennium.

From æI to æ?

During the turbulent twentieth century we have found, with æI as a sounding board, that æII and æIII have played their part in specific musical situations, but we have also developed æIV as an even broader and more common addition. The last-named factor developed as a result of the studies by popular music researchers highlighting the difference in rock/pop's meaning in its daily and "grounded" use. We passed by the thoughts that also reminded us that the aesthetic is a common human need. Willis's "grounded" aesthetic was seen to have its counterpart in æV^n. Simmel saw an aesthetic dimension in all social interactions.

As we soon shall see, there are two directions inherent in an extension of this Simmelian thesis. Either we see all of the everyday as aesthetified, or we see it as de-aesthetified because contemporary symbols have been completely emptied of meaning. A question that hangs in the air is, of course: "What do we listen to then?"

In the previous section we met sociological analyses of how postwar societies have contributed new ways of contemplating their environment. We have called attention to researchers like Habermas and Luhmann, who have proposed hypotheses about how society as an entity or as a system changes and we have met Beck and Ziehe who put their finger on how a society of open possibilities affects people. The sociologist Gerhard Schulze (1992) has, among others, used their theories as well as his own empirical material collected at the end of the 1980s, to build a synthesizing social model that has a high level of explanatory value.

Schulze shows how a high *bourgeois* mode of using culture or *Hochkulturschema* had its counterpoint in a *Trivialschema* already in the nineteenth century. Within the first mode we find art music and within the second we find salon music.[57] If this seems familiar and we can see that æII is mainly synonymous with the high culture mode and æIII has a certain relevance for the

---

[57] *Hochkulturschema*, writes Schulze, is marked by reserved bodily reactions, still observation, concentrated listening, the emphasis on education, and general knowledge, perfection, etc, while the trivial scheme is marked by a greater physical enjoyment, by comfort and friendliness, by being in a group, by singing along in gatherings, by living with song and music, etc (see further in 1992, 142-153).

trivial mode, then Schulze's third mode the *Spannungsschema* of excitement, adds something new. It adds what Schulze argues is a prerequisite for our new society, the *Erlebnisgesellschaft* or society of experience.

Society of Experience

As Beck points out, Schulze shows that during the 1960s a sweeping change in the western society can be observed, that is to say a transformation into the society of experience.[58] Schulze maintains that the choice of goods brought with it the development where goods no longer were seen as a means to an end, but as the end *itself*. Four-wheel drive vehicles that are only used in city traffic is one such example: the cars are seen to have attributes which became the main point, while functionality and necessary aspects become the accessories (Beck 1992, 13). We can illustrate this with the development of music systems with 150 watt power developed for home use in apartments. These changes are seen as a pseudo-aesthetification. Life has become more and more an experiential project. Our search for happiness stands in opposition to the earlier *bourgeois* view of the worthiness of delayed gratification in all of its forms.

Schulze underlines that today—in an overflow of impressions and products—it becomes more important to ask yourself: what do I want with this object? What is it that *I* want to experience (Schulze 1993, 33). It is said to be especially relevant that in this situation the individual to a greater extent than earlier must turn inward for the experiences. One puts the self—reflexively—in the center, which is why "outwardly-oriented" experiences are reduced in meaning. From the latter perspective a car, for example, is seen as a means of conveyance with which one moves from point A to point B. An "inwardly-oriented" experience, however, would mean that one wanted to experience something *thanks to* the journey. The dedicated music listening in cars can partly be understood as an "inwardly-oriented" behavior, which is strengthened by the fact that people often are very selective when it comes to what music they use when driving.[59]

Schulze further points out that experience's external side and people's inner experience of the same are not of the same kind"

---

[58] Schulze's analysis is very thorough and rich in different theories and sociological writings of different formations of taste and behavioral groups. Not least, a large body of empirical material is reviewed that relates to the connection between, on one hand, age and education, and on the other hand, behavior and preferences.

[59] For discussions of the use of music in the car from a musicological and psychological perspective see Casagrande and Risser 1992, and Öblad 2000, as well as for a general ethnological perspective on the car and its use, Andreasson 2000.

To be inwardly oriented ... has nothing to do with being introverted. Instead, it means here that a person begins processes that can be developed within the person..."inwardly oriented" is the same as experientially oriented. The project of finding beauty in life is the project of experiencing something (Schulze 1993, 38).

We have talked earlier about the concentrated listening to instrumental music (æII) as being thought of as work. What is new here is that enjoyment has now turned into work ["Das Vergnügen ist eine Arbeit geworden"] (Schulze 1993, 38).

Everyone's search for *beauty*, that is to say, in Schulze's meaning of positive inner experiences, leads to the search for experiential rationality. But one does not get a direct impression of something external, for example music, without *processing* the impression into an experience.[60] That which is experience will be understood as a *process* between an object-subject. There is, for example, a huge difference, according to Schulze, between wandering past painting after painting in an art museum and not experiencing anything in particular from the external world, and being in a situation where one is deprived of outer stimulation but still experiencing much in one's internal life. It is easy to discover an analogous point if we compare listening to, for example, industrially produced backgrounds music with concentrated listening in a concert situation.[61] The idea of the former is that it will be heard without being listened to, or better yet, that it is *noticed without being heard*.

If there was once a limited choice, people had to act externally according to the existing situation. Today it is different: *the subject characterizes the situation instead of the reverse*. Everyone would rather seek the environment that they like best (Schulze 1992, 298). In tempo with the increase in free time and choices, life becomes the development of the everyday into an aesthetic project. That life has changed into an experiential market has contributed to the fact that we live in a time of everyday aesthetics. The process of modernization has turned inward.

It is this social view where the third mode, the *Spannungschema*, enters in. Schulze suggests that the *Spannungschema*'s "semantic symbols" are "Rock music, Popular music, Blues and other music styles, film, discotheque, Comics

---

[60] Cf. the formulation "That the thought that there could be original experiences, that in themselves could be beautiful and interesting, is a popular philosophical mistake" ["Das es Ursprungserlebnisse geben könne, die an sich schön, intressant seien, ist eine populäre philosophische Irrtum"] (Schulze 1993, 53).

[61] Dissanayake finds that we do not identify what aesthetic effects Muzak (background music) creates because we do not listen consciously to the music. She also says that visitors to discos "who are overpoweringly aware of hearing sounds... cannot be said to be responding aesthetically to the pulses and insistent chords that bombard their bodies and provoke uninhibited, almost reflexive, physical action (Dissanayake 1992, 29)." According to my view, this is certainly doubtful; in any case æI is experienced, and, perhaps even æIV and eV^n as well.

and similar things." One "entertainment characteristic" he names is "action" and an important delimiting characteristic is "anti-conventional" as well as the dominating lifestyle characteristic "narcissism" (Schulze 1993, 746; cf. Schulze 1993, 153ff). The *Spannungschema* is a complementary voice in a new melodious sound: the society of experience. In this new symphony, other ways of acting and thinking can be heard from a "self-realizing perspective."

We recognize again in this description the form of aesthetic experience, æIV, that we found in Meltzer's and Willis's works, among other places. While æIV is already found in the introduction of the *Spannungschema*, it seems reasonable to see that the indeterminable and almost all-encompassing variant æV^n comes in during a later phase within this current scheme.

The traditional tension between "high culture" and "trivial culture" is, according to Schulze, already reduced during the later half of the nineteenth century (cf. middle music). At the same time, there was a tension between the cultural outer poles, which led to attempts by composers within the art music field to try continuously to differentiate themselves from other music. Within this process, as has been earlier stated, movements like *avant garde* and modernism arise.

It was later during this period that the third behavioral mode developed as an alternative, which *did not* mean that the other two disappeared. Schulze's point is in fact that these three modes exist simultaneously, and that all modes affect all generations. This contributes to the development of a leveling-out of the generations. The behavior of older people becomes younger, the younger people's behavior becomes older. Schulze and Beck both suggest that it is time to abandon the idea of a separate adult world.[62]

A consequence of peoples' reflexive and inwardly oriented way of relating to and understanding their lives is, however, that behavior simultaneously creates an *insecurity* (cf. Beck above and "risk") about what is actually achieved. This is true both for the "experience" industry that produces, and for the individual consumer that faces the difficulties of translating the impressions that the object— music, in this case—asserts on a thoroughly worked-out, realized and wished-for inner experience. It becomes problematic to separate music's use-value from its new, added experiential value. But, Schulze reasons, because experiential value is understood as definitive—and access to music experiences is thought to be inexhaustible—this leads to a reduction of pleasure over music's use-value. Under these living circumstances the beautiful experiences, the ones that we seek, are in danger of evaporating:

---

[62] As Schulze (1993, 369) writes, that with the abandonment of the goal of adulthood, adolescence also loses its sociological profile. Ziehe (1991, 142f) discusses in detail what the blurring of the categories of adult and youth means.

The more the quality of things is raised and the easier it is for someone to have access to them, the paler their use value becomes. The capacity for joy over the use value should involve a protection against disappointment. If one acts in an outwardly-oriented way, then it has not so much to do with happiness, although one senses it when something has fulfilled its purpose. In an inward orientation, the beautiful experience becomes the main point, usability is a sideline, that does not leave much room left over for the beautiful life. Thus a disappointment arises. The question becomes, therefore, at what minimum level can one hold the risk of disappointment, by applying an experientially rational mode of conduct (Schulze 1993, 64).[63]

Through the prioritizing of a society of experience in sense-oriented decisions, the aestheticization of everyday life is increased at the same time as the personal taste for increased legitimacy. Conversely, traditional aesthetic conventions have an increasingly reduced impact (Schulze 1993, 95). The *Hochkulturrschema* loses in meaning. There are groups within society whose behavior and preferences within the art field are not possible to understand with analyses that depart from an industrial class-based society. Today's society is multi-dimensional and makes possible that music is used in many different ways. If we interpret this analysis in the light of our aesthetic project, we can rediscover æIV, the broad, everyday form that we found in Meltzer's and Willis's works, but also æVn. We are reminded of processes that we earlier encountered from a postmodern perspective: that peoples' preferences when it comes to music have become increasingly varied from a sociological point of view, that to a much greater extent than earlier, independent of education, age, sex, and ethnicity, people can have both similar and different tastes.

What Schulze, in summary, finds troublesome is that additional attributes of different kinds obscure the view—in our case strongly reduces the possibilities of concentrating on the music—of deep structures in the content. The depth of meaning that he suggests can be experienced among the earlier rock and pop generation, had as its foundation not only a search for experience, *but also rested on a completely different philosophy of life.* The rebellious Rolling Stones have become what they were not—an article of entertainment.[64] The general social development

---

[63]"Je mehr sich die Qualität der Dinge gesteigert und je leichter man darüber verfügen kann, desto blasser erscheint ihr Gebrauchswert. Die Fähigkeit, sich über Gebrauchswert zu freuen, wäre eine sicherer Schutz vor Entäuschung. Handelt man ausserorientirert, kommt es auf Freude nicht an, gleichwohl verspürt man sie, wenn etwas einen Zweck erfüllt. Beim innenorientirerten Handeln wird das schöne Erlebnis zur Hauptsache, Brauchbarkeit zum Nebenaspekt, der für das Projekt des schönen Lebens wenig hergibt. Dadurch entsteht Enttäuschbarkeit. Die Frage ist nun, wie niedrig man das Entäuschungsrisiko durch erlebnisrationales Handeln halten kann."

[64]This does not mean, however, that many of the younger generation do not have a great interest in what views and attitudes are held by artists and musicians. It *is* for many an important reason to listen at all to an artist's or group's music. What Schulze sees is that the life philosophy and ideological interest generally is less among today's youth than it was for those who were young in

is an important reason why "Woodstock is over" (Schulze 1993, 547). Also within the act of experience itself one can sense a need to hear the next hit, and so forth. Perhaps like Schulze we can therefore consider the music industry's ideal consumer as a broadband channel to which they have free access.[65]

It can appear as if Schulze, in his analysis of the state of things, cannot resist holding at bay the feeling that it "was better before" and therefore, over-interpret the superficiality or the Sisyphusian quest for new experiences as something that the younger generation has especially become attached to. On the other hand, he also points out time and again that all in all there is a very broad spectrum of behaviors and preferences. The aesthetic realm should, therefore, have changed in a similar way. The aesthetic concept of æV^n, though, of course, difficult to delimit, can, as suggested, be placed within the eternal hunt after yet another experience as Schulze has pointed out.

If we extend this change to the limits of the imagination, we thus confront two completely different possibilities: "everything" is aesthetified, or the opposite is the case, everything is empty of aesthetic content.

One—or the Other

The concept "aesthetic/s," in DeNora's important work is used both singularly and in a number of word constellations, in total more than one hundred times in the book's 170 pages.[66] On a considerable number of pages the word appears in four to five different combinations, which taken together makes it possible to experience the book as thoroughly aestheticized without the reader being able to find a unifying definition. But it is completely clear that in music—which DeNora describes as an agent and a daily partner—as a personality-forming offering and a support, there is included an aesthetic part that in itself is both a means and an end. We often come upon formulations like:

> Aesthetic materials may provide paradigms and patterns for the construction of non-aesthetic matters... sociologists have been reluctant to consider aesthetic dimensions of social organization and that aesthetic materials can be understood to afford modes of action, feeling and embodiment....Focus is on materially and aesthetically configured spaces... Music provides a resource for establishing the prospective parameters of agency's aesthetic dimension (DeNora 2000, 109).

---

the 60s—an idea that naturally is problematic and leads me to believe that Schulze was probably born in the 1940s.

[65]Schulze writes in summary that enjoyment dominates today while the former high culture is almost gone. Waves of experiential opportunities flood the society. This means that the as you consume one thing, the next is already on the brink of presenting itself (Schulze 1993, 548).

[66]For example in compilations with "material." "technology," "realm," "forms," "reflexivity," "agents," "violence," "unconscious," "reflexive action," "charter of music," and so forth.

> To be an agent, in the fullest sense, is thus to be imbued—albeit fleetingly—with forms of *aesthesia*. Feeling and sensitivity—the aesthetic dimension of social being—are action's animators... To be aestheticized is to be capacitated, to be able to perceive or to use one's senses... It is this sense, then, that aesthetic materials such as music afford perception, action, feeling, corporeality (DeNora 2000, 153).

In summary, her use of aesthetic lies near the everyday way of viewing that is represented by examples like those given by Simmel and Willis, but does not exclude earlier forms either. Her use of language ensures that the concept is hardly possible to define unambiguously, but can as a chameleon develop appearances from æI, to æII, æIII, æIV and also to æV^n. For DeNora, the concept of aesthetics seems to stand for a grounded *everyday, tangible, engagement and personally positive experience*.

But the æV^n variant prepares us for further problems. If we see it as an individually variable concept in the society of experience—and related to the *Spannungsschema*, it is thus problematical to put a finger on the concept (cf. Schulze 1992, 39f). Perhaps we shall, with Schulze and Beck, see æV^n as a "risky concept," which is to say, as an experience that from a person's point of departure, can easily become a disappointment, leading the subject to seek a renewed positive experience. It implies that something is taking place on *the surface* rather than in *the depths*.

As a polar opposite to DeNora and the above-mentioned writers, we will also listen to the sociologist Jean Baudrillard who earlier occupied a completely different position. Baudrillard found that during the 1960s the character of all types of consumption began to be similar to the conditions within fashion: consumers of music, gardening, cars, and so forth were characterized by a cyclical thinking. New styles succeeded one another: "Culture is no longer made to last.... What affects the meaning of the work is the fact that *all significations have become cyclical*" (Baudrillard 1998, 102). A new product simulated an earlier one. People became accustomed to a consumption, that, according to Baudrillard, was a *structure* and where the object only functioned as a simulation, like artificial imitations of one another. People no longer saw the object as a symbol, but rather as a simple sign, and when the sign only was related to another sign, they lost all content through this process. If Benjamin and the circle around him in the 1930s were worried about the loss of aura around the art work in a time when it become possible to mass produce music and pictures, Baudrillard considered that people in the West did not understand that they had landed in an empty communications world where they (we!) probably were blinded by simulacra but nothing more:

> So art is dead, since not only is its critical transcendence dead, but reality itself, entirely impregnated by an aesthetic, which is inseparable from its own structure, has been confused with its own image. It no longer even has the time to take

on the effect of reality.... The cool universe of digitality absorbs the universe of metaphor and metonymy. The simulation principle dominates the reality principle as well as the pleasure principle (Baudrillard 1993, 75).[67]

For Baudrillard there is, therefore, only a surface to analyze, and no substance behind it. Because generally throughout history music has been the art form whose content has been most strongly doubted by philosophers, we could perhaps expect that he exemplified his thesis with musical simulacra. I have not really found any useful examples, but I have, in the following citation about art/painting simply exchanged words such as "painting," "visually," etc., to their parallel words within the music field in order to show how he draws out the consequences of his theses to the outmost limit:

> It is very difficult to speak of [*music*] today because it is difficult to [*hear*] it. Because generally it no longer wants exactly to be [*listened to*], but to be absorbed [*audibly*] without leaving any traces. In some way modern [*composition*] could be characterized as simplified aesthetic forms of the impossible exchange. So that the best discourse about [*music*] would be a discourse where there is nothing to say, which would be the equivalent of a [*composition*] where there is nothing to [*hear*]. The equivalent of an object, the object of art, that isn't an object any more (Baudrillard 1997, 9).

It is perhaps best to leave Baudrillard's theses hanging free in the air. If they are confronted with the empirical German sociology and the ideas extracted from it, his analysis could easily land in an intellectual vacuum. While the younger generation must hear yet one more song in their inner quest for experience which "actually" does not contain anything more than an empty surface of signs, what can the best-intentioned analysis of music's future say?[68] If this were a correct analysis, I cannot see anything other than that the aesthetic experience is also empty, which is why the concept of æ0 would be appropriate.

---

[67] As a citation from the middle of the 1970s it is in part an apt analysis of the future of the illusionary reality that our computer power can now simulate. With very few exceptions, Baudrillard does not, as far as I have found, discuss music culture's development, but rather art, photography and film. Nonetheless it is possible to see changes in music in a similar way. There is, of course a general difficulty in taking his theses seriously, as he often draws out their consequences to the extreme. When he, for example, discusses the contemporary technique's virtual possibilities he also comes upon the development of music technology and writes: "High Fidelity. Disappearance of the music by excess of fidelity, by the promiscuity of the music and its absolute technical model" (Baudrillard 1997, 25). I have translated that for myself to mean that today's sound technology has reached a level, where the music itself disappears and what is left is something else. Can this be what he is implying? The sentence that follows after the above citation seems to suggest that it is: "Holographic music, holophonic, stereophonic, as if it had swallowed its own genetic code before expelling it as an artificial synthesis — clinical music, sterile, purged of all noise" (Baudrillard 1997, 25).

[68] The sociologist Georg Ritzer writes, however, in his introduction to a translation of Baudrillard 1998, that several of Baudrillard's earlier theses have been fulfilled.

Baudrillard's theories are easily harmed by their own premise: they are also simulacra and relate, in my own opinion, little to the everyday reality of "normal" people. He simplifies an incredibly complex interplay and believes that he can see, like a prophet, society's hidden changes. And he does this in order to build his theoretical model. As I have repeated several times, there is often a bothersome empty space between the theoretical constructions that theoretical armchair researchers come up with, and the empirical reality upon which they build their constructions, that is to say, *on which they do not build their constructions*.[69] Researchers from both sides, the philosopher / cultural theoreticians and the ethnologist / sociologists, clearly have nourished a suspicion of one another, and have not made the situation better.

But, in the spirit of optimism, let us listen to yet another German philosopher, Wolfgang Welsch, and conclude this discussion of the aesthetification of society. Here, hopefully, we can find an "aesthetic" escape route.

Both—And

The title of Welsch's book is *Undoing Aesthetics*.[70] Welsch wants to tie together the different aesthetic knots he has found. We live in a time, he says, that is characterized by an aesthetic boom. But he makes a distinction between two forms of aesthetification: one shallow, and one deep. The shallow, surface form can be simply characterized as everything that is produced to be consumed and has a surface that diverts attention away from its content. To use a new Swedish word, everything *stylas* (everything is styled).

One could perhaps say that the packaging is the message. If we follow, as an example, the history of gramophone records, it is difficult to deny that the changes that have occurred during the twentieth century do suggest that surface aesthetics have expanded. 78 records were sold in hard mono-colored paper envelopes. What was on the record could be read from the round label, about seven cm in diameter. The record itself was, as a rule, completely black. The interest was focused on the content, the music. From the 1940s, however, exclusive records were produced whose labels had colorful pictures such as a beautiful woman dancing the carioca. But it was not until the 1950s that the record jacket—for EP and LP records—began to have a life of its own. Precisely as had always been the case earlier with illustrations designed to awake the consumer's interest, on

---

[69] The concept of "armchair researchers" comes from the English "armchair anthropologists," who, since the beginning of the twentieth century has been a description for the social anthropologists that mainly studied non-European cultures by sitting in their offices in Berlin, London, or Paris.

[70] Late in the process of writing the Swedish version of this book, I found that Welsch 1997 was very influential for Lars-Olof Åhlberg (2000) and Simo Säätelä (2000). These authors took Welsch's German work as a point of departure and give a thorough introduction to it.

printed sheet music and especially *schlager* tunes, now without a doubt many records were sold primarily on the strength of their jackets and not the music itself (I have chosen to ignore in this discussion music that might already be known by the buyer).[71] It has also become the rule—especially for records with jazz and art music—that the back side of the LP has an informative text about the artists and the tunes for jazz, or the composers, music and conductor (or the musicians themselves in smaller ensembles) for art music. These commentaries were similar to texts that concert listeners were already acquainted with at concerts.

This situation changed in part when the CD format was introduced. The attraction of the cover art was reduced because of the smaller format.[72] Other forms of external packaging during the twentieth century have increased in importance. The way artists look and dress has been an increasingly important factor since World War II with the introduction of an artist. How one plays and sings, presents oneself, and with what theatrical props, scenery and realization has been given increasing attention. In addition, it became increasingly important by the 80s to create a video made especially for a new song; the video in part came to function as an external packaging for the music, and became part of the experience of the music.[73]

Welsch suggests that what is the outer and the inner in a product, albeit in a less radical sense than Baudrillard, changes places in a world where economic motives dominate. Software and hardware changes places:

> In surface aestheticization the most superficial aesthetic value dominates: pleasure, amusement, enjoyment without consequence... Experience and entertainment have become guidelines for culture in recent years... The bond with aesthetics renders even the unsaleable saleable... The aesthetic aura is then the consumer's primary acquisition, with the article merely incidental (Baudrillard 1997, 3).

Similar ideas can also be found in the work of the Swedish cultural sociologist Sven Nilsson (1999). When he discusses the changes that have occurred within popular culture during the last decades, he presents the American literary scholar John

---

[71] Exhibitions at museums with reproductions from record albums have been a standing feature since the 1980s. For a discussion of the pictures on record jackets' supportive and marketing function for art music see Cook 1998.

[72] In recent years some music groups have, however, reduced the amount of information in the record's (CD's) booklet. Instead of publishing the songs text there are artistic illustrations and photos on several folded pages, giving the listener a corresponding visual experience. Cf., for example, Radiohead's double CD, "Kid A" and "Amnesiac" (EMI).

[73] Already in the era of silent films, well-known artists introduced their *schlager* tunes in short films where artists—silently—sung their melodies. On the screen the pictures were intermittently interleaved with parts of the song texts. The idea was that the silent film pianists or the orchestra more or less simultaneously would play the melody. With the advent of talking pictures artists could be both seen and heard to sing their own songs—whether they were relevant to the content of the film or not.

Fiske's well-known thesis that control over the meaning of a text is increasingly transferred to the readers and those who listen. As Willis, among others, has earlier pointed out, it is said that an aesthetification occurs within more and more areas. The aesthetic attitude that is linked to computer games is now also connected to music. And, as Nilsson argues, if ethnologists now see an aesthetic expression as other statements are normal cultural manifestations, one can also argue that "increasing numbers of cultural manifestations have become artistic and aesthetic expressions. Design has developed a greater importance in the forming of products and services and as a guiding principle in organizations (management by design)" (Nilsson 1999, 30).

Progressions like these are, at this point, well-known to us. We have since the beginning of time seen that sounding music has enriched people's lives. Music functioned later as a representative sound experience for nobility and for the church and was an important tool of religions, political movements and folk movements. Today music is also a sounding addition that contributes to an increasingly extensive *surface aesthetification*, but according to Welsch, also to a *deep aesthetification*. In his hypothesis Welsch departs from the idea that a beautification of everything has occurred and is occurring, which means that the aesthetic addition has become the main point. Today it is possible, through computer technology, to find, test and try out products (including art and music) in a *production* milieu. The negative sense of "simulation" that Baudrillard represents, is turned by Welsch into its opposite:

> Simulation - an aesthetic process… has no longer an imitational, but rather a productive, function. So, here too aesthetic shifts to the fore… Aesthetic processes don't only shroud already completed, given substances, but also the core. Aesthetics thus no longer belongs to the superstructure, but to the base. The material aestheticization… entails an immaterial aestheticization at the same time (Welsch 1997, 5).

It is not difficult to see (hear) a similarity with the computer milieu (hardware) and the software-controlled processes within which art music and popular music are often created. Music as a sounding material offers less resistance than before. Increasing numbers can be counted as composers thanks to these possibilities.[74] Corresponding processes (people-hardware-software) have, however, not occurred for those who write texts to music.

If we follow Welsch's ideas, we see that the forms of immaterial aestheticization that occur through computer work in daily and business life

---

[74] Note that the interactive music possibilities that exist thanks to the CD-ROM have recently been introduced. Paul Théberge writes: "Recent music releases on CD-ROM and CD-I… by artists such as David Bowie, Peter Gabriel and Todd Rundgren, offer consumer an expanded set of options for not only assessing certain types of material (text, sound or image) but, in some instances, for shaping and rearranging that material as well" (Théberge 1997, 253).

mean that a deep aesthetic process has found its way into our consciousness. This also occurs on the individual level, and it is therefore not a surprise that Welsch poses the rhetorical question about whether the "stylizing" of people and all the forms of life means that we are becoming *homo aestheticus*. The answer to this rhetorical question is, as we remember, a point of departure for the present work (cf. Dissanayake).

In a time when earlier etiquette and moral norms are watered down, Welsch sees, therefore, that the integration between people becomes increasingly aesthetically characterized. But he also views this process critically. He observes and writes:

> Where everything becomes beautiful, nothing is beautiful any more... aestheticization breaks into anaestheticization (Welsch 1997, 25; cf. above p. 215).[75]

If we now join Welsch's warning with Lash's view of what threatens the reflexive society, we remember the latter's misgivings about "things that think" and what the fusion between subject and object within network societies means. But Lash's and Welsch's message is still basically positive.[76] For, as Welsch formulates it: the sense of sight has dominated entirely too long, and not with completely successful results. It is, therefore, necessary that our present culture shall be a listening, an auditive one:

> Not only for reasons of equal treatment must hearing be emancipated following more than two thousand years of vision's dominance. Moreover, the person who hears is also the better person—one that is able to enter into something different and to respect instead of merely dominating it. A continued existence of the human species and the planet earth is to be hoped for only if our culture in future takes hearing as its basic model (Welsch 1997, 150).

It would be difficult to find a better wish to introduce our concluding section.

---

[75]Cf. Säätelä who, in his exposition on Welsch writes that surface aestheticization "is the same as the kitsch-ification of the world" and that "the package becomes more important than the product" (Säätelä 2000, 83), thoughts like those we have already seen in Schulze.
[76]Cf. Lash's work where he suggests a division into a) cognitive, b) aesthetic and c) hermeneutical reflection. Within the reflexive society the "reflexive aesthetic" becomes wide spread. The form of reflection that he means is not of the rational type as Habermas, Beck, and others, advocate. While the aesthetic reflexion is mimetic, a direct and, to a small extent, mediated form, the cognitive reflexion is critical (Lash 1994, 135-45). He criticizes also Habermas's focus on the cognitive/rational when Habermas discusses how contemporary people, through an expanded rational discussion shall escape from being trapped in a stifling, system-oriented world: "Of the theories of reflexive modernity Habermas'... is primarily a *critical* theory, in that transcendental, intersubjective and discursive truths of communicative rationality are explicitly aimed at a critique of the system in order to win space for the life-world" (Lash 1994, 140). Cf. also Fornäs 1995, 199f.

> *Musicology, like music, possesses persuasive powers; and these performative strategies need to be analysed to see how a particular approach pushes towards certain conclusions. That is a way of saying that musicology should be theoretically informed, that it cannot stand aside from its own strategies.*
>
> Alastair Williams

CONCLUSION

Tying up loose ends

Although it is not difficult to find the word aesthetics (aesthetic, aesthetification, esthete, and other compounds) in current academic discourse, we know by now that it can often be problematic to describe what is contained within this multifaceted concept. As Welsch formulates it, "the aesthetic's semantic ambiguity" is as old as the word itself. It is a word that we have seen occurs today within almost every area of musicology, not only in studies of art-music, pop and rock, but also in writings about West African traditional music or Swedish traditional dance music. In Nketia's book on West African music we find under the heading "Aesthetic values" that he uses the word to refer to the norms and rules that are followed within traditional West African music (Nketia 1974, 240). In Lundberg we find that for the older Swedish generation that cares about old dance music, there is an "aesthetically clearly marked border" excluding music with pounding beats, and that older peoples' "aesthetic preferences" are different from "the following generations" (Lundberg et al 2000, 420).

Paradoxically enough, the word appears in current written discourse both often and seldom, but as a rule readers are generally left to their own interpretations. The word is, as before, an unusual guest in people's everyday conversations.[1]

---

[1] To give two further examples from the word database at Göteborg Unviersity the Swedish word *estet* (aesthetic) appeared in the three major Swedish daily newspapers 226 times in 1998, only 13 times in relation to music (the database contains nine million words). We find here examples of use that suggest that a modern aesthetic thought process existed in the Middle Ages: "Here for the first time in the West, many composers took the first step from liturgically functional music to aesthetically independent music by decorating the monodic Gregorian choral with one or more voices" (cf. the earlier discussion on p. 16). In another example we meet an idea that takes us back to our discussion about "absolute music" and "autonomy": "And if Osterling and Bartok before the intermission represented music in absolute aesthetic form, then George Crumb contributed

The extent of the semantic field within which the concept has been active in the thousands of years through which we have passed is very large. Well into our own time we have seen that the use of music and song has probably never been so varied as it is today, which indirectly points to the expansion of the aesthetic field and its extent. To give three examples:

1. A young Sami reindeer herder in Lapland, while at top speed on a snow scooter with a loud motor can follow his reindeer herd in the otherwise quiet mountains and listen to Sami Techno music on an MP3 player, or for that matter, Beethoven's ninth symphony (Karajan's interpretation?). Like everyone that uses mobile stereos with earphones, he finds himself in his own individual soundtrack. It is a completely private experience where the impression from the outside environment becomes a part of the experience of the music—and/or the opposite, that the inner experience of the music is a part of the experience of the environment.

2. In Göteborg a newly retired Swedish person can dance to old-fashioned dance music in the morning and sit and listen in a concentrated way with aesthetic preparedness to Sweden's national symphony perform Shostakovich's Fifth Symphony before the orchestra's tour of Italy with its conductor Neemi Järvi. This public performance and the tour were commented on in a large article in the Swedish national newspaper *Dagens Nyheter* (DN 2/2 2001).

3. In Malmö several Assyrian immigrant women gather in Mrs. Moussa's house as usual on a Thursday afternoon and talk and drink tea. And naturally there is music in the background, music that encapsulates within itself the social activity taking place. Those who are captured by this quiet, discreet music perhaps know that it is a recording of the Stockholm group Qenneshrin.[2] From the upstairs, now and then, sound reaches them from someone—a young student at a local music school?—practicing the violin.

Within the gigantic field of music today there is a muddle of values and opinions about the need for different kinds of music. Song/music is created, packaged, distributed, sold, listened to, played, taught, experienced as background, and so forth, locally and globally in amounts as never before. New computer-based technique and software makes it possible to create new music styles where sound and text elements are combined in new ways. In a technologically unlimited

---

completely other dimensions" (www.gu.se/spraakbanken). As was seen in the Introduction, the word appears in widely differing contexts: pictures of food, movies, wind power generators, art, motorways, politics, literature, and on and on.

[2] See further in Lundberg et al 2000, 124f. Band members in the group "are young, between 20 and 24, and with some exceptions, second generation immigrants" (Lundberg et al 2000, 293). A normal way for Assyrians, like everyone else who has access to the internet, is to download music from home pages (Lundberg et al 2000, 296).

world, almost anything can be de-contextualized, broken up and tried in a new context. It is in this postmodern time that a traditionally *bourgeois* way of viewing culture as a way of holding culture together is questioned. The roles of researchers and writers as preservers of culture have been replaced by those of the interpreter and the critic. Lundberg et al 2000 coins a new Swedish word and calls researchers *vetare*, a word literally meaning "knowers" (derived from the word for science), those who practice culture he calls *görare* or "doers" and those who arrange culture he calls *makare* or "makers." At the end of their broad discussion of music in Sweden, a discussion that describes a great number of music styles (traditional Western art-music and middle music are, however, discussed only minimally), they throw out the idea that composers and musicologists find themselves on the periphery today. The authors also point out the following problem, albeit one that they themselves are not affected by thanks to their own triple competency as knowers/makers/doers:

> At the same time few have more space in public life than the musicians... This development can also be partly explained by the transference from knowers to doers and makers. The substantial increase in the number of doers and makers in the music field has brought about a very large growth in knowledge in areas like music and computers, or how one introduces music to special target groups. Academic knowledge has not expanded to the same extent, however, a fact that has led to an increasing uselessness for most of the participants in the field of music (Lundberg et al 2000, 416).

Their final point can be challenged. Academic knowledge has witnessed a substantial growth also within musicology, witnessed not least by the growth of academic musicological literature in Sweden during the 1990s. It has, however, become all the more difficult in a hardened commercial book and cultural climate to reach those who are, or should be, interested in this knowledge: musicologists in general, musicians, music journalists, music administrators, general music enthusiasts, and so forth. And perhaps many also feel that new scholarly books are constantly being written but do not know how to relate to their contents in a way helpful to them.[3]

   While the thought that there is value in the traditional *bourgeois* musical canon has not yet been abandoned, an obvious crisis of legitimacy will be even more clear when the 40s generation are no longer driving the culture. We have

---

[3] It is likely that this attitude extends to several areas. As if I had ordered it up, while writing this I am reading about a media project at a high school in Göteborg. In this project, high school students were asked to analyze rock texts, write their own poems and rock lyrics as well as *read novels* that concerned their contemporary culture. The latter left the students asking the teachers what value there could possibly be in reading books. An amazed teacher tried to explain the value of benefiting from other people's experiences through the written word and that the students could develop a richer and more nuanced control over their own language. The students were not impressed.

inherited a complex of cultural values and a global smorgasbord of cultural possibilities to surf between. Control and power increasingly come from other agents and through other forms of influence.

The three examples of how music is used given above can be multiplied—using factors like the type of music, music's use, time and place, who is playing and listening (according to gender, age, profession, class, ethnicity, etc.), so one could surely vary these examples to the point where they would fill at least a whole chapter all by themselves. The point is the same: within the large and shifting music culture, different aesthetic concepts live, side by side, sometimes entirely different lives. As we know by now, the concept of aesthetics has been and is still used ahistorically and from a value perspective in a delimiting way. It is not only that it is difficult to get a grip on, but above all that one often thought from a top-down perspective. The objective of this work has been try to turn this perspective around.

If we return to Welsch's analysis, we see that he also tried to create an overview of the field of aesthetics. It contains to a great extent a repletion of the factors that philosophers through the ages have made clear. He first sees the dual nature of the concept, that is "sensation," which is concerned with pleasure and feelings, as well as "perception," that he understands as a more cognitive process (Welsch 1997, 12-17; cf. above p. 37). Today, according to Welsch, it is enough that something affects our senses for it to be called aesthetic. We can add that people in the West can similarly think about and consider attractive material/music as aesthetic. But Welsch also puts emphasis on the other aspects: contemplation, the subjective aspect, the redeeming, the beautiful, the outer, the created and the creative, the educated, the emotional, the sublime, and so forth. With a sideways glance at Wittgenstein he concludes:

> In summary: the different usages of the expression 'aesthetic' are held together by family resemblances. There exist significant differences as well as overlaps and cross-connections between diverse meanings. Hence the polysemy of the expression 'aesthetic' is not, say, objectionable or threatening, but can be well understood; moreover the family resemblances guarantee a—loose—coherence of the expression 'aesthetic' as a whole (Welsch 1997, 17).

As we saw earlier, analytical philosophers often reject this form of definition for art. Family resemblance is, in practice, almost the same as an open definition, by which one cannot differentiate art from non-art. But the quotation above is about aesthetics, not art. If, therefore, we see a process-oriented definition of aesthetics, that is to say, as a function of its social use and placement in a culture, then Welsch's conclusions are appropriate. The five concepts of aesthetic experience that we have discussed in this work can be graphically summarized in the following way:

CONCLUSION

Time

$$æI \Rightarrow$$
$$æII \Rightarrow$$
$$æIII \Rightarrow$$
$$æIV \Rightarrow$$
$$æV^n \Rightarrow$$
$$? \Rightarrow$$

If æI is an eternal human form, then it was not until the Age of Enlightenment that æII appeared, and thereafter the other three forms of experience, æIII, æIV and æV^n followed one another with increasing speed. It is, however, of little value to try to define from a traditional philosophical and ahistorical perspective *what the aesthetic is*, because the contents of the concept vary with time, place and the varying uses and needs people have for song and music. As we have seen, all of these forms exist simultaneously in our current culture.

If we then try to collect the aesthetic observations that have been made through history into a concluding summary, we return to the overarching purpose of this work: to create a dialog between (a) a description and analysis of the concept of the aesthetic and, above all, its musical trajectory and (b) Western music's use, function and meaning on normal days and feast days.

The basic anthropological aesthetic experience named after Dissanayake's concept of 'making-special" as a *special experience*, æI, an experience that from different points of departure was and is positive for people as a social and biological entity. Support for this point of departure can also be found in the philosopher Noël Carrol, who thinks that the aesthetic experiences is grounded in our biological need to react to structures. The qualities of some structures have come to be singled out and strengthened in different ways through our shared cultural history:

> The interpretation of artworks is, most likely, an offshoot of this evolutionary opportunity—a training ground—for developing these adaptive powers with greater and greater subtlety. Inasmuch as aesthetic experiences of artworks are connected to our interpretative powers—both in terms of their origins and enhanced persistence—they are evolutionarily valuable instrumentally (Carrol 2000, 199).[4]

[4] Cf. also Carrol's definition: "An aesthetic experience is one that involves design appreciation and/

In the classical period of ancient Greece we next met the word *aisthesis* that described the ability to experience something with our senses, an ability that was not only applicable to art, but that was not used in the modern sense. With *aisthesis*, for example one could experience the different qualities of the modal scales (*modii*) and their mimetic dimensions in programmatic works of instrumental music. These sensory impressions stood in opposition to the intellectual ideas about music, music's acoustical qualities, the division of the scale into different steps for the different modes, and so forth. One did not hear something as beautiful in and of itself.

In chapter two, the Age of Enlightenment, we witnessed the rebirth of the word aesthetic and the development of the concept that happened in Baumgarten's lifetime. We observed how the nobility's way of understanding art, their thought processes and ways of behavior began to change, and a *bourgeois* economic and goal-oriented rational mode of thought slowly spread as society itself evolved thanks to the socio-cultural affects of the Enlightenment. In a society that changed constantly new *bourgeois* forms of using music developed: one played and sang during leisure time in circles of family and friends but the upper classes also listened to music in concert situations. Concert culture developed further on the musical foundations laid by musical activities in the church, as well as the opera tradition, two separate traditions that had different levels of importance in various parts of Europe.

What was considered art, and how social taste was formed were questions that we found were much debated by those thirsty for enlightenment. While the belief in God's omnipotence slowly receded, it fell to the individuals to find causes for the truths and values that they had inherited. One thought about what was beautiful, what was sublime. Not only was art defined as separate from handicraft in this new development, but different levels of value within art also appeared. In the most artistic sphere it was believed that specially gifted composers created *works* that were supposed to be listened to with an interested attitude and in a concentrated way. An aesthetic discourse developed, interpreted by a little minority of culturally and musically interested people around the turn of the nineteenth century. A number of factors—like the development of concert culture, within which observers and reviewers became important for the creation of a new musical language, changes within music's forms and structures as well as the development of an increasingly large musically educated and interested *bourgeoisie*—contributed to a complex interplay within an increasingly market-oriented and capitalistic social system. Within this process a complex weave of value judgments developed further, judgments that were passed on and managed

---

or the detection of aesthetic and expressive properties and/or attention to the ways in which the formal, aesthetic and expressive properties of the artwork are contrived" (Carrol 2000, 207).

both in spoken and written form by culturally interested people within the upper layers of society.

A larger demand for instrumental music and a slow change in attitude about what music was most valuable contributed to the attention granted by philosophers and music writers to the inner life of textless instrumental music. A subjective power was projected onto music that in turn could transport the listener to a metaphysical artistic world, far from the demands of everyday life. In these cases listening ideally became a sacred work. The new concert venues were likened to musical temples. Within this cultural discourse there developed the experience of an added *aesthetic dimension* æII. Among the factors related to one another and generating the prerequisites for this experience there are, among others (a) the view of music as art, (b) the idea that music was autonomous, (c) the belief that instrumental music expressed the inexpressible and (d) that one created a new way of listening in the contexts in which music was performed. Within the developing romantic era, in the contexts in which art-music was discussed and judged the word aesthetic gradually became a way of marking the specific and added dimension in the experience that one understood the word to represent. Gradually it came to have specific relationships to other value adjectives and nouns: pleasurable, joyful, well-being, enjoyable, piquant, etc.

The role played by song also remained strong during this period. People sang in an increasing number of contexts: schools, free churches, folk movements, etc. Secular choirs were founded by students, professional groups and within folk movements of various kinds. Music was seen as a part of the developing *bourgeois* culture, not least because music and song answered needs in a compensatory way that a competitive and goal-oriented social climate often denied. Song and music were simply an intimate part of people's lives, both cognitively and emotionally.

The aesthetic discourse that was present from the beginning within a little intellectual and educated *bourgeois* class, spread out during the nineteenth century slowly over larger and larger socio-cultural areas and through enculturation, education and socializing came to be a concept shared by a larger *bourgeois* group's world of ideas. Somewhat later it also became a part of a cultural tradition that the leaders of the working class took on and would gladly see that other members of their class would soon have access to as well. Within the *bourgeoisie* a person interested in the arts was expected to have opinions about the latest music and art, opinions that one could develop by reading the ideas of reviewers. It was also at this time that music historians and music theoreticians developed methods of analysis (formal, functional, stylistic, etc.) that supported opinions about music as an independent sounding world, where some composers and their works occupied a non-negotiable place of honor.

The ideas—perhaps most sharply formulated by Friedrich Nietzsche—that absolute facts do not exist, only interpretations, supported the development of a more individualist worldview. However, the people who invested all of their economic and symbolical capital in the artistic/aesthetic field were still a very small group, an *avant garde*. As in the eighteenth century, the majority of the nineteenth-century society was hardly affected at all by the aesthetic arguments that were being carried on by the *bourgeoisie*. The use of and access to new forms of music by the majority changed only very slowly during the nineteenth century.

During this *bourgeois* development, the aesthetic experience expanded to include æIII, within which there was often a strong emotional component. The aesthetic concept and the idea of artistically superior music were seen increasingly as synonymous. An expectation explicitly propagated through education as well as implicitly taken for granted by the culture at large, to acquire and understand higher art was, however, not accomplished in the way it was intended. On the contrary, already during the nineteenth century other forms of music dominated within the *bourgeoisie*: salon music of different kinds, operettas, dance music, etc. This music was also disseminated to other social class and during the first half of the twentieth century, together *schlager* and all other entertainment music became the completely dominant music forms. Schlager melodies became the new folk music.

During this process the number of people in the *bourgeoisie* that had the capacity to experience æIII in different music contexts increased greatly. Humanistically-influenced education and enculturation projects also got under way, like workers' concerts, so that the majority of people could experience the great aesthetic value that the *bourgeois* culture had produced. It became increasingly common and natural to entertain big ideas about Culture's and Art's higher aesthetic and ethical value.

On the other hand the group of people interested in art, those who aimed to experience the earlier form of æII when they listened to the latest art-music, did not expand in a similar way. This was due in part to the music's increased complexity. For the true—and as opposed to modernist music, well-meaning—seekers after æII, the more common and broader form of æIII was seen as a weakening of the authentic concentrated aesthetic experience. For many modernist art-music composers in the twentieth century it was long regarded as most important to be true to oneself and to one's own art. Aesthetics were understood more as an eternal category than a socially constructed one.

If people's access to music that occupied the foreground of a social situation (as a goal in itself) as well as to music that was found in the background of a social situation (music as a means) burgeoned during the nineteenth century, the latter form increased to colossal proportions during the twentieth. To give an economic measure, among the almost 300 people from STIM (the Swedish performing rights society) in the middle of the 1990s who received more than a hundred thousand kronor per year (roughly twelve thousand dollars), only fifteen

CONCLUSION

of them were composers. The other members worked in the popular music branch (Edström 1998, 371). This statistic is also evidence for the thesis for the primacy of vocal music.

Thanks to broadcast media and mechanical advances it has become possible for increasingly large groups to hear music. Music came to be used in new situations and contexts which in turn meant a faster evolution of the aesthetic project than during the previous centuries. As we have seen, one of the most important causes for these quick changes was that the *bourgeois* music education agenda did not achieve its intended success as a result of popular music's doubled ease of access through broadcast media's development and the music's own structure. While basically all popular music from the first half of the twentieth century, like earlier salon music, operettas, marches, music for choirs, and so forth, was regarded as middle music from a stylistic point of view, much of the contemporary art-music after the Second World War was quickly dismissed from this structural abode, regrettably for those who had earlier sought æII within this world.

Art music from earlier centuries—with the addition of some moderately modernist twentieth-century music—became the music that fulfilled the concert public's desire for beautiful, delightful, and/or exciting experiences. This "easy listening" art-music, like popular music in all of its stylistic variants, *schlager*, jazz, pop, rock, world music, etc., developed partly thanks to the music media that in less than fifty years managed to fill all available space. People are often surrounded today by music. Music is used in practically every imaginable situation in our lives. Music and song, more than ever before, are a part of our social lives, but at the same time remain a private meeting with a sounding experience.

Our lives have been filled with song and music. As in earlier centuries, it is important to stress the fact that song has always been a more common music form than instrumental music. At the same time song's textual-semantic dimension conveyed that it was experienced as a different discourse already from the beginning of the aesthetic project. The content of the aesthetic experience of the nineteenth century within *bourgeois* society expanded later in the twentieth century the "grounded" aesthetic experience of æIV as well as the "borderless" form of æV^n. Concurrently in this process an increasing number of non-instrumental aspects were integrated in the aesthetic experience. Our current music world is dominated by song. It was also this way in earlier centuries.

It is naturally no accident that the aesthetic process from æII to æIII, æIV societies æV^n, happens concurrently during the same period of time as the European society goes through change in three large phases, from a) the seventeenth- and eighteenth-centuries' pre-industrial courtly societies; to/via b) nineteenth-century capitalist industrial society; to c) twentieth-century global post-industrial society. æII appears under the stars of idealism and romanticism, while æIII develops during the rise of liberal-capitalism. æIV appears after the Second World War when industrial society's value system is called into question and æV^n in a "late modern" phase where the Western 'information society" rides toward unknown open country.

Modernism's hope that true art could make it possible for people to reach an authentic, metaphysical world, had to give way before other approaches. The educated *bourgeois* curiousity during the interwar period, the spirit of the age that animated the postwar period's enthusiastic followers, have been gradually replaced by other understandings in a time that cultural theorists, philosophers and others see as a time *after* (post) modernism, but that we found should more closely be understood as an aspect within modernity. The fact that collective judgments in society received increasingly limited exposure at the end of the twentieth century, resulted in the rise of a number of different groups for which questions about music/song's aesthetic value were answered in very different ways.

People's use of music varied most dependent upon two factors: education and age. The ways in which younger people's *psychogenesis* changed after the Second World War led to the use of culture in different ways. In part, it led to a daily, "grounded" and pleasure-oriented use of culture, the aesthetic experience æIV. This was understood as an expansion of æIII, but where the new elements were clear aspects that characterized the experiences as "fun," "irrational," "vulgar," and so forth. In part this also led to *reflexive* people's repeated search after external experience in an environment, where all the senses are bombarded by external stimuli, to another expansion of the conditions that could convey an aesthetic experience, æV^n.

Even if all forms of aesthetic experience are social constructions that are lived individually with variable degrees of intersubjective overlapping, it was stressed that æV^n had (has) a larger intrasubjective and contingent profile. This was due in part to the fact that opportunities now followed after people's inwardly oriented interests, and not the opposite as had been the case earlier, that people conformed outwardly to the more or less infrequent social cultural experiences that were offered.

In the form of aesthetic experience that Kant talked about during the eighteenth century, there was a clear differentiation between object and subject. This cultural ability was found (and is found) as an ingredient within the aesthetic addition æII. This objectivizing way of looking at music depended on the process of composition, that is as a written process rather than an oral one and thereby a very rationalized and controllable type of work. Here we can, once again, connect to one of Dissanayake's key ideas about the difference between and oral and a literate culture. Literacy facilitates objectification (Dissanayake 1990, 203). In relation to earlier periods it is likely that *musical* literacy started to increase first at the end of the eighteenth century, which suggests that this fact also could have played a role in the aesthetic process that we observe from the nineteenth century. It was at the end of the twentieth century that in the West it was no longer considered a great handicap if a musician or singer couldn't read music. Many musicians active within popular music could, during the last two decades of the twentieth century compensate this "lack" by learning to use electronic software and hardware, a modern form of musical literacy and performance. The increasing specialization within the music profession that has gone on for a long period, has not only grown among professional musicians who play art-music but also among those who perform popular music. Numerous musicians played both art-music and dance and entertainment music up to the 1950s, and thereafter "classical" musicians increasingly played only art-music, while some specialized only in historically-informed performance. The same type of specialization had also taken place within popular music. One musician might play New Orleans jazz but not free form. Another musician plays dance-band music but not punk. The developments within today's computer music world have now come so far that musicians do not even need to know how to *play* any traditional instruments in order to compose/play a composition/tune.

As we have recently discussed, the changes within contemporary culture have probably led not only to a surface aestheticization in everyday live, but also in all likelihood to a more profound form of aestheticization. A new "interface" between man-software-machine has been added, which influences the creation of artistic objects (pictures, music, etc.).

We have almost no deeper experience or empirical knowledge of what this last-named deep aesthetic process chiefly contains. Welsch talks in general about an "immaterial aesthetification" and that physical attitudes come in at an early stage in the creation process. Lash, for his part, talked about an erasing of the interface between object and symbol. The material object, it is pointed out, becomes both symbolic and active in the shaping of consciousness. He also considered that within the global information society borders are dissolving between human and non-human, between different cultures, as well as between the non-material and the material. With that and forever after, the romantic dream of art's autonomous position was torn apart.

As we have seen, it is problematical to try to describe more closely this current process. One stumbles so easily over the theoretical threshold trying to come into this open room. The conceptual content of the word aesthetic has expanded and mutated at the same tempo as social change in the West and with it the continuously all-embracing expansion of music as a part of basically all human activity. At the same time, the thought has struck me that we may have traveled in a giant spiral. At the beginning of this work we met the concept of *homo aestheticus*, "original," "special experience," æI. We emphasized the relationship between sociogenesis and psychogenesis, in other words, the close connection that exists between structural changes within a culture and the changing ways people think and react. Now many thousand of years later, through the changes that have been wrought in our culture, perhaps we have come in the door to a new room where everything is touched by a hegemonic surface aesthetics and where there exists a deep aesthetic *always-happening*, and thereby an *always aesthetic experience*, æVI?

***

In conclusion: it has been my aim to write a music history that could illuminate socio-cultural context and changing processes from the perspective of how song and music has been used in daily life. I have wished to give a *different* picture of Western music history. It has been a picture created by my own view of musicology as a discipline where music history including the analysis of music, ethnomusicology and popular music history are included as equally important ingredients.

I hope this work has also managed to give a clearer picture of the destiny of the word *aesthetic* and its adventures through time. It is a concept that is used with shifting motives and that is understood in very different ways. When it is used today it functions normally as a strengthening adjective in contexts where one speaks or writes about art in traditional ways and—along with the expansion of the cultural definition—about *everything*, that in some sense someone can experience as art or as having a sensual and/or an artistic dimension. The word can, with few exceptions, be replaced by "art" and related concepts like "artistry," "artistic view," "understanding art." or with "artistic" or "stylistic." It is often difficult to define, but as a rule it is a reinforcing word. At times those who use the word perhaps do not really know what they mean by it. It is my hope that this book has managed to shed new light on he multi-faceted history of this concept.

WORKS CITED

Adorno, Theodor W. 1952. *Versuch über Wagner.* Frankfurt am Main: Suhrkamp.
——. 1970. *Ästhetische Theorie.* Frankfurt am Main: Suhrkamp.
Ågren, Kurt. 1985. Ett nytt Europa 1500-1750. In *Bra Böckers Världshistoria* Vol. 8. Höganäs: Bra Böcker.
Åhlberg, Lars-Olof. 2000. Estetik mellan filosofi och konst: Fyra variationer. *Nordisk Estetisk Tidskrift* 20:55-76.
Ahlberger, Christer. 1996. *Konsumtionsrevolutionen: om det moderna konsumtionssamhällets framväxt 1750-1900.* Göteborg: Göteborg Universitet.
Allen, Warren Dwight. 1962. *Philosophies of Music History: A Study of General Histories of Music 1600-1960.* New York: Dover.
Alsmark, Gunnar. 1985. Ljus över bygden. In *Modärna tider: vision och vardag i folkhemmet.* Malmö: Liber Förlag.
Ander, Owe. 2000. Svenska sinfoni-författares karaktäristiska orkesteregendomligheter"– Aspekter på instrumentations-, orkestrerings- och satstekniken i Berwalds, Lindblads och Normans symfonier. Ph.D. diss., Stockholm University.
Andersson, Greger. 1998. Bland speldosor och trattgrammofoner på Krapperup. In *Kring 1900,* edited by S. Å. Nilsson and L. Vinge. Nyhamnsläge: Gyllenstiernska Krapperupstiftelsen.
Andreasson, Håkan. 2000. *Resande i bilsamhället: vardagligt resande i kulturell belysning.* Ph.D. diss., Göteborg University.
Arvidsson, Alf. 1991. *Sågarnas sång.* Ph.D. diss., Umeå University.
Aschenbrenner, K., and W. Hother, eds. 1954. *Reflections on Poetry: Alexander Gottlieb Baumgarten's Meditationes philosophicae de nonnullis ad poema pertinentibus.* Berkeley: University of California Press.
Axelsen, Doris. 1997. *Listening to recorded music: habits and motivation among high-school students,* Ph.D. diss., Göteborg University.
Baacke, Dieter. 1998. Der Welt der Musik und die Jugend. In *Handbuch Jugend und Musik.* Opladen: Leske und Budrich.
Baker, N. K. and Th. Christensen, eds. 1995. *Aesthetics and the Art of Musical Composition in the German Enlightenment: Selected writings of Johannes Georg Sulzer and Heinrich Christoph Koch.* Cambridge: Cambridge University Press.
Ballstaedt, Andreas and Tobias Widmaier. 1989. *Salonmusik: zur Geschichte und Funktion einer Bürgerlichen Musikpraxis.* Stuttgart: Steiner Verlag.
Baudrillard, Jean. 1993. *Symbolic Exchange and Death (1976).* London: SAGE.
——. 1997. *Jean Baudrillard: Art and Artefact.* Edited by Nicholas Zurbrugg. London: SAGE.
——. 1998. *Consumer Society: myths and structures (1970).* Translated by Georg Ritzer. London: SAGE.
Baugh, Bruce. 1993. Prologomena to Any Aesthetics of Rock Music. *The Journal of Aesthetics and Arts Criticism* 51:1, 23-29.

Batteux, Charles. 1747. *Les Beaux-arts réduits à un même principe*. Paris: Durand.
Beardsley, Monroe. 1981. *Aesthetics: Problems in the Philosophy of Criticism*. Indianapolis: Hackett.
Beck, Ulrich. 1992. *Risk Society (1986)*. Translated by Mark Ritter. London: SAGE.
——. 1997. *The Reinvention of Politics (1996)*. Translated by Mark Ritter. Cambridge: Polity Press.
Benestad, Finn. 1978. *Musik och tanke (1977)*. Translated by Nils Wallin. Stockholm: Rabén and Sjögren.
Bengtsson, Ingmar. 1973. *Musikvetenskap: en översikt*. Stockholm: Esselte.
Berg, Lars-Erik. 1998. "Den sociala människan: Om den symboliska interaktionismen." In *Moderna samhällsteorier: traditioner, riktningar, teoretiker*. Edited by P. Månsson. Stockholm: Rabén Prisma.
Berg, Wilhelm. 1914. *Bidrag till musikens historia i Göteborg 1754-1892*. Göteborg: Wettergren and Kerber.
Berleant, Arnold. 1994. "Beyond disinterestedness." *British Journal of Aesthetics* 34:3, 342-254.
Bernskiöld, Hans. 1986. Sjung, av hjärtat sjung: församlingssång och musikliv i svenska missionsförbundet fram till 1950-talet. Ph.D. diss., Göteborg: Göteborg University.
——. 1992. Vem som helst – Musiksyn och melodiskrivande i 1870 och -80-talets väckelsemiljö med utgångspunkt från Nils Frykman. *Svensk tidskrift för musikforskning* 1:61-106.
Bernstein, Jay M. 1992. *The Fate of Art: Aesthetic Alienation from Kant to Derrida and Adorno*. Cambridge: Polity Press.
Bjurström, Erling. 1997. Högt och lågt: smak och stil i ungdomskulturen. Ph.D. diss., Umeå: Boréa.
Björnberg, Alf. 1991. *Analyse af populærmusik: Teori og metoder*. Aalborg: Aalborg University.
——. 1996. Entertainment objects: konstmusik och populärmusik i 90-talet. In *Notera tiden: 8 essäer om ljudkonst, dans and estetik*. Edited by E. Wallrup. Stockholm: Kungliga Musikaliska Akademien, 1996.
——. 1998. *Skval och harmoni: Musik i radio och TV 1925-1995*. Stockholm: Norstedt/Prisma.
Boëthius, Ulf, Magdalena Czaplicka, and Mats Franzén. 1998. *Från Flygdröm till swingscen: Ungdom och modernitet på 1930-talet*. Edited by Per Olov Qvist and Olle Sjögren. Lund: Arkiv.
Bouij, Christer. 1998. Musik mitt liv och kommande levebröd": en studie i musiklärares yrkessocialisation. Ph.D. diss., Göteborg: Göteborg University.
Bourdieu, Pierre. 1977. *Outline of a Theory of Practice (1972)*. Translated by Richard Nice. Cambridge: Cambridge University Press.
——. 1984. *Distinction: a Social Critique of the Judgement of Taste (1979)*. Translated by Richard Nice. London: Routledge and Kegan Paul.
——. 1996. *The Rules of Art: Genesis and structure of the literary field (1992)*. Translated by Susan Emanuel. Cambridge: Polity Press.

Bourdieu, Pierre, A. Darbel and Dominique Schnapper. 1991. *The Love of Art –European Museums and their Public (1969)*. Translated by Caroline Beattie and Nick Merriman. Cambridge: Polity Press.

Bowen, José. 1997. Finding the Music in Musicology. In *Rethinking Music*. Edited by N. Cook and M. Everist. Cambridge: Cambridge University Press.

Brantner, Christina. 1991. *Robert Schumann und das Tonkünstler-Bild der Romantiker*. New York: Lang.

Broady, Donald. 1990. *Sociologi och epistemologi: Om Pierre Bourdieus författarskap och den historiska epistomologin*, Stockholm: HLS förlag.

Broman, Per F. 1999. "Back to the Future": towards an aesthetic theory of Bengt Hambræus. Ph.D. diss., Göteborg: Göteborg University.

Broman, Per O. 2000. Kakafont storhetsvansinne eller uttryck för det djupaste liv?: Om Ny musik och musikåskådning i svenskt 1920-tal, med särskild tonvikt på Hilding Rosenberg. Ph.D. diss., Uppsala: Uppsala University.

Brostrøm, Stig. 1994. Adorno i verkligheten: estetikens möjligheter idag. In *När det sköna och sanna inte längre sammanfaller: essäer om aktuell musikestetik*, Edited by Hans Gefors. Malmö: Ars Nova.

Bruér, Jan and Lars Westin. 1974. *Jazz : musik, människor, miljöer*. Stockholm: Prisma.

Bücken, Ernst. 1979. Die Musik des Rokokos und der Klassik. In *Handbuch der Musikwissenschaft* Vol. 2. Laaber: Laaber Verlag.

Bull, Michael. 2000. *Sounding out the City: Personal Stereos and the Management of Everyday Life*. Oxford: Berg.

Bujić, Bojan. 1988. *Music in European Thought 1851-1912*. Cambridge: Cambridge University Press.

Burke, Peter. 1992. *The fabrication of Louis XIV*. New Haven: Yale University Press.

———. 1994. *Popular Culture in Early Modern Europe*. Aldershot: Scolar Press.

Burney, Charles. 1959a. *The Present State of Music in France and Italy: or the Journal of a Tour through those Countries, undertaken to collect Materials for a General History of Music, 1771*. Edited by P. Scholes. London: Oxford University Press.

———. 1959b. *The Present State of Music in Germany, the Netherlands and the United Provinces. or the Journal of a Tour through those Countries, undertaken to collect Materials for a General History of Music, London 1773*. Edited by P. Scholes. London: Oxford University Press.

Carlsson, Anders. 1996. "Handel och Bacchus eller Händel och Bach?": Det borgerliga musiklivet och dess orkesterbildningar i köpmannastaden Göteborg under andra hälften av 1800-talet. Ph.D. diss., Göteborg: Göteborg University.

Carrol, Noël. 2000. Art and the domain of the aesthetic. *The British Journal of Aesthetics* 40:2, 191-208.

Casagrande, Renate and Ralf Risser. 1992. Musikhören im Privat-PKW: Demonstration des persönlichen Lebensstils oder Bedürfnis der musikintressierten Menschen? *Gesellschaft und Musik- Wege zur Musiksoziologie, Festgabe für Robert H. Reichardt zum 65. Geburtstag*. Edited by Wolfgang Lipp. Berlin: Duncker and Humblot.

Citron, Marcia. 1993. *Gender and the musical Canon*. Cambridge: Cambridge University Press.
Collinson, Diané. 1992. Aesthetic Experience. In *Philosophical Aesthetics: an Introduction*. Edited by O. Hanfling. Oxford: Blackwell.
Cook, Nicholas. 1990. *Music, Imagination and Culture*. Oxford: Clarendon.
——. 1998. The Domestic *Gesamtkunstwerk*, or Record Sleeves and Reception. In *Composition–Performance–Reception: Studies in the Creative Process in Music*. Edited by W. Thomas. Aldershot: Ashgate.
——, and M. Everist, eds. 1999. *Rethinking Music*. Cambridge: Cambridge University Press.
Crossley-Holland, Peter. 1960. Ancient Greece. In *The Pelican History of Music* Vol I. London: Penguin.
Dahlhaus, Carl. 1980. Die Musik des 19. Jahrhunderts. In *Neues Handbuch der Musikwissenschaft* Vol. 6. Laaber: Laaber Verlag.
——. 1983. *Foundations of Music History (1977)*. Translated by J. B. Robinson. Cambridge: Cambridge University Press.
——. 1988. *Klassische und Romantische Musikästhetik*. Laaber: Laaber Verlag.
Dahlstedt, Sten. 1986. Fakta and förnuft: svensk akademisk musikforskning 1909-1941. Ph.D. diss., Göteborg: Göteborg University.
Damasio, Antonio. 1994. *Descartes' Error*. New York: G.P. Putnam.
Danto, Arthur. 1997. *After the End of Art: Contemporary Art and the Pale of History*. Princeton: Princeton University Press.
Davies, Steven. 1994. *Musical Meaning and Expression*. Ithaca: Cornell University Press.
——. 1994. General Theories of Art versus Music. *British Journal of Aesthetics* 34:4, 315-325.
DeVeaux, Scott. 1997. *Bebop: a social and musical history*. Berkeley: University of California Press.
Dennett, Daniel. 1991. *Consciousness Explained*. London: Allen Lane.
——. 1995. *Darwin's Dangerous Idea: Evolutions and Meanings of Life*. New York: Simon and Schuster.
Dennis, Christopher J. 1998. *Adorno's Philosophy of Modern Music*. Lewiston: Edwin Mellen Press.
DeNora, Tia. 1995. *Beethoven and the Construction of Genius: Musical Politics in Vienna, 1792-1803*. Berkeley: University of California Press.
——. 2000. *Music in everyday life*. Cambridge: Cambridge University Press.
Dickie, George. 1997. *Introduction to Aesthetics: an Analytic Approach*. New York: Oxford University Press.
Diffey, T. F. 1995. A note on some meanings of the term 'aesthetic'. *British Journal of Aesthetics* 35:1, 61-66.
Dissanayake, Ellen.1988. *What is Art For?* Seattle: University of Washington Press.
——. 1992. *Homo Aestheticus: Where Art Comes From and Why*. New York: Free Press.

———. 2000. Antecedents of the Temporal Arts in Early Mother-Infant Interaction. In *The Origins of Music*. Edited by N. Wallin, B. Merker, and S. Brown. Cambridge: MIT Press.

Docker, John. 1994. *Postmodernism and Popular Culture: a Cultural History*. Cambridge: Cambridge University Press.

Dodd, Nigel. 1999. *Social Theory and Modernity*. Cambridge: Polity Press.

Dunbar, R. C. Knight and C. Power, eds. 1999. *The Evolution of Culture*. Edinburgh: Edinburgh University Press.

Dutton, Denis. 1994. Kant and the conditions of artistic beauty. *The British Journal of Aesthetics* 34:3, 226-239.

Eagleton, Terry. 1990. *Ideology of the Awesthetic*. Oxford: Basil Blackwell.

Edler, Arnfried. 1982. *Robert Schumann und seine Zeit*. Laaber: Laaber Verlag.

Edström, K Olle. 1979. Musikens ursprung–fåglar–människan. In *Skriftfest* Stockholm: Stockholm University.

———. 1982a. *På begäran: Svenska musikerförbundet 1907-1982*. Kristiansstad: Liber.

———. 1982b. The Roots of Music. In *Stencillerade skrifter från Musikvetenskapliga institutionen*. Göteborg: Göteborg University.

———. 1986. Till förståelsen av musikupplevelsen. *Svensk tidskrift för musikforskning* 17-38.

———. 1987. Hur schottis blev bonnjazz, eller hur svensk foxtrot besegrade jazzen, eller har afro-amerikansk musik funnits i Sverige? *Etnomusikologian Vuosikirja* 54-83.

———. 1989. "Vi skall gå på restaurang och höra på musik": om reception av restaurang- och annan "mellanmusik." *Svensk tidskrift för musikforskning* 77-112.

———. 1992. *Michael Jackson, Dangerous och dess mottagande*. Göteborg: Göteborg University.

———. 1992. The Place and Value of Middle Music. *Svensk tidskrift för musikforskning* 1:7-60.

———. 1996. *Göteborgs Rika Musikliv: en översikt mellan världskrigen*. Göteborg: Göteborg University.

———. 1997a. Musik som folkbildande projekt. Folkkonserternas upp- och tillbakagång. In *Musiken, folket och bildningen*. Edited by E. Öhrström. Linköping: Mimer.

———. 1997b. Fr-a-g-me-n-ts: a discussion on the position of critical ethnomusicology in contemporary musicology. *Svensk tidskrift för musikforskning* 1:9-68

———. 1998. *Harmoniskt samspel–sjuttiofem år med STIM*, Göteborg: STIM.

Ehrlich, Cyril. 1991. Taste, function and technology: some conjectures. In *Papers at the Second Anglo-Swedish Musicology Conference Cambridge 5-10 August 1989*. Göteborg: Göteborg University.

Elias, Norbert. 1978. *The Civilization Process (1939)*. Translated by Edmund Jephcott. Oxford: Blackwell.

———. 1983. *The Court Society (1969)*. Translated by Edmund Jephcott. Oxford: Blackwell.

———. 1987. *Involvement and Detachment*. Translated by Edmund Jephcott. Oxford: Blackwell.

———. 1991a. *The Symbol Theory*, Edited by Richard Kilminster. London: Sage.

———. 1991b. *Zur Sociologie eines Genies*. Edited by Michael Schröter. Frankfurt am Main: Suhrkamp.

———. 1998. *On civilization, power, and knowledge : selected writings*. Edited by Stephen Mennell and Johan Goudsblom. Chicago: University of Chicago Press.

Ellis, Katharine. 2001. A Dilettante at the Opera: Issues in the criticism of Julien-Louis Geoffroy, 1800-1814 In *Reading Critics Reading: Opera and Ballet Criticism in France from the Revolution to 1848*. Edited by R. Parker and M.A. Smart. Oxford: Oxford University Press.

Erlmann, Veit. 1999. *Music, Modernity, and the Global Imagination*. New York: Oxford University Press.

Etter, Brian K. 2001. *From Classicism to Modernism: Western Musical Culture and the Metaphysics of Order*. Aldershot: Ashgate.

Ewers, Heino. 1978. *Zur genesis des Bürgerlichen Kunstideals*. Stuttgart: Metzler.

Farstad, Per Kjetil. 2000. German galant lute music in the 18th Century. Ph.D. diss., Göteborg: Göteborg University.

Feld, Steven. 1982. *Sound and Sentiment: birds, weeping, poetics, and song in Kaluli expression*. Philadelphia: University of Pennsylvania Press.

Ferry, Luc. 1993. *Homo Aestheticus: The Invention of Taste in the Democratic Age*. Translated by Robert de Loaiza. Chicago: University of Chicago Press.

Fiske, Harold. 1990. *Music and Mind: philosophical essays on the cognition and meaning of music*, Lewiston: E. Mellen Press.

Fornäs, Johan. 1995. *Cultural theory and late modernity*. London: SAGE.

———, Ulf Lindberg, Ove Sernhede Fornäs. 1988. *Under rocken: musikens roll i tre unga band*. Lund: Symposion.

Foster, H., ed. 1983. *The Anti-Aesthetic*. Port Townsend: Bay Press.

Forte, Allan. 1995. *The American popular ballad of the golden era 1924-1950: a study in musical design*. Princeton: Princeton University Press.

Frisby, David. 1991. The Aesthetics of Modern Life: Simmel's Interpretation. *Theory, Culture and Society* 8:3, 73-93.

Frith, Simon. 1981. *Sound effects: Youth, Leisure, and the Politics of Rock'n'Roll*. New York: Pantheon Books.

———. 1987. Towards an aesthetic of popular music. *Music and Society: The politics of composition, performance and reception*. Edited by R. Leppert and S. McClary, Cambridge: Cambridge University Press.

———. 1998. *Performing Rites: Evaluating Popular Music*. Oxford: Oxford University Press.

——— and Howard Horne. 1987. *Art into Pop*. London: Methuen.

Frykman, Jonas and Orvar Löfgren, eds. 1979. *Den kultiverade människan*. Lund: Liber.

———. 1985. *Modärna tider: vision och vardag i folkhemmet*. Malmö: Liber Förlag.

Fubini, Enrico. 1997. *Geschichte der Musikästhetik (1987)*. Stuttgart: Metzler.

Gallie, Walter B. 1955. Essentially Contested Concepts. *Proceedings of the Aristotelian Society* 56:167-198.

Geck, Martin and Peter Schleuning. 1989. *'Geschrieben auf Bonaparte' –Beethovens 'Eroica': Revolution, Reaktion, Rezeption*. Reinek bei Hamburg: Rowohlt Taschenbuch.
Goehr, Lydia. 1992. *The Imaginary Museum of Musical Works: an essay in the philosophy of music*. Oxford: Clarendon.
—. 1994. Political music and the politics of music. *The Journal of Aesthetics and Art Criticism* 52:1, 99-112.
Gronow, Jukka. 1997. *The Sociology of Taste*. New York: Routledge.
Gruhn, Wilfried. 1998. *Der Musikverstand: Neurobiologische Grundlagen des musikalischen Denkens, Hörens und Lernens*, Hildesheim: Olms.
Haas, Walter. 1957. *Das Schlagerbuch*. München: List.
Habermas, Jürgen. 1984. *Borgerlig Offentlighet: Kategorierna 'privat' och 'offentligt' i det moderna samhället (1962)*. Lund: Arkiv.
Hanfling, Oswald, ed. 1992. The Problem of Definition. In *Aesthetic Experience: an Introduction*. Oxford: Blackwell.
Hanslick, Eduard. 2003. *Vom Musikalisch Schönen (1854)*. Translated by Geoffrey Payzant. New Zealand: Cybercorportions.
Hawkins, Stan. 2002. *Settling the Pop Score: Pop Texts and identity politics*. Aldeshot: Ashgate.
Heister, Hanns-Werner. 1983. *Das Konzert: Theorie einer Kulturform*. Wilhelmshafen: Heinrichshofen.
Heitmeyer, W. and T. Olk. 1995. The Role of Individualization Theory in Adolescence. In *Individualization in Childhood and Adolescence*. Edited by G. Neubauer and K. Hurrelmann. New York: de Gruyter.
Henderson, Isobel. 1957. Ancient Greek Music. In *The New Oxford History of Music: Ancient and Oriental Music*. Oxford: Oxford University Press.
Henriksson, Alf. 1934. *Röster om radio: intryck och erfarenheter av tio års svensk rundradio*. Stockholm: Sveriges Radio.
Higgins, Kathleen. 1991. *The Music of our lives*. Philadelphia: Temple University Press.
Hobsbawm, Eric. 1979. *Revolutionens tidsålder (1962)*. Translated by Jaak Talvend. Stockholm: Tiden.
—. 1981. *Kapitalets tidsålder (1975)*. Stockholm: Tiden.
—. 1994. *Age of Extremes: The Short Twentieth century*. London: Joseph.
Hogan, Patrick C. 1994. The Possibility of Aesthetics. *British Journal of Aesthetics* 34:3, 337-349.
Holecek, Josef. 1996. För Musikens Skull: studier i interpretativ gitarrspelteknik från tidsperioden cirka 1800 - cirka 1930 med utgångspunkt från gitarrskolor och etyder. Ph.D. diss., Göteborg: Göteborg University.
le Huray, Peter, and James Day, eds. 1981. *Music and Aesthetics in the Eighteenth and Early-Nineteenth Centuries*. eds. Cambridge: Cambridge University Press.
Hurtshouse, Rosalind. 1992. Truth and representation, *Philosophical Aesthetics: an Introduction*. Edited by O. Hanfling. Oxford: Oxford University Press.
Huyssen, Andreas. 1986. *After the Great Divide: Modernism, Mass Culture, Postmodernism*. Bloomington: Indiana University Press.

Inglis, Fred. 1993. *Cultural Studies*. Oxford: Blackwell.
Jameson, Fredric. 1991. *Postmodernism, or, The Political Logic of Late Capitalism*. London: Verso.
Jay, Martin. 1973. *The dialectical imagination: a history of the Frankfurt School and the Institute of Social Research, 1923-1950*. London: Heinemann Educational Books.
———. 1998. *Cultural Semantics*. Amherst: University of Massachusetts Press.
Jeanson, Gunnar and Julius. Rabe. 1927-31. *Musiken genom tiderna*, Stockholm: Hugo Gebers.
Jernhake, Klaes-Göran. 1999. Schuberts 'stora C-dursymfoni' – kommunikationen med ett musikaliskt konstverk. En tillämpning av Paul Ricoeurs tolkningsbegrepp. Ph.D. diss., Uppsala: Uppsala University.
Jonsson, Leif. 1990. Ljusets riddarvakt. 1800-talets studentsång utövad som offentlig samhällskonst. Ph.D. diss., Uppsala: University.
Jonsson, L. and A. Ivarsdotter Johnson, eds. 1993. *Musiken i Sverige II: Frihetstid och Gustaviansk tid 1720-1810*. Stockholm: Atlantis.
Kant, Immanuel. 1951. *Critique of Judgement (1790)*. Translated by J. H. Bernard. London: Hafner Press.
———. 1997. *Lectures on Metaphysics (1783)*. Translated and edited by K. Ameriks and S. Naragon. Cambridge: Cambridge University Press.
———. 1998. *Critique of pure reason (1781)*. Translated by P. Gyer and A. W. Wood. Cambridge: Cambridge University Press.
Karevold, Idar. 1996. Kontinentale impulser i en norsk musikerslekt før 1850: en studie i brever, musikalier og skrifter etter slekten Lindeman. Ph.D. diss., Göteborg: Göteborg University.
Keldany-Mohr, I. 1977. *"Unterhaltungsmusik" als soziokulturelles Phänomen des 19. Jahrhunderts. Untersuchung über den Einfluss der musikalischen Öffentlichkeit auf die Herausbildung einen neues Musiktypus*. Regensburg: Bosse.
Kilminster, Richard. 1998. *The sociological revolution: From the Enlightenment to the global age*. London: Routledge.
Kivy, Peter. 1993. Auditor's Emotions, Contention, Concession, and Compromise. *The Journal of Aesthetics and Art Criticism* 1:1-12
Kjørup, Søren. 1999. *Människovetenskaperna: problem och traditioner i humanioras vetenskapsteori*. Lund: Studentlitteratur.
———. 2000. *Kunstens Filosofi: en indføring i æstetik*. Roskilde: Roskilde University.
Klempe, Hroar. 1998. *Generative teorier i musikalisk analyse*. Oslo: Spartacus.
Knepler, Georg. 1977. *Geschichte als Weg zum Musikverständnis*, Leipzig: Reclam.
Kogan, Nathan. 1994. On Aesthetics and its Origins: Some Psychobiological and Evolutionary Considerations. *Social Research* 61:1, 139-165.
Kramer, Lawrence. 1992. The Musicology of the Future. *Repercussions* Spring, 5-18.
———. 2002. *Musical meaning: Toward a Critical History*. Berkeley: University of Califonia Press.
Kreitman, Norman. 1999. *The Roots of Metaphor: a multidisciplinary study in aesthetics* Aldershot: Ashgate.
van Krieken, Robert. 1998. *Norbert Elias*. London and New York: Routledge.

Kvist Dahlstedt, Barbro. 2001. Suomis sång: kollektiva identiteter i den finländska studentsången 1819-1917. Ph.D. diss., Göteborg: Göteborg University.
Kydland Lysdahl, Anne Jorunn. 1995. Sangen har lysning: Studentersang i Norge på 1800-talet. Ph.D. diss., Oslo: Solum forlag.
Köhler, Joachim. 1998. *Nietzsche and Wagner: A Lesson in Subjugation*. New Haven: Yale University Press.
Lagerroth, Erland. 1994. *Världen och vetandet sjunger på nytt: från en mekanisk värld till ett kreativt universum*, Göteborg: Korpen.
Lash, Scott. 1999. *Another modernity, a different rationality: space, society, experience, judgement, objects*. Oxford: Blackwell.
Lessem, Alan. 1988. Bridging the gap: Contexts for the Reception of Haydn and Bach. *The International Review of the Aesthetics and the Sociology of Music* 2:137-148.
Levinson, Jerrold. 1996. *The Pleasures of Aesthetics: Philosophical Essays*. Ithaca: Cornell University Press.
—. 1997. *Music in the Moment*. Ithaca: Cornell University Press.
Lesle, Lutz. 1984. *Der Musikkritiker: Gutachter oder Animateur?: Aspekte einer publikumpädagogischen Handlungstheorie der Musikpublizistik*. Hamburg: Wagner.
Liedman, Sven-Erik. 1997. *I skuggan av framtiden: modernitetens idéhistoria*, Stockholm: Bonniers.
Lilliestam, Lars. 1993. Om begreppen folkmusik, konstmusik och populärmusik. In *Musiklivet år 2002, rapport nr 4*. Stockholm: Kungliga Musikaliska Akademien.
—. 1995. *Gehörsmusik: blues, rock och muntlig tradering*, Göteborg: Akademiförlaget.
—. 1998. *Svensk rock: musik, lyrik, historik*, Göteborg: Bo Ejeby förlag.
—. 2002. *En dödsmetall-hardcore-hårdrocksgrej... Det är jättesvårt att förklara: Göteborgska gymnasister samtalar om musik*. Göteborg: Göteborg University.
Lindberg, Boel. 1997. Mellan provins och parnass: John Fernström i svenskt musikliv. Ph.D. diss., Lund: Lund University.
Ling, Jan. 1979. Folkmusik: en brygd. *Fataburen*, 9-34.
—. 1983. *Europas musikhistoria -1730*, Stockholm: Esselte.
—. 1989. *Europas Folkmusik*, Stockholm: Esselte.
—. 1999. Apollo Gothenburgensis: Patrick Ahlströmer och Göteborgs musikliv vid 1700-talets slut. *Svensk tidskrift för musikforskning* 53-94.
Lippman, Edward. 1964. Theory and Practice in Schumann's Aesthetics. *Journal of the American Society of Musicology* 17:311-345
—. 1986. *A History of Western Musical Aestethics: A Historical Reader*. Lincoln: University of Nebraska Press.
—. 1999. *The Philosophy and Aesthetics of Music*. Lincoln: University of Nebraska Press.
Leux-Henschen, Irmgard. 1958. Den musikestetiska debatten i Stockholms Posten 1779-80. *Svensk tidskrift för musikforskning* 61-135.
Lloyd, David. 1990. Analogies of the Aesthetic: the politics of culture and the limits of materialist aesthetic. *New Formations* 10:109-126.

Luhmann, Niklas. 1986. *Das Kunstwerk und die Selbstreproduktion der Kunst. Stil: Geschichten und Funktionen eines kulturwissenschaftlichen Diskurselements.* Edited by H. U. Gumbrecht and K. L. Pfeiffer. Frankfurt am Main: Suhrkamp.
——. 1994. How Can the Mind Participate in Comunication? *Materialities of Communication.* Edited by H. U. Gumbrecht and L. L. Pfeiffer and translated by William Whobrey. Stanford: Stanford University Press.
Lundberg, Dan, Krister Malm and Owe Ronström. 2000. *Musik Medier Mångkultur: Förändringar i svenska kulturlandskap.* Hedemora: Gidlund.
Lyas, Colin. 1997. *Aesthetics.* London: UCL Press.
Lyotard, Jean-Francais. 1984. *The Postmodern Condition: a report on knowledge (1979).* Translated by Geoff Bennington and Brian Massumi. Manchester: Manchester University Press.
Maegaard, Jan. 1967. *Musikalisk modernism*, Stockholm: Prisma.
Magee, Bryan. 1998. *En filosofs bekännelser (1997).* Translated by Hans Berggren. Stockholm: Wahlström and Widstrand.
Mannheim, Karl. 1968. *Essays on the Sociology of Knowledge.* Edited by P. Kecskemeti. London: Routledge and Kegan Paul.
Manoff, Tom. 1982. *Music: a living language.* New York: Norton.
Maquet, Jacques. 1986. *The Aesthetic Experience: an Anthropologist looks at the Visual Arts.* New Haven: Yale University Press.
Mathiesen, Thomas J. 2000. *Apollo's Lyre: Greek Music and Music Theory in Antiquity and the Middle Ages.* Lincoln: University of Nebraska Press.
McGinn, Colin. 1993. *Problems in Philosophy: The Limits of Inquiry.* Oxford: Blackwell.
McGuigan, Jim. 1997. Cultural Populism Revisited. *Cultural Studies in Question.* eds. M. Ferguson and P. Golding. London: SAGE.
Meltzer, Richard. 1987. *The Aesthetics of Rock.* New York: Da Capo Press.
Mennell, Stephen. 1989. *Norbert Elias: an introduction.* Oxford: Blackwell.
Merriam, Allan. 1964. *The Anthropology of Music.* Evanston: Northwestern University Press.
Meyer, Leonard B. 1973. *Explaining Music: essays and explorations.* Berkeley: University of California Press.
Middleton, Richard. 1990. *Studying Popular Music.* Milton Keynes: Open University Press.
Miller, Simon, ed. 1993. *The Last Post: Music after Modernism.* Manchester: Manchester University Press.
Milner, Andrew. 1994. *Cultural Theory: an Introduction.* London: UCL Press.
Moberg, Carl-Allan. 1973. *Musikens historia i västerlandet intill 1600.* Stockholm: Natur och kultur.
Moore, Allan F. 1993. *Rock: The Primary Text. Developing a Musicology of Rock.* Buckingham: Open University Press.
——. 1998. *Beatles: 'Sgt Pepper's Lonely Hearts Club Band*, Cambridge: Cambridge University Press.
Morgan, Robert P. 1991. *Twentieth-century Music: A History of Musical Style in Modern Europe and America.* New York: Norton.

Morrow, Mary Sue. 1997. *German Music Criticism in the late Eighteenth century.* Cambridge: Cambridge University Press.
de la Motte-Haber, Helga. 1989. *Musikpsychologie.* Laaber: Laaber Verlag.
Mulhall, Stephen. 1994. *Stanley Cavell: Philosophy's recounting of the Ordinary.* Oxford: Clarendon Press.
Müller, Harro. 1994. Luhman's Systems Theory as a Theory of Modernity. *New German Critique* 61:1, 39-54.
Neitzert, Lutz. 1990. *Die Geburt der Moderne, der Bürger und die Tonkunst.* Stuttgart: Franz Steiner Verlag.
Neubauer, G., and K. Hurrelmann, eds. 1995. *Individualization in Childhood and Adolescence.* Edited by New York: de Gruyter.
Nicholsen, Shierry W. 1993. Subjective Aesthetic Experience in Adorno and its Historical Trajectory. *Theory, Culture and Society* 10:89-126.
Nielsen, Steen K. 1999. Making a stand biting the hand: Steve Martland and British new music culture. Ph.D. diss., Aarhus: Aarhus University.
Nilsson, Sven. 1999. *Kulturens vägar: kultur och kulturpolitik i Sverige.* Malmö: Polyvalent.
Nketia, J. H. Kwabena. 1974. *The Music of Africa.* New York: Norton.
Nordin Hennel, Ingeborg. 1997. *Mod och Försakelse. Livs- och yrkesbetingelser för Konglig Theaterns skådespelerskor 1813-1863.* Stockholm: Gidlund.
Norlind, Tobias. 1916. *Allmänt Musiklexicon.* Stockholm: Wahlström and Widstrand.
———. 1922. *Allmän musikhistoria.* Stockholm: Wahlström and Widstrand.
Norris, Christopher. 1993. *The Truth about Postmodernism.* Oxford: Blackwell.
Nylöf, Göran. 1967. *Musikvanor i Sverige. Rikskonserter: konsertbyråutredningens slutbetänkande, Statens Offentliga Utredningar* 9. Stockholm: no pub.
Nässén, Eva. 2000. 'Ett yttre tecken på en inre känsla': studier i barockens musikaliska och sceniska gestik. Ph.D. diss., Göteborg: Göteborg University.
Öblad, Carin. 2000. Att använda musik: om bilen som konsertlokal. Ph.D. diss., Göteborg: Göteborg University.
Oesch, Hans. 1987. *Aussereuropäische Musik.* Neues Handbuch der Musikwissenschaft Vol. 9. Laaber: Laaber Verlag.
Öhrström, Eva.1987. Borgerliga kvinnors musicerande i 1800-talets Sverige. Ph.D. diss., Göteborg: Göteborg University.
Olsson, Bengt. 1993. SÄMUS: en musikutbildning i kulturpolitikens tjänst? En studie om en musikutbildning på 1970-talet. Ph.D. diss., Göteborg: Göteborg University.
Ong, Walter J. 1982. *Orality and Literacy: The Technologizing of the World.* London: Routledge.
Outhwaite, William. 1994. *Habermas: a critical introduction.* London: Polity Press.
Paddison, Max. 1993. *Adorno's Aesthetic of Music.* Cambridge: Cambridge University Press.
Paetzold, Heinz. 1983. *Ästhetik des deutschen Idealismus,: zur Idee ästhetischer Rationalität bei Baumgarten, Kant, Schelling, Hegel und Schopenhauer.* Wiesbaden: Steiner.

Panassié, Hughes. 1934. *Le jazz hot*. Paris: no pub.
Parret, Herman. 1998. Kant on Music and the Hierarchy of the Arts. *The Journal of Aesthetics and Art criticism* 56:3, 251-264.
Pattison, Robert. 1987. *The Triumph of Vulgarity*. New York: Oxford University Press.
Persson, Torgil. 2001. Den kommunala musikskolans uppkomst och turbulenta 90-tal. Ph.D. diss., Göteborg: Göteborg University.
Pinker, Steven. 1997. *How the Mind Works*. New Work: Norton.
Plumpe, Gerhard. 1993. *Ästhetische Kommunikation der Moderne*. Opladen: Westdeutscher Verlag.
Preussner, Eberhard, ed. 1949. *Die Musikalischen Reisen des Herrn von Uffenbach: aus einem Reisetagenbuch des Johann Friedrich A. von Uffenbach aus Frankfurt a.M. (1712-1716)*. Kassel: Bärenreiter.
Rackham, Henry, ed. 1932. *Aristoteles in twenty-three volumes*. Cambridge: Harvard University Press.
Ratner, Leonard. 1980. *Classic Music: Expression, Form, and Style*. New York: Schirmer Books.
Reichardt, Johann Fr. 1976. *Briefe, die Musik betreffend: Berichte, Rezensionen (1774-1776)*. Edited by Greta Herre and Walther Siegmund-Schulze. Leipzig: Reclam.
Riethmüller, Albrecht. 1989. Musik zwischen Hellenismus und Spätantike. *Die Musik des Altertums*. Neues Handbuch der Musikwissenschaft. Edited by F. Zaminer. Laaber: Laaber Verlag,
Rose, S. and H. Rose, eds. 2000. *Alas, poor Darwin... Alas, Poor Darwin, arguments against evolutionary psychology*. London: Jonathan Cape.
Rosen, Charles. 1980. *Sonata Forms*. New York: Norton.
Runciman, Walter C. 1998. *The Social Animal*. London: Harper Collins.
Russell, Dave. 1987. *Popular music in England, 1840-1914*. Manchester: Manchester University Press.
Ruud, Even. 1997. *Musikk og identitet*. Oslo: Universitetsforlaget.
Ryle, Gilbert. 1949. *The Concept of Mind*, London: Hutchinson.
Samson, Jim. 1999. Analysis in Context. In *Rethinking Music*. Edited by N. Cook and M. Everist. Cambridge: Cambridge University Press.
Schulze, Gerhard. 1988. Alltagsästhetik und Lebenssituation: eine Analyse kultureller Segmentierungen in der Bunderepublik Deutschland. *Kultur und Alltag*. Edited by H. G. Soeffner. Göttingen: Otto Schwartz.
——. 1993. *Die Erlebnis-Gesellschaft: Kultursoziologie der Gegenwart*. Frankfurt: Campus Verlag.
Schumann, Robert. 1877. *Music and Musicians*. London: no pub.
——. and Clara Schumann. 1987. *Tagebücher II, 1836-1854*. Edited by G. Nauhaus. Leipzig: Deutsche Verlag für Musik.
Scott, Derek. 1989. *The Singing Bourgeois: Songs of the Victorian Drawing Room and Parlour Music*. Milton Keynes: Open University Press.
Scruton, Roger. 1998. *The Aesthetics of Music*. Oxford: Clarendon.
Seboek, Thomas. 1979. Prefigurements of Art. *Semiotica* 3-73.

Shusterman, Richard. 1992. *Pragmatist Aesthetics: Living Beauty, Rethinking Art*. Oxford: Blackwell.
——. 1997. The End of Aesthetic experience. *The Journal of Aesthetics and Art Criticism* 55:1, 29-41.
Simmel, Georg. 1995. *Hur är samhället möjligt?–och andra essäer*. Introduction by Erik af Edholm. Göteborg: Korpen.
Singer, Peter. 2000. *A Darwinian Left: politics, evolution, and cooperation*. New Haven: Yale University Press.
Skuncke, M. C. and A. Ivarsdotter. 1998. *Svenska operans födelse: studier i gustaviansk musikdramatik*. Stockholm: Atlantis.
Sloboda, John. 1985. *The Musical Mind: The Cognitive Psychology of Music Psychology*. Oxford: Clarendon.
Sparshott, Francis. 1987. Aesthetics of Music: limits and grounds. In *What is Music? An Introduction to the Philosophy of Music*. Edited by P. Alperson. University Park: Pennsylvania State University Press.
Sponheuer, Bernd. 1987. *Musik als Kunst und Nicht-Kunst*. Kassel: Bärenreiter.
Stålhammar, Börje. 1995. Samspel: grundskola-musikskola i samverkan: en studie av den pedagogiska och musikaliska interaktionen i en klassrumssituation. Ph.D. diss., Göteborg: Göteborg University.
——. 1999. *Grounded theory och musikpedagogik: teorigenerering med empiri som grund*. Örebro: Musikhögskolan vid Örebro universitet.
Stigsdotter, Margareta. 1985. Den långa vägens män. *Modärna tider - vision och vardag i folkhemmet*. Lund: Liber.
Stockfelt, Ola. 1988. Musik som lyssnandets konst - en analys av W.A. Mozarts symfoni nr 40, g-moll K 550. Ph.D. diss., Göteborg: Göteborg University.
Stoljar, Margaret. 1985. *Poetry and Song in late 18th Century German: a Study in Musical Sturm und Drang*. London: Croom Helm.
Strindberg, August. 1913. *Likt och olikt*. Stockholm: Bonniers.
Subotnik, Rose R. 1991. *Developing Variations: Style and Ideology in Western Music*. Minneapolis: University of Minnesota Press.
Suppan, Wolfgang. 1984. *Der musizierende Mensch: eine Anthropologie der Musik*. Mainz: Schott.
Swingewood, Alan. 1998. *Cultural Theory and the Problem of Modernity*. Basingstoke and New York: St. Martin's Press.
Säätelä, Simo. 2000. "The Aesthetic Turn": Aisthesis och Somaestetik. *Nordisk Estetisk Tidskrift* 20:77-94.
Söderberg, Johan. 1997. Konsumtion, kön och preferenser i Sverige 1920-1965. In *Kultur och konsumtion i Norden 1750-1950*. Edited by J. Söderberg and L. Magnusson. Helsingfors: FHS.
Sörbom, Göran. 1994. Aristotle on Music as Representation. *Journal of Aesthetics and Art Criticism* 52:1, 37-46.
Tadday, Ulrich. 1993. *Die Anfänge des Musikfeuilletons: der kommunikative Gebrauchswert musikalischer Bildung in Deutschland um 1800*. Stuttgart and Weimar: Metzler.

———. 1997. Systemtheorie und Musik: Luhmanns Variante der Autonomieästhetik. *Musik and Ästhetik* 1:13-34.
———. 1999. *Das schöne Unendliche. Ästhetik, Kritik, Geschichte der romantischen Musikanschauung*. Stuttgart: Meltzer.
Tatarkiewicz, Wladyslaw. 1979. Geschichte der Ästhetik. Basel: Schwabe.
Tegen, Martin. 1955. Musiklivet i Stockholm 1890-1910. Ph.D. diss., Stockholm: Stockholms kommunalförvaltning.
———. 1986. *Populär Musik under 1800-talet*. Stockholm: Reimers.
Théberge, Paul. 1997. *Any Sound You Can Imagine: Making music, consuming technology*. Hanover: University Press of New England.
Thomsen, Rudi. 1983. *Högkulturerna tar form*. Höganäs: Bra Böcker.
Thyssen, Oe, ed. 1992. *Autopoiesis Autopoiesis: En introduktion til Niklas Luhmanns verden af systemer*. København: Politisk Revy.
Tillman, Joakim. 1995. Ingvar Lidholm och tolvtonsmusiken. Analytiska och historiska perspektiv på Ingvar Lidholms musik från 1950-talet. Ph.D. diss., Stockholm: Stockholm University.
Tittel, Ernst. 1965. *Harmonilehre*. Wien: Doblinger.
Touraine, Alain. 1995. *Critique of Modernity*. Oxford: Blackwell.
Valkare, Gunnar. 1997. Det audiografiska fältet: Om musikens förhållande till skriften och den unge Bo Nilssons strategier. Ph.D. diss., Göteborg: Göteborg University.
Volgsten, Ulrik. 1999. Music, Mind and the Serious Zappa. Ph.D. diss., Stockholm: Stockholm University.
Wallin, N., B. Merker, and S. Brown, eds. 2000. *The Origins of Music*. Cambridge: MIT Press.
Walter, Joakim. 2000. This heaving ocean of tones: nineteenth-century organ registration practice at S:t Marien, Lübeck. Ph.D. diss., Göteborg: Göteborg University.
Walton, Kendall L. 1993. How Marvelous! Toward a Theory of Aesthetic Value. *The Journal of Aesthetics and Art Criticism* 51:3, 499-510.
Weber, William. 1975. *Music and the Middle class: the social structure of concert life in London, Paris and Vienna*. New York: no pub.
———. 1997. Did people listen in the 18th century? *Early Music*. 25:4, 678-691.
———. 1999. The History of Musical Canon. *Rethinking Music*. Edited by N. Cook and M. Everist. Cambridge: Cambridge University Press.
Wegner, Max. 1963. *Musikgeschichte in Bildern*. Leipzig: Deutscher Vörlag für Musik.
Weiss, P. and R. Taruskin, eds. 1984. *Music in the Western World: a History in Documents*. New York: Norton.
Welsch, Wolgang. 1997. *Undoing Aesthetics*. London: Sage.
Wennhall, Johan. 1994. Från djäkne till swingpjatt: Om den moderna ungdomskulturens historia. Ph.D. diss., Uppsala, Uppsala University.
Wicke, Peter. 1982. Rock music: a musical-aesthetic study. *Popular Music* 2:219-243.
———. 1990. *Rock music: Culture, aesthetics and sociology*. Cambridge: Cambridge University Press.

Williams, Alastair. 2001. *Constructing Musicology.* Aldershot: Ashgate.
Willis, Paul, Simon Jones, Joyce Canaan and Geoff Hurd. 1990. *Common Culture: Symbolic work at play in the everyday cultures of the young.* Milton Keynes: Open University Press.
Wilson-Brown, S. and C. McCarthy. 1999. The Organization of Affect: Popular Music, Youth, and Intellectual and Political Life–An interview with Larry Grossberg. In *Sound identities–Popular music and the cultural politics of education.* Edited by Cameron McCarthy. New York: Peter Lang.
Witkins, Robert W. 1998. *Adorno on Music.* London: Routledge.
Wittgenstein, Ludwig. 1992. *Filosofiska undersökningar (1953).* Translated by Anders Wedberg. Stockholm: Thales.
Wolff, Christoph. 1991. *Bach: Essays on His Life and Music.* Cambridge: Harvard University Press.
Wolin, Richard. 1992. *The Terms of Cultural Criticism: The Frankfurt School. Existentialism, Poststructuralism.* New York, Columbia University Press.
Woodmansee, Martha. 1994. *The Author, Art, and the Market: Rereading the History of Aesthetics.* New York, Columbia University Press.
Zaminer, Frieder. 1989. Musik im archaischen und klassischen Griechenland. in *Die Musik des Altertums: Neues Handbuch der Musikwissenschaft* Vol. 1, Edited by F. Zaminer, Laaber: Laaber Verlag.
Ziehe, Thomas. 1975. *Pubertät und Narzissmus: sind Jugend entpolitisiert?.* Frankfurt am Main: Europäische Verlagsanstalt.
—. 1986. Inför avmystifieringen av världen. Ungdom och kulturell modernisering. *Postmoderna Tider.* Edited by M. Löfgren and A. Molander. Stockholm: Nordstedts.
—. 1991. *Zeitvergleiche: Jugend in kulturellen Modernisierungen.* Weinheim: Juventa Verlag.

INDEX

Symbols

æI ix, 11, 21, 27, 34, 44, 46, 53, 124, 125, 164, 174, 189, 200, 212, 262, 264, 268, 279, 286
æII 11, 21, 124-125, 149, 152, 163-165, 168-169, 172, 174-175, 186, 189, 197, 200-202, 217, 228, 246, 262, 264, 268, 279, 281-285
æIII 11, 21, 163-166, 174-175, 186, 189, 197, 200-201, 217, 228, 247, 250, 262, 268, 279, 282, 284
æIV 22, 247, 250, 252, 262, 264-266, 268, 279, 283-284
æV^n 22, 252, 262, 265-268, 279, 283-284

A

Adorno, T. 106, 109-119, 149, 172, 179, 181-183, 185, 187, 189, 196, 199, 204, 225, 228-229, 238, 242, 259
aesthesis 39, 46, 51
Ågren, K. 27, 28, 29, 33
Ahlberg, L. 24, 130, 270
Ahlberger, C. 218, 220, 221
aisthesis 21, 37, 83, 280
Ambros, A. 148, 156
Ander, O. 71, 121, 124, 140, 148, 155, 159
Andreasson, H. 263
Aristotle 21, 36-48, 163
Aristoxenos 42, 45, 48
art music 12, 14, 15, 19, 74, 93, 108-110, 112, 115, 117, 124, 126, 133, 134, 141, 142, 145, 149, 150-153, 155, 157, 158, 166, 171, 172, 179-181, 184-190, 192, 199, 200, 204, 206, 208-210, 217, 223, 227-232, 238, 240-241, 244, 246, 248-250, 257, 261, 262, 265, 270-272, 275, 277, 281-283, 285
Arvidsson, A. 207
autonomous music 170
Axelsen, D. 225-226

B

Baacke, D. 234
Bäck, S. 74, 207, 228
Ballstaedt, A. 135, 142-146
Bartok, B. 187, 245, 276
Batteux, C. 59, 60
Baudelaire, C. 154-155, 259
Baudrillard, J. 241, 243, 268-272
Baugh, B. 246, 250
Baumgarten, A. 51, 52, 54, 57, 61-63, 84, 92, 95
Beardsley, M. 214
Beatles 15, 17, 191, 232, 235-236, 238
Beck, U. 254-258, 262-268, 273
Beethoven, L 14, 72, 95, 103, 113-121, 132-150, 156-157, 159, 164, 166, 168, 170-172, 176
Benestad, F. 15, 36, 39, 45, 129, 176
Bengtsson, I. 13, 14
Benjamin, W. 196, 215, 259, 268
Berleant, A. 202
Bernskiöld, H. 167, 170
Bernstein, J. 182, 183

Berwald, F. 141
Birtwistle, H. 228
Bizet, G. 130
Björnberg, A. 188
Bjurström, E. 225, 226,
Blomdahl, K. 228
blues 16, 264
Bourdieu, P. 45, 127, 140, 154, 155, 162, 163, 174, 208, 227
Bowen, J. 134
Brahms, J. 149, 153, 156, 158, 161, 162, 167, 168, 200
Brantner, C. 152
Brendel, F. 156
Broady, D. 174
Broman, P. 157, 228
Brostrøm, S. 187
Bruér, J. 231
Bücken, E. 76
Bujić, B. 15, 129, 147, 148, 155, 156, 157
Bull, M. 157, 234, 242, 247
Burke, P. 55, 56, 90, 91, 205
Burney, C. 67, 68, 69, 70, 71, 79, 81

C

Caldara, A. 66
Campagnoli, B. 73
Carlsson, A. 71, 95, 107, 137, 138, 139, 142, 146, 168
Carrol, N. 279
Casagrande, R. 263
Cassirer, E. 75
Chopin, F. 153
Citron, M. 171
Collingwood, R. 211
Collinson, D. 37, 38
Confrey, Z. 229
Cook, N. 89, 109, 270
Crossley-Holland, P. 42
Czapek, J. 138

D

Dahlhaus, C. 15, 87-88, 94, 100, 102, 112, 123, 130, 136-137, 156-157, 163-171, 190, 210-211, 216
Dahlstedt, S. 93, 140, 141
Damasio, A. 25, 165
Danto, A. 186, 187, 211, 212, 217
Darwin, C. 29, 30, 32
Davies, S. 187, 214, 228
Day, J. 15, 58, 59, 88, 89, 100, 117, 129, 130, 147, 148, 199
de la Motte-Haber, H. 33
Dennet, D. 25, 29
Dennis, C. 111
DeNora, T. 117, 118, 119, 220, 224, 225, 226, 227, 230, 267, 268
Descartes, R. 24, 25, 57, 75, 92, 101
DeVeaux, S. 230
Dewey, J. 212, 236
Dickie, G. 75, 129, 210, 211, 212, 213, 214, 215, 216, 217
Diffey, G. 18, 130
Dissanayake, E. 14, 23, 24, 25, 26, 27, 28, 29, 30, 33, 34, 36, 37, 44, 46, 96, 100, 202, 211, 212, 243, 264, 272, 279, 285
Docker, J. 178
Dodd, N. 111, 115, 229, 241, 243
Doucet, C. 229
Du Bos, J. 58, 59
Duchamp, M. 196
Dutton, D. 97

E

Edler, A. 151, 152, 156
Edström, O. 3, 4, 5, 27, 96, 107, 110, 112, 137, 151, 157, 159, 162, 184, 188-190, 193-195, 198-199, 201, 204, 207-208, 220, 222-223, 228-231, 245, 247, 283
Ehrlich, C. 194
Elias, N. 20, 25, 48, 51, 54-57, 60-61, 63, 77, 81, 83, 100-101, 105-106, 116, 134, 163, 174, 179,

184, 254-255
Ellis, K. 119, 292
Englund, P. 55
Eno, B. 247
Erfahrung 51, 166, 215-216, 234
Erlebnis 215, 216, 234, 266
Erlmann, V. 179
Etter, B. 185
Ewers, H. 117

F

Farstad, P. 76, 79, 80
Feld, S. 14
Fernström, J. 217
Ferry, L. 24, 52, 57, 58, 60, 63, 75, 81, 84, 92, 97, 98, 106, 129, 182, 184, 185
Fiske, H. 213, 214, 271
Flaubert, G. 154, 155
folk music 52, 204
Fornäs, J. 183, 255, 257, 273
Forte, A. 15
Freud, S. 182
Frisby, D. 253, 254
Frith, S. 221, 223, 226, 237, 239, 244, 245, 246, 247, 248, 249, 250, 252
Frykman, J. 205
Fubrini, E. 15, 57

G

Gallie, W. 11, 233
Geck, M. 117, 119, 143
Gershwin, G. 15, 191, 229
Goehr, A. 228
Goehr, L. 92, 96, 97, 100, 101, 123, 134, 172, 173, 181, 228
Goethe, W. 56, 87, 95, 134, 143, 203
Goodman, N. 35, 214, 245
Göteborg 33, 71-73, 86, 95, 107, 121, 137-142, 144, 155, 162, 168, 170, 185, 188-189, 192-193, 195, 198, 201, 203, 208, 275-277

Goudsblom, J. 48
Gounod, C. 166, 210
Grétry, A. 67
Grieg, E. 148, 168, 201
Gronow, P. 175, 253, 254
Grossberg, L. 245, 250
Grout, D. 45, 170

H

Haas, W. 192
Habermas, J. 77, 85, 106-107, 110, 112, 114, 179, 183, 186, 241, 254-255, 262, 273
Hamnquist, H. 193
Händel, G. 77, 78
Hanfling, O. 36, 39, 59
Hanslick, E. 99, 134, 148, 156-158, 161-162, 169
Hawkins, S. 67, 237
Haydn, J. 72, 74, 80, 85, 87, 89, 94-95, 103, 113, 118, 136, 145, 156, 197, 201
Hegel, G. 47, 48, 117, 130, 133, 148, 152, 157, 179, 238
Heidegger, M. 37, 242
Heister, H. 71, 82-83
Heitmeyer, W. 258
Henderson, I. 40, 42-43, 45-46
Henriksson, A. 198, 202
Herder, J. 90
Higgins, K. 99
Hindemith, P. 16, 187
Hobsbawm, E. 129, 131-132, 178, 198, 229, 234, 244, 260
Hogan, P. 209
Holecek, J. 144
Horne, H. 221, 223, 226, 239, 244, 247
Hume, D. 57, 75, 76, 84, 97
Hurtshouse, R. 38

I

Ingles, F. 178
instrumental music 20, 40, 42, 43-44,

46, 48, 58, 60, 77, 78-79, 85-87, 89, 92-94, 96-97, 102, 106, 114, 117, 120, 122-124, 129, 146, 151, 154-155, 157, 168-171, 173, 186, 192, 206, 208, 223, 264, 280-281, 283
Ivarsdotter, A. 73

J

Jackendorff, T. 32
Jameson, F. 189, 216, 240-241
Jay, M. 37, 182, 196, 216
Jeanson, G. 15, 187
Jernhake, K. 216
Jonsson, L. 93
Josephson, J. 71

K

Kant, E. 47-48, 75-76, 84, 95, 88, 84, 97-101, 105, 125, 129, 140, 202, 214, 246, 253, 259, 285
Karevold, I. 66
Kenner 91
Kilminster, R. 255
Kivy, P. 26, 213-214
Kjørup, S. 15, 51, 86, 165
Klempe, H. 36
Klopstock, F. 90
Knepler, G. 23
Kogan, N. 29
Köhler, J. 130
Kramer, L. 171, 237
Kreitman, N. 97
Kvist Dahlstedt, B. 93
Kydland Lysdahl, A. 93

L

Lagerroth, E. 77
Langer, S. 26, 211
Lash, S. 253, 258-260, 273, 285
le Huray, P. 130
Lerdahl, F. 32
Leux-Henschen, I. 128

Levinson, J. 89, 215
Lezle, L. 126
Lidholm, I. 217, 228
Liebhaber 75, 91
Lied 87, 104, 122, 151, 168-169, 215
Liedman, S. 52, 59-60, 90, 126, 172, 178, 259
Lilliestam, L. 17, 35, 221, 225, 232, 240, 250, 258
Lindberg, B. 217, 257
Lindgren, A. 141
Ling, J. 15, 43, 45, 52-53, 73-74, 205
Lippman, E. 4, 15, 40, 150
Liszt, F. 135-136, 147, 149, 153, 156-157, 201
Lloyd, D. 105
Löfgren, O. 205
Louis Ferdinand, 72
Luhmann, N. 77, 94, 101, 106-110, 114, 127, 153, 179, 183, 188, 228, 254, 262
Lundberg, D. 275-277
Lyotard, J. 242-243

M

Maegaard, J. 185
Magee, B. 129-130
Mahler, G. 130
Mannheim, K. 48, 69
Manoff, T. 15-16
Maquet, J. 18
Marcus, G. 236
Marx, A 157
Marx, K 175
Mathiesen, T. 39, 42
Mattheson, J. 48, 58, 76
Mayerl, B. 229
McCarthy, C. 173
McGinn, C. 31
Mellers, W. 235
Meltzer, R. 15, 235-237, 239, 245, 247, 250, 265-266
Mendelssohn, F. 59, 95, 138, 142, 147, 149

INDEX

Mennel, S. 48
Merriam, A. 14, 17, 33, 46, 127
Messiaen, O. 4, 227
Meyer, L. 13, 122
middle music 137, 190-192, 198-200, 206-207, 217, 265, 277, 283
Middleton, R. 174
mimesis 38-39, 57, 60, 85, 88, 108, 116, 243
Moberg, C. 41, 43-44, 51
modernism 63, 107, 117, 150, 178-179, 181-182, 185, 188-189, 215, 228, 230, 239-243, 265, 284
Moore, A. 15, 247
Morgan, R. 185
Moritz, K. 59, 87-88, 95-96, 109, 114
Morrow, M. 85-89, 119, 127, 132, 171
Moscheles, I. 72, 147
mousiké 39-40, 43, 45-46
Mozart, W. 15, 17, 48, 72, 80, 87, 94-95, 113, 119, 121, 134, 136-138, 149, 156-157, 171, 186, 248
Mulhall, S. 88
Müller, H. 108, 137, 152

N

Nässén, E. 15, 93, 141
Naumann, J. 73
Neefe, C. 91, 117
Neitzert, L. 66, 77-81, 107-108, 111-113, 120, 149
Nicholsen, S. 242
Nilsson, B. 217, 271
Nketia, K. 275
Nono, L. 228
Nordin Hennel, I. 160
Norlind, T. 15, 93, 141
Norman, L. 141
Norris, C. 241-242
Nylöf, G. 261
Nystroem, G. 152, 197

O

Oblad, K. 263
Oesch, H. 26
Öhrström, E. 27-29, 33
Ong, W. 35
opera 52, 56-58, 63-74, 91, 93, 103, 119, 121, 128, 133, 135-138, 140, 142, 149, 151, 160, 165, 169, 171, 231, 244, 280

P

Paddison, M. 112, 229
Paetzold, H. 99
Parret, H. 99
Pascal, B. 57, 92
Pattison, R. 236
Persson, T. 220
Plato 21, 34, 36-45, 47, 71, 72, 75, 97, 172, 243
Plumpe, G. 36, 37, 51, 52, 59, 98, 125, 131
Pollock, J. 12
popular music 14-16, 33, 112, 168, 137, 146, 149, 150, 187-192, 208, 220-223, 283, 286, 232-250, 258, 261
postmodernism 189, 216, 239-244
Presley, E. 14, 232
Profet, M. 30
Pugnani, G. 68
Pythagoras 36

R

Rabe, J. 15, 157, 197, 204
Rackham, H. 43
radio 177, 180, 185, 188, 190-199, 201, 206, 207, 209
Rangström, T. 203
Ratner, L. 13, 51, 58, 80
Reichardt, J. 70-75, 81, 82, 85, 89, 91
Risser, R. 263
Rochlitz, J. 119

Romberg, B. 72
Rose, S. and H. 30
Rosen, C. 80
Runciman, W. 30
Ruud, E. 224-226
Ryle, G. 25

S

Säätelä, S. 270, 273
Said, E. 179, 241
salon music 142-153, 157, 166, 168, 190, 262, 282, 283
Samson, J. 158
Satie, E. 243, 244
Schenker, F. 12, 15, 32
Schiller, F. 51, 62, 148
Schleuning, M. 117, 119, 143
Schnittke, A. 240
Schönberg, A. 112, 146, 149, 150, 158, 182, 184-187, 189, 201, 217, 242
Schopenhauer, A. 129, 130, 148
Schubert, F. 103, 143, 149-150, 169-170, 242
Schultz, J. 89
Schulze, G. 91, 248, 262-268, 273
Schumann, C. 71, 135, 146, 147
Schumann, R. 71, 138, 142, 146, 149-156, 166, 168, 210, 225
Scott, D. 168, 230, 258
Scruton, R. 15, 130
Seboek, T. 33
Shusterman, R. 35, 37, 44, 202, 211-217, 252
Sibelius, J. 152, 180
Sims, L. 229
Singer, P. 30
Sjögren, E. 193
Sjögren, O. 205, 222
Skuncke, M. 73
Sloboda, J. 33
Smetana, B. 95, 140, 142, 146
socialization 112, 258
sociogenesis 48, 253, 261, 286

Söderberg, J. 218, 220
songs 15, 27, 33, 39, 40, 43, 53, 65-72, 80, 89-93, 117, 124-125, 141-150, 167, 169, 185, 191, 198-205, 231, 233, 239, 245, 261, 271
Sörbom, G. 37, 39, 44, 46, 51
Sparshott, F. 122, 180-181, 214
Spohr, L. 71, 134
Sponheuer, B. 132-134, 149-152
Stenhammar, W. 186
Stern, D. 26, 28, 29
Stigsdotter, N. 194, 205
Stockfelt, O. 119, 151
Stockhausen, K. 228
Stoljar, M. 80, 90-92, 94, 106, 148
Strauss, J. 137, 168
Strauss, O. 204
Strauss R. 157
Stravinsky, I. 187, 189, 240
Sturm und Drang 80, 91, 92, 94, 122
Subotnik, R. 99-100, 113-114, 119, 171-172
Sulzer, J. 58, 70, 79, 86-89, 96
Suppan, W. 23, 26, 33, 35, 40
Swingewood, A. 111, 185, 240-244

T

Tadday, U. 102-104, 110, 126-127, 155, 171
Taruskin, R. 68
Tatarkiewicz, W. 36
Tchaikovsky, P. 158
techné 36, 46
Tegen, M. 137, 143-144, 168
Théberge, P. 272
Thomsen, R. 41, 42, 45
Thyssen, O. 108, 109
Tourraine, A. 178-179, 259

U

Uffenbach, J. 65-67, 71, 74, 81

INDEX

V

Valkare, G. 187, 217, 228
Verdi, G. 132, 151, 153
virtuosi 42, 44, 45, 64, 66, 71, 103, 115, 134,-138, 142, 160, 176
vocal music 42, 57-58, 70, 76, 93, 96, 124-125, 152, 157, 168-170, 208, 247, 283
Vogler, G. 73
Volgsten, U. 27, 28, 29, 33, 137, 157, 168, 204, 251
von Leibniz, G. 27, 28, 29, 33
von Wolff, C. 52

W

Wackenroder, J. 94, 152
Wagner, R. 111, 130, 134, 138, 148-151, 153, 156, 157, 167, 171, 184
Walter, J. 11, 30, 35, 119, 196, 215
Walton, K. 249
Weber, W. 71, 121, 134, 136-137, 139-140, 144, 149, 159, 166, 186, 242
Wegner, M. 42
Weiss, P. 68, 152
Weitz, M. 211
Welsch, W. 270-273, 275, 278, 285
Wennerberg, G. 159
Wennhall, J. 219-220, 230
Westin, L. 231
Wicke, P. 169, 237-239, 245, 250
Williams, A. 115, 118, 233, 275
Williams, R. 241
Willis, P. 192, 246, 250-254, 259-260, 262, 265, 266, 268, 271
Wittgenstein, L. 105, 173, 211, 242, 278
Wolff, C. 79
Wolin, R. 112, 131
Woodmansee, M. 51, 60-62, 87

Z

Zaminer, F. 40
Zappa, F. 232
Zelter, C. 89
Ziehe, T. 254-258, 262, 265